Calviniana:
Ideas and Influence of
Jean Calvin

Habent sua fata libelli

Volume X
of
Sixteenth Century Essays & Studies
Robert V. Schnucker, Editor

ISBN: 0-9404474-10-7

Composed by Paula Presley, NMSU, Kirksville, Missouri
Printed by Edwards Brothers, Ann Arbor, Michigan
Text is set in Bembo II

Calviniana

Ideas and Influence
of
Jean Calvin

Robert V. Schnucker
Editor

Volume X
Sixteenth Century Essays & Studies

Table of Contents

Part II: His Influence

Cataloging-in-Publication Data

Calviniana: ideas and influence of Jean Calvin.
  (Sixteenth century essays & studies; v. 10)
  Includes index.
  1. Calvin, Jean, 1509-1564. 2. Calvinsim. I. Schnucker, Robert V.   II. Series.
BX9418.C38   1988   284'.2'0924   88-18310
ISBN 0-940474-10-7

Preface

As part of a long line of Reformed clergy extending back to the 1840s in America, I've always been sensitive to the importance of John Calvin and the role of the Reformed movement in Christian history. Early in my life I became fascinated by the courage of those who belong to the Reformed faith and by their sense of discipline. The restraint and care that is found in the Presbyterian motto of "decently and in order" has been a refrain that continually echoes through the memory of my religious heritage. Yet as I attempted to study that heritage, I soon discovered that it is easier to study the Lutheran heritage, at least in the English language, due to the tremendous number of books and articles that have poured forth from that branch of the Christian tradition. There has not been a similar outpouring in the Reformed tradition. When I made inquiries about why this has been the case, Eugene Rice suggested that the Reformed tradition really did not find the person Calvin as interesting as the ideas of Calvin. Thus although the Reformed tradition nods its head in the direction of Calvin as its founder, it immediately moves on to his ideas and their impact upon the world.

Perhaps this is the way it ought to be. Rather than give devotion to the founder in various biographies and in a minute exploration of every phrase he wrote, it is better to show that devotion by using the founder's ideas to precipitate change in the world. Certainly the early followers of Calvin did attempt to change the world by using his ideas and principles as the basis for change. They soon became a vigorous international movement and adapted his ideas to fit their own environments.

The combination of Calvin's ideas and their adaptation by his followers to the world is found in this collection of essays. The first part gives some of the key ideas of Calvin, from a case study of his theological method to his handling of marriage. The second part explores the application of his ideas by followers in various parts of Europe, moving from Calvin's influence in England to the contemporary scene in South Africa. These essays are the result of a series of letters and conversations between myself and W. Fred Graham. We both felt strongly that a volume ought to be brought into existence that would be part of an effort to revitalize an interest in the history of the Reformed tradition prior to its appearance in the New World.

I wish to acknowledge the solid work of my friend and colleague W. Fred Graham in the creation of this book; the encouragement and support of the Reverend William Keesecker who made a contribution to its production before any essays had been assembled; the considerable support of the H. H. Meeter Center for Calvin Studies and its Director, Richard Gamble; to the incredible patience, diligence, intelligence, and good cheer of our typographer, Paula Presley. To all the readers, I hope you find this modest volume to be a window that opens onto part of the fascinating world of the Reformed tradition.

Robert V. Schnucker

Kirksville, Missouri
May, 1988

8 *Calviniana*

Introduction

Robert M. Kingdon

In the past two decades The Sixteenth Century Journal Publishers has issued symposium volumes focused on aspects of the Reformation launched by Martin Luther early in the sixteenth century. On the anniversaries of the Formula of Concord (1977) and the Augsburg Confession (1980), special issues of *The Sixteenth Century Journal* were published. Then James D. Tracy edited Volume VIII of the Sixteenth Century Essays and Studies series, *Luther and the Modern State in Germany*, published in 1986. To this date, however, we had not issued a similar symposium volume on the later phase of the sixteenth-century Reformation which was dominated by John Calvin. Yet Calvin and the movement he launched obviously deserve and get scholarly attention. In the world today several scholarly societies and journals are supported by interest in Calvin and Calvinism. Some believe that the Protestant message as interpreted by Calvin still has relevance in the modern world. Many recognize that the version of Protestantism most widely accepted during the sixteenth century, outside of the Holy Roman Empire of the German nation, was Calvinist. Even within Germanic Europe, second and later generations of Protestants in the late sixteenth and early seventeenth centuries found a version of Calvinism attractive. In fact, so significant a number of Germans turned to Calvinism that noted German scholars, such as Heinz Schilling, have urged us to label this development a Second Reformation.

To remedy a lack of balance in its publication program, The Sixteenth Century Journal Publishers presents this volume. It is designed to be a sampling of current work on Calvin studies similar to earlier samplings of current Luther studies. The project was conceived of and brought to fruition by Robert V. Schnucker, the managing editor of the *Journal* and the Essays and Studies series. Professor Schnucker was ably assisted by W. Fred Graham, of Michigan State University, and Howard Rienstra, the first director of the H. H. Meeter Center for Calvin Studies in Grand Rapids, Michigan. Completion of the project was unfortunately delayed by Professor Rienstra's fatal illness. His successor at the Meeter Center, Richard C. Gamble, fortunately found time and mobilized financial support necessary to complete the project. We are grateful to them all.

In recent years, studies of Calvin and Calvinism have become to an unprecented degree interconfessional, interdisciplinary, and international. Evidence of each of these elements will be found in the present volume.

Most of the contributors to this volume who have confessional commitments come from churches that still claim allegiance to Calvinist theology, and some of them explicitly hope their work will prove valuable to contemporary Reformed theologians. Yet most of the contributors also draw from the works of scholars in other confessional traditions. Both John Hesselink and Merwyn Johnson, in analyzing Calvin's third use of the law, are careful to set it in the context of work by Lutheran theologians on Luther's concept of law and gospel. Timothy George points out some intriguing parallels between the early ideas of Calvin and Menno Simons, drawing upon the work of specialists from the Anabaptist tradition. Several contributors utilize the work of such sensitive contemporary Catholic interpreters of early Calvinism as Alexandre Ganoczy.

Most of the contributors to this volume are academic theologians or historians, and accordingly offer us technical analyses either in historical theology or in intellectual history. Some examine the fine points of Calvin's own theology, such as David Foxgrover, Richard Gamble, John Hesselink, Mervyn Johnson, and James Torrance. Others examine the implications of Calvin's ideas: Wayne Baker considers ecclesiology; Charmarie Blaisdell, feminist studies; Fred Graham, politics; and Christopher Kaiser, science. They branch out into other types of history, as in Bodo Nischan's use of the history of education. They go beyond the normal methods used by theologians and historians, to borrow methods from literary critics, as does Claude-Marie Baldwin, and from analytical bibliographiers, as does Ian Hazlett.

In national background, most of the contributors are American; but some Scots offer variety, too. Many, however, have studied in Europe, and all are aware of current work by Europeans in Calvin studies. For example, Brian Armstrong considers Calvin's home country of France; Dan Danner, Ian Hazlett, and Donald McKim examine neighboring Britain; and Bodo Nischan, Germany. We deal not only with Calvin's own century, but continue well beyond his lifetime, into the seventeenth century in France (Armstrong), Germany (Nischan), and England (McKim).

To be sure, this volume makes no attempt to give equal time to all the current approaches to the study of Calvin and Calvinism. It does contain some reaction to insights of William Bouwsma's provocative recent psychological portrait of Calvin, but only of a rather preliminary sort. Less attention is given to current work drawing on the insights of anthropology and sociology, on the model of Natalie Zemon Davis for example. Still we trust *Calviniana* will prove to be a useful sample of one spectrum of work on the Calvinist tradition and that it will stimulate further work on this important facet of sixteenth-century life. In that hope we offer it to our readers. In that hope we also invite your comments.

Dedicated to
Anna Mae Schnucker
whose unstinting seventeen years of service
as financial officer has strengthened
the SCJ, HEME, and this monograph series.

11

This book has been brought to publication with the generous
support of
the H. H. Meeter Center for Calvin Studies,
Northeast Missouri State University,
and the Reverend William Keesecker.

The paper used in this publication meets the minimum requirements of the American National
Standard for Permanence of Paper for Printed Library Materials Z39.48, 1984.

I

Ideas

Law and Gospel or Gospel and Law?
Calvin's Understanding of the Relationship

I. John Hesselink

Usually the subject of Law and Gospel has been the domain of the Lutherans. This chapter considers Calvin's approach to the subject and concludes by showing that Calvin's approach is tempered by the various meanings given to the terms "law" and "gospel"; that he perceived an opposition between the two; and that his position is rather complex with a law-gospel-law paradigm as a key to his thought.

THE SUBJECT OF LAW AND GOSPEL has been a special Lutheran interest. Check any book on Luther or a Lutheran dogmatics and there will usually be a section or chapter on law and gospel.[1] This is not true of studies of Calvin or dogmatics (theologies) written in other traditions. There will be references to, and occasionally treatments of, the law–but rarely will there be a special section entitled "law and gospel" as such.[2] Thus, for centuries this theme has been largely a Lutheran domain.

It has been generally recognized that Calvin also had a special interest in the law but primarily in the third use of the law (the law as a guide for believers) which for him was "the principal use."[3] Although Calvin was in full accord with Luther on the first and second uses of the law (*usus civilis* and *usus elenchticus*), Lutheran scholars tend to denigrate the seriousness with which Calvin takes the accusing function of the law (second use for Calvin, the first for Luther).[4] When Calvin does take up the theme of law and gospel in the larger context of the witness to Christ under the old and new covenants

---

[1]See, for example, Philip Watson, *Let God be God. An Interpretation of the Theology of Martin Luther* (London: Epworth, 1947), 152 ff.; Paul Althaus, *The Theology of Martin Luther* (Philadelphia: Fortress, 1966), Chap. 19; Eric W. Gritsch and Robert W. Janson, *Lutheranism: The Theological Movement and Its Confessional Writings* (Philadelphia: Fortress, 1976), 42 ff.; Helmut Thielicke, *The Evangelical Faith* (Grand Rapids: Eerdmans, 1982), vol 3, chap. 11.

[2]In *Calvin: Institutes of the Christian Religion*, ed. John T. McNeill, trans. Ford Lewis Battles, Vols. 20 & 21, Library of Christian Classics, (Philadelphia: Westminster, 1960), 1677, there is a very detailed listing of topics related to the simple heading "Law," one of which is "and gospel." Unless indicated otherwise, quotations from *Institutes,* will be from the McNeill & Battles translation of 1960.

[3]*Institutes* II.7.12.

[4]See Werner Elert, *Law and Gospel* (Philadelphia: Fortress Facet Books, 1967), 7 ff. Some Lutheran theologians view Melanchthon as the villain for introducing a third use of the law into Lutheran theology. Gerhard Ebeling, for example, maintains that Melanchthon first followed Luther's approach, which was a *duplex usus legis* but then in order "to suit the intentions of his own doctrine of the law . . . remodeled it into the scholastic schema of the *triplex usus.* (*Word and Faith,* [Philadelphia: Fortress, 1963], 74).

However, the Danish ethicist, N. H. Søe, maintains that neither of the reformers is correct in positing a second (first for Calvin) use of the law. Søe, following Barth and Bonhoeffer, maintains that it is not the law but the gospel–and the Spirit–which brings about a sense of sin and unworthiness.

in the *Institutes,* in Book II,[5] the Lutheran Old Testament scholar Emil Kraeling tartly comments that here "Calvin really abandons Paul's (and Luther's) antitheses of law and gospel."[6]

For inexplicable reasons Calvin scholars and Reformed theologians generally have not been very interested in defending Calvin on this issue, so the issue has not really been joined in regard to the law-gospel question except briefly by Wilhelm Niesel in his symbolics, *The Gospel and the Churches.*[7] His treatment is brief and is influenced by Barth as can be seen in the title of the chapter dealing with this theme: "Gospel and Law."

This issue might have remained dormant had it not been for Barth's controversial monograph *Evangelium und Gesetz* which first appeared in 1935.[8] Its impact in German-Scandinavian Lutheran theological circles was almost as great as his earlier Romans commentary which was compared to a bomb dropping on a children's playground. By reversing the traditional order, law-gospel, to gospel-law, Barth had attacked a sacrosanct pillar of faith in Lutheranism. The editors of the symposium *Gesetz und Evangelium* explain in their preface that, as a result of Luther research in the nineteenth century, the theme of law and gospel became a "fundamental" theological issue and "was elevated to a central, even distinctive doctrine within Protestantism (*innerevangelischen Unterscheidiungslehre*)."[9]

In the Luther renaissance after World War I, the political notion of a people's law (*Volks-Gesetz*) became an issue which prompted a renewed interest in the broader issue of law on the part of Protestant theologians in Germany. It was in this context that Barth's monograph appeared and "opened . . . a new period of systematic theological discussion and consideration of this original and genuine reformation theme which has lasted until today."[10] The symposium *Gesetz und Evangelium* reflects that discussion and contains seventeen essays which are largely a response to Barth's *Evangelium und Gesetz* (also included). Not surprisingly, almost all of the contributors are German and Scandinavian Lutheran historians and theologians. There are two exceptions, the Dutch Reformed theolgian Hendrikus Berkhof and the Roman Catholic theologian Gottlieb Søhngen.

[5]The title of this chapter is "Christ, Although He Was Known to the Jews Under the Law, Was at Length Clearly Revealed Only in the Gospel."

[6]Emil Kraeling, *The Old Testament Since the Reformation* (London: Lutterworth, 1955), 31.

[7](Philadelphia: Westminster, 1962).

[8]The English translation, "Gospel and Law," appears in *Community, State and Church,* ed. Will Herberg (Garden City: Doubleday, Anchor Books, 1960), 71-100.

[9]Ernest Kinder and Klaus Haendler, Hg. *Gesetz und Evangelium. Beitrage zur gegenwartigen theologischen Diskussion* (Darmstadt: Wissenschaftliche Buchgesellschaft, 1968), xx. Translation mine.

[10]Ibid., xxi.

In 1969, a year after the appearance of *Gesetz und Evangelium*, Gerhard
O. Forde's revised Harvard dissertation was published: *The Law-Gospel Debate*.
It covers much the same ground, although the scope is much larger.
However, as was true in the German symposium, the genesis of the
contemporary debate is Barth's reversal of the law-gospel scheme. For, as
Forde points out, "Karl Barth startled theologians, especially Lutherans, by
suggesting a basic reorientation of the law-gospel dialectic. His essay was the
first major attempt at a redefinition of the problem."[11]

Calvin is mentioned only once in passing in Forde's work, and rarely in
the German symposium, but Werner Elert is not alone in thinking that
Barth's position is basically a Calvinian-Reformed one. He declares that
Barth's much-cited assertion in *Evangelium und Gesetz*–that the law is only
the form of the gospel–"coincides exactly with the view of Calvin."[12] That
this is not true will become apparent in the substance of this essay. Calvin,
no less than Luther, recognizes an accusing function of the law and even an
antithesis between the law and the gospel. There are similarities between
Calvin and Barth but there are also fundamental differences. Consequently,
a treatment of Calvin's position in regard to this debate is long overdue. The
primary purpose of this essay is to attempt to clear up a common
misunderstanding regarding Calvin's view of the relation of law and gospel.
Indirectly, this brief analysis should also help to clarify the relation between
the views of Calvin and Barth which have often been confused.

What is often overlooked by Lutheran scholars who write on this subject
and who compare Luther and Calvin is that they are not always talking about
the same thing when they use the expression "law and gospel." Neither of
them uses the expression in a fixed way, so that depending on the situation
or context, law and gospel can mean any one of a number of things. When
the reformers confine themselves to exegesis of given passages, the results
are surprisingly similar. As I have demonstrated elsewhere, when they
exegete key passages relating to the law and the gospel in their respective
Galatians commentaries, Calvin is no less "Pauline" than Luther[13] The
similarities are also striking in their expositions of the ten commandments
in their catechisms where Luther's praise of the law is even more exuberant
than Calvin's.

The Different Meanings of Law for Luther and Calvin
When Luther uses the expression "law and gospel" he is most often
thinking in terms of the question of justification and works righteousness.
The law accordingly stands either for righteousness by works in opposition

[11]Gerhard O. Forde, *The Law-Gospel Debate* (Minneapolis: Augsburg, 1969), 137.

[12]Elert, *Law and Gospel*, 8.

[13]John Hesselink, "Luther and Calvin on Law and Gospel in Their Galatians Comm.aries,"
Reformed Review 37/2 (Winter 1984).

to the righteousness of faith or is likened to the "hammer" of God's demands which crushes self-righteous sinners and drives them to the gospel where they experience the free grace of God. The law in this context stands for God's demand, the gospel for God's gift. Therefore the gospel cannot be preached without first preaching the law.[14]

Calvin, on the other hand, often uses the words promise and curse rather than law and gospel when dealing with this issue.[15] He uses the expression "law and gospel" more often to describe the relation between the two covenants. Hence the misunderstanding of Emil Kraeling noted earlier, in reference to the title of Chapter 9 of Book II of the *Institutes,*: "Christ, Although He Was Known to the Jews Under the Law, Was At Length Clearly Revealed Only in the Gospel." That "law" and "gospel" here refer to the two covenants or dispensations comes out clearly in the next chapter, "The Similarity of the Old and New Testaments."

Calvin's emphasis on the basic unity of the two Testaments is well known. A common charge is that he so stressed their unity that the differences between the two are severely underestimated. Reinhold Seeberg, for example, in his *Dogmengeschichte* declares that "a consequence of Calvin's legalism is that he tends to blur the boundaries between the Old and New Testaments."[16]

What such interpreters fail to recognize is that here Calvin is using the word "law" in a comprehensive sense, in which case the substance of the two covenants is the same: Christ. Only the form of administration differs. For "the covenant made with all the fathers is so much like ours in substance and reality that the two are actually one and the same. Yet they differ in the mode of administration."[17]

It is this sort of statement that has led many scholars to conclude that Calvin does not appreciate or accept what would appear to be the Pauline antithesis between law and gospel. What is not recognized in such cases is precisely in what the difference consists and, most importantly, that for Calvin there is not only a *difference* between the law and the gospel, but also an *antithesis* insofar as the law is opposed to the gospel. (With Calvin the phrase "insofar as" [*quatenus*] is crucial in understanding the nuances of his position.)

---

[14]Watson, *Let God be God,* chap. 5; Gerhard Heintze, *Luthers Predigt von Gesetz und Evangelium* (München: Chr. Kaiser Verlag, 1958), chap. 9.

[15]See *Institutes,* II.8.4

[16]Reinhold Seeberg, *Lehrbuch der Dogmengeschichte* IV, 2, 5. Auflage (Basel: Benno Schwabe, 1960), 566. Subsequently, Edmund Schlink, confusing Calvin and Barth, asserted that both of them "water down" the 'heilsgeschichtliche' distinction between the two covenants and law and gospel ("Gesetz und Paraklese," in *Antwort,* Festschrift zum 70. Geburtstag von Karl Barth [Zollikon-Zurich: Evangelischer Verlag, 1956], 332).

[17]*Institutes* II.10.2.

Thus, for example, when the Apostle Paul in Gal. 3:19 opposes the law given to Moses to the promise given to Abraham, Calvin observes that the law here is separated from the promises of grace and is being considered only in view of its "peculiar office, power, and end."[18] This law, the law which is the antithesis of the gospel, is the narrow, peculiar sense of the law, the "bare law" (*nuda lex*).[19] The law, so conceived, is separated from its original context, the covenant; it is a bare letter without the Spirit of Christ. It has nothing but rigorous demands which place all humanity under the curse and wrath of God.[20] Concerning the law, so understood, Calvin is no less compromising than Luther in opposing the law to the gospel. Everything depends on what is meant by "law."

The relation between law and gospel, therefore, is not simply a twofold distinction between form and substance, but a threefold distinction:

1. A *unity* of the substance of the doctrine.

2. A *distinction* in the form or mode of instruction (*forma docendi*).[21]

3. An *antithesis* of letter and Spirit.[22]

In the remainder of this essay I shall develop more fully the nature of these distinctions.

Unity of Substance

It is impossible to discuss the unity of substance without discussing to some extent the difference in the form of law and gospel. For Calvin invariably makes such distinctions in the context of the same passage. Also,

---

[18]Comm. Ex. 19:1, *Harmony of the Last Four Books of Moses,* I: 314. Generally I am using the old Edinburgh edition of Calvin's Old Testament Commentaries (Eerdmans reprint, 1948-50) and the recent Torrance edition of the New Testament commentaries (Grand Rapids: Eerdmans, 1959-72), but occasionally I have altered the translations for the sake of consistency and greater precision.

[19]*Institutes* II.7.2. The contrast here is with the law "clothed (*vestita* translated by Battles as "graced") with the covenant of free adoption" Cf. Comm. Gal. 4:24.

[20]See Comm. Deut. 30:11; Ps. 19:7-8; Rom. 10:5; and 2 Cor. 3:6.

[21]Comm. Isa. 2:3 and Mk. 1:1.

[22]I have adopted this division from Werner Krusche, *Das Wirken des Heiligen Geistes Nach Calvin* (Gottingen: Vandenhoeck & Ruprecht, 1957), 184-202; but I have given these terms a somewhat different content. For Krusche limits the antithesis almost exclusively to a discussion of 2 Corinthians 3, an unwarranted limitation of the scope of this contrast. Andrew J. Bandstra has used the same divisions, based on my Basel University dissertation, "Calvin's Concept and Use of the Law" (1961). Bandstra, professor of New Testament at Calvin Theological Seminary, investigates whether Calvin is a faithful Paulinist in his discussion of law and gospel and concludes affirmatively. See his essay, "Law and Gospel in Calvin and Paul," in *Exploring the Heritage of John Calvin: Essays in Honor of John Bratt,* ed. David E. Holwerda (Grand Rapids: Baker, 1976).

when Calvin discusses the common substance of the law and gospel, another topic frequently enters the picture: the experience of the fathers (i.e., the Old Testament believers) with Christ and the gospel.

It was noted above that the covenant made with the Old Testament "fathers" or patriarchs has the same substance and reality as that made with believers in the New Testament era. This key statement in the *Institutes,* (II.10.2) distinguishes Calvin from opponents on two sides: the Roman theologians on the one hand, and the Anabaptists on the other. Calvin, however, was no innovator in this respect, for Zwingli, Bucer, Melanchthon, and Bullinger had made similar distinctions prior to this time.[23]

For Calvin the issue at stake is not only the unity of revelation but the unity of God himself. In those places where the law is opposed to the gospel, Calvin readily recognizes the antithesis, but at the same time he is quick to warn his readers that it would be erroneous to conclude that God is "unlike" or "inconsistent"[24] with himself.[25]

> When we learn that the doctrine of the gospel 'came forth out of Zion' (Isa. 2:3), we conclude from this that it is not new, or a recent innovation, but that it is the eternal truth of God of which a testimony had been given in all ages before it was brought to light. We also gather that it was necessary that all of the ancient ceremonies should be abolished and that a new form of instruction (*nova docendi forma*) should be introduced, although the substance of the doctrine (*doctrinae substantia*) continued to be the same. For the law formerly proceeded out of Mount Sinai (Ex. 19:1), but it now proceeded 'out of Zion,' and therefore it took on a new form.
>
> Two things, therefore, must be observed: First, that the doctrine of God is the same and always agrees with itself (*et sui perpetuo similem*); that no one may accuse God of changeableness (*variationis*) as if he were inconsistent. Although the law of the Lord is the same as always, yet it came out of Zion with new garments (*veste*). Second, when the ceremonies and shadows had been abolished, Christ was revealed in whom their reality was perceived.[26]

In this one quotation it becomes apparent what Calvin means by both the unity and diversity of the covenants. For him there is essentially only

[23]See Gottlob Schrenk, *Gottesreich und Bund im alteren Protestantismus* (Darmstadt: Wissenschaftliche Buchgesellschaft, 1967 [reprint of 1923 ed.]).

[24]Comm. Gal. 3:12; Sermons on Gal. 2:15-16; and Gal. 3:11-14.

[25]Comm. Hab. 2:4; Heb. 1:1-2.

[26]Comm. Isa. 2:3. Cf. Comm. Isa. 42:4; Comm. Micah 4:7.

one covenant, the covenant of grace, which unites both Testaments. Here Calvin stands on firm ground, for the one covenant promise–"I will be your God and you shall be my poeple"–is repeated throughout Scripture.[27]

However, Jeremiah and Ezekiel speak of a "new covenant," and in Heb. 8:6-13 we read that this new covenant, which is ratified by the blood of Christ, makes the "old covenant" obsolete. Calvin still insists that the so-called "new covenant" is not contrary to the first covenant. To draw such a conclusion would imply that God is not true to himself and is somehow inconsistent. "For he who once made a covenant with his chosen people has not changed his purpose as though he had forgotten his faithfulness."[28]

What is "new" about the new covenant only refers to its form. The covenants made with Abraham, Moses, and David, and the new covenant promised by Jeremiah and Ezekiel, are all united by the one promise which finds its culmination and fulfillment in Christ. He is the *fundamentum, anima, spiritus, perfectio, scopus,* and *finis* of the law.[29]

Since Christ is the substance of the law, and thereby also of the two Testaments, they are inseparable and interdependent. The gospel does not supplant or supesede the law but rather confirms it and gives substance to the shadows. Consequently, "where the whole law is concerned, the gospel differs from it only in clarity of manifestation."[30]

Distinction in Form

The distinction between law and gospel–between the old and new covenants, as we saw earlier–consists principally in the mode of dispensation or manner of instruction. Calvin treats this subject in Book II, chapter 11 of the *Institutes,*, although he had already dealt with this matter provisionally in chapter 9. The title of this chapter indicates what the principal distinction is: "Christ, although he was known to the Jews under the law, was at length clearly revealed only in the gospel."

The *tota lex* is still the object of inquiry. In this context, the difference between the covenants is only relative, a matter of more or less; the substance is the same. Only the form or manner of God's self-revelation and our understanding and experience of it varies.

In view of all this, it might seem that Calvin has so moderated or smoothed out the differences betwen the Testaments, or the law broadly conceived, and the gospel, that the distinctions are not really significant. Before dealing directly with that objection, we should examine the five differences or distinctions which Calvin lists in chapter eleven.

[27]See Lev. 26:12; Jer. 31:31; Ezek. 37:27; 2 Cor. 6:16; Heb. 8:10.

[28]Comm. Jer. 31:31; Cf. Comm. Ezek. 16:61.

[29]Comm. 2 Cor. 3:6-7; Comm. Jer. 31:31-32; Comm. on Matt. 17:3; Comm. Rom. 10:4-5. Cf. *Institutes* II.7.l.]

[30]*Institutes* II.9.4.

1. The Jews were given the hope of immortality under the figure of earthly blessings, but now this inferior method has been suspended.

2. Truth was exhibited by types in the Old Testament, but is now openly revealed in the New, as we see in the Epistle to the Hebrews. This was due to the fact that the Jews were in a state of tutelage, except for the patriarchs who were in advance of their time.

3. The old covenant has the character of the letter, the new, of the Spirit; the old lacks the Spirit whereas the new is engraven on the heart (Jer. 31:31 ff.). The old is deadly because it includes the curse, the new is an instrument of life. The old is a shadow which must pass away; the new will stand forever.

4. The old covenant produces fear and trembling, except for the promises in it which properly belong to the new (so Augustine), whereas the new produces freedom and joy.

5. The revelation of the Old Testament was confined to the Jewish nation. In the New Testament the Gentiles are also invited to share in its blessings.[31]

A careful reading of these five differences shows that the third and fourth differences are not of the same character as one, two, and five. These three are of a less radical, more "evolutionary" type of difference whereas three and four come close to representing an antithesis between law and gospel. That is, the difference between the letter and the spirit, works and faith, bondage and freedom, are far greater than the movement from a more limited and obscure revelation to that which is clearer, fuller, and more universal. As Calvin himself points out, "Where the whole law (*tota lex*) is concerned, the gospel differs from it only in clarity of manifestation."[32]

When one speaks of an "antithesis," as in the next section, a much sharper contrast or break is implied. However, even in this case the break or antithesis is never absolute because even the law (although not the *nuda lex*) is *adventitiously* invested with certain qualities of the gospel. This qualification is crucial for understanding Calvin's view of law and gospel and will be illustrated later.

First, however, it is necessary to explore further the nature of the differences between law and gospel. In the following quotation we have a succinct, yet comprehensive, description of that difference in terms of the "more" of the gospel over against the "less" of the law.

---

[31]This paragraph contains the main points and arguments of *Institutes* II.11.

[32]*Institutes* II.9.4.

Both [law and gospel] attest that God's fatherly kindness and the graces of the Holy Spirit are offered us in Christ, but ours is clearer and brighter. In both Christ is shown forth, but in ours more richly and fully, that is, in accordance with that difference between the Old and New Testament which we have discussed above. And this is what Augustine means . . . in teaching that when Christ was revealed, sacraments were instituted, fewer in number but more majestic in signification (*significatione*), more excellent in power (*virtute*).[33]

Hence the Old Testament "fathers" also enjoyed God's grace, but they were granted only a small portion, its perfection being deferred until the time of Christ.[34] Calvin uses many similes and metaphors to describe this relative difference. One he employs frequently is that of the shadow (*umbra*) which he contrasts with truth or reality (*veritas*) and body (*corpus*) or substance (*substantia*). Christ is the reality of the shadows and ceremonies of the law which are abolished when he appears.[35] "For the shadows immediately vanish when the body appears.[36] Commenting on John 4:23–". . . will worship the Father in Spirit and truth"–Calvin observes:

Although the worship of God under the law was spiritual, it was wrapped up in so many outward ceremonies that it had the flavor of carnality and earthliness . . . . Hence we may well say that the worship (*cultus*) of the law was spiritual in its substance, but with respect to its form was somewhat carnal and earthly. For that whole economy (*ratio*) whose reality is now openly manifested to us was shadowy.[37]

The difference between the two ages or dispensations is also described commonly in terms of distance. The simile of a shadow is sometimes used here, too; but in this case the idea is not so much that of insubstantiality as obscurity. That which was distant and obscure is now near at hand. That which was concealed under the law is visible under the gospel.[38]

Col. 2:17 is particularly relevant in this connection: "These are only a shadow of what is to come; but the substance belongs to Christ." According to Calvin, the apostle here

[33]*Institutes* IV.14.26.
[34]Comm. Heb. 11:39.
[35]Comm. Isa. 2:3; cf. Comm. Heb. 4:8.
[36]Comm. Heb. 4:10.
[37]Comm. Jn. 4:23.
[38]Comm. Zech. 13:1; Comm. 1 Pet. 1:10.

contrasts shadows with revelation and absence with manifestation. Those, therefore, who adhere to those 'shadows' act like someone who judges a man's appearance by his shadow when in the meantime the man himself is personally present before his eyes. For the substance of those things which the ceremonies anciently prefigured is now presented before our eyes in Christ.[39]

Another way in which Calvin likes to describe the difference between the fathers' experience of God's grace and ours is in terms of eating a meal. The Old Testament believers drew from the same fullness of Christ that we do, but "they had a more scanty taste of the benefits of God." However, when Christ appeared in the flesh, "the blessings were poured out, as it were, with a full hand."[40] They had but a "slight taste" of the grace to which they bore witness. But now that this grace "is placed before our eyes" we "can more richly enjoy it."[41]

Nevertheless, although the fathers had only a taste of that grace which has been so generously poured out on us, even though they saw Christ only through types and figures, and therefore obscurely and at a distance, "yet they were satisfied . . . ."[42] At the same time they desired to see the things which we see, and hear the things which we hear (Lk. 10:24; Mt. 13:17; 1 Pet. 1:10-12). For although they "were content with their lot and enjoyed a blessed peace in their own minds, this did not prevent their desires from extending further (cf. Jn. 8:56; Lk. 2:29) . . . . Due to the burden of that curse by which the human race is crushed, it was impossible that they should be anything but inflamed with the desire of a promised deliverance.[43]

This brings us to the most significant difference between the status of believers under the old covenant and the new, one that was alluded to earlier when it was said that the fullness of God's grace was "deferred until the time of Christ."[44] For all the grace which the Old Testament believers enjoyed was in a sense "suspended" (*suspensa*) grace.[45]

It is not simply a matter of more or less, although their knowledge was far more obscure, their experience of God's grace far more scanty. What they knew and experienced was real, not illusory. They had more than bare

---

[39]Comm. Jn. 4:23.

[40]Comm. Jn. 1:16.

[41]*Institutes* II.9.1; cf. Comm. Acts 13:32; Comm. Isa. 1:19.

[42]Comm. Heb. 11:13.

[43]Comm. Lk. 10:24.

[44]Comm. Heb. 11:39.

[45]I have developed this theme of "suspended grace" in Calvin's thought more fully in an essay, "Calvin and Heilsgeschichte," contributed to a festschrift for Oscar Cullmann's sixty-fifth birthday, ed. Felix Christ, *Oikonomia Heilsgeschichte als Thema der Theologie* (Hamburg: Herbert Reich, 1967).

promises. The promises themselves, being the living Word of God, contained life and provided a genuine hope. But whatever they had, whatever they received and experienced, was all contingent upon the manifestation of the Son of God in the flesh. "Whatever God at that time conferred [on the fathers], it was so to say adventitious (*quasi adventitium*), for all those benefits were dependent on Christ and the promulgation of the gospel."[46]

Those who lived under the law were partakers of the promise; "there was a participation (*societas*) in the same grace" which we enjoy. But "their faith stood, as it were in suspension (*in suspensa*) until Christ appeared in whom all the promises of God are yea and amen."[47] Calvin takes this "suspension" so seriously that he even says that "in a certan sense (*quodammodo*) grace was suspended until the advent of Christ."[48] For "under the law there was no true and real expiation of sins."[49]

"Suspension," therefore, means that "the ceremonies [i.e., of the old covenant] sketch (*adumbrarent*) Christ as though he were absent whereas to us he is represented as actually present."[50] One should not conclude, however, that the Old Testament faithful didn't have some share in the grace of Christ. Calvin, as we have seen, affirms that in various ways. They "possessed him [Christ] but as one hidden and absent . . . because he was not yet manifest in the flesh."[51]

The differences thus are real and significant. All the criticisms about Calvin levelling the differences between the two testaments and failing to recognize the newness of the gospel are seen to be groundless in view of this notion of "suspended grace" which has been overlooked even by sympathetic Calvin scholars like Wilhelm Niesel and François Wendel.

Calvin often warns about confusing different ages (*confusio temporum*),[52] i.e., the two dispensations. However, as to the antithesis of law and gospel, more narrowly conceived, we should keep in mind a characteristic concern and motif of Calvin: the "constancy of God" in all his dealings with humanity.[53]

Antithesis Between Letter and Spirit

Now we come to that aspect of the law which most Protestants take for the whole. This law, the law opposed to the gospel, is the law separated from Christ and the Holy Spirit. This is the bare law (*nuda lex*), the accusing

[46]Comm. Jer. 3:34.
[47]Comm. Acts 13:32.
[48]Comm. Col. 2:14.
[49]Comm. Ex. 24:4; Cf. Comm. Ex. 25:8; Comm. on Dan. 9:25.
[50]Comm. Gal. 3:23.
[51]Comm. I Pet. 1:12.
[52]Comm. Jn. 4:20; Cf. Genesis *Argumentum* (i.e., the preface to his Genesis Commentary).
[53] *Institutes*, II.11.13.

law that troubles the conscience, the law in itself (*per se*) and as such which is isolated from the covenant and the promises. This law requires perfection, and where that is lacking, it curses, condemns, and kills. Over against the gospel, when each is taken in its narrower and peculiar sense, this law demands what only the gospel can give.

Does Calvin recognize such a law? Or is this only a minor motif in Calvin's theology, grudgingly conceded because of the strong Pauline evidence in favor of such a view? Is J. S. Whale correct when he affirms that "the gospel as it appears in Paul and John" is found "in clearer and brighter form in Luther than in Calvin"?[54]

The best way to answer such questions is to examine Calvin's exegesis of a few key Johannine and Pauline texts. The first is John 1:17: "The law was given through Moses; grace and truth came through Jesus Christ." On the one hand, Calvin notes that "Moses' contribution was extremely scanty compared to the grace of Christ." This sounds like the comparisons we saw in the last section; it is simply a matter of more and less. But Calvin does not stop here. He proceeds to point out,

> But we must notice the antithesis in his contrasting of the law to grace and truth; for he means that the law lacked both of these. . . . Here we are dealing with . . . the validity of the law in itself (*per se*) and apart from Christ. The evangelist denies that anything substantial is to be found in it until we come to Christ. Moreover, the truth consists in our obtaining through Christ the grace which the law could not give.[55]

A key Pauline text in this regard is Rom. 4:15: "For the law brings wrath, but where there is no law there is no transgression." This is a very negative text, one where Calvin might be tempted to soften its sharpness. But he states unequivocally that

> since the law generates nothing but vengeance, it cannot bring grace. The law would, it is true, point out the way of life to men of virtue and integrity, but since it orders the sinful and corrupt to do their duty without supplying them with the power to do it, it brings them in their guilt to the judgment seat of God.[56]

[54] J. S. Whale, *The Protestant Tradition* (Cambridge: Cambridge University Press), 1955, 164.

[55] Comm. Jn. 1:17. Cf. *Institutes* II.7.16.

[56] Comm. Rom. 4:15.

In any discussion of Paul's view of the law two other texts of a similar nature are always brought forward: Rom. 5:20 and Gal. 3:19. The former reads, "The law came in to increase the trespass . . . ." Calvin begins his comments by making a characteristic distinction: Paul here, he maintains, "is not describing the whole office and use of the law, but is dealing only with the one part which served his present purpose."[57]

This qualification is crucial to an understanding of Calvin's view of the law: that when Paul speaks in this way of the law, he is not referring to the original meaning of *Torah*, the revelation of God's will for his people. Rather, he is limiting himself to only one aspect and function of the law. Another example of this qualification is seen in his commentary on Rom. 7:2-3. Here, too, Calvin cautions, the apostle "refers only to that part of the law which is peculiar to the ministry of Moses."[58]

The other text which seems to indicate an exclusively negative and secondary role for the law is Gal. 3:19: "Why then the law? It was added because of transgressions." Calvin again begins with characteristic cautions and qualifications.

> The law has many uses, but Paul confines himself to one which serves his present purpose. He did not intend to inquire how many ways the law is of advantage to men. It is necessary to put readers on their guard on this point; for I have found that many make the mistake of acknowledging no other use of the law than what is expressed here. Paul himself elsewhere speaks of the precepts of the law as profitable for doctrine and exhortation (2 Tim. 3:16). Therefore *this definition of the use of the law is not complete and those who acknowledge nothing else in the law are wrong.*[59] [Italics mine]

The closing warning might be viewed as a criticism of Luther or some of his followers. However, a careful comparison of Luther's and Calvin's exegesis of key law-gospel passages in Galatians shows that the two reformers are in fundamental agreement on this issue.[60] In regard to this text (Gal. 3:19), for example, he continues with this commentarie.:

> However much the law may point out true righteousness, yet, due to the corruption of our nature, its teaching merely increases transgressions until the Spirit of regeneration comes and writes it

[57]Comm. Rom. 5:20.

[58]Comm. Rom. 7:2-3.

[59]Comm. Gal. 3:19.

[60]See Hesselink, "Luther and Calvin on Law and Gospel in Comm. on Galatians," cited in n 13.

on the heart; and the Spirit is not given by the law but by faith. The reader should keep in mind that this saying (*dictum*) is not philosophical or political but expresses a purpose of the law which the world has never known.[61]

In Calvin's commentary on Gal. 2:19 one would think that this was Luther, not the Genevan reformer. The text goes: "For I through the law died to the law, that I might live to the law."

We must not ascribe to Christ what is properly the task of the law. It was not necessary that Christ should annihilate the righteousness of the law, for the law slays its own disciples . . . . It is the law which forces us to die to itself; for by threatening our destruction it leaves us nothing but despair and thus drives us away from trusting in it.

This passage will be better understood by comparing it with Romans 7. There Paul describes superbly how that no one lives to the law but he to whom the law is dead, i.e., is idle (*otiosa*) and without effect. For as soon as the law begins to live in us it inflicts a fatal wound by which we die, and at the same time it breathes life into the person who is already dead to sin. Those who live to the law, therefore, have never felt the power of the law, or even tasted what it is all about; for the law, when truly understood, makes us to die to itself. It is from this source, not from Christ, that sin proceeds.[62]

It is necessary to examine Calvin's exegesis of one more passage, for here, more than anywhere else, the distinctive nuances of Calvin's understanding of the law are clearly delineated. The passage is 2 Cor. 3:6-7: "For the letter [written code," RSV] kills, but the Spirit gives life." Calvin concludes that "letter" or "written code" (*gramma*) here refers to the Old Testament and "Spirit" refers to the gospel. "By the word 'letter' Paul means preaching which is external and does not reach the heart; by 'Spirit' he means teaching which is alive, which works mightily in the souls of men by the grace of the Spirit."[63]

[61]Comm. Gal. 3:19.

[62]Ibid. These and similar commentary should suffice to show that Helmut Thielicke errs when he says, "The Law-Gospel antithesis [in Calvin] is thus to be understood as being quite relative, not unconditional," *Theological Ethics,* Vol. 1 (Philadelphia: Fortress, 1966), 122.

[63]Comm. 2 Cor. 3:6.

It seems out of character for Calvin to identify the external letter with the Old Testament, but he is convinced that Paul here has Jer. 3:31 in mind and accordingly likens the old covenant to something external whereas in the new covenant the law is written on the heart through the Spirit.

But this raises the question of the faith of the Old Testament believers. Did God only speak to them externally without touching their hearts by his Spirit? Given all that Calvin has affirmed earlier about this subject, this would appear to contradict those affirmations. The first answer to this question is that Paul has in mind here "a special characteristic (*proprium*) of the law."

Although God was at that time working by his Spirit, he did so not through the ministry of Moses but through the grace of Christ. As we learn from John 1:17, 'The law was given by Moses, but grace and truth by Jesus Christ.' Of course, all that time the grace of God was not inactive; but it is also clear enough that it was not the peculiar blessing of the law. Moses fulfilled his office when he gave the way of life, with its threats and promises. Paul calls the law 'letter' because in itself it is dead preaching; and he calls the gospel 'Spirit' because its ministry is alive and makes alive.

Secondly, I answer that Paul is not speaking of the law and the gospel absolutely (*non simpliciter*), but only *insofar as* they are opposed to one another for even the gospel itself is not always Spirit. Still, when it comes to a comparison between the two, one must say truly and properly that the nature of the law is such that it teaches literally without penetrating beyond the ear; on the other hand, it is the nature of the gospel to teach spiritually (*spiritualiter*) because it is the instrument of the grace of Christ.[64]

Calvin sharpens the antithesis as he takes up the description of the law as a "ministry (or dispensation) of death" in verse 7. After analyzing various aspects of the comparison, he draws up a summary.

Let us now examine briefly the characteristics of the law and the gospel. But let us remember that the point at issue is neither the whole of the teaching we find in the law and the prophets, nor the experience of the fathers under the Old Testament but rather the peculiar function of the ministry of Moses. The law was engraved on stones and thus it was literal teaching. This defect of the law had to be corrected by the gospel, since the law could not but be breakable, having been consigned to tablets of stone. The gospel,

[64]Ibid.

therefore, is a holy and inviolable covenant because under God it was promulgated by the Spirit. It follows that the law as a ministration of condemnation and death, for when men are taught of their duty and are told that anyone who does not satisfy God's justice is cursed, they are guilty and found guilty of sin and death. Therefore, they receive nothing from the law but condemnation, for in the law God demands his due (*exigit quod sibi debetur*), but does not confer the power to perform it. The gospel, on the other hand, by which we are regenerated and reconciled to God through the free forgiveness of sins, is the ministration of righteousness and consequently of life itself.[65]

The real problem, however, is not that of demonstrating that Calvin takes the accusing, condemning function of the law seriously. Far more difficult is the matter of showing how he integrates this concept of the law with his understanding of the law as a whole. He frequently reconciles the apparent contradiction between the views of David (as in Psalm 119) and Paul concerning the law by suggesting that David is speaking of the whole law whereas Paul is speaking of the law in a limited sense.

Thus, when David praises the law, he is thinking not only of precepts and commandments but also of the promises of salvation as well. He rejoices in the law of the covenant, God's gift to Israel. Paul, however, is dealing with people who perverted and abused the law. They saw it as a means toward achieving righteousness rather than as a gift to a people already redeemed. They separated it from the grace and Spirit of Christ and hence experienced the law as sheer demand and therefore as deadly.[66]

However, with this explanation we still have not come to the crux of the matter. It is not just a question of the misunderstanding and perversion of the law by the Judaizers (so Barth). Nor is it only a question of the narrower and broader concepts of the law. There is something intrinsic in the law which distinguishes it from the gospel. The antithesis lies in the peculiar office, function, and ministry of the law. When the law is separated from the promises and the gospel, when it is viewed according to its peculiar properties in contrast to those of the gospel, the antithesis is radical and profound.

The explanation lies in the two "offices" (*munera*) of Moses, as Calvin understands them. One was general (*in universum*), "to teach the people the true role of piety." In this sense he was a minister of the whole law and preached repentance and faith. In fact, he proclaimed the promises of free grace and was thus a preacher of the gospel (*evangelii praeconem*)![67]

[65]Comm. 2 Cor. 3:7.
[66]Cf. Comm. Ps. 19:7-8; Comm. Acts 7:38; Comm. 2 Cor. 3:14-17.
[67]Comm. Rom. 10:5.

However, Moses also had another "office," which unlike his general office, he did not have in common with Christ.

> This office was particularly imposed upon him, to demand perfect righteousness of the people and to promise them a reward, as if by compact, upon no other condition than that they should fulfill whatever was enjoined upon them, but also to threaten and declare judgment against them if they ever fell from the way .... Therefore, it is important to distinguish between the general doctrine (*generalem doctrinam*) which was delivered by Moses and the special commission (*mandatum*) which he received.[68]

When this distinction is understood, it is possible to see how Paul can speak on the one hand of the law as holy and good and on the other as the law of sin and death. The apostle, because of the situation in which he found himself, often pointed to that which was peculiar to Moses and distinct from Christ, even though they are in agreement as far as the substance of their doctrine is concerned.[69] However, when Paul thus refers to that office of the law which was peculiar (*propria*) to the ministry of Moses, he is not referring to the ten commandments, "For the will of God must stand the same forever."[70]

This closing comment may sound like a softening of the antithesis, but Calvin makes two other distinctions which show that the antithesis is real and radical. One concerns the matter of justification. Here Calvin is as uncompromising as Luther. There are two kinds of promises and two kinds of righteousness: legal promises and evangelical promises, the righteousness of works and the righteousness of faith.[71] These are two opposing systems which are totally irreconcilable. For the law requires works; directs us to Christ. This is why Paul often opposes the law to faith when it comes to justification.[72] The law is not contrary to faith. Were that the case, God would be unlike himself! But as far as the cause and method of justification are concerned, the law is completely at variance with faith.[73]

The other difference between the law and gospel relates to sin. Whereas both the law and the gospel can be empty and useless apart from the Spirit of regeneration, there is an inherent quality in the law which makes it

[68]Comm. Ex. 19:1.

[69]"The End and Use of the Law," in *Comm.ary on the Last Four Books of Moses*, 3: 1978. cf. Comm. 2 Cor. 3:6-10.

[70]Comm. Rom. 7:2.

[71]*Institutes* III.11.17; III.17.6.

[72]Comm. Lev. 10:5; Comm. Acts 15:11; *Institutes* II.9.4.

[73]Comm. Gal. 3:12.

particularly deadening. For the law is a less appropriate vessel for the Holy Spirit than the gospel. Therefore, Calvin approves of Augustine's statement, "If the Spirit of grace is absent, the law is present only to accuse and kill us."[74] The same could not be said of the gospel, for

> it is the nature of the gospel to teach spiritually, because it is the instrument of the grace of Christ. That depends on God's appointment (*hoc ex Dei ordinatione pendet*) for it has pleased him to reveal the power of the Spirit more through the gospel than through the law; for it is the Spirit alone who can teach the hearts of men effectively.[75]

The haunting question that has lurked in the background must now be faced. If the original purpose of the law was to condemn and kill–even though its eventual result was salutary–it would reflect both on the law and on God for having willed something which could only hurt and bring a curse. Calvin's answer–and this brings us to the final reason for the antithesis–is that this negative aspect of the law is "accidental" (*accidentale*) and therefore must be attributed to ourselves.[76]

> When Paul calls the law the ministration of death (2 Cor. 3:6), it is accidental on account of the corrupt nature of man. For the law itself does not create sin; it finds it in us. It offers life to us, but because of our corruption we derive nothing but death from it. It is therefore deadly (*mortifera*) only in relation to man.[77]

Consequently, it is not the law as such that is defective, but the weakness of our flesh.[78] The fact that we are not justified by works is not due to the imperfection of the law. The promise is made of no effect by our sin and corruption. It is possible to speak of the "defect" of the law but that defect arises from human infirmity.[79] It was for this reason that the first covenant was made void[80] and only resulted in condemnation.[81]

---

[74]Quoted in *Institutes,* II.7.7.

[75]Comm. 2 Cor. 3:6.

[76]"The End and Use of the Law," p. 198; cf. Comm. Deut. 30:19.

[77]Comm. Acts 7:38.

[78]*Institutes* III.17.7.

[79]Comm. Lev. 26:9. Cf. Comm. Rom. 8:3.

[80]Comm. Lev. 26:9.

[81]Comm. Deut. 7:12.

If we had not sinned, *if* our nature had remained pure, then "the law would not have brought death on us."[82] But this is all hypothetical, reminiscent of that crucial phrase which provides the clue to the interpretataion of the first five chapters of the *Institutes,*: "If Adam had remained upright" (*si integer stetisset Adam*).[83]

Sin may be an intrusion, contrary to the purpose of the Creator, but it is an established reality. Hence the curse and deadly wound of the law is "not only accidental but perpetual and inseparable (*perpetuum et inseparabile*) from its nature. The blessing which it offers to us is excluded by our depravity, so that only the curse remains."[84] "Since our carnal and corrupted nature contends violently against God's spiritual law and is in no way corrected by its discipline, it follows that the law which had been given for salvation, provided it met with suitable (*idoneos*) hearers, turns into the occasion for sin and death."[85]

The gospel is good news, however, because this "defection" of ours is "accidental" and "therefore cannot abolish the glory of God's goodness" in his generous promises. Our failure cannot nullify the steadfast love of the God who condescended to covenant with his people. "God exhibited a remarkable proof of his goodness in promising life to all who kept his law–and this will always remain inviolate (*integrum*).[86] However, since in fact no one has kept the law, the "wickedness and condemnation of us all are sealed by the testimony of the law. Yet this is not done to cause us to fall down in despair, or completely discouraged, to rush headlong over the brink–provided we duly profit by the testimony of the law."[87]

Thus, driven by the law to seek God's grace, we have an even greater evidence of God's goodness and faithfulness–despite our sin and faithlessness. "Thereby the grace of God, which nourishes us without the support of the law, becomes sweeter, and his mercy, which bestows that grace upon us, becomes more lovely."[88]

Conclusion

This investigation has shown at least three things:

[82]Comm. Rom. 7:19. Cf. *Institutes.* II.7.7.

[83]*Institutes* I.2.1.

[84]Comm. Gal. 3:10. Cf. Comm. Rom. 7:10; Comm. 2 Cor. 3:7f. It is failure to take this reality into account that results in Daniel Fuller's thesis that law and gospel represent a continuum rather than an antithesis. See his *Gospel and Law: Contrast or Continuum?* (Grand Rapids: Eerdmans, 1980), x-xi. In particular, the passages I have just cited show how wrong Fuller is when he concludes: "Calvin never sensed, as biblical theology has begun to perceive, that Paul used the same term 'law' in two ways that are very opposite to each other because of the complicating factor of the power of sin," 204.

[85]*Institutes* II.7.7.

[86]Comm. Ezek. 20:11.

[87]*Institutes* II.7.8.

[88]*Institutes* II.7.7.

1. One cannot make any judgments at all about Calvin's understanding of law and gospel without recognizing the various meanings each of those terms connotes and the various qualifications made within those meanings.

2. Calvin does indeed recognize an antithesis or oppostion between law and gospel, as those terms are generally conceived.

3. Accordingly, Calvin is far closer to Luther than to Karl Barth in regard to the whole law-gospel, gospel-law debate. Any schematization fails to do justice to the nuances of Calvin's position, but it might be depicted as law-gospel-law. In any case, at one level, as we have seen, there is an antithesis between law and gospel, something Barth would not acknowledge. For Barth, the antithesis is only apparent, in that Paul's negative strictures relate only to a *misuse* and *distortion* of the law.[89] For Calvin, as for Luther, there is something intrinsically different between the law and the gospel, and hence neither would probably agree with Barth's famous dictum that "the law is nothing else than the necessary *form* of the gospel, whose content is grace"[90]

---

[89]*Community, State and Church,* 89-91.
[90]Ibid., 80.

Calvin's Handling of the Third Use of the Law and Its Problems

Merwyn S. Johnson

The task of this article is to discern how Calvin avoids re-erecting the law for Christians while establishing the legitimacy of the "third use of the law." Calvin supplements and extends Luther's—and Paul's—understanding of law and gospel as the cornerstone of his own theology, but refuses to allow humans any "additions" to the work of grace. Calvin does show how the "demand" character of the law is removed by Christ and instead is used as a means of participating in Christ's redemptive work. The contents of the article may also suggest an agenda for further study and reflection to see that the theme of law and gospel is as important for Reformed theology as it is for Calvin.

THE "THIRD USE OF THE LAW" TYPICALLY rubs a raw nerve in Reformation studies. The subject touches on the larger issue of law and gospel, which in turn provides the foundation for the Reformation accent on justification by grace through faith. For Protestants in the Reformation heritage there is no question that there are "two" uses of the law, both pertaining to human sin, whereby the law stands over against the gospel. If justification comes by the gospel or faith-union with the righteousness of Jesus Christ, *apart from* the works of the law (Rom. 3:23), then the possibility of a further use of the law for those who are justified threatens the whole dialectic of law and gospel and the efficacy of justification as well.[1]

Such is the Lutheran complaint against John Calvin and the whole Reformed tradition of theology. From 1539 on Calvin refers to the third use of the law as the "principal use, which pertains more closely to the proper purpose of the law."[2] "Calvin, and those who followed in his tradition," says Paul

---

[1] The literature pertaining to the theme of law and gospel is almost endless, most often between Lutheran and Reformed authors. The latest round of discussion was triggered by Karl Barth's essay, "Gospel and Law," in 1935. An extensive bibliographical listing of writings on the subject, both historical and current, can be found in *Gesetz und Evangelium*, ed. Ernst Kinder and Klaus Haendler (Darmstadt: Wissenschaftliche Buchgesellschaft, 1968). More recently I. John Hesselink has cited relevant treatments of the topic law and gospel with a special accent on the Reformed context, in his helpful article, "Luther and Calvin on Law and Gospel in Their Galatians Commentaries," *Reformed Review* 37 (1983/84): 69–82. See also I. John Hesselink, "Christ, the Law, and the Christian: An Unexplored Aspect of the Third Use of the Law in Calvin's Theology," in *Readings in Calvin's Theology*, ed. Donald K. McKim (Grand Rapids: Baker, 1984), 179–91; and Edward A. Dowey, "Law in Luther and Calvin," in *Theology Today* (July 1984): 146–53.

[2] The primary sources used in this article are (1) John Calvin, *Institutes of the Christian Religion*, ed. John T. McNeill, trans. Ford Lewis Battles (Philadelphia: Westminster, 1960); and (2) John Calvin, *Institutes of the Christian Religion: 1536 Edition*, Rev. Ed,. trans. and annotated by Ford Lewis Battles (Grand Rapids: Eerdmans, 1986). References to each of these will be made in the text itself, prefaced by "1559" for (1) and "1536" for (2) where needed for clarity. References

Hoyer, reflecting his Lutheran sources, "lost the distinction between Law and Gospel and, in effect, advocated a type of justification by works."[3]

The matter is raised already by Paul in his letter to the Galatians. The question was whether new Christians, especially Christians of Greek or Gentile background, had to perform all the rites and rituals of the Old Testament–circumcision or eating only "clean" foods, for example–in order to become Christians. Paul says "no they don't," for Christians are justified by Jesus Christ, not by doing what the laws of the Old Testament command. To have to obey the laws of the Old Testament would make Christ subordinate to the law: union with Christ would be merely an aid to help the Christian do what the law required all along. For Paul, on the other hand, union with Christ is the aim and a truly sufficient means to relationship with God, which the continued demands of the law only disrupt. "If I build up again those things which I tore down," he says, "then I prove myself a transgressor" (Gal. 2:18).[4]

The task of this article is to discern what Calvin does with the third use of the law. How in particular does he avoid re-erecting the law? How does he establish the legitimacy of the "third use of the law" and guard against its pitfalls? What difference does the "third use of the law" make to the larger shape of Reformed theology? The working thesis of the article is that Calvin's handling of the "third use of the law" supplements and extends without denying Luther's treatment of law and gospel and thereby establishes some of the most distinctive features of Reformed theology in his train. The article has been written in the hope that there is something here to be gained both by Calvin's proponents and by his detractors.

The Situation in 1530

By 1530 Protestant theology was being forced both from within and from without to consider a third use of the law. The early irruption and fever of Luther's "protest" were over. The Protestant cause was pressed to consolidate its gains in both church and society, and in the aftermath of the Peasants' Uprising in 1525 also to withstand the heavy criticism that justification by faith leaves no room or need for good works. Luther and his colleagues moved

to (1) will generally be in three numbers, e.g., 2.7.12 for the quote in the text, reflecting Book II, Chapter 7, Paragraph 12. References to (2) will be in two numbers, reflecting chapter and paragraph. The critical apparatus in (1) makes clear that the expression quoted in the text comes from Calvin's 1539 Latin edition of the *Institutes*.

[3]Paul M. Hoyer, "Law and Gospel: With Particular Attention to the Third Use of the Law," in *The Concordia Journal*, (September 1980): 189. See also, pointedly, Walter Elert, *Law and Gospel* (Philadelphia: Fortress, 1967), 7f, 38–43, 44–48.

[4]See the entire passage, Gal. 2:11–21. All Biblical quotations are taken from the Revised Standard Version, under copyright protection of the National Council of Churches, 1946 and 1952.

quickly to fill the breach. Luther initiated a "visitation" to determine the condition of the churches of Saxony. For this purpose, under Luther's direction, Melanchthon drafted a set of "Instructions for the Visitors of Parish Pastors in Electoral Saxony" (1528), which hints at a third use of the law.[5] In 1529 Luther wrote a large and a short catechism for the instruction of the faithful. Both catechisms include an exposition of the Ten Commandments. The Large Catechism in particular describes the importance of the commandments also for Christian believers.[6] The same point is made in *The Augsburg Confession* (1530), a public defense of the Lutheran position ordered by the Emperor Charles V and written by Melanchthon. Article XX, "Of Good Works," begins:

> Our teachers are falsely accused of forbidding good works. Their publications on the Ten Commandments and others of like import bear witness that they have taught to good purpose about all stations and duties of life, indicating what manners of life and what kinds of work are pleasing to God in the several callings.[7]

The *Confession* goes on to distinguish between the good works of believers and those of unbelievers. Good works pleasing to God proceed only from a believing heart moved by the Holy Spirit. It is no less necessary for the believer to do good works, "not that we should trust to merit grace by them but because it is the will of God."[8]

Understood precisely in these terms Calvin launches into the third use of the law. The first two uses are respectively for "all men" and "certain men . . . untouched by any concern for what is just and right." The third use is for "the believers, . . . in whose hearts the Spirit of God already lives and reigns" (1536:1.35–36). In the heat of the Antinomian controversy between Luther and Agricola (1537-40) Calvin restates the key sentence: "The third and principal use, which pertains more closely to the proper purpose of the law, finds its place among believers in whose hearts the Spirit of God already lives and reigns" (1559:2.7.12, reflecting the additions of 1539).

[5]See *Luther's Works*, vol. 40, ed. Conrad Bergendoff (Philadelphia: Muhlenberg, 1958), 277: "These two are the first elements of Christian life: Repentance or contrition and grief, and faith through which we receive the forgiveness of sins and are righteous before God. Both should grow and increase in us. The third element of Christian life is the doing of good works; To be chaste, to love and help the neighbor, to refrain from lying, from deceit, from stealing, from murder, from vengefulness, and avenging oneself, etc." Ibid., 275, contains the formula worked out to smooth the first antinomian challenge of John Agricola in 1527. The challenge became a public debate in 1538-1540.

[6]See *The Book of Concord*, trans. and ed. Theodore G. Tappert (Philadelphia: Fortress, 1959), 360f.

[7]Ibid., 41, following the Latin text.

[8]Ibid., 45.

36   *Calviniana*

Calvin, then, is responding to the sense of the matter as it emerged overall in the Protestant arena, as much from within as from without, as much from Luther as from Melanchthon, at the time when he–Calvin–came on the scene in the early 1530s.[9] And at that moment the issue of the third use of the law was ambiguous. Is the law only for use with non-believers, to reveal their sin and the wrath of God against them, then to drive them to the gospel for mercy and salvation? To leave the matter there invites the antinomian conclusion that the law has application to unbelievers but none at all to believers. Not only Calvin but also Luther, Melanchthon, and the whole Protestant cause were forced to move away from that position.

Is the third use of the law simply a re-application of the first two uses of the law to the believer? To the extent that the believer is not yet fully regenerated, continues to sin, and needs further forgiveness and repentance, such a reading of the third use of the law is highly plausible. Under this reading the law continues to function to restrain sin (*usus civilis*) and to reveal sin (*usus theologicus*), so that *believers* might be moved constantly toward the gospel and an ever-closer union with Christ. The law does not terrify believers in the same way as unbelievers, because believers know already the grace in store for them. The law thus functions together with the gospel simply as part of the believers' on-going experience or walk with God, something to be sought and not avoided. Luther's perception that the law needs to be preached first and then the gospel, the two together in tandem, invites such a meaning of the third use of the law. Where Luther himself does not discuss the matter in terms of the third use of the law, Melanchthon and the later *Formula of Concord* (1576/84) do.

According to the last edition (1555) of *Loci Communes* Melanchthon asserts that the third use of the preaching of the law is "concerned with those saints who are now believers."[10] "The law in this life is necessary," he says, "that saints may know and have a testimony of the works which please God."

[9]Both Elert, *Law and Gospel*, 38ff; and Gerhard Ebeling, "On the Doctrine of the *Triplex uses legis* in the Theology of the Reformation," *Word and Faith* (Philadelphia: Fortress, 1963), 62–64 including especially n 2 on 62f; show that all references to a third use of the law in Luther's writings are spurious. Ebeling concludes, 69–75, that Luther never embraced a third use of the law as such and, 65–69, that the language and concept of the third use stems from Melanchthon. Besides the writings cited in the text Melanchthon makes another reference to the use of the law in the Christian life in the *Apology of the Augsburg Confession* (*Apology*, 136–142, in *The Book of Concord*, 126f), but not as a third use; the *Apology* was first published in 1531. In elaborated form a third use of the law does not appear until the 1535 edition of Melanchthon's *Loci Communes* and successive editions of this work. Calvin completed his work on the *Institutes* of 1536 in August of 1535, which makes it highly unlikely that he borrowed his already well-developed view of the three uses of the law from Melanchthon.

[10]For this and subsequent quotes in this paragraph see *Melanchthon on Christian Doctrine: Loci Communes 1555*, trans. and ed. Clyde L. Manschreck (New York: Oxford University Press, 1965), 127. See also Melanchthon's treatment of the law in contrast to the gospel, 144–49; and the place and importance of preaching the law, 154f.

But the real thrust of the law for believers is increased "penance before God" and lamentation over "our false security and impurity." "Such can come about through the divine word, through a consideration of the punishments on others, or through our own punishment." Indeed, the function of the law among believers is directly parallel to its function among unbelievers: humanity needs "a divine testimony of what is right and of what sin is; so that through the punishment of sin in all men, the unconverted may be converted, and the converted be strengthened in the fear of God."

The *Formula of Concord* is even clearer in Article VI, "Of the Third Use of the Law." "Both for penitent and impenitent, for regenerated and unregenerated people the law is and remains one and the same law, namely, the unchangeable will of God."[11] Obedience to the law may be distinguished according to whether accomplished by the regenerate and the unregenerate. The obedience of the former falls under the heading of fruits of the Spirit, while obedience of the latter is called works of the law. But the working of the law, even the third use of the law, is the same: the law helps the regenerate wrestle with the remnants of the Old Adam within and carry forward their regeneration and renewal, which "is incomplete in this world . . . in fact, only begun." The law, that is, in the third use of it, exposes "self-decreed and self-chosen acts of serving God" (*usus theologicus*). The law must also coerce the will (*usus civilis*) so that "not only by the admonitions and threats of the law, but also by punishments and plagues, . . . he [the regenerate] will follow the Spirit and surrender himself a captive."[12]

However, the treatment of the third use of the law by Melanchthon and the *Formula of Concord* does not exhaust the possibilities of Luther's thought. Suppose the third use of the law were indeed for believers only, as Luther suggests, but more than just a re-application of the first two uses. Can the law have a constructive value for believers as a guide to the Christian life? Such was the proposal Calvin made.

To substantiate Calvin's proposal and square it with Luther, the required steps are to show (a) that Calvin takes seriously the first two uses of the law in Luther's sense of them, (b) that Calvin retains Luther's extraordinary accent on grace both in justification and in sanctification, and (c) that a constructive use of the law can be sustained without making the law again "the power of sin" (1 Cor. 15:56). The rest of this article will trace these foundations of Calvin's handling of the third use of the law.

---

[11]*Formula of Concord*, Article VI, paragraph 6, quoted from *The Book of Concord*, 481.

[12]On the distinction between works of the law and fruits of the Spirit see *Formula of Concord*, Article VI, paragraphs 4–5. The quotes are taken from *Formula of Concord*, Article VI, paragraph 3, *Book of Concord*, 480. Elert *Law and Gospel*, 34–43, concurs with stating the third use of the law as a re-application of the first two uses to the Christian.

The Institutes of 1536

The first place to look in Calvin is the *Institutes* of 1536. Not only is this one of the very first avowedly Christian publications by Calvin but also the early edition of this work makes crystal clear Calvin's starting point, critical categories, and essential lines of argument on the subject of the third use of the law. The chapter divisions of the 1536 edition follow closely the ordering of material in Luther's Small and Large Catechisms of 1529.[13] The germane parts of the *Institutes* of 1536 are Chapter I, "The Law: Containing an Explanation of the Decalogue," and Chapter VI, the first thirteen paragraphs dealing with Christian freedom. These portions present the basic interplay of law and gospel, breathing the same air as that of the young Luther, Melanchthon, and the early Reformation more generally.

An outline of Chapter I shows plainly how central are law and gospel as the critical categories with which Calvin is working:[14]

The knowledge of God and the knowledge of man, 1.1–3;

The law (1.4) and the gospel (1.5) set forth/defined;

The ten commandments expounded (1.7–23) and the Lord's teaching on the commandments(1.24–25);

The righteousness of the law (1.26–29) and its futility contrasted with the righteousness based on the mercy of God in Christ and the way of faith (1.30–32);

The three uses of the law spelled out (1.33);

Discipleship and the rightful place of good works in the Christian life (1.34–38).[15]

[13]The point comes from A. Ganoczy, *Le Jeune Calvin* (1966), 139, as cited in Battles, 1536 Ed., 243f. The *Institutes* of 1536 and Luther's *Large Catechism* consider in the same order (1) the law including the Ten Commandments, (2) what Christians believe in terms of the Apostles' Creed, (3) prayer focusing on the Lord's Prayer, and (4) the sacraments of Baptism and the Lord's Supper. Calvin then adds a chapter on the five false sacraments. The "Table of Duties" in the *Small Catechism* corresponds roughly with a further chapter, "Christian Freedom," by Calvin.

[14]This outline differs from that of Battles, who inserts the following sub-headings into the translation:
   A. Knowledge of God (1.1)
   B. Knowledge of Man (1.2–3)
   C. The Law (1.4)
   D. God's Love in Christ (1.5–6)
   E. Exposition of the Decalogue (1.7–23)
   F. Summary (1.24–25)
   G. Justification (1.26–32)
   H. Uses of the Law (1.33)
   I. Justification (continued) (1.34–38)
Calvin, of course, provides no sub-headings beyond the paragraph numbers. Battles' sub-headings draw less from the substance of the material than from Calvin's reorganization of the same material in later editions of the *Institutes*.

[15]Calvin added eleven chapters to the edition of 1539 and another four chapters to the edition of 1543, but simply expanded the basic material and order of the edition of 1536. The *Institutes* received its final form from Calvin's hand in 1559, when he recast the whole work, greatly

According to Calvin's identification of the three uses of the law (1536:1.33) the first one corresponds to Luther's second: in the *usus theologicus* the law reveals and increases human sin–following Paul in Rom. 3:20 and 5:20. The second use of the law for Calvin corresponds to Luther's first: in the *usus civilis* the law restrains human sin by threatening punishments for offenses committed. These two uses apply to all people, whether Christian or non-Christian. The third use of the law, however, applies only to believers: it teaches them "more thoroughly each day what the Lord's will is like" (1.33), and it prompts them by exhortation "like a whip to an idle and balky ass" (1.33).

Like Luther, Calvin's treatment of the *usus theologicus* follows Paul very closely. The law sets forth "those things that God either requires of us or forbids us do, both toward himself and toward others," summed up in the one word 'love,' love for God and love for neighbor (1.24). But the promise of the law, righteousness and life with God, takes place only if humans fulfill the law in every respect, for the law requires perfect obedience (Gal. 3:10). To violate the law in any one respect violates the whole law, and any transgression of the law condemns the transgressor utterly. The transgressor becomes liable to a just punishment and a curse that lasts until restitution can be supplied or the legitimate demands of the law can somehow be fulfilled.

The dilemma is not simply that humans violate particular commandments, committing particular sins or omitting to do what the commandments say to do. Having committed particular sins, humans assume they can make restitution for their sins and otherwise still fulfill the law. However, their efforts to achieve restitution and fulfillment only bind them more closely to the law. They focus their attention more and more on what they can and must do to accomplish what the law demands, so that "He who does them [works of the law] shall live by them" (Gal. 3:12, quoting from Lev. 18:5). Tragedy arises inasmuch as the curse upon sins committed in the past cannot be removed by human efforts at restitution, and the law once violated cannot ever be fulfilled by trying harder to do so. The law itself, then, by the very efforts of humans to fulfill it, traps humans in their sins, increases their trespass (Rom. 5:20), makes them slaves to sin (Rom. 6:17, 20; John 8:34), renders them "sin-

---

expanded its contents, and redistributed the material from the 1536 edition. The paragraph on the knowledge of God (1536:1.1), expanded, remains at the beginning of the whole work (1559:1.1–2). The rubrics of law and gospel (1536:1.27, 33) are buried in the middle of Book II (1559:2.7.1–17. See also chapters 6 and 9) followed by the exposition of the decalogue and Jesus' summary of the law (cf. 1536:1.3–27 and 1559:2.8.1–59). The interplay between law and gospel (1536:1.6, 27–32, 34–38) forms the heart of the later treatment of justification (1559:3.11–18). The thirteen paragraphs on Christian freedom (1536:6.1–13) are taken up with only minor verbal revisions in subsequent editions (1559:3.19.1–16). On the editions of 1539 and 1543 see John Calvin, *Opera Selecta*, vol. III, 2d rev. ed., ed. Peter Barth and Wilhelm Niesel (Monachii in Aedibus: Christian Kaiser Verlag, 1957), ix–xv, xviii–xxii.

ful beyond measure" (Rom. 7:13), and binds them all the more to the curse of the law (Gal. 3:10).[16]

Of course, Paul argues all through the book of Romans that there is nothing intrinsically wrong with the law.[17] The law is spiritual (Rom. 7:14), righteous altogether (Rom. 7:12), a true expression of the will of God for humanity. The destructive "power of the law" (1 Cor. 15:56, and 1536:1.30) arises from a false estimation of human capacities. With the law in their own hands humans consider themselves able to achieve a righteousness which comes from God alone. The false estimation of themselves and their attempts to satisfy the demands of the law turn the law into a self-sufficient rule of morality with no real regard for its origin or its purpose. At that point, however, the law ceases to function as an avenue to life with God and becomes instead the avenue of self-righteousness and self-justification for sinful humans. The law, which is good in its origin, becomes a tyrant in its effects. No longer morally neutral, the law becomes in Paul's view a substitute for God, the basis for the worst of all sins—idolatry, and a euphemism for human sin, evil, and death.

Calvin embraces Paul's line of thinking in the section 1.26-32. "If we look merely to the law, we can only be despondent, confused, and despairing in mind, since from it all of us are condemned and accursed" (1.27).

> The fact, then, remains that through the law the whole human race is proved subject to God's curse and wrath, and in order to be freed from these, it is necessary to depart from the power of the law and, as it were, to be released from its bondage into freedom (1.30).

> All men, without exception, are puffed up with insane confidence in their own powers, unless the Lord proves their vanity. When all this stupid opinion of their own power has been laid aside, they must needs know they stand and are upheld by God's hand alone. Again, since by the righteousness of their works they are aroused against God's grace, it is fitting that this arrogance be cast down and confounded that, naked and empty-handed, they may flee to God's mercy, repose in it, hide within it, and seize upon it alone for righteousness and merit. (1.33).

---

[16]This is Luther's line of thinking in the Heidelberg Disputation (1518). See the Karlfried Froehlich translation of the theses in Martin Luther, *Selections from His Writings*, ed. John Dillenberger (Garden City: Doubleday, 1961), 500-3. Thesis 16 is especially appropriate: "A man who thinks that he wants to attain righteousness by doing what is in him is adding sin to sin, so that he becomes doubly guilty."

[17]Melanchthon's statement that "the law always accuses" comes close to making the law intrinsically sinful, which exceeds Paul's meaning. Elert, *Law and Gospel* 11-13, quotes Melanchthon and the *Apology to the Augsburg Confession* on the subject, but never mentions Luther.

Calvin extends his understanding of the *usus theologicus* of the law to the far reaches of his theology. Clearly *any* trust in human capacities to accomplish the purposes of God is suspect. In the section 1.26–32 Calvin specifically refers to the activities of monks (1.26), works of satisfaction or superogation (1.27–29), or any notion of human response to God's grace (1.32). The point obtains explicitly to what is usually assumed to be Calvin's position on the third use of the law.[18] "God does not," says Calvin,

> as many stupidly believe, once for all bestow on us this forgiveness of sins in order that, having obtained pardon for our past life, we may afterward seek righteousness in the law; this would be only to lead us into false hope, to laugh at us, to mock us. For since no perfection can come to us so long as we are clothed in this flesh, and the law moreover announces death and judgment to all who do not achieve perfect righteousness in works, it will always have grounds for accusing and condemning us unless, on the contrary, the Lord's mercy counters it, and by continual forgiveness of sins repeatedly acquits us. (1.30)

Notice that Calvin deliberately allows the full severity of the law to take effect ("false hope . . . accusing and condemning us") and relates reliance upon good works also for the Christian back to the issue of justification ("the Lord's mercy . . . acquits us").

In his mature theology Calvin applies these thought patterns to other aspects of Christian experience, specifically to the innate sense of divinity, natural revelation, and the Scriptures. Concerning religion Calvin says that "God has implanted in all men a certain understanding of his divine majesty" (1559:1.3.1). At the same time "this seed is so corrupted that by itself it produces only the worst fruits" (1.4.4) and "no real piety remains in the world" (1.4.1), because humans make their own "zeal for religion . . . sufficient," which quickly turns to idolatry (1.4.3). When elevated to a self-sufficiency in the hands of humanity, religion becomes *like the law* the occasion for human sin.

Calvin follows the same reasoning toward natural revelation. The "skillful ordering of the universe is for us a sort of mirror in which we can contemplate God, who is otherwise invisible" (1.5.1). But the problem of the law recurs. Humans begin to regard nature as sufficient to itself and focus their attention upon creatures instead of the creator(1.5.6) "Such is our stupidity that we grow increasingly dull toward so manifest testimonies, and they flow away without profiting us" (1.5.11) or worse, lead to "an immense crowd of

[18]So Elert, *Law and Gospel*, 44: Calvin "puts the third use of the law in the position which, according to Luther belongs to the *usus theologicus*. Elert's whole treatment of Calvin hinges on this point, 44–48.

gods [flowing] forth from the human mind" (1.5.12). The "inner revelation of God through faith" is required here also: such a perception of God is not available to humans by nature or by their own efforts (1.5.14). Natural revelation, that is, functions *like the law* in the *usus theologicus* and locks humans onto the fixations of their sinful affections.[19]

Finally, Calvin makes the same point about the Scriptures, or the written law. The Scriptures are for humans the spectacles through which the Spirit can lead us to the knowledge of God we otherwise lack (1.6.1–4). Even though the Scriptures manifest a whole series of perfections and are inspired by God as the author, the secret testimony of the Holy Spirit is yet required for the Scriptures to be of any help (1.7.4, 1.8.13). "Even if it wins reverence for itself by its own majesty, it seriously affects us only when it is sealed upon our hearts through the Spirit" (1.7.5). And Calvin sharply criticizes those humans, whether collectively as the church (1.7.1–2) or privately as individuals (1.9.1), who attempt to take the interpretation or exercise of the Scriptures into their own hands. The Scriptures, that is, handled by humans as a self-sufficient means of revelation, become *another law* which arouses human sin all the more.

In these several ways Calvin is simply tracing out Paul's arguments in Rom. 1:18–2:16 and 2 Cor. 3:1–6. The law for Paul is, after all, not only the Ten Commandments but also the natural law written upon the hearts of humankind, the basis of religion, and the Pentateuch of the Old Testament Scriptures (as in the expression "the law and the prophets"). The scope of the law and its use is worth spelling out at least in passing, however, to show that Calvin takes the *usus theologicus* of the law with utter seriousness. Not only in 1536 but also in his mature theology Calvin develops, enhances, and makes the *usus theologicus* an operational part of the larger structure of his theology.

Jesus Christ and the Law

How, then, can Calvin sustain a third use of the law without re-erecting the power of the law in the sense of the *usus theologicus*? The basic argument is that in Christ the law itself undergoes a transformation. Christ fulfills all the requirements of the law, takes them up into himself, and supercedes them.[20]

---

[19]Elert, *Law and Gospel*, 4, suggests that the law is "*the* other Word of God" (italics Elert's) besides Christ, and further, 14–15, that the law belongs in its own realm, namely nature, while the Gospel belongs in its own realm, namely grace. A dichotomy of law and gospel along the lines of nature and grace is what Calvin seeks to avoid. To grant the law a realm like nature or culture apart from the realm of grace gives the law precisely the self-sufficiency which transforms the law into "the power of sin" (I Cor. 15:56). The whole dynamic of law and gospel as understood by Paul and Luther as well as Calvin comes in to play whenever such a "self-sufficient realm" emerges.

[20]Elert, *Law and Gospel*, 16–33, concurs with Calvin in seeing the gospel largely in terms of the accomplishments of Christ in his life, death, and resurrection.

For those united with Christ in faith the righteousness of Christ is substituted for the righteousness attempted by human works according to the strictures of the law. In Christ God gives what he commands (1.26), so that human righteousness like human salvation "consists in God's mercy alone" (1.32). But then by Christ the demand character of the law is removed, and the attention of a regenerated humanity shifts from what the law requires of human behavior to the mercy of God, what Christ has in fact accomplished, and where God is presently active.

The basic lines of Calvin's argument are, again, already clear in the *Institutes* of 1536. Calvin never tires of saying that the righteousness of the Christian is no more and no less than the righteousness of Jesus Christ. "By Christ's righteousness then are we made righteous and become fulfillers of the law. . . . Christ's righteousness, which alone can bear the sight of God because it alone is perfect, must appear in court on our behalf, and stand surety for us in judgment" (1.32). The righteousness of Christ consists in *his* fulfilling the requirements of the law in every respect.

Christ's fulfillment of the law covers three critical junctures. First, Jesus lived out in his own human behavior what the law requires of humankind. "Though he was one God with the Father," says Calvin, "Jesus Christ our Lord . . . put on our flesh, to enter a covenant with us and to join us (far separated from God by our sins) closely to him" (1.5). "The example of Christ embraces both this [patience and gentleness associated with taking up one's cross and denying oneself] and all other duties of piety and holiness. He presented himself to the Father as obedient even to death" (1.35). Calvin also considered Jesus to be "the law's best interpreter" (1.25): in his teaching Jesus "added nothing to the old law, but only declared and recleansed the law" (1.25).

Second, Jesus took upon himself the curse of the law on human sins and sinfulness, and by his death upon the cross discharged the punishment due to all humanity. "By the merit of his death [he] paid our debts to God's justice, and appeased his wrath. He redeemed us from the curse and judgment that bound us, and in his body the punishment of sin, so as to absolve us from it" (1.5, 1.32, 1.36, and *passim*). Just so does the work of Jesus Christ point us to the *mercy of God alone* (1.32), because God satisfies the just demands of righteousness as presented by the law and thereby provides a different foundation for human righteousness.

Third, Jesus re-creates the image of God in humanity, previously corrupted by sin, so that those who are joined with Christ enter in to new possibilities of doing what the law required all along. The re-creation of humanity is properly what Jesus accomplishes in his resurrection, notably the resurrection of the body. Calvin refers to the resurrection itself, as when he says, "We have been raised with Christ that we may live for righteousness" (1.37. Cf. Rom. 6:4 and 1 Pet. 2:24). He also connects Paul's language of a "new creation" (2 Cor. 5:17) with being conformed to "the image of his Son" (Rom. 8:29) as the point where Christians "pass from the realm of sin into the realm of righteousness" (1.35). Most often, however, Calvin speaks of adoption:

> Through him we are reborn, wrested from the power and chains of the devil, freely adopted as children of God, sanctified for every good work. Through him also—so long as we are held in this mortal body—there are dying in us the depraved desires, the promptings of the flesh, and everything the twisted and corrupt perversity of our nature brings forth. Through him we are renewed from day to day, that we may walk in newness of life and live for righteousness. (1.5)[21]

The overarching point is, of course, that Jesus Christ fulfills the law in every respect, whether living it out, submitting to the curse of the law to satisfy the law's demands for punishment on transgressors, or reestablishing on other grounds the possibility of doing what the law required.[22] Christ, in other words, has accomplished everything that the law has ever required or ever will require of humanity. The righteousness that was attached to the law now belongs in full to Christ. The righteousness of Christ, therefore, is the only righteousness a sinful humanity will ever have, and that by imputation, gift, and participation in the accomplishments of Christ (see 1.32).

In later editions of the *Institutes* Calvin expands on the notion of Christ fulfilling the law. Calvin makes repeated reference to Rom. 10:4, "For Christ is the end of the law" (1559:1.6.2, 2.6.4, 2.7.2, 3.2.6).[23] On the one hand Christ is the purpose of the law. The whole law points toward Christ as the basis of the human knowledge of God and likewise as the basis of human salvation (see 2.6.2, 2.7.1–2). Said in other words: Christ fulfills the *promises* of God made in the law; "The gospel . . . is a new and unusual sort of embassy by which God has fulfilled what he had promised; that the truth of his promises

[21]"Him" in this quote could refer to the Holy Spirit. For Calvin, however, the Holy Spirit joins us with the life of Jesus Christ, the whole incarnation embracing Jesus' birth, active life, death, and culminating in his resurrection. So reads the following: "In short, if we partake of Christ, in Him we shall possess all the heavenly treasures and gifts of the Holy Spirit, which lead us into life and salvation" (1.6). See also 1.32, 1.34, 1.35, 1.37, and 6.3.

[22]Elert, *Law and Gospel*, 8, contends that "God promises his grace only on the condition that the law is fulfilled." Calvin's point—and Luther's—is that *Christ* does the fulfilling on behalf of sinners and in the process takes care of both the rewards and the punishments, the promises and the curse, that pertain to doing the works of the law.

[23]All these references to Rom. 10:4 were added in the edition of 1559, according to the McNeill/Battles textual apparatus, as were the two chapters VI and IX in Book II. The former chapter asserts that Christ, who conveys the knowledge of God and human redemption, is the one who was promised in the Law. The latter chapter asserts that the gospel of Jesus Christ simply makes plain what the Law had promised all along. The chapters in between these two derive directly from the *Institutes* of 1536, pertaining to the uses of the law (Chapter VII) and an elaboration of the Ten Commandments (Chapter VIII).

would be realized in the person of the Son" (2.9.2). The law, then, has no independent meaning apart from Christ, to whom the law refers by way of purpose and accomplishment.

On the other hand Christ is the conclusion of the law. By fulfilling the law, Christ provides for humankind an avenue of relationship to God "apart from the law" (Rom. 3:21). Christ, who accomplished the law, also abolished it (3.2.6) as a requirement for human salvation, in order that humans might focus their attention upon him instead of themselves, his accomplishments instead of their own futile strivings, his righteousness instead of their persistent sins. The accomplishments *of Christ* become for Christians the floor upon which they walk, the air that they breathe, the new standard by which they measure their efforts and attainments. Christ himself does not thereby become a new law, because Christians are not duplicating the accomplishments of Christ. Being united with Christ in his death, resurrection, and new life, Christians share his accomplishments. The accomplishments of Christ are *given* without further demand or requirement, so that Christians live always and only by the mercy of God freely extended to them.

Calvin's Handling of the Third Use of the Law

Christ's fulfillment of the law brings to a head Calvin's argument concerning the third use of the law. The first two uses still obtain for both believers and unbelievers. Both deal with sin, one with the inner sins of self-righteousness and the other with the outer, flagrant sins of public behavior. But in the light of Christ's fulfillment, the law takes on a different meaning for the Christian. Specifically, the demand character of the law is removed, together with its curse. The law, says Calvin, "is not for them what it formerly was: it may no longer condemn and destroy their consciences by confounding and frightening them with the message of death" (1.33; 2.7.14). Calvin makes the same point repeatedly in the chapter on Christian freedom:

> The consciences of believers, while having to seek assurance of their justification before God, should rise above and advance beyond the law, forgetting all law-righteousness. (6.2)

> Where consciences are worried how to make God favorable, what to respond and with what assurance to stand, if called to his judgment—there we are not to reckon what the law requires, but Christ alone, who surpasses all law-perfection, must be set forth for righteousness. (6.2)

> See how all our works are under the curse of the law if they are measured by the standard of the law! But how, then, would unhappy souls gird themselves eagerly for a work for which they

might expect to be able to receive only a curse? But if, freed from this severe requirement of the law, or rather from the entire rigor of the law, they hear God calling them with fatherly gentleness, they will cheerfully and with great eagerness answer his call, and follow his leading. (6.3)[24]

How, then, does the law function for Christians whose relationship with God depends on Christ's accomplishments and no longer on doing what the law demands? Calvin mentions two specific ways. Both are present in the *Institutes* of 1536, receive some clarification in the 1539 edition, but do not change through the edition of 1559.

First, from the law Christians "learn more thoroughly each day the nature of the Lord's will to which they aspire" (2.7.12, 1.33). Calvin offers the illustration of the servant, who, "already prepared with all earnestness of heart to commend himself to his master, must search out and observe his master's ways more carefully in order to conform and accommodate himself to them" (*ibid.*). The law, that is, functions as an *indicator* of the character and activity *of God*.[25] The servant does not wait to be told what to do, but uses the law to anticipate the master's wishes, to get a reading on the master's purposes, character, and habits, and to direct his own actions accordingly. The law is not God, but points to God: What kind of God wants humans to behave this way? What does God like and not like, want or not want? Precisely as a reflection of the will of God, the law points to where God might be and what God might be doing and indicates the scope and intent of God's activities.

Such a use of the law opens up perhaps the primary avenue of human piety before God. The law, most notably as covenant formula or as ethical instruction, points the Christian to specific ways and places where God is present and active, so that ethical behavior becomes the principal arena of communion with God. Christians serve the Lord not to appease wrath, earn righteousness, be good for its own sake, give a proper response, or some other way of presenting a leveraged demand upon humans. Christians "meditate on the law day and night" (Ps. 1:2) to help them discern the presence and activity of God in the midst of their lives, relationships, opportunities, current events, and the like, so that they can—by the gift of participation—live with God and God with them.[26]

[24]The relevant sections of the *Institutes* of 1536, 6.1–13, carry over into the *Institutes* of 1559, Book III, chapter 19, with only minor revisions.

[25]Elert, *Law and Gospel*, seriously misunderstands Calvin when he says that "the law is understood only as God's legislation," 9, and reduces Calvin's treatment of the third use of the law to "the desired information on all the practical questions of our life," 46. Calvin here turns the focus of the law away from human behavior altogether and shines it upon Godself and upon the "practical questions" of God's life.

[26]This meaning of the law shows up in the Old Testament formulary, "do this, and live" (Lev. 18:5), where the point of doing is not goodness for its own sake but life, interacting with

Calvin's whole teaching on the Christian life follows the opening developed by this rendering of the third use of the law. The reliance is still upon Christ: "because all his [Christ's] things are ours and we have all things in him, in us there is nothing" (1.34). Any good works done are gifts from God, both the goodness and the works:

> These good works are given to them [believers] by God and are theirs because they have been given by God. At the same time, they are taught that the works are acceptable to God, and the believers are pleasing to him in these: not that they are thus deserved, but because the divine goodness has established this value for them. (1.36)

Christians are released from the narrow calculation of rewards and punishments (1.37), because they are "sons"—children—in God's family (6.3) who are entering in to their inheritance, not earning a wage (1.38). "Good works" for Calvin mean a participation in Christ, sharing in his self-denial, sufferings, and cross (1.35), as well as his wisdom, righteousness, purity, power, and life (1.34). The glory of God takes the place of human merit or self-interest as the primary motivation in the Christian life (1.37): the incentive to greater efforts comes from the joy of deeper levels of experience and communion in the activities of God.

Calvin's lengthy exposition of the Decalogue (1.7–25; 2.8.1–59) carries out the rubrics of the previous two paragraphs and deserves further, careful scrutiny along with his sermons on the Ten Commandments,[27] and his whole treatment of repentance (regeneration, sanctification, adoption) and of the Christian life (1559:3.1–10).

Exhortation is the other way in which the law carries out its third use. "The law," says Calvin, "is to the flesh like a whip to an idle and balky ass, to arouse it to work" (1559:2.7.12, 1536:1.33). Because Christians continue to sin, even they need a "constant sting" (1.33) to get them moving. Exhortation recalls the imperative mood of a command and may even entail posing a threat or emphasizing the consequences of a certain course of action ("Stop the car! before you go through the intersection, hit a car, get hurt, or kill someone!") An exhortation appeals to the prudence of an action and properly takes the form of a prudential imperative. The force of such an imperative, however,

others and with God through the covenant framework. The same meaning shows up in the New Testament formulary, "abide in me and I in you" (John 15:4), in which union with Christ is linked with keeping the commandments (vs. 10. See also John's constant reference to "words," which refer both to the "ten words" of the OT and to the "words of Jesus'" teaching.).

[27]See *John Calvin's Sermons on the Ten Commandments*, ed. and trans. Benjamin W. Farley (Grand Rapids: Baker, 1980).

falls short of an absolute demand which binds the conscience or brings Christians under the curse of the law. To raise an exhortation to the level of an absolute demand would indeed re-erect the law and declare that Christ has accomplished nothing, or make of Christ a mere enabler of the works of the law.

Calvin does not lose sight of the proximate character of exhortation, nor of the grace required to hear and obey. "The Lord instructs by their reading of it [the law]," says Calvin, "those whom he inwardly instills with a readiness to obey" (2.7.12). And a short time later: "*Through Christ* [italics added] the teaching of the law remains inviolable; by teaching, admonishing, reproving, and correcting, it forms us and prepares us for every good work" (2.7.14). The law, though abrogated, thus remains a focus of human "veneration and obedience," but for those engrafted in Christ it cannot become again the occasion for human bondage (see 2.7.14–15).

As understood by Calvin, all three uses of the law—the *usus theologicus, usus civilis*, and *tertius usus*—exist side by side without contradicting one another. The first two uses complement each other inasmuch as both pertain to human sin, the one to the deeper, inner sin of self-righteousness and the other to the outer sins of blatant misbehavior. The latter calls forth community structures for regulating behavior in a civil society. The former raises the urgent need for redemption and conversion of the human affections from the inside out.

The first and third uses of the law complement each other, too. In fact the third use of the law parallels directly the first use of the law. The *usus theologicus* initially points to the kind of human being—obedient and righteous according to the requirements of the law—that God created humans to be. The law actually desciibes the fullness of a healthy humanity, not only as an individual but also as a society. The law manifests human sins and sinfulness by showing humans specifically where they fall short of the law's demands and then how humans pervert the law into a self-sufficient instrument of moral attainment. Without displacing this profound meaning of the law, the *tertius usus* allows the descriptive force of the law, to fall also upon God, asking the reflective question, "What does the law tell us about the Lawgiver and the Lawgiver's character, modes of presence, and active directions?" The law functions as a guide to the Christian life not by telling humans again what they have to do but by pointing to God and what *God* is now doing. Such information serves both to clarify and to motivate strenuous efforts at Christian living. But the information is never self-sufficient: it still relies upon being engrafted into Christ and the urging of the Spirit to meditate upon the law and interpret present situations with the faith that God is truly present and active in them. "To be Christians under the law of grace," says Calvin,

> does not mean to wander unbridled outside the law, but to be engrafted in Christ, by whose grace we are free of the curse of the law, and by whose Spirit we have the law engraved upon our hearts. (1.26).

Conclusion and Further Agenda

The article has shown several things so far. (a) From his earliest Christian writings on, Calvin understood the law, especially the *usus theologicus*, in much the same way Luther did. Calvin also understood the Gospel in terms of Jesus Christ, Christ's accomplishments, and the utterly undeserved mercy of God to a sinful humanity, just like Luther. In a real sense Calvin begins with Luther's—and Paul's—basic understanding of law and gospel as the cornerstone of his own theology. Further, (b) for Calvin the grace of God alone redeems and sustains Christians, by uniting them with Christ and his accomplishments. Grace is not triggered or affected by any efforts of humans either to believe or after believing to respond with good deeds. Calvin is clear, consistent, and unequivocal in refusing to allow humans any "additions" to the work of grace. Humans *participate* in what Christ has done, what God is doing: they do not achieve anything of their own. But then Calvin retains the same accent on grace in both justification and sanctification that is Luther's hallmark as well. Finally, (c) Calvin shows how, once the demand character of the law and its curse have been removed by Christ, the law can have a constructive use for Christians without reverting to the law's role as the deadly accuser against a sinful humanity. As a reflection not upon the strictures of human behavior, but upon the nature, presence, and activities of the Lawgiver, the law supplies both clarity and positive motivation to ardent Christian living in communion with God. The third use of the law in this sense neither nullifies the *usus theologicus* nor establishes any self-sufficient claims for the law.

These several points lead to the conclusion that Calvin's treatment of the law picks up where Luther's left off and extends Luther's thought in a valid, consistent direction. The contents of the article may also suggest an agenda for further study and reflection.

First, in the light of the material presented here the differences between Lutheran and Reformed perspectives on law and gospel do not appear to be mutually exclusive. The differences are real and have important consequences for each tradition. Law and gospel in the Lutheran tradition focus on the condition of humanity in sin, as the law makes plain, and the condition of humanity in grace, as the gospel reaches out to people. Elaborating the third use of the law, the Reformed tradition accentuates how redeemed humans can serve the purposes of God while participating in God's plans, presence, and activities.[28] These differences, however, may be a matter of ethos, more "connotative" than "denotative," as Professor Dowey puts it.[29] Both traditions can

---

[28] As the Westminster Shorter Catechism (1647) aptly puts it, "Man's chief end is to glorify God, and to enjoy him forever." Quoted from *Creeds of Christendom*, vol. 3, 4th ed. Revised and Enlarged, ed. Philip Schaff (Grand Rapids: Baker 1919), 676. See also John 15:1–17 and Eph. 2:8–10.

[29] Dowey, "Law in Luther and Calvin." Hesselink, "Luther and Calvin on Law and Gospel in Their Galatians Commentaries," supports the same conclusion.

legitimately trace their theological roots back to Luther. The differences—and the similarities—are worth exploring further.

Second, Calvin's treatment of law and gospel, including specifically the third use of the law, offers another handle for picking up Calvin's theological methodology, the structure of his thought, and the distinctive positions he takes. For example, the dialectic of the knowledge of God and the knowledge of humanity ("nearly all the [true and sound] wisdom we possess," 1559:1.1.1 and 1536:1.1) arises from his treatment of law and gospel. Calvin identifies law as a kind of boundary line where God and humanity meet, from which he extrapolates a theological reflection upon humanity (first two uses of the law) and a theological reflection upon God (third use of the law). These connections in Calvin's thinking become matters of explicit self-awareness in the *Institutes* of 1539 and later editions.[30] The ramifications of this thought process for Calvin's theology deserve to be worked out. It just may be that the issue of law and gospel is as important for Calvin as it is for Luther.

Third, if the previous agenda item bears fruit for Calvin, the question is worth posing whether a similar investigation might bear fruit also for the history of Reformed theology, inasmuch as the distinctive features of Calvin's theology have impressed themselves on Reformed theologians down through the years. Surely more than common positions on the various loci of theology bind together such disparate figures as the Westminster Divines in seventeenth-century England, Friedrich Schleiermacher in eighteenth-nineteenth-century Germany, Charles Hodge in nineteenth-century America, and Karl Barth in twentieth-century Switzerland. Is there here also a distinctive methodology, emanating from a distinctive treatment of law and gospel? It just may be that the theme of law and gospel is as important for Reformed theology as it is for Calvin.

[30]See notably 1559: II.8.1-11.

Calvin and the Political Order:
An Analysis of the Three Explanatory Studies

W. Fred Graham

There is little doubt that the genius of Calvin did not extend to his analysis of political order, especially to his advice to Christians who labored under rule so unjust that their very lives were in jeopardy. Students (like myself) who appreciate his balanced, supple, and insightful work in Christian doctrine and scripture exegesis are suddenly brought up short at his impoverished and traditional views of political order, and his injudicious use of the Bible as he tries to explicate hard cases, such as Huguenots who daily walked down the valley of death in his beloved France. In this essay I shall examine three recent interpretations of Calvin and see whether they help us understand the shortcomings of the political Calvin. After a brief examination of Calvin's political theory in the *Institutes*, we shall in turn look at the studies of Harro Höpfl, Suzanne Selinger, and William Bouwsma, and conclude with a word about how each provides insights that may help us understand Calvin's thought in this arena.

THERE HAVE BEEN plenty of studies of Calvin's political thought.[1] The modern reader can read through his major statement in Chapter 20 of Book IV of *Institutes of the Christian Religion* in a few minutes. There one will find a traditional separation of church and state expounded, with a strong defense of magistrates against the calumnies of Anabaptistic anarchists, "who would have men living pell-mell like rats in straw."[2] As a practical matter Calvin recognizes different kinds of government and expresses his own preference for "a system compounded of aristocracy and democracy" because it is safer not to entrust political power to only one man, or even a few.[3] Like most sixteenth-century thinkers Calvin thought princes and magistrates ought not to neglect national piety and the general care of religion.[4] Indeed, throughout his exposition of the calling of magistrates, their various duties, the right to make war under certain conditions, taxation, the writing and enforcing of laws, the judicial process, and the like, there is little that one can take exception to, unless Calvin is to be judged according to later doctrines of our more absolute separation of church and state.

---

[1]Two places to find quick bibliographies in this area are *Calvin: Institutes of the Christian Religion*, ed. John T. McNeill, trans. Ford Lewis Battles, Library of Christian Classics (Philadelphia: Westminster, 1960), Book IV, where Chapter xx, "Civil Government," begins, and in the bibliography of Harro Höpfl, *The Christian Polity of John Calvin* (Cambridge: Cambridge University Press, 1982).

[2]*Institutes* IV.20.7 footnote gives his French translation.

[3]*Institutes.* IV.20.8.

[4]*Institutes.* IV.20.9.

51

Where Calvin is less helpful is when he turns in IV: 20: 23, to the question of the obedience citizens owe to unjust rulers. Calvin knew well enough how bad slothful and wicked rulers could be:

> But it is the example of nearly all ages that some princes are careless about all those things to which they ought to have given heed, and, far from all care, lazily take their pleasure. Others, intent upon their own business, put up for sale law, privileges, judgments, and letters of favor. Others drain the common people of their money, and afterward lavish it on insane largesse. Still others exercise sheer robbery, plundering houses, raping virgins and matrons, and slaughtering the innocent.[5]

The Stalins, Somozas, Amins, Pinochets, Duvaliers—Calvin knew his history and he knew the corruption of power. Rule had always attracted or produced people in whom there is "no trace of that minister of God, who had been appointed to praise the good, and to punish the evil."[6]

But it is at this point that his advice sours in our ears, as it did to his Huguenot compatriots:

> We are not only subject to the authority of princes who perform their office toward us uprightly and faithfully as they ought, but also to the authority of all who, by whatever means, have got control of affairs, even though they perform not a whit of the princes' office.

And what is the calling of the wicked ruler?

> They who rule unjustly and incompetently have been raised up by him to punish the wickedness of the people; that all equally have been endowed with that holy majesty with which he has invested lawful power. . . . In a very wicked man utterly unworthy of all honor, provided he has the public power in his hands, that noble and divine power resides which the Lord has by his Word given to the ministers of his justice and judgment. Accordingly, he should be held in the same reverence and esteem by his subjects, in so far as public obedience is concerned, in which they would hold the best of kings if he were given to them.[7]

---

[5]*Institutes.* IV.20.24.
[6]*Institutes.* IV.20.25, citing 1 Pet. 2: 14.
[7]*Institutes.* IV.20.25.

Calvin, ever the minister of God's Word, can find scripture to support his position. Nebuchadnezzar, surely a most wicked ruler, was nevertheless praised by both Ezekiel and Daniel. In Jeremiah we read that even the Babylonian ruler was God's servant and the Hebrew people were enjoined to serve him and live. So eager is Calvin for scriptural support for a position that persecuted Protestants found repugnant, if not farcical, that he is driven to twist Samuel's warning to Israel that the king they desire will oppress them, by translating *mishpat* as *ius* and (in French) a more neutral *puissance*, when in context it clearly means 'order' or (in an ironic sense) 'justice.' Hence, instead of Samuel uttering a warning that their desire for monarchy would bring on a succession of bad kings, Calvin reads Samuel as saying "this shall be the *right* of the king that will reign over you . . . ," or some such translation which converts warning into royal privilege.

After also noting that wives and children must obey husbands and fathers who fail to live up to God's demands, he concludes by saying that we must look within at our own sinfulness, and it appears that Calvin simply sees such bad governors as the natural judgment of God upon those who are so oppressed. That is, he places the blame on those who are abused:

> Therefore, if we are cruelly tormented by a savage prince, if we are greedily despoiled by one who is avaricious or wanton, if we are neglected by a slothful one, if finally we are vexed for piety's sake by one who is impious and sacrilegious, let us first be mindful of our own misdeeds, which without doubt are chastised by such whips of the Lord. By this, humility will restrain our impatience. Let us then also call this thought to mind, that it is not for us to remedy such evils; that only this remains, to implore the Lord's help, in whose hand are the hearts of kings, and the changing of kingdoms.[8]

Is there not insult added to injury here? Calvin, relatively safe in Geneva, tells persecuted brothers and sisters that they must not only accept their lot peaceably, but must consider their state to be the result of their own misdeeds. One feels that Calvin's empathy or imagination for the oppressed has fled him here. It is because this is so antithetical to his general teaching that the sympathetic student of Calvin shakes the head in bewilderment.

It is true that in the last two sections—which form the brief conclusion to his long exposition of Protestant theology—he suggests that duly elected magistrates may restrain the willfulness of kings, and all commentators assume he has parliaments in mind. Indeed, he goes further and says such magistrates

---

[8]*Institutes*. IV.20.26, citing 1 Sam. 8: 11.

must not "wink at kings who violently fall upon and assault the lowly common folk."[9] But not every land had a parliament–France's had not met for decades–and Calvin's admonition must have been read as a sop by those who bitterly resented unjust or anti-Protestant rule.

There are two other negative observations that can be made about Calvin's view of government. The first is the brevity of his treatment; it appears almost to be an afterthought. A glance at the title to the last book of the *Institutes* gives the impression that church and state will be given balanced treatment: "The External Means or Aids by which God Invites Us into the Society of Christ and Holds Us Therein." But as a matter of fact the church receives 93 percent of the attention, the state only 7 percent, or about thirty-five pages in the *Library of Christian Classics* translation. So it appears *prima facie* that Calvin is not much interested in the state, even if every sixteenth-century Christian lived under a mixed church-state jurisdiction.

The second additional negative is the actual practice of politics in Calvin's Geneva. There is much positive that should be said about his influence on Genevan life, as I and others have detailed rather exhaustively.[10] Calvin clearly held to what some today call "preference for the poor and oppressed" in his social and economic views. But there was a tendency to over-legislate and to call for penalties for unsocial behavior that most people in his day and ours would call excessive. In my own disappointment at some legislation and its enforcement under his influence, I wrote:

> The success, the positive results of his views . . . are not so puzzling. If the Christian gospel, which proclaims the love of God to be inextricably bound up with Jesus Christ, whose compassion for humankind took him even to the Cross, if this good news will not have a beneficial effect on men in society when once it grips a man of Calvin's stature–then it is of dubious value. . . . But the gospel at times became a club, an excuse for foolishness and insensitivity, for torture, even death. What went wrong? . . . Contemporaries of lesser acumen than Calvin in neighboring cities were perplexed by this rigor that, had St. Paul applied it (Haller said), would have excommunicated every person in Corinth.[11] [Haller was chief pastor in Bern.]

[9]*Institutes.* IV.20.31.

[10]See, for example, W. Fred Graham, *The Constructive Revolutionary: Calvin's Socio-Economic Impact* (East Lansing: Michigan State University Press, 1987); William C. Innes, *Social Concern in Calvin's Geneva* (Allison Park, Pa.: Pickwick, 1983); Elsie McKee, *John Calvin on the Diaconate and Liturgical Almsgiving* (Geneva: Droz, 1984).

[11]Graham, *Constructive Revolutionary*, 174–76.

To what can we attribute the neglect of the political order, his poorly imagined advice to persecuted Protestants, and the harsh measures Geneva instituted under his influence to keep the body politic and ecclesiastic relatively pure? Earlier writers tended to treat his views in this arena as simply a hangover of medieval thought, something tangential to his real concerns, which were religious, not social or political. James B. Torrance, in a contribution to this book, follows Karl Barth in attributing it to a failure to understand that Christ is lord over the state as well as the church. Torrance argues that if Christ is not understood as head of the state, then other norms apply to its operation, and the role of citizens within it, than those that are found in Christ's gracious rule.

Without disagreeing with this position, one could still ask why Calvin exempts the state from Christ's rule, if indeed he does. In the last five years three excellent studies of Calvin have appeared, all of which attempt to get behind general categories of analysis, such as "he was too much a thinker of the Middle Ages," or "he had a harsh and unyielding temperament," and to focus in sharply and specifically those aspects of his life or thought that illumine larger areas, such as the one we are concerned with. The first is Harro Höpfl's very helpful *The Christian Polity of John Calvin*[12]; next, Suzanne Selinger's largely neglected *Calvin against Himself: An Inquiry in Intellectual History*[13]; and quite recently William J. Bouwsma, *John Calvin: A Sixteenth Century Portrait*.[14] I shall present thumbnail sketches of the three studies of Calvin, and then explicate what each scholar says or might say about my thesis that Calvin's political theory is weak and unhelpful, his practice as an influencer of the magistrates of Geneva overly harsh, lacking in the generally pragmatic approach Calvin took toward matters that were not at the heart of the gospel.

In a chronological study that examines Calvin's views of the state from the first edition of the *Institutes* right through the French translation of his last edition, Höpfl correlates the development in Calvin's thought with his experience of the political realm. Taking the *Institutes*, the commentaries and sermons, the various *Ordonnances*, and occasional writings together, Höpfl is puzzled that, while these touch on a very wide range of political topics, "it . . . remains a question, precisely in view of the quantity of this material, why he should never have drawn it all together in a more comprehensive fashion than book 4, chapter 20 of the *Institution*."[15] So careful to spell out church order; so

---

[12]Harro Höpfl, *The Christian Polity of John Calvin* (Cambridge: Cambridge University Press, 1982). This is one in a series of Cambridge Studies in the History and Theory of Politics.

[13]Suzanne Selinger, *Calvin against Himself: An Inquiry in Intellectual History* (Hamden, Ct.: Archon [The Shoestring Press], 1984).

[14]William J. Bouwsma, *John Calvin: A Sixteenth Century Portrait* (New York: Oxford University Press, 1988).

[15]Höpfl, *The Christian Polity* 148.

[16]Ibid., 212.

negligent about the political. This would be unexceptional today, Höpfl argues, but in Calvin's day the close relationship between the two, indeed, the overlapping jurisdictions, overlapping disciplines, and Calvin's own Genevan work in law-writing and diplomacy beg for a more careful analysis than the "pieties" Calvin enunciated. Even the 1562 massacre of the Huguenots at Vassy did not stir him to further exposition. It is not surprising, Höpfl notes wryly, that Huguenot disciples abandoned their master's doctrine of political obedience within a decade of his death in 1564.

When he poses an answer to his own questions about why Calvin did not analyze political order more cogently and why he leaves his friends in such distress—especially in his beloved France—Höpfl's answer is that "anabaptists and apostates are a much graver menace than papists, and divisions amongst the custodians of purity of doctrine are graver than either."[16] What this means is that schisms, sects, and irreligion could never be prevented simply by the discipline administered by clergy, hence it was the secular magistrate who had to be counted on for unity in the church. Schism was more a problem to Calvin than were external threats. As Höpfl points out, such a conclusion makes far more sense in the little Genevan republic than it did in France, where the ruler was a papist and as likely to destroy the church as he was to quench the raging fires of Anabaptism and atheism, or prevent Protestant schisms.

I confess that Höpfl's excellent study appears uncertain and tentative at the end. Why should Calvin have made a choice that left his followers so exposed? Why insist on obedience to wicked rule to preserve the church's unity, when the aim of the ruler is to abolish the church? Höpfl scorns scholars who say Calvin had a "pathos of order" (p. 212), but one has the impression that the cause was something deeper than the practical consideration that Höpfl outlines and at the same time acknowledges made no sense given the realities of religious persecution in the sixteenth century.

Suzanne Selinger's *Calvin against Himself* needs more discussion than it has gotten so far. Anyone who has read Calvin very long has, I think, felt the power of his language, whether used in advocating a position or fighting an erroneous one, and knows that Calvin can sometimes fight more bitterly than the argument seems to warrant. It is as if something in him impels rhetorical overkill. One ploy he uses is to attack something sharply and then say that true religion nevertheless requires one to take that position. For example, he will say terrible things about the body, "that bag of worms," and then say that if you want to have anything in common with Christ you must not despise the body.

Selinger argues that the power of this rhetoric is rooted in a deep dualism that pervades his psyche, a dualism expressed in such conflicts as that between our foulness and God's glory, between despair and faith, emotion and intellect,

[16]Ibid., 212.

body and spirit. The latter duality is the key, she argues, and the struggle not to surrender to a manichaeism of body and spirit is the dynamo that powers his rhetoric. That is, temperamentally Calvin is a dualist, who values the spiritual more than the physical, and is quite overcome at times by the foulness of the body. But theologically he does not accept the dualism that his temperament inclines him toward. Instead, he is a good disciple of Luther and maintains Luther's solid integration of spirit and flesh. She traces that integration in Calvin's doctrines of the Word-made-flesh, in the sacraments, and the church. In all of these, she says, it would have been easy for Calvin to tilt toward spiritualist interpretations, following Zwingli rather than Luther in the matter of the Real Presence, for example. But he stays with the physical, even though the cost is great, and it is a cost that psychically pays off in powerful rhetorical expression.

> Calvin is disgusted with the foulness of the human nature; Luther despairs at its weakness. Calvin, like Luther, uses the term 'flesh' to characterize mind and spirit as well as body. But he seems to have had a horror of the flesh in itself and as sheer matter, in a Platonic sense, as Luther did not. This seems to me [Selinger] to make more impressive the strength of the Lutheran influence: it was persuasive enough to overcome psychic resistance.[17]

Much of Selinger's argument is not central to this study. Perhaps it suffices to say that for her Calvin is "almost all right psychologically." What is not quite all right expresses itself in unpleasant remarks about the physical, a bitter combativeness toward what is strange or seen as enemy, a censorious attitude toward sins, especially sexual ones. She finds this rooted in a psychological type that Carl Jung denominated "the introverted thinker." Such a person has difficulty with emotion, with temper, and with life in the public eye. All of these, of course, were problematic for Calvin, for whatever reason. She attributes his internal state to an oedipal ambivalence due to the loss of his mother by death, when he was five or six, compounded by his father's quick re-marriage. The resulting betrayal feelings, she holds, produced passions of hatred, of yearning and jealously, of fury and fear, that could not be directly expressed. Hence, they get expressed in admissable ways, for Calvin primarily

---

[17]Selinger, *Calvin against Himself* 62. One wishes that negative statements Calvin makes about the human body would be read together with his own medical record. Competent physicians who have looked at the list of medical problems he sent to a group of consultant physicians at Montpelier the year of his death have diagnosed him as suffering from migraine headaches, gout, kidney stones, pulmonary tuberculosis, with its accompanying quartan fever, intestinal parasites, thrombosed hemorrhoids, and a spastic bowel condition. For him to call the body pejorative names in the light of the pain he daily experienced seems the mark of normalcy. Cf. "Calvin's Illnesses," Charles L. Cooke, M.D., in forthcoming *Calvin Studies IV*, papers presented at the fourth Calvin Colloquium, Davidson College, N.C.

in the power of his written and spoken rhetoric. Bouwsma, who is too careful to be accused, like Selinger, of writing psychobiography, also makes a good deal of Calvin's coldness toward his father and believes that Calvin created surrogate fathers and mothers out of the city council and even the city itself.

Even if one disagrees with Selinger's analysis, or some part of it, it is a brilliant piece of argument. And one piece of it seems to me uniquely useful as a clue to Calvin's cavalier treatment of the political order, and the tendency toward harshness in his role as chief pastor of the people of Geneva. She argues that the introverted intellectual divides the world into trustworthy and hostile parts and abstracts these into good and evil (p. 88). In addition, the introvert tends to be on the defensive against a threatening world and this produces a need for control. Now, many introverts find that controlling some part of their private lives or environment suffices to alleviate this need. But Calvin was cast willy-nilly into the role of moral arbiter for his city, a role he did not relish. In fulfilling the call God had given him—the God who would not allow him "to fight and wrestle in the shade"—he was put in a situation where an untrustworthy citizenry threatened seriously the charge of God. Control of hotheads was necessary, and after 1555 and the defeat of the Perrinist party he was able to exert that control. No wonder the political order was felt as hostile and no wonder Calvin gave it short shrift in his writing, even when (as Höpfl demonstrates) the absolute need for church and state to function together in Calvin's social and religious economy demanded he make a fuller account.

So Selinger's identification of Calvin's psychological type not only rings true, but goes some way toward answering the questions about Calvin's dismissal of political order as a part of theology, and his harshness in dealing with dissent and disorder.

What about the other aspect of Calvin's failure as a political theorist: his wretched advice for the poor persecuted Protestants? Here William Bouwsma's portrait is helpful. Like Selinger, Bouwsma detects a split in Calvin's thought and personality, but he locates it differently. She finds Calvin temperamentally a dualist with a disdain for the physical, which he overcomes by his forceful allegiance to Luther's non-dualistic theology. But Bouwsma finds the split in the two streams of influence that flowed into the lives of most intellectuals of Calvin's century. On the one hand, was the long medieval tradition, with its optimism about human ability to know the truth, its belief in order and hierarchy with its consequent absolutism and authoritarianism, and its trust in reason. Sixteenth-century thinkers were an anxious lot because this long tradition no longer described their world. Nor did they feel at home in its claustrophobic embrace. So they turned to the second strand of classical tradition available to them, the work of the rhetoricians. Like Erasmus and other Renaissance humanists, Calvin drank at their stream more gratefully than he did the philosophic one. Here the art of persuasion replaced the medieval attempt to order truth into intelligible systems of thought. With *persuasio* went *eruditio*, the stress (in his case) on the biblical as well as the classical languages, and with that a belief that knowledge should be useful, even if one-to-one correlation between language and truth could no longer be fully maintained.

If Selinger stresses the agonies of the introverted intellectual, Bouwsma sees Calvin as an anxious man in a world of anxious people, trying to escape the claustrophobic "Labyrinth" of medieval thought by teetering on the "Abyss" of humanist freedom. Selinger stresses Calvin's Lutheran inheritance; Bouwsma, whose studies in Italian humanism are celebrated, stresses his closeness to Erasmus. For Selinger, the struggle is between a theology that approves the physical with a temperament that abhors it. For Bouwsma it is the anxiety of one caught in the confluence of two streams of tradition which tossed everyone to and fro like woodchips that might be sucked under by a maelstrom of social unrest and loss of direction. Catholicism will return to the medieval tradition and work from that tradition, in a world that will increasingly find that base irrelevant, until a pope comes along and throws the church's windows open for *aggiornamento*. Protestantism will follow, reluctantly, the humanist tradition—except in those cultural eddies that allow small Protestant traditions to catch the bank and stay in place. So Bouwsma holds that Calvin's humanism is not peripheral to his achievement, as some have supposed, but is crucial to his thought.[18] "It constantly challenged his traditional culture, and Calvinism had its origins in his struggle to come to terms with the double legacy of philosophy and humanism."[19]

It is at this point that Bouwsma's insights into Calvin's psychology are most helpful in explaining Calvin's sluggishness in coming to the help of his persecuted fellow-religionists, especially in France. Let this be put into a single sentence that will then be parsed: Calvin's traditional inheritance taught him a respect for political order that, for reasons psychological, his biblically informed humanism was unable to inform or reform. Classical cosmology revealed a super-lunary harmony that was rooted in hierarchy. For Calvin the order of the heavens was deeply consoling: "On earth, there often appears dreadful confusion and the works of God, so far as we can understand them, appear mutually discordant; but whoever raises his eyes to heaven will see the greatest harmony."[20] Nature dictates a similar harmonic subordination for most people. "Those who cannot submit themselves to the magistrates, who rebel against their fathers and mothers, who cannot bear the yoke of masters or mistresses sufficiently show that they cannot join with anyone who does

---

[18]For example, David E. Demson, "The Image of Calvin in Recent Research," in *In Honor of John Calvin, 1509-64* ed. E. J. Furcha, Faculty of Religious Studies, McGill University: Montreal: ARC Supplement no. 3, 1987.[19]Bouwsma, *John Calvin: A Sixteenth Century Portrait* 113.

[19]Bouwsma, *John Calvin: A Sixteenth Century Portrait* 113.

[20]Ibid., 73, in Comm. Ezek. 1: 11.

not reverse the whole order of nature and jumble heaven and earth, as people say."[21]

Why does this traditionalist language stand unopposed in Calvin's writings? After all, many of the strong statements Bouwsma finds to exemplify Calvin's dependence on his received philosophic tradition, he finds negated in another place by the humanist Calvin. Not so his views on the political order. Why, then, does not a more flexible humanism inform this area of his life? Bouwsma gives us the hint when he argues that Calvin's anxiety, like many of his fellow savants, was rooted in social psychology. In particular, Calvin hated *mixing* things that should not be mixed together (e.g. women taking gunnery practice!) and consequently approved strongly of setting boundaries. He liked to order things into antithetical categories, black and white, we and they, foul and pure, and any crossing of boundaries he called pollution. Indeed, most sin for Calvin can be put under the heading of impurity or pollution.[22] That same language pervades his discussion of political order at the end of the *Institutes.* For a citizen to resist a ruler is to remove all the proper boundaries that order our lives below the heavens. It is to negate God's callings, where one is ruler and another is not:

> subjects should be led not by fear alone of princes and rulers to re-
> main in subjection under them (as they commonly yield to an
> armed enemy who sees that vengeance is promptly taken if they re-
> sist), but because they are showing obedience to God himself when
> they give it to them; since the rulers' power is from God.
>
> I am not discussing the men themselves . . . but I say that the
> order itself is worthy of such honor and reverence that those who
> are rulers are esteemed among us, and receive reverence out of re-
> spect for their lordship.[23]

In addition, his primary source as a theologian of the humanist stripe failed him here. The easiest place for Calvin to find the proper relationship between state and subject is the thirteenth chapter of Romans. There an obedience to governing authorities is put in language that for an anxiety-prone Calvin must have seemed unequivocal: obey the ruler, pay your taxes, show your respect. Already committed to boundaries, wary of 'mixture'—in this case commingling the roles of ruler and ruled—Romans spoke straight to his mind as well as his need. One wonders what he might have written on this subject had he allowed Revelation 13 to guide him. There the Roman rule is no longer God's minister (or 'deacon', as Paul wrote), but is the Beast, the hand-

---

[21]Ibid., 74, in Sermon No. 46 on Deuteronomy.

[22]For this discussion, see all of chapter 2.

[23]*Institutes.* IV.20.22.

work of the Dragon (Satan). Would Calvin's respect for the 'order itself' have kept him from countenancing rebellion against Satan? But Calvin was not given to much study of the Book of Revelation, his only reference to Revelation 13 coming in a discussion of the pope as Antichrist.

Conclusion

Höpfl is correct in saying that it is not useful to speak simply of 'medieval heritage' or 'pathos of order' when examining Calvin's palpably deficient work on political order. The solid studies of Suzanne Selinger and William J. Bouwsma get far enough beneath Calvin's skin for us to understand, in part at least, the psychological and cultural strains he lived with, and the effect those tensions produced on an area of life he found alien, even frightening. One comes from their studies with a deeper sense of the genius of "that Picard," who, although hurried and distant when he addressed the political order, yet in his proclamation of the gospel spoke a language that engaged people of his epoch, a message still compelling today.

Calvin writing *Institutes of the Christian Religion.*

Calvin's Theological Method: Word and Spirit, A Case Study

Richard C. Gamble

The goal of this essay is to elucidate Calvin's theological methodology. This will be accomplished by the examination of a test case–investigating the relationship between the word and the Spirit via Calvin's polemics with the Anabaptists or Spiritualists on the one hand and the Roman Catholics on the other.

TO FULLY UNDERSTAND THE PROPER RELATIONSHIP between word and Spirit in Calvin, broader methodological questions must be addressed. Calvin's teaching on the word and Spirit, as with his other positions, must be viewed within his whole theological system. The primary question here is whether a specific theological structure or system can be found in Calvin's writings. Numbers of attempts have been made to determine such a system, with the result that it seems apparent that scholars can only agree to disagree.[1] Can our discussion of the relationship between the word and Spirit aid us in determining that structure? It is evident that it can.

Prior to any analysis of the "structure" of Calvin's theology, the advice of William Bouwsma should be heeded. Bouwsma wants us to "recognize the degree to which Calvin abhorred systematic theology as a matter of principle."[2] He calls for us to see Calvin identifying himself more with Renaissance humanism.[3] Is it possible to both attempt to determine a "structure" to Calvin's theology *and* understand him within the context of Renaissance humanism? It is readily seen that a proper historical/theological analysis will have to endeavor to do both.

The ideal of Renaissance humanism has been considered "the pursuit of eloquence"[4] or "rhetoric, the art of persuasion."[5] Without spending much time on the nature of eloquence or persuasion, one can easily see how this Renaissance idea would dovetail into Calvin's desire to persuade his

---

[1]Wilhelm Niesel, *Theology of Calvin* (Grand Rapids: Baker, 1980), 9-21 and Benjamin C. Milner, *Calvin's Doctrine of the Church* (Leiden: Brill, 1970), 2, analyze three basic approaches to the history of Calvin studies.

[2]William Bouwsma, "Calvinism as Renaissance Artifact," in *Calvin Studies II*, ed. John Haddon Leith and Charles Edward Raynall III (Papers presented at a Colloquium on Calvin Studies at Davidson College Presbyterian Church and Davidson College, Davidson, North Carolina, 1984), 27.

[3]William Bouwsma, *John Calvin: A Sixteenth Century Portrait* (Oxford: Oxford University Press, 1988), 113. "His humanism was thus not merely peripheral or auxiliary to his achievement, as has commonly been supposed."

[4]Hanna H. Gray, "Renaissance Humanism: The Persuit of Eloquence," in *Renaissance Essays*, ed. Paul Kristeller and Philip Wiener (New York: Harper & Row, 1968), 199-216.

[5]Bouwsma, *John Calvin*, 114. Cf. Quirinus Breen, "John Calvin and the Rhetorical Tradition," *Church History* 26 (1957): 12.

64   *Calviniana*

opponents. The polemical writings of Calvin should therefore lend themselves quite well to exhibiting this characteristic of Renaissance humanism.

Turning to his polemical writings, note that there has been extensive analysis of some of them, most recently Calvin's *Reply to Sadoleto*. Here the utilization of rhetorical finesse for the purpose of convincing argument has been clearly demonstrated.[6] Since eloquence and persuasion are intimately connected, and are part and parcel of Renaissance humanism, Calvin's implementation of rhetorical devices toward that goal may be seen as being influenced by Renaissance humansim.

As Calvin seeks to persuade his readers, he will use various literary devices. For the purposes of this study, it would be helpful to focus on one aspect of Calvin's devices, namely the application of what may be called "antithesis" or "paradox." This will be done–not on the basis of analysis of one particular text, but rather by developing our test case regarding Calvin's analysis of word and Spirit.

Much attention has been focused on "paradox" in Calvin's theology over the last twenty years. Having roots in H. Bauke's 1922 study, *Die Probleme der Theologie Calvins*, Alexandre Ganoczy's important *The Young Calvin* (1966) ET (1987) devotes a short chapter to "the dialectical structure of Calvin's thought."[7] Ford Lewis Battles has since then produced the definitive work in this area.[8] Some of their ideas on paradox and antithesis have also been observed by William Bouwsma and Francis Higman.[9] Very recently Carlos M.N. Eire has stated, "Calvin systematically juxtaposed the divine and the human, contrasted the spiritual and the material, and placed the transcendent and omnipotent *solus* of God above the contingent multiple of man and the created world."[10] W. Stanford Reid has also recently asserted: "Calvin's stand [on natural science] was midway between two extremes. . . ." On the next page he says: "Based on his view of the Scriptures, Calvin steered a middle course between deism and pantheism."[11] It can therefore be concluded that

[6]James Payton, "History as Rhetorical Weapon: Christian Humanism in Calvin's *Reply to Sadoleto*," in *In Honour of John Calvin, 1509-64* (Papers from the 1986 International Calvin Symposium, McGill University, Montreal, ed. E. J. Furcha), 110.

[7]Alexandre Ganoczy, *The Young Calvin* (Philadelphia: Westminster, 1987), chapter 18.

[8]Ford Lewis Battles, "Calculus Fidei" in *Calvinus Ecclesiae Doctor*, ed. Wilhelm Neuser (Kampen: Kok, 1978), 85-106.

[9]William Bouwsma, "Calvin and the Renaissance Crisis of Knowing," *Calvin Theological Journal* 36 (1982) as cited in R. Gamble, "Exposition and Method in Calvin," *Westminster Theological Journal* 49 (1987): 157. Francis Higman, ed., *Three French Treatises of John Calvin*, as cited in Gamble, "Exposition and Method," 161.

[10]Carlos M.N. Eire, *War Against the Idols* (Cambridge: Cambridge University Press, 1986), 197.

[11]W. Stanford Reid, "Calvin's View of Natural Science," in *In Honor of John Calvin*, ed. E. J. Furcha, 238 f.

there is a relatively broad base of support underlining Calvin's implementation of paradox or antithesis.

To further substantiate and underline the importance of "paradox" or "antithesis" in Calvin, noteworthy are two pertinent passages from the Commentaries. These two passages are randomly selected from a number of available ones:

> And thus it is sure, for all the mysteries of God are paradoxes to the flesh; . . . We are here reminded that if we desire to become capable of understanding them, we must especially labor to become freed from our own reason.

> And surely in general nothing is more absurd in the view of human reason than to hear that God has become mortal.[12]

As noted by Eire, for example, Calvin juxtaposed spiritual and material. This rhetorical device is an effective tool of persuasion. Yet these two, spiritual and material, stand in a relationship impossible to reconcile. But Calvin would at times, as has been demonstrated by Battles with scores of examples,[13] set off two antithetical options, both false, and attempt to demonstrate that the proper (hence biblical) response was a *via media* between these two extremes.

This *via media* between two extremes, based upon Aristotle's notion of falsity consisting in excess or defect of truth, was used extensively by Calvin. We will be using this rhetorical device as a model for analyzing Calvin's teaching on the relationship between the word and the Spirit. Our purpose in selecting this model is not to demonstrate the epistemological foundations of Calvin's theologizing, as did Battles, but rather to view this type of analysis as a sixteenth-century rhetorical device.[14]

It must be acknowledged from the outset that the polemical tracts lend themselves most easily to structuring within this antithetical relationship. Whether or not one can deduce the entire structure of Calvin's theology

---

[12]John Calvin, *Commentaries on the Epistle of Paul the Apostle to the Romans* (Edinburgh: Calvin Translation Society, 1843; reprinted, Grand Rapids: Baker, 1981), 191. Cf. John Calvin, *Commentary on the Epistles of Paul the Apostle to the Corinthians* (Edinburgh: Calvin Translation Society, 1843; reprinted, Grand Rapids: Baker, 1981), 85.

[13]Ford Lewis Battles, "Calculus Fidei" (1978, unpublished manuscript located in the H. H. Meeter Center for Calvin Studies, Calvin College and Seminary, Grand Rapids, Michigan). Some examples given by Battles concern Calvin's analysis of: the marks of the Church, the government of the Church, the nature of prayer, the final resurrection, and providence.

[14]It is interesting to note that Bauke sees major support for the idea of the *complexio oppositorum* precisely in Calvin's analysis of word and Spirit. He also notes that it was seen earlier by Karl Heim, *Das Gewissheitsproblem* (Leipzig: J. C. Hinrichs, 1911), 274f. Bauke says: "Dadurch komme Calvin zu keiner klaren Entscheidung über die Begrundung der Schriftwarheit." *Die Probleme der Theologie Calvins* (Leipzig: Hinrichs, 1922), 55.

from this antithetical structure is not the purpose of this article; nevertheless it is a helpful method of investigating the particular topic at hand and could provide for some fruitful discussion. Therefore, since Calvin emphasized parallel antithetical structures in his theology, a test case can be made for using word and Spirit to see if it also falls within this structure.

Word and Spirit: Defining the Terms

Prior to any beneficial analysis of theological topics, it is imperative that terms under discussion be properly defined. Concerning the word of God, is the letter of scripture for Calvin the very "word of God"? To fully analyze this hotly debated subject would take us beyond our space limitations. On the one hand there is the statement of Rupert E. Davies that "Calvin committed himself to a completely verbal and mechanical theory of inspiration."[15] This agrees with the view of the Princeton theologian of the nineteenth century, Benjamin Warfield, who states: "nothing is more certain than that Calvin held both to 'verbal inspiration' and the 'inerrancy of Scripture,' however he may have conceived the action of God which secured these things."[16] Yet it is precisely the second half of this phrase which causes problems. Warfield did not properly investigate that important aspect of Calvin's teaching on the nature of scripture which is commonly called "accommodation" as articulated by a number of Calvin scholars, preeminently Ford Battles.[17] On the other hand there is the equally unsatisfactory view of John T. McNeil, who says: ". . . quite inadequate [is] any bald statement that [for Calvin] the letter of Scripture is the Word of God. . . . God's Word and the Bible are not convertible terms in Calvin's thinking, even though in many contexts attention is not called to the distinction."[18]

These later Calvin scholars can be criticized in light of the conclusions of men like Edward Dowey, who says: "To Calvin the theologian an error in Scripture is unthinkable. Hence the endless harmonizing, the explaining

[15]Rupert E. Davies, *The Problem of Authority in the Continental Reformers* (London: Epworth, 1946), 114.

[16]Benjamin B. Warfield, *Calvin and Augustine* (Philadelphia: Presbyterian and Reformed Publishing Co., 1974), 61 n36.

[17]Cf. Ford Lewis Battles, "God Was Accommodating Himself to Human Capacity," *Interpretation* 31 (1977): 19-38, and Dirk Jellema, "God's 'Baby-Talk': Calvin and the 'Errors' of the Bible," *Reformed Journal* 30/4 (1980): 24-27. Cf. also Ronald S. Wallace, *Calvin's Doctrine of the Word and Sacrament* (Edinburgh: Oliver & Boyd, 1953), 2 ff.

[18]John T. McNeil, "The Significance of the Word of God for Calvin," *Church History* 27 (1959): 132-33. This theory was earlier asserted by Heinrich Heppe, *Reformed Dogmatics* (German edition, 1861; English trans., London: Allen & Unwin, 1950) and then again by J. Chapuis, *Le temoignage du Saint-Esprit dans la theologie de Calvin* (Lausanne: Bridel, 1909). A cautious reply to the question is given by Walter Kreck in his "Wort und Geist bei Calvin," in *Festschrift für Gunther Dehn*, ed. Wilhelm Schneemelcher (Neukirchen: Verlag des Buchhandlung des Erziehungsvereins, 1957), 170, in which he writes: "Aber Calvin identifiziert keineswegs einfach *verbum* und *scriptura*."

and interpreting of passages that seem to contradict or to be inaccurate."[19] Brian Gerrish as well asserts: "For Calvin, in fact, the whole Bible is the 'Word of God,'"[20] and demonstrates that there is plenty of ammunition for both sides of the debate on Calvin's view of the scriptures.

An important treatise which will be the object of our investigation is Calvin's work *Against the Libertines*. Here Calvin discusses the word of God and at least in the context of that particular treatise he undoubtedly refers to the words of scripture. Not only does Calvin mean in fact the words of scripture, but furthermore, he intends them in the "plain sense," that is not in an allegorical sense. Therefore, limiting ourselves to this one important polemical tract, one can speak of the word of God and the Bible as being one and the same for Calvin. Nevertheless, such a limited investigation is insufficient to provide solid conclusions.

Mention also needs to be made concerning Jesus Christ as word of God. The primacy of Jesus Christ, the "word made flesh,"in the theology of Calvin is well documented.[21] A discussion of "word and Spirit" in Calvin would be incomplete without this important point being underlined.[22]

Praedicatio Dei verbum Dei est is also an important tenet of Calvin's theology. As Dr. Parker[23] among others has made clear, the preached word may also be considered the word of God. Parker's analysis is very helpful; he finds two antagonistic views as to the relationship between the preached word of God and the written word of God. On the one hand is Luther who asserts that the word of God preached "meant no less than the Word of God written. . . . In both cases it is, in all literalness, God himself who speaks."[24]

[19]Edward Dowey, *The Knowledge of God in Calvin's Theology* (New York: Columbia University Press, 1952), 104.

[20]Brian Gerrish, "Biblical Authority and the Continental Reformation," *Scottish Journal of Theology* 10 (1957): 353. He also says ". . . Calvin is obliged by his view of inspiration to think of the Scriptures as inerrant" (p. 354). François Wendel maintains "the word of God, and the Holy Spirit which inspired its writers bears witness in us to the faithfulness with which they accomplished their task." He does not go on to assert, like Gerrish, that Calvin held to inerrancy, even though he equates the Bible with the word of God. *Calvin: The Origins and Development of His Religious Thought*, trans. P. Mairet (New York: Harper & Row, 1963), 159.

[21]Thomas H. L. Parker's article, "Calvin's Concept of Revelation: The Revelation of God the Redeemer," *The Scottish Journal of Theology* 2 (December 1949): 337-51 is especially helpful here. Cf. also Charles Partee, "Calvin's Central Dogma Again," *Sixteenth Century Journal* 18 (Summer 1987): 194, where he says: "Nevertheless, the exposition of his theology finds the presence of the union with Christ in so many places and in such a significant way that that "union with Christ" may be usefully taken as the central affirmation." Partee is arguing here for "union with Christ" as a/the central motif of Calvin's theology, not necessarily the "incarnation" as such.

[22]Cf. in full, E. David Willis, *Calvin's Catholic Christology*, Studies in Medieval and Reformation Thought, vol. 2 (Leiden: Brill, 1966).

[23]Thomas H. L. Parker, *The Oracles of God: An Introduction to the Preaching of John Calvin* (London: Lutterworth, 1947), 45-56.

Zwingli, on the other hand, rejected Luther's theory as to the intimate connection of the word and Spirit and he, along with his colleagues Oecolampadius and Bullinger, developed the notion of the *Verbum Dei externum* and *Verbum Dei internum*. The preached word (as well as the word of the Bible) are the former.

Despite the polemics of the various theological camps, agreement can be made on the issues important for this article. Someone like Ronald Wallace is right on target when he says:

> Calvin no doubt means to emphasize that, though the resultant Word was really the Word that God intended would be uttered in all its details, nevertheless the prophet acted throughout as one who really experienced all that he said and who gave forth the message as one coming naturally from his own heart through a process of thought, on a psychological level, no different from that of ordinary human authorship. . . . However much on a human level the mental process of the inspired writer may be, Calvin insists that in the resultant Word there is freedom from human error and from the marks of human infirmity.[25]

When defining the word "Spirit," it can be said that Calvin is referring to the Holy Spirit; there is not the controversy over meaning with that word. Nevertheless, the role of the Spirit or Holy Spirit in Calvin's theology is not only noteworthy, but also complex. Especially the relationship between word and Spirit is of fundamental importance. A working definition at this point will still be simple: the Holy Spirit is understood and more particularly focus will be placed upon the work of the Holy Spirit in the lives of the Christian community which reads the Bible.

Word and Spirit: The Scriptures and the Internal Testimony

Having determined that the Bible is authoritative in Calvin's theology, the question to be answered is precisely how the Bible is authoritative. More specifically, what is the Holy Spirit's role in establishing the authority of scripture? This is the question of the internal testimony of the Spirit.

Is it the internal testimony of the Spirit which establishes the authority of the scriptures, according to Calvin? The proper answer here is "yes and no." We are convinced that Calvin taught that there is an intrinsic authority

---

[24]Ibid., 47.

[25]Ronald Wallace, *Calvin's Doctrine of the Word and Sacrament* (Tyler, Texas: Geneva Divinity School Press, 1982), 108. Cf. also Henry J. Forstman, *Word and Spirit* (Stanford: Stanford University Press, 1962), 22.

to the scriptures.[26] Yet the internal testimony of the scriptures is absolutely vital to his teaching as well. It is the internal testimony of the Spirit which persuades us that it is authoritative.[27] It is the internal testimony which makes it authoritative with us. Calvin discusses the internal testimony of the Spirit extensively in the *Institutes* I.7, and the chapter headings given there are helpful in underlining the importance of the subject matter:

> By what testimony ought the Scripture to be established, namely of the Spirit: in order that its authority may remain certain; and that it is a wicked invention to say that the faith of Scripture depends upon the judgment of the church.

That the internal testimony of the spirit is of vital importance to Calvin's doctrine of Scripture and authority rests upon a sure foundation. This point needs to be remembered in proceeding. There is a reciprocal relationship between the word of God, the Bible, and the Holy Spirit of God. They cannot and should not be separated.

One cannot separate the Spirit from the word.[28] Looking ahead to what we will later investigate, it is the spiritualists who separate visions or oracles from the Bible.[29] Forstman has a powerful conclusion:

> The full impact of such a conception of authority is an absolute certainty which towers over the vicissitudes of history and trembles not in the least at the most overwhelming human weaknesses. An authority is expounded which is dependent in no determinative way upon human beings. The authority is God. He communicates

[26]"Auch Calvin hat seit der 2. Ausgabe der Institutio diesen Gedanken der Selbstmanifestation der Schrift vertreten und in der letzten Ausgabe ausdrücklich das Prinzip der Autopistie eingeführt." Werner Krusche, *Das Wirken des Heiligen Geistes nach Calvin* (Göttingen: Vandenhoek & Ruprecht, 1957), 203.

[27]"According to Calvin, the persuasion that God was the author of Scirpture was established in people by the internal testimony of the Holy Spirit," Jack B. Rogers and Donald S. McKim, *The Authority and Interpretation of the Bible: An Historical Approach* (New York: Harper & Row, 1979), 104. "The authority of Scripture is authenticated by the inner witness of the Holy Spirit. The reverence which the Church gives to the Scripture is due primarily to the influence of the Holy Spirit in giving inward testimony to the believer that this word is the Word of God," Wallace, *Calvin's Doctrine*, 101-2.

[28]Walter Kreck, "Wort und Geist," 170, writes "Es besteht eine gegenseitige Verbindung von Wort und Geist." Rogers and McKim, *Authority*, 106, tell us: "For Calvin, the Word and Spirit belonged inseparably together." Anthony N. S. Lane, "John Calvin: The Witness of the Holy Spirit," in *Faith and Ferment* says: "Calvin's cure for those who have either the word without the spirit or vice versa is to stress their inseparability." Papers read at the 1982 conference. (London: Westminster Conference, 1982), 5.

[29]Richard C. Prust, "Was Calvin A Biblical Literalist?"*Scottish Journal of Theology* 20/3 (1967): 312-28. "The Word is inseparable from the Spirit: for this reason the radical reformers are in error when they forsake Scripture for a direct access to the Spirit" (p. 315).

himself to prophets and apostles through the Holy Spirit, and under the overpowering influence of this Spirit these men are led to write. The collection of these writings is then recognized by men as the true knowledge of God through the internal agency of the same Holy Spirit. The writers have not ceased to be human beings, nor have those who accept their writings and believe them ceased to be men, but the human element in each instance has been so circumscribed that it is no longer a real peril to the authority.[30]

Word and Spirit: The Anabaptists

Willem Balke has written the magisterial work, *Calvin and the Anabaptist Radicals.* Although a complete treatment of Cavlin and Anabaptism deserves a dissertation like Balke's, still his section on word and Spirit is immediately relevant to us.

In the 1539 edition of the *Institutes*, Calvin first criticized his opponents who despised those who follow the "dead and killing letter"[31] Calvin and his colleagues would be the objects of that criticism. He held that the opinion of the Holy Spirit is revealed in Scripture and that the Holy Spirit is not imparted except through the scriptures. Calvin summarizes: ". . . he [the Spirit] would have us recognize him in his own image, which he has stamped upon the Scriptures. He is the Author of the Scriptures: he cannot vary and differ from himself. Hence he must ever remain just as he once revealed himself there. This is no affront to him, unless perchance we consider it honorable for him to decline or degenerate from himself."[32] The Holy Spirit does not work outside the Word.

Focusing on the topic of the Anabaptist conception of word and Spirit we take a quick look at what was happening in Anabaptism during this time. It appears that Paul's statement in 2 Cor. 3:6-7 was a prime area of debate. This debate did not initiate in the sixteenth century, but has a long-standing history in the church. In A.D. 412 Augustine wrote *De Spiritu et Littera.* This book was eagerly studied by the Protestants; Luther, Bucer, Zwingli as well as Calvin and the Anabaptists saw Augustine as their champion.

Within the group that may generally be called "anabaptists" there is another group which has been called the "spiritualists." There is, of course, a lot of discussion among scholars as to how any one different group should be named, and one must be sensitive to that debate. For our limited purposes here, we will simply refer to that group of Christians who are identified by tendencies to separate the word and the Spirit. Generally speaking this group

---

[30]Forstman, *Word and Spirit*, 19.

[31]Cf. *Calvin: Institutes* of the Christian Religion, ed. John T. McNeill, trans. Ford Lewis Battles, Vols. 20 & 21, Library of Christian Classics, (Philadelphia: Westminister, 1960), I.9.1, which includes the 1539 change.

[32]*Institutes* I.9.2.

could be called the Swiss Brethren or the "Spiritualists."[33] In a marvelous article, William Klaasen has pointed out that this group of believers, holding to the Schleitheim confession, entered into debate with Pilgram Marpeck. Klaasen sees the Swiss Brethren as biblicists with whom Marpeck had serious problems. Klaasen writes: ". . . for on this battleground was fought the hardest battle between biblicism and spiritualism, the letter and the spirit, law and gospel, freedom and enslavement."[34] The context of Calvin's 1539 edition of the *Institutes* is specifically referring to a group which one would term "spiritualists" in his polemics against the separation of the word and the Spirit.

Word and Spirit: The Proper Relationship

One of the best sources of Calvin's teaching on the word and spirit is summarized in *Against the Libertines*. There he writes:

> In order that every Christian might be warned to resist such a pernicious temptation, we must note to what end our Lord has promised us his Spirit. Now he did not promise the Spirit for the purpose of forsaking Scripture, so that we might be led by him and stroll amid the clouds, but in order to gain its true meaning and thus be satisfied. In Jesus Christ's own words: 'when the spirit of truth comes, he will enable you to understand the things which you have heard from me.' (Jn. 14:26) [Hence] we see that he does not promise his apostles a spirit that will create new doctrines for them; rather the Spirit only confirms them in the gospel which was preached to them.[35]

> Furthermore, after his resurrection, when he opened the understanding of his disciples, it was not in order to inspire them with strange subjects not found in Scripture, but in order to help them understand Scripture itself.[36]

[33]Cf. the work of George H. Williams, *The Radical Reformation* (Philadelphia: Westminster, 1962), especially 821-28.

[34]William Klaasen, "Anabaptist Hermeneutics: The Letter and the Spirit," *Mennonite Quarterly Review* 40 (1966): 91. Cf. also Lowell Zuck, "Letter and Spirit in the Reformation," *Theology and Life* 4/4 (1961): 289.

[35]This passage is very similar to what Calvin says elsewhere in the *Institutes*: "But in promising it [the Holy Spirit], of what sort did he declare his Spirit would be? One that would speak not from himself but would suggest to and instill into their minds what he had handed on through the Word. Therefore the Spirit, promised to us, has not the task of inventing new and unheard of revelations, or of forging a new kind of doctrine, to lead us away from the received doctrine of the gospel, but of sealing our minds with that very doctrine which is commended by the gospel" (I.9.1).

[36]Cf. *Institutes* I.9.3. "In this manner Christ opened the minds of two of his disciples, not that they should cast away the Scriptures and become wise of themselves, but that they should know the Scriptures."

In fact, to whom has been given the greatest abundance of the Spirit, if not to the Apostles? Nevertheless, the Spirit did not cause them to lay aside Scripture or create in them mistrust for it. On the contrary we see that the Scripture became the focus of their entire study and obedience. And we hold to the same obedience.[37]

What do we learn about Calvin's teaching from this particular passage? At this place Calvin is stressing that the primary purpose of the Holy Spirit in relationship to the scriptures is to enlighten the writers and to give those who currently read the scripture access to its "true meaning." A primary function of the Holy Spirit seems to be illuminating the pages of scripture for the Christian reader. What would happen if that purpose were discarded? Such appears to be the case with both the Anabaptists and the Roman Catholics. Walter Kreck maintains that Calvin's teaching of the word and Spirit must be seen within these tensions. Commenting on the double front against Rome and the Schwärmer, "on the one hand he defends the union of the word against the inner light of the Schwärmer, on the other he must warn against idolizing the church."[38]

It is clear that the Anabaptists represent for Calvin a false extreme in their analysis of the relationship between the word and the Spirit. Instead of seeing that the Holy Spirit is united to the word, meaning the Bible, the spiritualists "despise" the word. They put emphasis on the work of the Holy Spirit apart from his work in the Bible. An implication of this teaching is that they fail to see the unity of activity between the three Persons of the Trinity.

At the other extreme is the Roman Catholic church.[39] It has a similar fault of not putting proper emphasis upon the word, in this case, not by over-emphasizing the activity of the Spirit but by under-emphasizing it. The Roman Catholic church does not sufficiently see the power of the Holy Spirit at work in the word and therefore feels the need for some other, additional, source of authority to establish the authority of the word.

[37]Calvin, *Treatises against the Anabaptists and against the Libertines*, trans. and ed. Benjamin Wirt Farley (Grand Rapids: Baker, 1982), 224. This is similar to a passage in the *Calvin: Institutes*: "Besides this Paul, 'caught up even to the third heaven; yet did not fail to become proficient in the doctrine of the law and the Prophets, just as also he urges Timothy, a teacher of singular excellence, to give heed to reading." I.9.1. Other important passages that would relate to this one as seen in the *Calvin: Institutes* would be: I.9.3; IV.14.9f; III.1.4.

[38]"Er kämpft wie de Reformation überhaupt in der doppelten Frontstellung gegen Rom und gegen die Schwärmer. Hier mus er die Bindung ans Wort gegenüber dem inneren Licht der Schwärmer verteidigen, dort mus er vor der Vergötzung einer kirchlichen Gegebenheit warnen" ("Wort und Geist,"178).

[39]It is Calvin's interaction with the Roman Catholic church which is very helpful in elucidating his theory of the word. Niesel mentions his polemics with the Roman Catholics as one of the three places in Calvin's *corpus* which deals with this issue. (*Theology of Calvin*, 31).

Seeking authority for the teaching of the church outside of Christ and the scriptures is clearly wrong in Calvin's view. He is convinced that the first task of ministers is to teach the word of God,[40] and that one of the prime tenets of the Roman Catholic church is to deny what the scriptures teach concerning Christ.[41] He believes that the power of the church is subject to the scriptures[42] and that in the Old Testament church God gave the Word to teach the people.[43] The same principles are to be found in the New Testament church.[44]

Calvin places his finger precisely at the point of the question of the relationship between the word and the Spirit as the fundamental one in discussing the problem of the Roman Catholic church. The pivotal passage comes from the *Institutes* (IV.8.13).

> Their statement that the church cannot err bears on this point, and this is how they interpret it–inasmuch as the church is governed by the Spirit of God, it can proceed safely without the Word; no matter where it may go, it can think or speak only what is true; accordingly, if it should ordain anything beyond or apart from God's word, this must be taken as nothing but a sure oracle of God.

He summarizes the problem more precisely when he says:

> This then is the difference. Our opponents locate the authority of the church outside God's Word; but we insist that it be attached to the Word, and do not allow it to be separated from it.

Or again, he says:

[40]"The first task of the bishop's office is to teach the people from God's word." *Institutes* IV.7.23.

[41]"The second [article of the papacy]: everything written and taught about Christ is falsehood and deceit," *Institutes* IV.7.27.

[42]"The power of the church, therefore, is not infinite but subject to the Lord's Word and, as it were, enclosed within it." *Institutes* IV.8.4.

[43]"But where it pleased God to raise up a more visible form of the church, he willed to have his Word set down and sealed in writing, that his priests might seek from it what to teach the people, and that every doctrine to be taught should conform to that rule." *Institutes* IV.8.5. ". . . and to this standard [the scriptures], priests and teachers, even to the coming of Christ, had to conform their teaching. And it was not lawful for them to turn aside either to the right or to the left, for their whole office was limited to answering the people from the mouth of God." *Institutes* IV.8.6.

[44]Cf. *Institutes* IV.8.8, IV.8.9.

It is this inviolable decree of God and of the Holy Spirit which our foes are trying to set aside when they pretend that the church is ruled by the Spirit apart from the Word.

As the Anabaptists represent for Calvin the extreme of over-emphasis upon the Spirit's influence upon the individual.[45] So the other side of the scale is the Roman Catholic church,[46] guilty of error in that it has over-emphasized the work of the Spirit in the church. Both of these extremes had failed to realize the proper unity of the word and the Spirit.

Both of the extremes produce false teaching. The spiritualists have in many ways the root problem of the improper separation of the word and the Spirit. From that separation flows a host of theological problems as outlined specifically in Calvin's work *Against the Libertines*. In that work he mentions, among others, their errors concerning providence, Christ, regeneration, and the resurrection.[47]

Calvin finds significant errors accruing from the mistaken teachings of the Roman Catholic church. In regard to the consubstantiality of the Son to the Father, he reminds us that the Roman Church taught that the concept is not found in the Bible, but is from the teaching of the church.[48] After admitting that the word "consubstantial" is not in fact found in the Bible, he avows that the idea itself is, and that the authority for the term must come from the Bible and not from church teaching. Likewise concerning infant baptism, the Roman church taught that there was no clear mandate from the scriptures regarding the practice, but that it also comes from a decree of the church. Calvin spends quite a number of pages of the *Institutes* demonstrating that this teaching too is dependent upon the clear instruction of the scriptures, rather than upon church teaching or tradition.[49]

In conclusion, it is possible to see in Calvin's analysis of the word and Spirit that:

[45]"Gegenüber der *schwärmerischen* Berufung auf ein Geisteszeugnis gegen die Schrift-autorität wird die Frage nach einem Kriterium für die Unterscheidung zwischen wahrem und falschem Geisteszeugnis wach, und dieses Kriterium wird in der Schrift gefunden: der Geist ist am Wort zu messen." Werner Krusche, *Das Wirken des Heiligen Geistes*, (Gottingen: Vandenhoeck & Ruprecht, 1957), 204.

[46]"Calvin verweist gegenüber der *römischen* Ableitung der Schriftgewissheit aus der Kirchenautorität auf die Selbstevidenz der Schrift und auf das Zeugnis des Heiligen Geistes, ohne dass die Zuordnung dieser beiden Grössen eindeutig geklärt würde." Ibid.

[47]Other errors mentioned concern: the consicience, liberty, vocation, and fellowship.

[48]*Institutes* IV.8.16.

[49]*Institutes* IV.16., in toto. In connection with this, Krusche says of Calvin, "Gegenüber der papistischen Behauptung, die Schrift habe keine Autorität ohne die Kirche, der Grund für die certitudo scripturae sei also das kirchliche Dekret, wird mit Nachdruck festgestellt, dass die Schrift keiner ausser ihr liegenden Instanz zur Verbürgung ihrer Göttlichkeit bedürfte." *Das Wirken des Heiligen Geistes*, 206.

1. The work of the Holy Spirit is closely associated with the written word of God.

2. The Bible is to be the source book for instruction within the Christian church and that the Holy Spirit guides the church in her understanding of that source.

3. The "spiritualists" are theologically mistaken in separating the work of the Holy Spirit from the Bible and depending upon the Bible for their source of authority.

4. The Roman Catholics are theologically mistaken in separating the work of the Holy Spirit from the Bible and depending upon church authority or tradition, rather than the Bible, to instruct the church, or, put another way, mistaken in their need to establish the authority of the Bible by another means than the Spirit.

Conclusion

Calvin's analysis of word and Spirit has provided a good model to demonstrate his *via media* approach. Both the libertines and catholics have been guilty of an extreme, and therefore of error. Calvin persuasively presents his own analysis as the safe and moderate way between both falsehoods. This methodological approach should be seen as following Renaissance humanism's ideals.

How are those ideals summarized? The Renaissance was concerned with rhetoric and rhetoric was concerned with persuasion. Employment of antithesis, which is very clear and leaves no doubt in the reader, is an excellent tool of persuasion.

We have briefly analyzed Calvin's theological method through the implementation of a test case. Our analysis of word and spirit elucidates Calvin's methodology, one which is in many ways dynamic and strongly influenced by sixteenth-century thinking. Calvin's use of antithesis, for the purpose of persuading, is not an ancillary element of his theological method but rather, as Francis Higman says, "the style of his treatises becomes an integral part of their message."[50] This article still leaves a number of questions unanswered, however: from which historical sources does Calvin draw as he develops his methodology?[51] If Calvin is in some ways dependent upon Renaissance humanism for his methodology, in which ways did he modify it and why?[52] These important questions would need to be addressed before a more complete picture of Calvin's theological method could be drawn.

[50]Francis Higman, *The Style of John Calvin in his Polemical Treatises* (London: Oxford University Press, 1967), 46.

[51]Possible candidates would be Agricola, Sturm, and Melanchthon. The work already done on their literary and theological styles could be compared with Calvin.

[52]Q. Breen reminds us that Calvin enjoyed reading Cicero but claims uniqueness for his own style. "John Calvin and the Rhetorical Tradition," 6.

Farel confronts Calvin in Geneva, 1536.

Calvin's Understanding of Aristotelian Natural Philosophy: Its Extent and Possible Origins

Christopher B. Kaiser

Even though contemporary science did not have such an impact on everyday life as it does now, medieval Aristotelian cosmology was perceived in Calvin's day to be a challenge to faith in a personal God as much as Newtonian physics in the eighteenth century and evolutionary biology in the late nineteenth. Calvin did not directly confront the Aristotelian view of natural philosophy, but a careful reading of the reformer's works will show that his varied comments on scientific issues of his day demonstrate a clear faith in the providence of God in the ordering of the universe. Calvin cited the Aristotelian distribution of the elements, the system of homocentric spheres, and the problem of the stability of the earth. His understanding of the issues was limited, judged by late medieval standards. Nonetheless it played an important role in his discussions of divine providence. Its origins seem to go back to his college days in Paris.

CALVIN'S PRINCIPAL INTERESTS WERE IN THE REFORM of the Church and society, not in matters of natural philosophy.[1] The same is true of the majority of Calvin scholars today. Quite properly, most contemporary treatments of Calvin have concentrated on issues of theology, the sacraments, church discipline, and the socio-political order. Very little attention has been given to the background material made increasingly available by recent studies in the history of medieval and Renaissance science.

However, Calvin had to establish the credibility of his reform program in a culture for which natural philosophy was as much a concern as it is for us today. Though contemporary science did not have such an impact on everyday life as it does now, its findings regarding the structure of the cosmos had implications for the sacraments and were widely held to provide analogies to the ideal structure of society.

[1] In addition to logic (included in the medieval *trivium*) and the practical branches of philosophy (ethics and politics), there were three theoretical branches of Aristotelian science: metaphysics; mathematics (the medieval *quadrivium*); and natural philosophy (physics, cosmology, and meteorology); Sir David Ross, *Aristotle* (London: Methuen, 1923; fifth ed., 1949), 20, 47, 156. Here we are concerned only with natural philosophy. On Calvin's use of Aristotelian categories and logic, see Joseph C. McLelland, "Calvin and Philosophy," *Canadian Journal of Theology* 11 (1965): 46–47.

78 *Calviniana*

The paradigm for natural philosophy in the middle ages (as of the thirteenth century) and Renaissance (through most of the seventeenth century)
was based on the texts of Aristotle and others, such as Sacrobosco, who popularized Aristotle's cosmology.[2] Aristotelian science was perceived by many to be
a challenge to faith in a personal God much as Newtonian physics was later to
become in the eighteenth century and evolutionary biology in the late
nineteenth.[3] Calvin's own concern with the challenges of science was most evident in his doctrines of creation and providence (Book I, chapters xiv and xvi
of the 1559 *Institutes*), but it thereby affected his concept of God and his entire
theology, which was rooted in the doctrines of God, creation, and providence.
The fact that we no longer subscribe to Aristotelian physics and cosmology
today ought not lead us to ignore this important dimension to the articulation
of religious faith in the sixteenth century.

For purposes of understanding Calvin, the physics and astronomy of
Aristotle can be summarized in three points: (1) the concept of "natural place"
for the four elements comprising sublunar bodies; (2) the system of revolving
homocentric spheres for celestial bodies; and (3) the problem of the immobility of the earth. We shall briefly inventory Calvin's knowledge of, and attitude
towards, Aristotelian natural philosophy under these three headings. An interesting paradox arose, as we shall see, concerning the dual role of the earth: on
one hand, it was the heaviest and most stable of the sublunar elements; on the
other hand, it was the center of the system of revolving spheres. What kept
it from being moved?[4]

The Concept of Natural Place

Aristotle's treatment of sublunar bodies was based on the idea that there
were four terrestrial elements—earth, water, air and fire—and that these natu-

[2]On the continued influence of Aristotelian ideas in the sixteenth century, see, e.g., Arnold
Williams, *The Common Expositor: An Account of the Commentaries on Genesis, 1527-1633* (Chapel
Hill: University of North Carolina Press, 1948), 47-50, 183-94; Paul Oskar Kristeller, *Renaissance
Thought: The Classic, Scholastic, and Humanist Strains* (New York: Harper & Row, 1961), chap. 2;
Eugene F. Rice, Jr., "Humanist Aristotelianism in France: Jacques Lefèvre d'Etaples and his Circle," in *Humanism in France at the End of the Middle Ages and in the Early Renaissance*, ed. A. H. T.
Levi (Manchester: University of Manchester Press, 1970), 132-49; Charles B. Schmitt, "Towards
a Reassessment of Renaissance Aristotelianism," *History of Science* 11 (1973); 159-93; idem,
Aristotle and the Renaissance (Cambridge: Harvard University Press, 1983); Edward Grant,
"Aristoteliansim and the Longevity of the Medieval World View," *History of Science* 16 (1978):
93-106.

[3]The 1277 Paris condemnation of propositions associated with Aristotelian physics and
Averroist philosophy is the most dramatic instance of a conservative Christian response to Aristotelian natural philosophy. In Calvin's immediate background is Zwingli's attempt to mediate
between the astronomers (whose prognostications were based on Aristotelian cosmology) and
their critics, the preachers (*De providentia* 7).

[4]We still have no evidence that Calvin was concerned with or even aware of the work of
Copernicus; C. B. Kaiser, "Calvin, Copernicus, and Castellio," *Calvin Theological Journal* 21
(1986): 5-31.

rally distributed themselves in spherical shells, with earth at the center, because it was the heaviest, and fire at the perimeter of the sublunar realm, just beneath the sphere of the moon. In comparison to earlier medieval cosmologies, like that of the Venerable Bede (earth, air, ether, Olympus, fire), this was a more rational, naturalistic account. Not only did it explain the distribution of the elements in terms of the concept of natural place, but it suggested that human beings were confined to the lowest sphere by nature rather than by divine ordinance.

Calvin cited the Aristotelian distribution of the elements quite frequently and seems not to have been aware of earlier systems like Bede's: earth was naturally at the center of the cosmos because it was the heaviest of all the elements;[5] the waters naturally formed a spherical shell between the earth and the atmosphere;[6] the fiery realm came last, just beneath the sphere of the moon.[7] Also following Aristotle, Calvin held that comets were formed from warm exhalations rising from the earth, those that did not go into the making of thunder, lightning, and wind.[8] Vapors rising from earth produced clouds, and these were what Moses had in mind when he referred to waters above the firmament in Genesis 1:7—this in contrast to the majority of medieval writers who took the supracelestial waters to refer to a transparent crystalline sphere beyond the sphere of the stars.[9]

But, though Calvin accepted the Aristotelian ordering of the elements and alluded to the concept of natural place, he did *not* accept the idea that a natural propensity for each element was a self-evident or a complete explanation of the elements' behavior. For example, Calvin cited the fact that the earth was not entirely covered with water but that clouds held back the rain and ocean basins contained the waters on earth. This containment could not be accounted for, he argued, on strictly Aristotelian principles; it was solely due to the ordinances of God described in Gen. 1:6 ("Let there be a firmament in the midst of the waters. . . .") and Gen. 1:9 ("Let the waters be gathered together

---

[5]Sermons on Job 26 (*Calvini Opera*, ed. William Baum et al. [hereafter *CO*; 59 vols., Brunswick and Berlin, 1863-1900] 34:430, 434); Third Sermon on Genesis (Richard Stauffer, *Dieu, la création et la Providence dans la prédication de Calvin* ([Berne: Peter Lang, 1978]), 225, n 77); Comm. Psalm 104:5 (James Anderson, trans., *Commentary on the Book of Psalms* [5 vols., Edinburgh, 1845-9] 4:148–89); Comm. Jer. 10:12-13 (John Owen, trans., *Commentaries on the Book of the Prophet Jeremiah and the Lamentations* [5 vols., Edinburgh, 1850-55] 2:34). On these and other texts on the place of the earth in relation to the sun, see Edward Rosen, "Calvin's Attitude toward Copernicus," *Journal of the History of Ideas* 21 (1960): 438–40; Stauffer, *Dieu*, 186-88.

[6]Comm. Gen. 1:9 (John King, trans., *Commentaries on the First Book of Moses* [2 vols., Edinburgh, 1847] 1:81); Comm. Psalm 104:5, 9, (Anderson, trans., 4:148-52); Comm. Jer. 5:22, (Owen, trans., 1:294).

[7]Comm. Gen. 1:15 (King, trans., 1:86); Comm. Jer. 10:12-13 (Owen, trans., 2:37).

[8]Comm. Jer. 10:12-13 (Owen, trans., 2:37); cf. Aristotle, *Meteorologica* I.4,7; II.4-5.

[9]Comm. Gen. 1:7 (King, trans., 1:79-80); cf. Basil, *Hexaemeron* III.7-9.

unto one place, and let the dry land appear").[10] In other words, Calvin wanted to show that the established order of nature was not strictly "natural" in the sense of being self-evident or determined by natural propensities. Rather, it was highly contingent, having been ordained by God in ways that would not necessarily have occurred to natural philosophers and sustained by God's direct operation or particular providence.

Even the fact that earth occupied the central position in the cosmos was not self-evident, Calvin argued, for, though earth was surely the heaviest of the four elements, the center of the cosmos was not the biggest part of creation. So why should it attract the heaviest element in the first place?[11] Here again Calvin attempted to press natural philosophers to question their own first principles and to see God as the free creator who established things that seem self-evident to us.

Calvin's varied comments on scientific issues might sound contradictory at first reading. On the one hand, Calvin used Aristotelian ideas and obviously appreciated their value as an antidote to Academic relativism and Epicurean indeterminism. On the other, he repeatedly challenged their self-evidence and pointed out gaps or contradictions in the purely naturalistic account.[12] When understood as an argument for particular providence, as distinct from strict naturalism, however, Calvin's varied comments make a good deal of sense. Calvin stressed the natural order when he felt that would strengthen faith in God; he qualified it when he felt it would become self-contained and detract from faith.

How extensive was Calvin's reading in the literature concerning Aristotle's concept of natural place? Of the problems Calvin raised, that of the elevation of dry land above sea level had been discussed most extensively by earlier scholars. Albert the Great (mid-thirteenth century) treated the problem as one of the lowering of the seas, rather than an elevation of land, in certain parts of the globe. The fact that the seas were lowered and the underlying

[10]Comm. Gen. 1:6-9; 7:11-12 (King, trans., 1:80-81, 270-71); Comm. Psalm 33:7; 104:5-9 (Anderson, trans., 1:544; 4:148-52); Second Sermon on Job 26 (*CO* 34:434-5); Third Sermon on Genesis (Stauffer, *Dieu*, 225, n 78); Comm. Jer. 5:22 (Owen, trans., 1:294-6); cf. *Institutes* I.5.6 The idea was expressed by the church fathers: e.g., Athanasius (*Contra gentes* 36) and Basil (*Hexaemeron* III.8; IV.2-3), but without the strict Aristotelian framework assumed by Calvin. Indeed, Athanasius (*Contra gentes* 9) and Gregory of Nyssa (*De opificio hominis* 3) used a system of elements more like Bede's than Aristotle's. So Calvin clearly received his Aristotelian physics and cosmology through late medieval and Renaissance sources, not from the fathers.

[11]Comm. Jer. 10:12-13 (Owen, trans., 2:34).

[12]E.g., wind, rain, thunder, and lightning are not fortuitous but subject to God's *potentia ordinata*; Comm. Psalms 104:3-4; 148:7-9 (Anderson, trans., 4:146; 5:307); Comm. Jer. 10:12-13 (Owen, trans., 2:37: "fire generates water"; "the sun attracts vapors"; etc., after Aristotle). On the other hand, "the power of God cannot be excluded, when we say that anything is done according to nature," as evidenced by the fact that winds rise suddenly even when it is calm and rain does not inundate the earth as it would on natural principles alone; Comm. Jer. 10:12-13 (Owen, trans., 36-38); cf. Comm. Gen. 1:6-8; 7:11-12 (King, trans., 1:80, 270-71).

earth exposed in the temperate and tropical zones was due to the greater intensity of sun and starlight there.

But then the waters should flow back from the polar regions to cover the land again, objected an early fourteenth-century treatise, *Quaestio de aqua et terra*. The only logical solution was that the stars above the temperate and tropical zones exerted some special elevating influence on the lands beneath them.[13]

A third suggestion was offered by John Buridan (mid-fourteenth century): once land masses had somehow risen above sea level they would be stabilized there by the drying effect of the sun: the portion of earth exposed to sunlight and air (by erosion) would become rarefied and hence lighter than water.[14] Buridan's treatment was adopted by Nicole Oresme and Albert of Saxony, among others, and must be granted the status of "best science" of the late medieval period.[15]

It is doubtful that Calvin was aware of these late medieval discussions. He gave no account of the various possible explanations and consistently referred to the gathering of the waters and the emergence of dry land as a "miracle" (*miraculum*) and "beyond nature" (*praeter naturam*)[16]. The only answer the natural philosophers could give, according to Calvin, was that the natural tendency of the waters to cover the earth is counteracted by the special providence of God.[17] Calvin's approach to Aristotle's natural philosophy appears to be a return *ad fontes* typical of the Renaissance (cf. Lefèvre, Reuchlin, Melanchthon), more than a *quaestio* typical of the late middle ages.

The System of Homocentric Spheres

The feature of Aristotle's science that had the greatest influence on the medieval doctrine of God was the cosmology of homocentric spheres as modified by the Arabic natural philosophers, Thebit (Ibn Qurra) and Alpetragius (al-Bitruji). As a rule there were thought to be nine or ten celestial spheres surrounding the earth; seven for the sun, the moon, and the five known planets; an eighth sphere containing the stars; an optional ninth sphere to allow for

[13]M. A. Orr, *Dante and the Early Astronomers* (London: Allan Wingate, 1913; rev. ed., 1956), 298-305. The relevant loci in Aristotle are *Meteorologica* II.2.23-26; *De caelo* II.4.287a.30-287b.14.

[14]*Quaestiones super libris de caelo et mundo* II.7; Ernest A. Moody, "John Buridan on the Habitability of the Earth," *Speculum* 16 (1941): 415-25 (the relevant text is given on 424-25); reprinted in idem, *Studies in Medieval Philosophy, Science, and Logic* (Berkeley: University of California Press, 1975), 111-26.

[15]E.g., Nicole Oresme's *De l'espère*; George W. Coopland, *Nicole Oresme and the Astrologers* (Liverpool: University of Liverpool Press, 1952), 17.

[16]E.g., Comm. Gen. 1:9 (*CO* 23:19); Comm. Psalm 33:7 (*CO* 31:328); Second Sermon on Job 26 (*CO* 34:435); Comm. Jer. 5:22 (*CO*37:63).

[17]Comm. Psalm 104:5 (*CO* 32:86; Anderson trans., 4:149).

anomalies ("trepidation") in the motion of the stars in the eighth; and a tenth containing the supracelestial waters of Gen. 1:7.[18]

The abode of God was located in the empyrean, beyond the outer boundary of the outermost sphere. According to Aristotle, God was the First Mover, that is, the ultimate formal and final cause, whose very presence was enough to activate the rotation of the outermost sphere of the cosmos. The latter was, therefore, the "first moved sphere" (*primum mobile*), the only object with which God was normally in any kind of immediate relationship. Inner spheres were moved by virtue of their proximity to outer ones, thus forming a chain of influence extending to the innermost celestial sphere, that of the moon, and even to the cycles of generation and corruption on earth.[19]

Since God was located, symbolically at least, beyond the outermost created heaven, the effect of the medieval assimilation of Aristotelian cosmology with its nine or ten heavens was that his action appeared to be rather more remote from terrestrial events than was traditionally thought to be the case. We are concerned here only with the normal mode of God's activity (*de potentia ordinata*), not with his occasional use of his absolute power (*de potentia absoluta*), as in miracles, or with his indirect operation through angels.

So with the influx of Aristotelian thought a spatial and causal gap threatened to open up between the normal activity of God and events on earth. Grosseteste (d. 1253), for instance, held that the diurnal rotation of the *primum mobile* was communicated to it by God in such a way that energy and motion were transmitted through the lower spheres all the way to the earth.[20] The same idea appears in Roger Bacon, William of Auvergne, Bonaventure, Albertus Magnus, and Thomas Aquinas in the thirteenth century.

The remoteness of God's providence suggested by the new cosmology, of course, had to be counterbalanced, even with respect to the normal mode of God's activity, if Aristotelian science was to be acceptable to Christian faith. This was done in several ways. Bonaventure, Albert, and Thomas all attempted to restore the balance by limiting the influence transmitted through the celestial spheres to the physical, secular aspects of life. So the configuration

---

[18]For background, see Nicholas H. Steneck, *Science and Creation in the Middle Ages* (Notre Dame: University of Notre Dame Press, 1976), 70-71; Edward Grant, "Cosmology," in *Science in the Middle Ages*, ed. David C. Lindberg (Chicago: University of Chicago Press, 1978), 273-75. A convenient source on the system of homocentric spheres in the sixteenth century was Gregorius Reisch's *Margarita philosophica* first published in 1503; A. Rupert Hall, *The Scientific Revolution* (2d ed., Boston: Beacon Press, 1966), 11-17.

[19]Aristotle, *De generatione* II.10.337a; 11.338b; *Meteorologica* II.2.354b.26-31. With the development of medieval machinery, models of the cosmos became so mechanical that they could be driven by a single weight; Coopland, *Nicole Oresme*, 15-16.

[20]Clare C. Riedl, trans., *Robert Grosseteste: On Light* (Milwaukee: Marquette University Press, 1942), 6-7, 15-16. Note that God became the efficient cause of motion for Grosseteste and other thirteenth-century scholastics, not just the formal and final cause as for Aristotle.

of the heavens was responsible for the creation of worms and insects from pu-
trefaction, for instance, and the sun could influence the birth and death of
higher animals—all, of course, under God's ultimate control. There were two
channels open, however, for the more immediate influence of God in human
life under normal conditions (*de potentia ordinata*): God could enlighten the
soul or affect the will directly, and he could, and regularly did, infuse grace
through the seven sacraments, particularly through the Eucharist.[21]

Calvin had difficulties, as did many of his contemporaries, with the Aristotelian cosmology, even in its medieval Christian version. Yet it was too well
entrenched in Western thought to be dismissed altogether. Even critics of
medieval Aristotelianism like Lefèvre, Reuchlin, and Melanchthon were concerned to restore the original texts and their meaning in keeping with the humanist program of bypassing scholasticism and returning to the ancient
sources.

Calvin made no mention of the optional ninth sphere which was added by
Arabic commentators, and, as noted, he rejected the medieval notion of a tenth
(crystalline) sphere containing the supra-celestial waters. Here again his stance
was consistent with that of the humanist litterati.[22] But Calvin accepted the
basic outline of Aristotle's cosmology: "astronomers make a distinction of
spheres," he said in his *Commentary on Genesis*, "and . . . teach that the fixed
stars have their proper place in the firmament." Beneath the firmament of the
fixed stars were the planetary spheres ranging from Saturn to the moon and
the outer boundary of the sublunar realm.[23] The whole structure was fitted together and interlocked like a great machine with the lower spheres subordinated to and driven in various ways by the upper ones; at the outer limit was
the *primum mobile*, the sphere which moved all the others and was, in turn,
driven by God. God was thus the Prime Mover, the "beginning and cause of
all motion," from that of the outer stars to that of the moon.[24]

---

[21]E.g., Aquinas, *Summa theologiae* Ia.115.3-4; Theodore Otto Wedel, *The Mediaeval Attitude
Toward Astrology* (New Haven: Yale University Press, 1920), 64-68; N. Max Wildiers, *The Theologian and His Universe* (New York: Seabury Press, 1982), 46-48, 53-55, 64,72. Cf. Calvin's comment on the necessity of transubstantiation for a realization of the presence of Christ within the
scholastic framework; *Institutes* IV.17.15.

[22]Treatises like Nicole Oresme's *L'espère* and Luther's *Lectures on Genesis* had already questioned the need for the ninth and tenth spheres; Coopland, *Nicole Oresme*, 16; *Luther's Works*, ed.
Jaroslav Pelikan and Helmut Lehmann, 55 vols., (Saint Louis: Concordia and Philadelphia: Fortress, 1955-76) 1:26-29. The point is that Calvin rejected the tenth outright and did not even
mention the ninth.

[23]Comm. Gen. 1:15, 16 (King, trans., 1:86); Comm. Psalm 19:4-6 (Anderson trans., 1:315).

[24]*Institutes* I.14.21; 16.1-5 (the quote is taken from Battles trans., *Institutes of the Christian
Religion*, ed. John T. McNeill 2 vols., [Philadelphia: Westminster, 1960], 1:200). Here Calvin cri-
tiques the philosophers' restriction of God to the role of prime mover but does not reject the role
itself as one aspect of God's operation; cf. Comm. Gen.3:17 (King, trans., 1:173); Comm. Psalm
68:31-33 (Anderson, trans., 3:43).

Here, again, we find Calvin delighting in the orderly presentation of the universe offered by the natural philosophers. But, also, we find him drawing the line in order to counteract the suggestion that God was separated from the ordinary events of life on earth by a long chain of second causes. This was one of the reasons for his opposition to judicial astrology. In astrological determinism, the chain of cause and effect was regarded as extending not only to the seasonal cycles of generation and corruption, but to all terrestrial events. Grosseteste's theory of the inward radiation of light and other material forms provided a plausible physical basis for such cosmic influences on everyday events. "The heavens," as A. M. Hunter put it, "were threatening to put their maker out of sight."[25]

Calvin, like his scholastic forebears, was quite specific in pointing out the limits of such astrological influence. Terrestrial bodies were subject to the order of the heavens, he allowed, and they drew their qualities and basic dispositions from the configurations of the celestial realm. But stellar influence could only account for events that occurred within the ordinary course of nature and not for "accidental" happenings, particularly those with possible spiritual consequences, which Calvin saw as coming under the direct control of God.[26] Examples of the latter were: (1) the determination of heredity—here God acted directly and made use of the means of parental seed more than of the stellar configurations at birth; (2) the regeneration of believers through his Spirit; and (3) the bestowal of special gifts or talents among humans for the benefit of his people. In short, Calvin limited astrological determination to the behavior of subhuman creatures and, in the case of humanity, to everyday matters of the body like physical illness and healing.[27] Stellar influences were a part of God's universal providence, but had little or nothing to do with particular providence, inner grace, or the care of the Church.

In all of these ways, Calvin, like Aquinas, Bonaventure, and others before him, tried to prevent the Aristotelian account of the massive world machine

---

[25]A. M. Hunter, *The Teaching of Calvin*, 2d ed. (London: James Clarke & Co., 1950), 291. Melanchthon, for example, allowed a degree of astrological determination; Clyde Manschreck, *Melanchthon, the Quiet Reformer* (Nashville: Abingdon, 1958), 102-12; Bruce Moran, "The Universe of Philip Melanchthon: Criticism and Use of the Copernican Theory," *Comitatus* 4 (1973): 8-10. On the differences between Calvin and Melanchthon, see Josef Bohatec, *Budé und Calvin* (Graz: Hermann Böhlaus Nachf., 1950), 276-78.

[26]*Advertissement contre l'astrologie* (Mary Potter, trans., "A Warning Against Judicial Astrology and Other Prevalent Curiosities, by John Calvin," *Calvin Theological Journal* 18 [1983]: 166-69, 181-83); cf. *Institutes* I.16.3, 5.

[27]*Advertissement* (Potter, trans., 170-71, 182); cf. Hunter, *Teaching*, 291-93; Wayne Shumaker, *The Occult Sciences in the Renaissance* (Berkeley: University of California Press, 1972), 44-46. The importance of natural astrology for medicine was based on, though not limited to, the humoral pathology of Galen. It had been a commonplace in Western Europe since the time of Isidore of Seville (seventh century) and was restated by Oresme among others; Wedel, *Mediaeval Attitude*, 28, 36, 67, 71-73; Coopland, *Nicole Oresme*, 23-24 (n 63 compares Calvin's *Advertissement*).

from embracing all of life and to secure a preserve for the direct action of God in human affairs. A cosmological interest and an understanding of the problematics of the Aristotelian worldview must be taken into consideration, therefore, in our interpretation of his theology.

But all of the ways just cited in which God affected human affairs directly were under the heading of special graces or *potentia Dei absoluta*.[28] If that were all, the realm of God's *potentia ordinata* would still have been governed by the great world machine, and in the everyday events of the natural world ("accidents" aside) God's activity would have seemed as remote as the distant *primum mobile*, just as it seemed (to their critics) to be in the theology of the medieval schoolmen.[29]

However, there were also several ways in which Calvin saw particular providence as affecting terrestrial events, even within the ordinary course of nature (the sphere of *potentia ordinata*) and these were wonderful signs to him that the direct expression of God's sovereignty and fatherly love were not limited to special graces but were evidenced in the basic conditions of everyday life. Two of these signs have already been discussed in our treatment of the sublunar elements: the confinement of the terrestrial waters to restricted areas and the restraint of the rain by the formation of clouds. Without these providential ordinances of God, waters would completely cover the earth in accordance with their nature, as they did in the great flood of Noah's time.[30]

Yet there was a third, even more astounding way in which God's immediate supervision affected everyday terrestrial affairs, and the evidence for this was incontrovertible. In fact, it was immediately at hand (or under foot) for everyone to see and feel—the immobility of the earth. This is the third point of Aristotelian natural philosophy that we need to consider.

The Immobility of the Earth

What Calvin noticed was that the earth played a dual role in medieval cosmology. On the one hand, earth was the heaviest of the elements; hence, it naturally settled in the center of the world system, according to Aristotle, and

---

[28]*Advertissement* (Potter, trans., 170); cf. *Institutes* I.5.11; *Comm. Gen.* 48:17; Charles Partee, *Calvin and Classical Philosophy* (Leiden: Brill, 1977), 129-30. On the relevance of the scholastic distinction between *potentia absoluta* and *potentia ordinata* to Calvin's theology, see Heiko A. Oberman, "The 'Extra' Dimension in the Theology of Calvin," *Journal of Ecclesiastical History* 21 (1970): 62-64; idem, "*Via antiqua* and *Via moderna*: Late Medieval Prolegomena to Early Reformation Thought," *Journal of the History of Ideas* 48 (1987): 38-39; Alister E. McGrath, "John Calvin and Late Medieval Thought," *Archiv für Reformationsgeschichte* 77 (1986): 77-78 with notes promising further details.

[29]The thirteenth-century scholastics also found scope in the sphere of everyday life for the immediate activity of God (*de potentia ordinata*), but this was primarily through the sacraments administered by the Church as noted earlier; see n 21. Calvin, obviously, would have to seek another solution.

[30]See n 10.

it was supposed to be stable there by nature. On the other hand, the earth was also the hub of the cosmic machine, the center of the system of homocentric spheres, with nothing but the surrounding elements of air and water to stabilize it. Why, then, should the earth not turn and twist along with the rest of the cosmic machinery?

Calvin phrased the question in two rather different ways, but, in each case, he saw the stability of the earth against any kind of rotation or wobble as a clear sign of God's continuous intervention in the regular course of nature. First, here is how Calvin put the question in his 1557 *Commentary on Psalm* 93:1, "He hath established the world; it shall not be moved":

> The psalmist proves that God will not neglect or abandon the world from the fact that he created it. A simple survey of the world should of itself suffice to attest a divine providence. The heavens revolve daily [*quotidie volvitur*], and, immense as is their fabric [*in mole tantae magnitudinis*], and inconceivable the rapidity of their revolutions [*in tante celeritate*], we experience no concussion—no disturbance in the harmony of their motion. . . . How could the earth hang suspended in the air were it not upheld by God's hand? By what means could it maintain itself unmoved [*staret immobilis*], while the heavens above are in constant rapid motion, did not its divine maker fix and establish it?[31]

In other words, Calvin argued, the massive motion of the heavenly spheres would inevitably disturb the equilibrium of the earth if God did not act continuously to keep it stationary. As the text cited shows, the issue was an existential one for Calvin: the incredible stability of the earth in the midst of the swirling heavens was a sign that God had not left terrestrial affairs to follow their own course or made them entirely subordinate to stellar influences—a sign of God's particular providence even in the everyday course of nature.

One problem with this passage is the absence of any mention of the fact that Aristotle had a simple explanation for the earth's immobility: the *primum mobile* moved all of the lower spheres by a series of mechanical linkages (with some degree of angelic supervision), but these linkages extended only as far as

---

[31]Comm. Psalm 93:1 (*CO* 32:16-17; Anderson, trans. 4:6-7; the French text is given in *Commentaires de Jehan Calvin sur le Livre des Psaumes*, 2 vols. [Paris, 1859], 2:205). Compare the following passage which first appeared in the 1543 edition of the *Institutes*: ". . . who so proportioned the inequality of days, which we daily observe [*quotidie cernimus*], that no confusion occurs. It is so too when we observe his power in sustaining so great a mass [*tanta mole*], in governing the swiftly revolving [*tam celeri . . . volutatione*] heavenly system," (*CO* 1:509; *Calvini Opera Selecta*, ed. P. Barth and W. Niesel [hereafter *OS*; 5 vols., Munich: Chr. Kaiser Verlag, 1926-36], 3:172; Battles, trans., 181). This earlier discussion of the swirling heavens may have raised the problem of the stability of the earth discussed in Calvin's later writings like the Commentary on Psalms.

the sphere of the moon. Beneath the moon, all motions were naturally up or down. Only the outermost part of the terrestrial atmosphere was dragged along with the lunar sphere. Why, then, did Calvin apparently assume that the rotational forces of the celestial spheres would extend all the way to earth? Why did he not even mention the Aristotelian explanation as he often did even if he wished to challenge the self-evidence or completeness of that explanation?[32]

Was Calvin's knowledge of Aristotelian science simply deficient at this point? Or, is it possible that he was trained to look for contradictions in the Aristotelian worldview in a speculative manner?[33] If the latter, could this critical approach to Aristotle reflect on the liberal arts instruction he received at the Collège de Montaigu in the 1520s?

There had been significant modifications in physical science since the thirteenth century, when Aristotelian physics and cosmology reigned supreme in Western thought. One of the leading arts masters at the Collège de Montaigu, John Major (1469-1550), was well known as an advocate of anti-Aristotelian concepts like an extra-cosmic void and an infinity of worlds that had developed in the fourteenth and fifteenth centuries.[34] However, I have not been able to find evidence of awareness on Calvin's part of these late medieval developments sufficient to confirm such an explanation of the apparent discrepancy in his understanding of Aristotelian cosmology.[35] There is an interesting (derogatory) reference to the idea of an extra-cosmic void in the 1559 edition of the *Institutes*,[36] but it is not specific enough to be differentiated from traditional Stoic speculations that might have been available to Calvin from

[32]See n10 above. Calvin may have been aware of passages in Aristotle's *De caelo* (II.13-14) where the possibility of the earth being swirled about by the heavens was discussed and rejected. An edition of the *De caelo* was published at Basel in 1553, the same year as Calvin's first discussion of the problem of the earth's stability (Twelfth Sermon on Psalm 119, delivered on 9 April 1553); Alexandre Ganoczy, *La Bibliotèque de l'Academie de Calvin* (Geneva: Droz, 1969), 263.

[33]Possible instances are cited in nn10-12 above.

[34]Edward Grant, *Much Ado About Nothing* (Cambridge: Cambridge University Press, 1981), 149-52. On the possibility of Major's influence on Calvin, see Alexandre Ganoczy, *Le jeune Calvin* (Wiesbaden: Franz Steiner Verlag, 1966), 186-92; A. N. S. Lane, "Calvin's Use of the Fathers and the Medievals," *Calvin Theological Journal* 16 (1981): 151-55; McGrath, "John Calvin and Late Medieval Thought," 66, 71.

[35]Compare Calvin's treatment of the rainbow which, of course, was a sign of the covenant between God and Noah. Here Calvin merely cited the classical explanation (reflection by water droplets) that had been offered by Aristotle (*Meteorologica* III.4) and repeated by Seneca (*Quaest. nat.* I.3) and Pliny (*Nat. hist.* II.1x.150) and made no mention of the new theory (refraction and internal reflection) developed by thirteenth- and fourteenth-century perspectivists like Theodoric of Freiburg (d. 1311). He merely insisted that the meaning of the rainbow was not exhausted by a naturalistic explanation, however complete: *Institutes* IV.14.18 (IV.8 in 1536 edition.); Comm. Gen. 9:13 (King, trans., 1:299). On the medieval theory of the rainbow, see A. C. Crombie, *Augustine to Galileo*, 2d ed. (Cambridge: Harvard University Press, 1961), 1:114-24.

[36]*Institutes* I.14.1. For the late medieval background of this idea, see Edward Grant, *Much Ado*, 129-52.

other sources. We do not yet know enough about the training Calvin received or about the sources he used to give a more detailed interpretation of his cosmological interests at this point.

The second way in which Calvin raised the paradox of the earth's immobility was based on the inability of the fluid elements—air and water—to provide the earth any firm support, rather than on the possible torque exerted by the whirling heavens. The two versions of the problem are logically independent and occur in different contexts, though there is no inconsistency between them, and they could quite easily be combined.

This second argument occurs in two slightly different forms both dating from the mid-1550s. First, in the *Twelfth Sermon on Psalm 119*, which was delivered on 9 April 1553 and published in 1554, we read:

> I beseech you to tell me what the foundation of the earth is. It is founded both upon the water and also upon the air: behold its foundation! . . . Behold the whole earth founded only in trembling, indeed poised above such bottomless depths that it might be turned upside down at any minute [*qu'elle pourroit renverser à chacune minute de temps*] to become disordered. Hence there must be a wonderful power of God to keep it in the condition in which it is.[37]

A second, slightly longer form appears in the corresponding passage in Calvin's *Commentary on Psalms*, which was published a few years later (Latin, 1557; French 1558). Here the ideas of the natural instability of earth and the overwhelming power of the rotating heavens are combined:

> . . . and now he [the psalmist] again teaches us, by experience, that, though the world is subject to revolutions [*quamvis volvatur mundus*; French: *combien que le monde soit sujet à révolutions*], yet in it bright and signal testimonies to the truth of God shine forth, so that the steadfastness of his word is not exclusively confined to heaven, but comes down even to us who dwell upon the earth. For this reason, it is added, that the earth continues steadfast, even as it was established by God at the beginning. . . . for, though it is suspended in the midst of the sea, yet it continues to remain in the same state. . . . for earth the which otherwise could not occupy the position it does for a single moment [*quae alioqui momento uno non staret*; French: *laquelle autrement ne pourroit subsister une seule minute*

---

[37]Twelfth Sermon on Psalm 119 (*CO* 32:620; Thomas Stocker, trans., *Two and Twentie Sermons . . . The Hundredth and Nineteenth Psalme* [London, 1580], fol. 99v; quoted and modernized by Edward Rosen, "Calvin's Attitude," 439); cf. Basil, *Hexaemeron* I.8 and Ambrose *Hexaemeron* I.vi.22 for the thought.

de temps], abides notwithstanding steadfast, because God's word is the foundation on which it rests.[38]

The emphases in these two passages are slightly different. The first stresses the instability of the terrestrial sphere, with clearly existential undertones ("founded in trembling," "poised above bottomless depth," etc.), as befits a sermon on the Psalms.[39] The second passage, on the other hand stresses the steadfastness of the earth, based on the care and faithfulness of God, in the midst of revolutionary cosmic forces ("subject to revolutions").

In all these ways, Calvin came to associate the apparent immobility of the earth with the immediate presence and power of God in ordinary events as a bulwark against revolution and disorder. The particular providence of God could be seen by all in the stability of the earth just as universal providence could be seen in the regular motions of the heavens. For Calvin, of course, there was a clear correlation between the concept of stability and order in the natural sphere and the sense of God's protection in the personal and social spheres. The believer could take comfort in the midst of social instability and ecclesiastical disorder knowing that God held the whole world in his hands.[40]

We have established that Calvin knew and accepted the basic tenets of Aristotelian natural philosophy, particularly those dealing with the terrestrial elements, meteorology, and the celestial spheres. The basic ideas he accepted include the concept of natural place, the natural sphericity of elemental distributions, and subordination of terrestrial cycles to the revolutions of the heavenly spheres, and the driving force of the *primum mobile.*

It should be stressed that there was nothing wrong with Calvin's ideas about natural philosophy: they had been accepted as well-established facts in the West for over three centuries and would not become "out of date" until a century later. Even Calvin's apparent ignorance (or disregard) of late medieval refinements of the Aristotelian cosmology was perfectly in keeping with Renaissance humanist efforts to bypass the subtleties of medieval scholasticism and work from original sources.

[38]Commentary on Psalm 119:90 (*CO* 32:253-4; *Commentaires sur le Livre des Psaumes* 2:419; Anderson, trans., 4:469). I take the word "world" (*mundus*) to refer to the world-system of celestial spheres (rather than to the earth) for two reasons: (1) that was the meaning of the term for late medievals like John Major; Pierre Duhem, *Medieval Cosmology* (Chicago: University of Chicago Press, 1985), 504; and (2) we have no evidence that Calvin was aware of Copernicus's work; Kaiser, "Calvin, Copernicus, and Castellio," 31. Cf. Comm. Psalm 90:2 (*volvanturomnia; CO* 31:834; Anderson, trans., 3: 462-63).

[39]Cf. William J. Bouwsma, "John Calvin's Anxiety," *Proceedings of the American Philosophical Society* 128 (1984): 254. I agree with Bouwsma that Calvin's sense of the instability of nature reflected his own anxieties (which had objective, as well as purely personal, grounds), but would also call attention to his concern to avoid total determination by forces (natural or ecclesiastical) other than God. See now Bouwsma's *John Calvin* (New York: Oxford University Press, 1988), 85.

[40]*Institutes* I.16.3-4; cf. Comm. Gen. 7:11 (King, trans., 1:270); Comm. Psalm 115:17 (Anderson, trans., 4:358).

The Origins of Calvin's Understanding
This leaves us with the question of when and how Calvin became interested in the specific problems of Aristotelian science. A brief review of the material cited above shows that most of Calvin's discussions of Aristotelian natural philosophy were written in the 1550s. They occur in both sermons (on Psalm 119, Job, and Genesis) and commentaries (on Genesis, the Psalms, and Jeremiah), as well as in the 1559 edition of the *Institutes*.[41]

Some of the most detailed descriptions of Aristotelian scientific issues are the meteorological material found in the *Commentary on Jeremiah*, which was begun in 1560 and published in 1563. A series of sermons on Jeremiah had been delivered as early as 1548-50, but, unfortunately, only the twenty-five sermons on Jer. 14:19 to 18:23 have survived in manuscript, whereas the meteorological material mentioned appears in the commentary on Jer. 10:12-13.[42] If the sermon on Jer. 10:12-13 dealt with problems of Aristotelian meteorology, then it may have been the earliest such discussion on Calvin's part, dating from December 1549 or January 1550.[43] The earliest surviving indications (of which I am aware) of a detailed interest in the cosmology of Aristotle occurred in the *Commentary on Genesis*, begun in July 1550 and published in 1554.[44] Here we find the first extant discussion by Calvin of the containment of terrestrial waters and the differentiation of celestial spheres.[45] The issue of the stability of the earth was first treated in the sermons and commentary on Psalms in the mid-1550s.[46]

It is difficult to know just how much significance to attach to these dates. They represent the mature Calvin, to be sure. Indeed, the publication dates all fall within five years of the last major Latin edition of the *Institutes* (1559). It may also be noted that the detailed expression of Calvin's interest in Aristotle's cosmology began just about the time Girolamo Zanchi arrived in Geneva (1552-53) and Peter Martyr Vermigli returned from Oxford to Strasbourg

---

[41]In roughly chronological order the writings cited above as discussing natural philosophy are: Commentary on Genesis (begun 1550; published 1554); Twelfth Sermon on Psalm 119 (preached 9 April 1553; published 1554); Commentary on Psalms (exposition begun 1552; published 1557); Sermons on Job (begun 1554; published 1563); *Institutes* I.14.1; 16.3-5 (1559); Sermons on Genesis (preached 1559-60; not published); and Commentary on Jeremiah (exposition begun 1560; published 1563). On the manuscripts and dates of the unpublished sermons on Genesis, see Richard Stauffer, "Les sermons inédits de Calvin sur le Livre de la Genèse," *Revue de théologie et de philosophie*, 3d ser., 15 (1965): 26-36. On the dates of the expositions or lectures related to the commentaries, see T. H. L. Parker, *Calvin's Old Testament Commentaries* (Edinburgh: T. & T. Clark, 1986), 29.

[42]See n 8.

[43]Rudolphe Peter, ed., *Sermons sur les Livres de Jérémie et des Lamentations* (*Supplementa Calviniana* 6, ed. Erwin Mülhaupt, Neukirchen-Vluyn: Neukirchener Verlag, 1971), xiv-xvi.

[44]Letter to Farel, July 1550 (*CO* 13:606). Parker ventures that Calvin wrote the first few chapters of the Genesis commentary (including Genesis 1:6-9) in his own hand in 1550; *Calvin's Old Testament Commentaries*, 25-26.

[45]See nn 10 and 23.   [46]See nn 31, 37, and 38.

(1553). Both Vermigli and Zanchi were trained in Italian Aristotelianism and lectured and wrote on Aristotelian natural philosophy, among other things.[47] It is conceivable that Calvin's interest was stimulated by their ideas, though I find no evidence of any discussions of natural philosophy in their written correspondence.

It is more likely that the appearance of passages dealing with Aristotelian physics and cosmology in the early 1550s was fortuitous. After all, it was not until the late 1540s that Calvin had his sermons systematically recorded and began regular work on his Old Testament commentaries.[48] So it would be worthwhile asking whether the ideas about natural philosophy expressed in Calvin's sermons and commentaries could have had their origins in earlier stages of his work.

Passing references to Aristotelian meteorology had occurred already in the 1532 Commentary on Seneca's *De clementia*, Calvin's first published work,[49] and in the first edition of the *Institutes* (1536).[50] The first reference (to my knowledge) to the rotation of the celestial spheres appeared in the 1543 *Institutes* along with the first extant citation of Basil's *Hexaemeron* as a model for the "history of the creation of the universe."[51] Then, Luther's first *Lectures on Genesis*, published in 1544, treated some of the same points of Aristotle and in relation to the same verses of Genesis 1 as those found in Calvin's later *Commentary on Genesis*.[52]

Based on the evidence cited here, a plausible account of the origins of Calvin's understanding of Aristotelian natural philosophy would be as follows. Calvin probably became interested in and informed about the subject

[47]Marvin Walter Anderson, *Peter Martyr: A Reformer in Exile* (Nieuwkoop: De Graaf, 1975), 175-77, 196-98, 372; John Patrick Donnelly, "Italian Influences on the Development of Calvinist Scholasticism," *Sixteenth Century Journal* 7 (1976); 86-88, 93-94.

[48]Nicolas Colladon, "Vie de Calvin" (*CO* 21:70); T. H. L. Parker, "Calvini Opera sed non Omnia," *Scottish Journal of Theology* 18 (1965): 196-97; *John Calvin: A Biography* (Philadelphia: Westminster 1975), 129-30; *Calvin's Old Testament Commentaries*, 9, 24-25.

[49]Ford Lewis Battles and André Malan Hugo, trans., *Calvin's Commentary on Seneca's "De Clementia"* (Leiden: Brill, 1969), 135. In another work, Battles concluded, "In the Commentary [on Seneca] can be seen the beginnings of Calvin the exegete. . . . The tools of exegesis: grammatical and rhetorical analysis, a wide background in history, philosophy, literature, and other studies—these characterize the young Calvin as they will more fully the later Calvin"; "The Sources of Calvin's Seneca Commentary," *John Calvin*, ed. G. E. Duffield (Appleford, Abingdon, Berkshire: Sutton Courtenay Press, 1966), 56-57.

[50]1536 *Institutes* IV.8 (IV.14.18 in 1559 ed.); cf. n 35 above.

[51]*Institutes* 1.14.20, 21 (*OS* 3:170, 172); cf. Basil, *Hexaemeron* I.11 for the ideas of the beauty of creation and God as the Artificer. The similarity of the wording of the 1543 *Institutes* passage to that in the later *Commentary on Psalms* 93:1 suggests that it may have raised in Calvin's mind the problem of the stability of the earth (also treated by Basil in *Hexaemeron* I.8) taken up in the latter; cf. nn 31 and 37 above.

[52]Luther, *Lectures on Genesis* 1:6, 9; 7:11-12 (*Luther's Works* 1:26-29, 34; 2:93-94). The Melanchthonian character of the redaction of Luther's commentary is noted by Pelikan in his Introduction to Vol. 1 of *Luther's Works*, x-xii.

during his college days in Paris; his approach to Aristotle's natural philosophy appears to be that of a humanist like Jacques Lefèvre d'Etaples or François Vatable, who may have been his Hebrew instructor at the Collège Royal in 1531-32.[53] Calvin's interest and understanding were heightened by his study of Seneca (early 1530s), his reading of Basil's *Hexaemeron* (early 1540s),[54] and by the publication of Luther's *Lectures on Genesis* (1544). This led to his first treatment of the distribution of the terrestrial elements and the mechanics of the celestial spheres. The fact that our texts do not give detailed evidence of this interest until the early 1550s is merely the result of his adopted schedule of preaching and writing.

Finally, in the mid-1550s, Calvin thought more deeply about the problem of the stability of the earth in the midst of a whirling cosmos. This further development may reflect the influence of Vermigli and Zanchius. It could also be related to Calvin's concern about the threat of Academic skepticism which was raised in his mind by the writings of Castellio and which occasioned his scornful rejection of the notion that the earth might turn in space in a sermon he preached in 1556.[55] It should be stressed that this is a tentative reconstruction. The identification of additional texts will serve to verify or improve on it.

Calvin was surely not a specialist in natural philosophy, but he did make an attempt to do justice to the subject in his biblical expositions and occasionally went into more detail than was absolutely necessary. His general stance was one of genuine dialogue reminiscent of that of one of his principal models, the *Hexaemeron* of Basil of Caesarea.

---

[53]Quirinius Breen, *John Calvin: A Study in French Humanism* (Grand Rapids; Eerdmans, 1931), 61-66. Vatable had translated several of Aristotle's scientific works, including the *Meteorologica*, in cooperation with Lefèvre d'Etaples in 1518; Rice, "Humanist Aristotelianism," 135-36.

[54]Calvin cited the Hexaemera of Basil and Ambrose in his *Psychopannychia* (*CO* 5:180, 181), written in 1534, but the earliest extant edition is that of 1545; Hughes Oliphant Old, *The Patristic Roots of Reformed Worship* (Zurich: Theologischer Verlag, 1970), 144-45.

[55]Eighth Sermon on 1 Corinthians 10-11 (*CO* 49:677); Kaiser, "Calvin, Copernicus, and Castellio," 23-31.

The Humanity of Christ:
Within Proper Limits

David Foxgrover

For the past thirty years, theologians and historians have argued that, on one hand, Calvin diminished the humanity of Christ in his role as Mediator or, on the other hand, that Calvin assigned a most important role to Christ's humanity in his doctrine of Reconciliation. This essay will show that Calvin recognized Christ's sinlessness even while He experienced human emotions, but that He kept His human emotions within "proper limits." This will be done by examining Calvin's interpretations of Jesus' grieving over the death of Lazarus and His prayer in Gethsemane, the statement in Hebrews that Christ "was heard for his godly fear," Calvin's Seneca commentary and his exegesis of Matthew 26:37 ff. where Christ may have gone beyond "proper limits," and Hebrews 5:7 ff. to show that Christ's divine nature controlled his human emotions.

FRANÇOIS WENDEL, WRITING ON "Christ and His work of Redemption," states:

> we may wonder whether, by thus depriving the obedience and the passion of Christ of any value independent of the divine will, Calvin did not too much diminish the humanity of Christ to the advantage of the divinity.[1]

His musing represents a common interpretation of Calvin's view of the humanity of Christ. For example, Max Dominicé contended that "the humanity of Jesus as such has no value for Calvin except by its union with the divine nature."[2] E. David Willis makes two criticisms of Dominicé's view. First, there is no humanity of Jesus that is not united with the divine nature. In other words, the only Jesus Calvin knows is he who is "Son of God and Son of Man, two natures in one person."[3] Second, Willis argues that since Calvin is speak-

---

[1] François Wendel, "Christ and His Work of Redemption," in *Calvin. The Origins and Development of His Religious Thought*. Tr. Philip Mairet (New York: Harper, 1963), 228.

[2] Max Dominicé, *L'humanité de Jésu d'après Calvin* (Paris: Je Sers, 1933), 48. Quoted by E. David Willis, *The Function of the So-Called 'Extra-Calvinisticum' in Calvin's Theology* (Leiden: Brill, 1966), 79 n 2.

[3] Cf. Calvin's comments on I Tim. 3:16. Comm. I Tim., 10:233; *Ioannes Calvini opera quae supersunt omnia* (hereafter cited *CO*), 52:290. References to Calvin's New Testament commentaries are to the Torrance edition: *Calvin's New Testament Commentaries*, ed. David W. Torrance and Thomas F. Torrance, 12 vols. (Grand Rapids: Eerdmans, 1960-1972). References to Calvin's Old Testament commentaries are to the Eerdman's (1948-) reprint of the 1848-1854 Calvin Translation Society edition. We also note the *Calvini Opera* references.

ing about the One Person of Jesus Christ in his office as Mediator, he does assign a special function to the humanity of Christ."[4]

Paul Van Buren goes further than Willis in stressing the importance of Christ's humanity in the work of redemption. Writing on "Christ's Union with Us," Van Buren observes that "the humanity of Christ plays a most important role in Calvin's doctrine of Reconciliation, for . . . it is precisely in His humanity that Christ performs his atoning work."[5] Later Van Buren writes; "We cannot speak of the obedience of Christ in Calvin's theology without speaking of the strong emphasis he puts on the idea that this obedience was performed in Christ's human nature only."[6]

We wish to argue that Calvin—within the framework of his Chalcedonian Christology—did not "too much diminish" the humanity of Christ. In fact, Calvin went so far in asserting the authentically human character of Christ's struggles that he risked denying the sinlessness of Christ. Calvin insists that Christ redeemed all dimensions of human nature, not bodies alone; therefore, Christ not only suffered physical pain, but emotional torment as well. Christ's sinlessness did not mean that he was free of human emotions, but that he kept his human emotions within what Calvin calls "proper limits."[7] Human emotions are not sinful *per se*, but only when they are excessive and "unbridled."

To set forth Calvin's views we will examine Calvin's interpretations of Jesus' grieving over the death of Lazarus and his prayer in Gethsemane, as well as the statement in Hebrews that Christ "was heard for his godly fear." The comments of John 11:33 affirm that since Christ assumed human nature, it was inevitable that he be affected by all human emotions. However, the emotions or passions of Christ were different in that they were composed and moderate. Moreover, the disorder of human emotions is accidental; they are not sinful *per se*. We turn to Calvin's Seneca commentary to see how the reformer depends on and differs from the classical notions of self-control. We examine next Calvin's exegesis of Matthew 26:37 ff., for there it seems that Christ went beyond "proper limits." Finally, we turn to Calvin's treatment of Hebrews 5:7 ff. in order to see whether Christ's divine nature made it inevitable that his affections remained composed.

---

[4]Willis, *Extra-Calvinisticum*, 79 n 2. Cf. E. P. Meijering, *Calvin wider die Neugirde . . .* (Nieuwkoop: DeGraaf, 1980), 86 ff.

[5]Paul van Buren, *Christ in Our Place: The Substitutionary Character of Calvin's Doctrine of Reconciliation* (Edinburgh: Oliver and Boyd, 1957), 14.

[6]Ibid., 38.

[7]Calvin's most frequently used words are: *finis*, *modus* and *meta*. Words used to described "excess" include: *impotens*, *vitiosus*, *intemperiens*. Only van Buren and the Dutch scholar E. Emmen refer to Christ remaining within "proper limits." However, neither van Buren nor Emmen examine Calvin's exegesis to see if Calvin's comments support this notion. Cf. E. Emmen, *Christologie van Calvijn* (Amsterdam: H. J. Paris, 1935), 96 ff.

In the first passage, Calvin describes the norm, while in the second and third he takes up two key issues: first, did Christ go beyond the limit and thereby sin? Second, is the ordering of Christ's emotions the result of an ontological distinction between Christ's humanity and that of others? Or is Christ's obedience a genuine, human act? It appears to us that in the comments on Matthew Christ's humanity is maintained, but his sinlessness is not. In the comments on Hebrews, Christ's sinlessness is upheld, but the genuineness of his struggle is not. However, Calvin was aware of these problems, and we will discuss briefly his attempt to deal with them in his notion of a "partial comparison."

Jesus' "groaning in the spirit" (John 11:33) prompts Calvin to consider several issues. First, Calvin states that Christ shows his sympathy by voluntarily mourning Lazarus' death: "He shows by His groaning in spirit, by a strong emotion of grief and by tears, that He is as much affected by our ills as if He had suffered them himself."[8] But, this demonstration of sympathy leads Calvin to ask: "how do groaning and trouble of mind belong to the Son of God?"[9] Calvin rejects Augustine's view that Christ selected the occasions when he would allow himself to be moved by human passions. Augustine thought, "that Christ, otherwise calm and free from all passion, summoned groaning and grief of His own accord."[10] Other people are carried away by their feelings, whereas Christ troubled himself.[11] In contrast, Calvin argues that when Christ put on human flesh, he voluntarily put on human feelings. Thus, Christ differed from other people in no way—"sin only excepted."[12]

Calvin then counters the objection that sinful passions cannot be shared by the Son of God. Calvin affirms that there is a difference (as well as a similarity) between the passions of Christ and others, and that the sinfulness of the passions is accidental. Human passions are sinful because they "rush on unrestrainedly and immoderately," while in Christ they were "composed and regulated in obedience to God and were completely free from sin."[13] Human emotions are vicious and perverse because they are confused and immoderate, and because they arise from illegitimate causes and aim at illegitimate ends.[14]

---

[8]Comm. Jn. 11-21, 11; *CO*, 47:265: "fremitu spiritus, arto doloris sensu et lacrymis testatur malis nostris perinde se affici ac si ea in se pateretur."

[9]Ibid., "fremitus et perturbatio"

[10]Ibid.

[11]Ibid.

[12]Ibid.

[13]Comm. Jn. 11-21, 12; *CO*, 47:265, "Ideo enim vitiosi sunt nostri affectus, quia intemperanter ruunt nec modum ullum tenent: in Christo autem, quia compositi fuerunt in Dei obsequium et moderati, vitio prorsus carebant."

[14]Ibid., primum quia turbulento motu feruntur, nec ad veram modestiae regulam ordinati sunt: deinde quia non semper oriuntur ex legitima causa, vel saltem non referuntur ad finem legitimum.

Calvin employs two favorite expressions to portray this lack of order: there is "excess" because no one rejoices or grieves as God allows, and many shake off the "bridle" of restraint. But the passions of Christ are "nothing like this," for "no passion of Christ ever went beyond its proper bounds."[15] Calvin observes that it is accidental that emotions are disorderly and rebellious, for prior to the Fall, the emotions were obedient to reason. The clear implication is that emotions are not sinful *per se*, but part of God's creation.[16] Calvin reaffirms that "Christ took upon Him human emotions, yet without *ataxia* [disorder],"[17] and reminds his readers that Paul does not demand "stony numbness" but admonishes them to "grieve in moderation."[18] There is similarity and difference between Christ and others: "if you compare his passions with ours, they are as different as pure, clear water flowing in a gentle course from muddy and thick foam."[19]

Two passages from Calvin's Seneca commentary show how Calvin is dependent on classical authors for this notion of emotions within proper limits. Commenting on Seneca's phrase, "And desires are never so well controlled," Calvin draws on Epicurus's threefold division of *cupiditas*, where the third division is defined as "neither natural nor necessary." To define this desire, Calvin refers to Cicero: "Of this, as Cicero says, neither measure nor limit can be found." Seneca is also quoted: "Desire which overleaps natural measure must develop into measurelessness."[20] Here are the words *modus, finis*, and *immensam* which Calvin will use in later writings to define the moderate emotions of Christ.

In many passages Calvin presents favorably the Senecan ideal person, moderate and self-controlled, whose reason no emotion disturbs. Writing on the phrase "from even the most tranquil souls," Calvin admonishes his reader that these words are "not to be neglected," for both "Our Seneca" and Cicero illustrate what tranquility means "to us."[21] Calvin says that "a tranquil soul is composed, and subject to no emotions . . .,"[21] adding that "moderation of mind," "equanimity," "security," "peace," and "euthymia" are synonymous terms. Calvin adds laconically: "The theologians almost always call it 'peace'."[22] It is noteworthy that Calvin does not criticize the Stoic ideal of apathy.

---

[15]Ibid., "Intemperiem esse dico . . .; multi etiam fraenum potius excutiunt." *CO*, 47:266: "In Christo nihil tale: nulla enim passio ultra suum modum unquam erupit. . . ."

[16]Comm. Jn. 11-21, 12; *CO*, 47:266, "quod autem nunc sunt imcompositi et rebelles, accidentale est vitium."

[17]Ibid.   [18]Comm. Jn. 11-21, 13; *CO*, 47:266   [19]Comm. Jn. 11-21, 12; *CO*, 47:266.

[20]*Calvin's Commentary on Seneca's de Clementia*, with introduction, translation, and notes by Ford Lewis Battles and Andre Milan Hugo (Leiden: Brill, 1969), 58-59, "insatiabili; cuius (ut ait Cicero) nec modus nec finis inveniri potest. Et Seneca . . . Necesse est in immensum exeat cupiditas, quae naturalem modum transilit."

[21]Ibid., 40-13.   [22]Ibid.

A second passage in the Seneca commentary is of interest because it deals with "pity," which is condemned by Seneca but later attributed to Christ by Calvin; and it shows Calvin's disinterest in resolving the issue of whether the wise man is emotionless. The Senecan line, "pity is a sickness of the mind," moves Calvin to write: "The Stoics reject pity, because it is a sickness of the mind. But passions, because they disturb the health and tranquility of the mind, are always vicious."[23] In order to complete Seneca's argument, Calvin comments on four lines in the remainder of the chapter. Calvin presents Seneca's argument that the wise man is subject to no emotion, and then declines to affirm or deny Seneca's position. On the phrase "his mind is serene," Calvin says: "Here he now attributes [to the wise person] *apathia* and *analgesia*, so that no emotions may touch the wise man at all. Whether this is true is not part of our present purpose to discuss."[24] Although Calvin claims that his purposes preclude an evaluation of Seneca's view, he observes that "passions cannot persist alongside reason."[25] However, Calvin is probably making a distinction between "passions" and "affections"; he is certain that passions should not exist in the wise person, but he is not certain about emotions. That distinction may be valid for Calvin, but it does not apply to Seneca who views *misericordia* as a passion. Seneca's point is that since emotions and passions are never well-controlled, the wise person must be free of them. In his later writings, Calvin is quite clear that natural, human emotions are not evil *per se*, but must remain within proper limits.

Two passages from the *Institutes* show Calvin affirming, in vocabulary reminiscent of the Seneca commentary, the naturalness of the affections and their perversion due to excess and intemperance. In III.3.12, Calvin says that "all man's faculties" are "so vitiated and corrupted that in all his actions persistent disorder and intemperance threaten. . . ."[26] Calvin aptly presents his view on the sinfulness of the naturally good affections: "all human desires are evil . . .–not in that they are natural–but because they are inordinate."[27] The proper order and integrity of the affections is described in Calvin's discussion of the image of God:

> the integrity with which Adam was endowed is expressed by this word [image], when he had full possession of right understanding, when he had his affections kept within the bounds of reason, all his senses tempered in right order, and he truly referred his excellence to exceptional gifts bestowed upon him by his Maker.[28]

[23]*Seneca's de Clementia*, 366-67.   [24]*Seneca's de Clementia*, 368-69.

[25]Ibid.   [26]*Institutes* III.3.12 ; *CO*, 2:132.   [27]*Institutes* III.3.12; *CO*, 2:132-43.

[28]*Institutes*III.15.3; *CO*, 2:138, "integritas qua praeditus fuit Adam quum recta intelligentia polleret, affectus haberet compositos ad rationem, sensus omnes recto ordine temperatos. . . ." Cf. Comm. Gen. (1:26), 1:95; *CO*, 23:26, where virtually the same words are used.

In Adam there was no excess, for the affections remained within "proper limits."

Calvin affirmed the goodness of human affections which remain within limits in vocabulary similar to the Stoics; but for the Stoic the ideal was emotionlessness, while for Calvin it was emotions within limits. Jesus embodies Calvin's ideal: human feelings in Christ were pure and free from sin, for they were "composed and regulated to the obedience of God."[29]

Now we turn to Calvin's extensive consideration of Christ's agony in Gethsemane, for there, it seems, Christ went beyond the "proper limits" and sinned.[30] Calvin asserts that Christ suffered beyond measure, but his emotions remained within limits. The crux of Calvin's exegesis of Matthew 26:37 ff. is that Christ's suffering and anguish are authentic, but not contrary to faith. Calvin begins by saying that "though God had trained his Son in some preliminary bouts, now at the closer aspect of death he deals a heavier blow and strikes him with unaccustomed terror."[31] Calvin first affirms that "those who pretend the Son of God was immune from human passions do not seriously and truly acknowledge Him as a man."[32] If Christ were not subject to passions and terror, he could not have fulfilled the "mystery of our salvation,"[33] for he would have redeemed bodies alone. Next, Calvin emphasizes the difference between Christ's affections and those which others experience: "let us keep the distinction; Christ in his fear and grief was weak, but without any spot of sin, while all our emotions bubbling out to excess are sinful."[34] In others the affections exceed their proper limits and are intemperate, but in Christ they are restrained: "None of our feelings are free of sin, for they all exceed the limit and proper moderation. Though Christ was troubled by sadness and fear, yet he did not rebel against God, but remained composed in the true rule of restraint."[35]

Third, Calvin describes "the kind of emotion with which Christ was tried. . . ." According to Matthew Christ experienced "grief and sorrow (or trouble of mind)" Luke says that we was "seized with anguish"; and Mark adds that Christ was "dismayed."[36] However, Christ did not experience such sor-

---

[29]Comm. Jn. 11-21 (12:27), 40; *CO*, 47:292, "compositi erant et temperati ad Dei obsequium."

[30]Calvin considers Matthew 26:37 ff. and other relevant passages in the *Institutes* II.16.10-12, where he is discussing the meaning of the *descensus.*

[31]Comm. Gospels 3, 147; *CO*, 14:719.

[32]Ibid.

[33]Comm. Gospels 3, 147-8. *CO*, 14, 719.

[34]Comm. Gospels 3, 148. *CO*, 14, 720, "nostros autem omnes affectus, quia in excessum ebulliunt, esse vitiosos. Cf. *Institutes* II.15.12; *CO*, 2:378, "omnes affectus turbido impetu modum excedunt . . . in cunctis eius [Christi] affectibus viguit moderatio, quae excessum cohiberet."

[35]Ibid., "quia omnes [affectus] modum ac rectum temperamentum excedunt: Christus . . . sed maneret compositus ad veram temperantiae regulam." Cf. *Institutes* II.15.12; *CO*, 2:378: "quia se [Christus] intra obedientiae fines continuit." [36]Ibid.

row and grief because of the "simple horror of death, the passing away from the world"; his awareness that he must face the tribunal of God, bearing the sins of the world, causes such acute grief. It is "the sight of the dread tribunal of God that came to Him. . . . No wonder if death's fearful abyss tormented him grievously, with fear and anguish."[37]

Now Calvin considers Christ's prayer, "O My Father, if it be possible, let this cup pass from me" (Matt. 26:39).[38] Although the words are abrupt, Calvin has "no doubt that Christ's call was a prayer." One can expect that the torment of Christ will express itself in a halting, intense prayer. Calvin writes that prayers "do not always keep an even moderation, and are not always composed in strict order, but rather are involved and confused, and even in conflict with themselves. . . ." Calvin hastens to add that "we must remember . . . that Christ's emotions were not turbulent in the way that ours shake pure moderation from our minds."[39] One wonders how Christ's prayers could have strayed from "an even moderation," while his emotions did not depart from "a pure moderation."

After this caveat about Christ's affections, Calvin states that Christ was "so struck with fright and seized with anguish" that he is compelled to shift from one prayer to another. First, he prays to be spared death, then "he holds himself in check, submits himself to the Father's command, and corrects and revokes the wish that had suddenly escaped him."[40] How could Christ pray to God to rescind a decree of which he (Christ) was not ignorant? Calvin responds that there is "nothing odd if Christ, following the way of the faithful, did not turn his eyes to the divine plan but rested his desire that burned within him upon His Father's knees."[41] In other words, Christ is so overwhelmed with grief that he does not rest in the divine plan (which he knows!), but puts forth his own desires which run counter to that plan. Christ not only ignores the divine decree, but "for a moment He did not think how He was sent to be the redeemer of the human race."[42] Is Christ keeping within the "bounds of obedience and moderation" here? Is there no "excess"? Calvin strives to maintain Christ's sinlessness: "there is nothing strange if in his prayers he did not maintain an immediate attention to everything and keep them in due proportion." Then he quickly reassures us: "We see how Christ from the very start checks his feelings and in good time brings himself back into line."[43]

---

[37]Ibid.

[38]Comm. Gospels 3, 149; *CO*, 14, 721.

[39]Ibid., "non semper aequabile temperamentum servant, non semper etiam distincto ordine sunt compositae, quin potius . . . confligunt secum . . . qui more nostro eius animo puram moderationem excuterent. . . ."

[40]Comm. Gospels 3, 149-150; *CO*, 14, 722.

[41]Comm. Gospels 3, 150; *CO*, 14, 722.

[42]Ibid.

[43]Ibid., "non semper occurrit praesens omnium rerum attentio, ut distinctus ordo teneatur. . . . ab ipsis carceribus affectum suum cohibeat, seque ipsum mature cogat in ordinem."

Calvin cannot leave behind this troublesome prayer, for he is still both-ered by the fact that Christ offers a prayer contrary to the known will of God. He has just offered the explanation that Christ's grief was so intense that he looked only to his own desires. Now Calvin offers another solution: there is an "indirect dissent" which is not sinful."[44] A prayer which differs from God's will may still be holy, for God "allows us to beg from him what our intelli-gence can grasp as desirable."[45]

Calvin is still dissatisfied: "But this does not dispose of the question alto-gether." Calvin asks the essential question: does not the offering of this prayer imply that Christ has exceeded the "bounds of obedience?" Calvin writes: "Since it was just said that all Christ's desires were properly controlled, how does he now correct himself? The way he brings his emotions into obedience to God suggests that he had transgressed the limit."[46] Calvin admits that in Christ's first cry there is not "quiet moderation"; his first emotion had to be "checked" and was not as "controlled" as it should have been. However, Calvin affirms that Christ's grief remained within the "bounds of obedience": "in Christ there exists a remarkable example of balance between the wills of God and of man; they differ from each other without conflict or contradiction."[47] Here it is the human will of Christ that is in question: "His human soul had different desires from the hidden purpose of God."[48] Calvin's unstated assumption is that Christ's affections were not in keeping with God's will, but as long as Christ does not oppose God's will he has not transgressed the bounds of obedience. Our interpretation is substantiated when Calvin writes: "This is faith's due limit, to allow God to decide differently from what we desire."[49]

As he concludes his comments on Matt. 26:39, Calvin writes; "It is then asked, What advantage prayer was to Christ?" In response Calvin quotes Heb. 5:7, "He was heard for his fear."[50] But does this fear come from lack of faith? To answer this objection Calvin introduces another distinction, that between Christ's "fleshly sense" and his "faith": "When Christ was struck with the horror of the divine curse His fleshly sense was affected, while His faith re-mained undamaged and unshaken."[51] The word "sense" appears to mean "un-derstanding," a not uncommon use of the word. Christ's fleshly understand-ing is "touched" (or "overwhelmed"!) by the affections of grief and fear; but his faith, his determination to obey God's will, remains firm.

[44]Ibid., "obliquae dissensionis. . . ."

[45]Comm. Gospels 3, 151; *CO*, 14, 723.

[46]Ibid., "quasi modum excesserit."

[47]Ibid.

[48]Ibid., "humanae eius animae suos fuisse affectus ab arcano Dei consilio distinctos."

[49]Comm. Gospels 3, 151; *CO*, 14, 724, "fidei modestia . . ."

[50]Comm. Gospels 3, 152; *CO*, 14, 724.

[51]Ibid., " . . . tactum fuisse carnis sensu, ut fides illaesa et incolumis maneret."

Calvin also uses the distinction between "fleshly sense" and "faith" in his exposition of Matt. 27:46 ("Jesus cried with a loud voice").[52] Although death is fearful because God is absent, faith "sees" God as still present. Calvin writes: "Although the physical senses feared death, faith was firmly set in his heart; for by it he saw God present, while he complained of His absence."[53] If we have any doubt about the meaning of "fleshy sense," Calvin helps us by employing the phrases "natural sense" and "ordinary sense" a few lines later: "We have noted a difference between natural sense and the intelligence of faith: so nothing prevents Christ, as far as ordinary sense dictated, taking thought of His estrangement from God, and at the same time, by faith, realizing that God was on his side."[54]

Calvin's allusion to Heb. 5:7 in his exegesis of Matt. 26:37 leads us to consider Calvin's comments on Heb. 5:7-9. There Calvin affirms that Christ has remedied Adam's disobedience with a contrary act of obedience, and that his sufferings refer properly to his human nature.[55] Calvin wishes to assert the genuine humanity of Christ and the authenticity of his sufferings. However, when we examine Calvin's thinking on what Christ learned and why he was heard "out of his fear," we cannot help but question Calvin's affirmation that Christ was "like man in all ways." Calvin's exegesis calls into doubt his own assertion that the obedience and learning of Christ were authentic. In his exegesis of Matt. 26:37 ff. Calvin could not convince us that Christ's emotions remained within "proper limits," and in Heb. 5:7-9, where the obedience of Christ is affirmed (and therefore his sinlessness), Calvin ends up emphasizing how Christ differs from others.

Calvin's masterful exegesis is neatly structured: the apostle distinguishes two reasons why Christ had to suffer, first, that he learn obedience, and second that he be consecrated a priest.[56] Under the first reason, Calvin presents three points of explanation: first, that Christ did take upon himself human infirmities (though he has now laid them aside in heaven); second, that Christ sought a remedy in order to be liberated from evil; and third, that Christ's prayer was not rejected even though he was not promptly delivered from evil. Throughout his exegesis, Calvin has a strong, pastoral concern, describing how believers may profit from Christ's example.

Calvin first asserts that Christ was "subject to human trials and infirmities" for people's good.[57] In commenting on Heb. 4:15, Calvin says "infirmities" means the emotions of the soul, such as "fear, sorrow, dread of death, and

[52]Comm. Gospels 3, 208; *CO*, 14, 779.

[53]Ibid.

[54]Ibid.

[55]Comm. Heb., 12:66; *CO*, 55:63.

[56]Comm. Heb., 12:63; *CO*, 55:61.

[57]Comm. Heb., 12:63; *CO*, 55:61.

the like."[58] There can be no doubt about the authenticity of Christ's humanity; Calvin makes his point quite forcefully: "It is one thing to be truly man, [and yet] endowed with a blessed immortality. It is a quite different thing to be subject to the human trials and infirmities which Christ underwent as long as He lived in the world. . . ."[59]

Second, Calvin states that Christ sought a remedy for his troubles. Calvin goes to great lengths to demonstrate the depth of Christ's suffering, just as in his comments on Matt. 26:37 ff. Christ, Calvin says, did not have "an iron spirit which felt nothing."[60] Calvin uses the strongest language he can muster to portray Christ's agony: "bitterest agonies of spirit," "supreme anguish of spirit," the "force of his grief," and "utter extremity." Calvin concludes: "He was oppressed by real sorrows, and prayed the Father in all earnestness to send help."[61] Christ is reduced to "utter extremity," but he does not go beyond the limit.

The third point Calvin makes is that Christ's prayer was not rejected even though he was not immediately delivered from his troubles. "At no time was He deprived of God's mercy and help," Calvin writes.[62] To explain the phrase "having been heard for his godly fear," Calvin writes that the correct translation suggests that "Christ was heard out of that which he feared. . . ."[63] That is, he was not heard *because* of his fear. The apostle implies that Christ "was not overwhelmed by and did not give way to these evils, nor was he overcome by death."[64] There is a difference between our fear of death and that of Christ:

> The Son of God descended to this struggle, not because he labored under unbelief, the source of all our fears, but because he underwent in mortal flesh the judgment of God, the terror of which cannot be overcome without laborious effort[65]

To answer "In what way was Christ heard out of his fear . . .?", Calvin in no way mitigates the magnitude of Christ's "laborious effort." Calvin looks to the "point of His fear": Christ dreaded death because he saw in it the curse of God,

---

[58]Comm. Heb., 12:55-56; *CO*, 55:54.

[59]Comm. Heb., 12:63; *CO*, 55:61, "Aliud enim est, esse verum hominem, tam etsi beata immortalitate praeditum. . . ." We diverge from Johnston's translation: "It is one thing to be truly human, even though endowed. . . ." The contrast is rendered senseless by that translation of *tam etsi*.

[60]Comm. Heb., 12:64; *CO*, 55:62.

[61]Ibid.

[62]Comm. Heb., 12:65; *CO*, 55:63.

[63]Comm. Heb., 12:65; *CO*, 55:62.

[64]Ibid.

[65]Ibid.

and because "He had to wrestle with the total sum of human guilt, and with the very powers of darkness themselves."[66] Whether one reads the *de Psychopannychia*, the *Institutes*, or the Matthew and Hebrews commentaries, Calvin's teaching is the same: Christ feared death because in death he beheld the curse of God, and this fear is genuine. In the Hebrews passage, more than anywhere else, Calvin stresses the idea that Christ overcame this fear through "laborious effort" or a "contrary act of obedience," which refers to his human nature.[67]

However, when we read Calvin's descriptions of what Christ learned through his suffering, we cannot help but question the genuineness of Christ's sufferings. Calvin's puzzling explanation comes to this: Christ learned obedience for the sake of others. Calvin begins with a contradictory statement: although Christ was "made accustomed to obedience," he was not compelled to obey, and he had no "need of such practices, in the way that the fierceness of oxen or horses is tamed."[68] He needed to be accustomed to obedience, but there is no need for exercises to accomplish this. In reality, Christ had nothing to learn. Christ rendered obedience to God "for our benefit, to give us the instance and the pattern of His own submission. . . ."[69] In other words, it is other people—not Christ—who have to learn obedience through suffering. Christ is the paradigm, though he had nothing to learn.

Calvin's next lines are contradictory as well. Calvin states that "it was in his death that Christ fully learned what it meant to obey God, since that was the point at which He reached His greatest self-denial."[70] It appears that Christ did have something to learn, and something beyond what he learned when he took upon himself human flesh. But when Calvin summarizes his point he says that what Christ learned is how far *other people* must submit to God: "The meaning is, therefore, that by the experience of His sufferings Christ was taught how far we ought to submit to and obey God."[71] It is strange that Christ must learn how far sinful man must submit to God. Calvin ends up describing how *other people* must learn obedience, when he set out to show in what way *Christ* had to learn obedience.

At the outset we noted that in this Hebrews passage where Calvin affirms the humanness of Christ's suffering and obedience, he cannot help but show how Christ differs from others. In a passage such as Matt. 26:37-39, where Calvin describes the authenticity of Christ's agony, he cannot help but admit that Christ went beyond the limit. Perhaps what we sense as an inconsistency,

[66]Comm. Heb., 12:65; *CO*, 55:63.
[67]Comm. Heb., 12:66; *CO*, 55:64.
[68]Comm. Heb., 12:65; *CO*, 55:63.
[69]Comm. Heb., 12:66; *CO*, 55:63.
[70]Ibid.
[71]Ibid.

Calvin would describe as a "partial comparison." In other words, Calvin wishes to affirm that Christ is like others in that he took upon himself human infirmities, but he is unlike others in that he accepted these infirmities willingly and kept them within proper limits. We would like to push Calvin into saying that Christ is human in all respects, but as long as Calvin wishes to assert "sin only excepted," that complete comparison will never be attained.

For Calvin, it is not necessary that the comparison between Christ and others correspond in every part. Writing on 1 Pet. 4:1 ("Forasmuch . . . as Christ suffered in the flesh, arm yourselves also. . . ."), Calvin perceives that some might object that human suffering in the flesh does not correspond completely to Christ's, since there was nothing sinful in Christ which needed correction. "The answer is obvious," Calvin opines, "that it is not necessary that a comparison should correspond in every part."[72] The work of redemption is fulfilled in the humanity of Christ, even though there is not a complete correspondence between the humanity of Christ and that of others.

Another passage in the Hebrews commentary which admirably illustrates this "same as, but different" theme is Heb. 2:13, where Calvin is contending that Christ did have faith. Some might object that Christ did not need faith. Calvin responds that the Psalm quoted by the apostle does apply to Christ, and that Christ's condition is the same as others: "if He had not been a man subject to human needs, He would have no need of such faith. Since He depends on the help of God, His condition is . . . the same as ours."[73] Although there is this common dependence on God in faith, there is a difference between Christ and others: "At the same time we differ from Christ, because the infirmity which is laid on us of necessity was undergone by Him of His own accord."[74]

In the Hebrews commentary, then, Calvin describes ways in which Christ is the same as, yet different from, others: he is subject to infirmities, but he accepted them voluntarily;[75] he had to be taught by the experience of suffering, but not because he needed that instruction;[76] he took on himself the affections of the soul, but in him they always were ordered to the true rule of justice;[77] he bore our infirmities, but he was free from sin;[78] and he struggled and was afraid, but not because of unbelief.[79] In spite of the differences between Christ and others, it can still be affirmed that Christ is truly human and that he accomplished redemption in his human nature. For Calvin, it is not necessary that Christ and others be alike in all respects.

---

[72]*I Peter*. 12:299; *CO*, 55:271, "quod necesse non sit hanc similitudinem per omnia congruere. . . ."

[73]Comm. Heb., 12:28; *CO*, 55:30.   [74]Ibid.

[75]Comm. Heb., 12:28; *CO*, 55:30.

[76]Comm. Heb., 12:55; *CO*, 55:54.

[77]Comm. Heb., 12:56; *CO*, 55:55.

[78]Comm. Heb., 12:60; *CO*, 55:60.

[79]Comm. Heb., 12:65; *CO*, 55:62.

As Calvin puts it in his comments on Psalm 22, the affirmation of this "sameness" and "difference" are "wonderfully joined together." Calvin states that the terror which proceeds from a sense of God's curse, and the patience which arises from faith are in Christ "wonderfully conjoined."[80] It is true, Calvin observes, that although others should be courageous, they "are not endued with the like power."[81] Calvin also contends that Christ's status as the Son of God and His experience of grief "can agree."[82] In other words, Christ is the same as others in that he experiences grief; but he is different as well in that he is the Son of God whose "perfection of . . . nature preserved him from all excess."[83] Even if we grant that "same" and "different" in Christ "wonderfully agree," we cannot help but wonder if the "differences" do not invalidate the authenticity of Christ's struggles.[84]

Our review of Calvin's detailed comments on three New Testament passages makes it clear that Calvin strongly affirmed that redemption was carried out in the humanity of Christ. Christ's emotions were authentically human and his torment was real, while His sinlessness consisted in keeping his emotions within "proper limits." This notion of emotions within proper limits is a creative expression of the orthodox confession of Christ's true humanity and divinity, for it emphasizes a dynamic, rather than an ontological, interpretation of sinlessness.

What is noteworthy, and troublesome, about Calvin's exegesis is that in one passage he cannot avoid questioning the sinlessness of Christ, while in the other he cannot help undermining the genuineness of Christ's humanity. Perhaps Calvin could have avoided the problem if he had clearly affirmed that Christ remained sinless through the aid of the divine nature, rather than suggesting that Christ's humanity differed from that of others. Christ's humanity was not sinless because it was ontologically unique, but because its emotions remained within limits. The modern interpreter is less troubled by Calvin's exegesis where he struggles to maintain the "proper limits" idea than the exegesis where the reformer suggests that Christ's humanity is ontologically unique.

---

[80]*Psalms*, 1:373; CO, 31:228.

[81]Ibid.

[82]*Psalms*, 1:361; CO, 31:222.

[83]*Psalms*, 1:362; CO, 31:222.

[84]Cf. van Buren, *Christ in Our Place*, 35-36.

Farel and Calvin banned from Geneva in 1538.

Christian Discipline and the Early Reformed Tradition: Bullinger and Calvin

J. Wayne Baker

After breaking with Rome, reformers grappled with the problem of the relationship of the church and the civil government. In the Reformed communities two basic answers were put forth. From Zurich and Zwingli came the idea of a close relationship between civil government and the church, and this idea was carried forward after 1531 by Bullinger. The other viewpoint, that the church and civil society were separate entities, was introduced in 1530 by Johannes Oecolampadius in Basel. John Calvin's approach in Geneva was nearly identical to Oecolampadius's theories.

These differing approaches were exemplified in Calvin's struggles with the magistrates in Geneva during the 1540s and his eventual victory in early 1550s over the Perrinists. Ironically, Bullinger's support of Calvin and his approach to church discipline during the Berthelier affair was instrumental in Calvin's victory in Geneva. Further, even though the Zurich and Genevan church traditions of discipline and relationship with the civil governments continued to compete through the sixteenth and seventeenth centuries, in the end the Oecolampadian-Calvinist system dominated the Reformed tradition.

THE QUESTION OF THE NATURE OF the church and its relationship with the civil community emerged as a burning issue from the very beginning of Reformed Protestantism. After the break from Rome, both reformers and governments had to grapple with the problem of Christian discipline. Who would discipline the laity, a civil court or an ecclesiastical court? Would the church or the civil authority control excommunication? What would be the respective roles of the church and the civil government in such a system? In the early Reformed communities there were two basic answers to these questions, the first coming from Zurich and the other from Basel and Geneva.

Zurich was the first Reformed city, and Huldrych Zwingli was the father of the Reformed tradition. Given the relationship between the civil government and the church just prior to the Reformation, the predictable result of the reform in Zurich was a close identification of the church and the civil community. The *Ehegericht*, the marriage court created by the Zurich council in 1525, was the institutional reflection of that identification. It soon became a true morals court, with all moral offences under its jurisdiction. From its inception it was a magisterial court, not an ecclesiastical tribunal. Church discipline in Zurich was civil discipline, under the authority of the Christian magistracy, from the beginning of the Reformation. Similar systems were adopted by other Swiss cities, such as Basel, Bern, and Schaffhausen, as they became Protestant.[1]

The system of magisterial discipline developed at Zurich mirrored Zwingli's own theory, which resembled that of Marsilius of Padua. Zwingli's point of view was molded in the crucible of late medieval civic corporatism and antipapal theory.[2] He argued that the Christian magistrate was supreme over all affairs in the Christian community, even over religion. Equating the elders of the New Testament with the Christian magistrates of his own day, he opposed any ecclesiastical jurisdiction independent of the magistracy. Even excommunication—and only the most flagrant sinner could be excluded from the Eucharist—fell under the authority of the Christian magistrate. Finally, he felt that neither the Supper nor the church was in any way polluted when sinners took part in the Eucharist. For Zwingli, the church was equivalent to the Christian city and the Christian, to the citizen. The purpose of discipline was to check evil, crime, and disorder in the Christian community, not to create a pure church.[3] Zwingli's was the first Reformed position on Christian discipline, and up until 1530 there was no competing theory in Switzerland.

In June 1530, Johannes Oecolampadius articulated an important new approach when he asked the Council at Basel to initiate a new form of discipline. Oecolampadius was convinced that the church and the Christian city were not identical, that the church and civil society were separate entities. There was, therefore, an essential difference between civil and ecclesiastical authority. Christ himself had instituted excommunication, and excommunication was absolutely necessary in the church. The purpose of excommunication was to

[1]For the situation in Zurich prior to the Reformation, see Hans Morf, "Obrigkeit und Kirche in Zürich bis zu Beginn der Reformation," *Zwingliana*, 13 (1970): 164–71; and Robert C. Walton, *Zwingli's Theocracy* (Toronto: University of Toronto Press, 1967), 3–16. For the statute creating the *Ehegericht*, see Emil Egli, *et al.*, *Huldreich Zwinglis sämtliche Werke* (Berlin/Leipzig/Zürich; Schwetschke und Sohn, 1905), 4:182–87 (Hereinafter cited as *ZW*). (English translation: Samuel Macauley Jackson [ed.], *Ulrich Zwingli 1484–1531; Selected Works* [Philadelphia: University of Pennsylvania Press, 1972], 118–22). For a study of the court, and those of other Swiss cities, see Walther Köhler, *Zürcher Ehegericht und Genfer Konsistorium*, 2 vols. (Leipzig: Heinsius Nachfolger, 1932 and 1942). Robert C. Walton has rightly asserted that in terms of magisterial authority over the church in Zurich "the Reformation marks the end rather than the beginning of the process." "The Institutionalization of the Reformation at Zurich," *Zwingliana*, 13 (1972): 497.

[2]Some scholars have argued that there was a definitive shift in Zwingli's position on discipline after 1525. Oskar Farner argues that Zwingli asserted congregational autonomy in the thirty-first of his "Sixty-Seven Articles" of 1523 (*ZW* 1:462) and in 1525 in his major theological treatise, "Commentary on the True and False Religion" (*ZW*, 3:877). *Die Lehre von Kirche und Staat bie Zwingli* (Tübingen: Mohr [Paul Siebeck], 1930), 15–18. See also Roger Ley, *Kirchenzucht bei Zwingli* (Zurich: Zwingli–Verlag, 1948), 33. However, Walther Köhler, in his comments on the section on excommunication in his essay introducing the "Commentary," disagrees: "Es gibt nur eine Obrigdeit, nicht geistliche (priesterliche) und weltliche (Laien-) Gewalt." *ZW*, 3:617. Although there may have been some development in Zwingli's position on the issue, it is clear that his later position was already evident in 1523. Walton agrees that Zwingli's later point of view was "only a further elucidation of the position taken before 1523." *Zwingli's Theocracy*, 214.

amend the life of the offender and to purify the church as much as possible. The most significant element of Oecolampadius's plan was his plea for a separate ecclesiastical court consisting of twelve presbyters or elders, men of impeccable life who would judge sinners according to the law of Christ in Matthew 18. This court would deal with sin while the magisterial court could only deal with crime[4]

Oecolampadius thus introduced the second Reformed position on Christian discipline, a point of view that would have enormous consequences during the next one hundred and fifty years. He failed to persuade Zwingli, however, and a Zwinglian type of discipline continued to prevail in the Swiss Reformed cities, including Basel, long after the deaths of Zwingli and Oecolampadius.

The person most responsible for perpetuating the Zwinglian point of view was Heinrich Bullinger, who succeeded Zwingli as leader of the Zurich church in 1531. Bullinger, however, was more consistent than Zwingli on the issue of discipline. He completely rejected the idea of excommunication in the sense of exclusion from fellowship and from the Eucharist. Instead, he thought in terms of public morality. The magistrate alone was responsible for guarding the good and punishing the evil in the Christian community. To treat a person "as a heathen and a publican" meant to count him among the criminals and to punish him as such. The models for Bullinger in the matter of discipline were Moses and the Old Testament kings, not the church of the New Testament. The New Testament church, since there were no Christian magistrates, had found it necessary to handle its own discipline. But when rulers became Christians, the proper magisterial discipline, following the Old Testament model, had been reinstated. For Bullinger, then, Christian discipline was external, physical punishment by the magistrate; it was public punishment of public crimes.[5] For over forty years Bullinger defended his point of

[3]See especially *ZW*, 9:451–67. For a more detailed analysis of Zwingli's position on discipline, see J. Wayne Baker, "Church Discipline or Civil Punishment: On the Origins of the Reformed Schism, 1528–1531," *Andrews University Seminary Studies* 23 (1985):3–18. See two recent studies for detailed analyses of Zwingli's development as a reformer and for his theology: Ulrich Gäbler, *Huldrych Zwingli: His Life and Work* (Philadelphia: Fortress, 1986); and W. P. Stephens, *The Theology of Huldrych Zwingli* (Oxford: Clarendon, 1986).

[4]Ernst Staehelin, ed., *Briefe und Akten zum Leben Oekolampads, Bd. 2: 1527–1593* (Leipzig: Heinsius Nachfolger, 1934) no. 750, pp. 448–61; no. 782, pp. 494–98. For a more detailed sketch, see Baker, "Church Discipline of Civil Punishment." For a complete study of Oecolampadius on discipline, see Akira Demura, "Church Discipline according to Johannes Oecolampadius in the Setting of His Life and Thought" (Th.D. dissertation, Princeton Theological Seminary, 1964).

[5]For Bullinger's early arguments on discipline, see his letter to Berchtold Haller of July 6, 1531; *Heinrich Bullinger Werke. Zweite Abteilung: Briefwechsel, Band 1* ed. Ulrich Gäbler and Endre Zsindely (Zürich: Theologischer Verlag, 1973), 205–16. For a detailed analysis of Bullinger's position on discipline and how it fit into his larger thought, see J. Wayne Baker *Heinrich Bullinger and the Covenant: The Other Reformed Tradition* (Athens: Ohio University Press, 1980), esp. 55–140.

view on discipline, first against the Anabaptists, but then, increasingly, against the Calvinists.

John Calvin was the most important disciple of Oecolampadius in the matter of Christian discipline. Although it is difficult to establish absolutely a direct influence, Calvin's approach was nearly identical with that of Oecolampadius, and there is evidence that makes such an influence probable. First, Calvin was familiar with Basel, having lived there in 1535 and 1536. He thus had access to Oecolampadius's point of view, especially after the publication, in 1536 in Basel, of the correspondence between Oecolampadius and Zwingli, which included their letters on the matter of discipline as well as Oecolampadius's oration before the Basel council.[6] Second, William Farel, Calvin's colleague in Geneva from 1536 to 1538, had also spent time in Basel and had personally known Oecolampadius. In January 1537 Calvin and Farel composed the "Articles concerning the Organization of the Church and of Worship at Geneva," which clearly stated the necessity of excommunication in the hands of the pastors, aided by faithful laymen.[7] The only missing elements were the Consistory and the use of the term "elder"—these were added in the "Ecclesiastical Ordinances" of 1541, after Calvin returned to Geneva from Strasbourg.

This has suggested to scholars that Martin Bucer had greatly influenced Calvin on the matter of church discipline during his stay in Strasbourg.[8] Even here, however, we discover the shadow of Oecolampadius, under whose influence Bucer himself stood. Initially Bucer opposed Oecolampadius's new plan for discipline.[9] But in 1531 he began to move in the direction of Oecolampadius when he participated, along with Oecolampadius and Ambrosius Blarer, in writing a new church ordinance for the city of Ulm that recommended the creation of an ecclesiastical court made up of pastors and laymen to handle church discipline and excommunication.[10] During the early 1530s he also attempted to institute such a system of discipline in Strasbourg, but to no avail.[11] Bucer had thus moved from a Zwinglian point of view on church discipline to the new Oecolampadian approach during the 1530s.

[6]*DD Ioannis Oecolampadii et Huldreichi Zwinglii epistolarum libri quatuor* (Basel, 1536).

[7]*Ioannes Calvini opera quae supersunt omnia*, XX.1.5–10 (hereinafter cited as *CO*). For an English translation, see J. K. S. Reid, trans. and ed., *Calvin: Theological Treatises*. The library of Christian Classics, vol. 22 (Philadelphia: Westminster, 1954), 48–52.

[8]This is the position of Jaques Courvoisier, *La notion d'Eglise chez Bucer dans son développement historique* (Paris: Librairie Felix Alcan, 1933), 133ff; and Gustav Anrich, *Strassburg und die calvinischen Kirchenverfassung* (Tübingen: Mohr, 1928), 27.

[9]Bucer to Zwingli, October 19, 1530: *ZW*, 11, 199.

[10]Demura, "Church Discipline according to Johannes Oecolampadius," 133–38.

[11]Miriam Usher Chrisman, *Strasbourg and the Reform: A Study in the Process of Change* (New Haven and London: Yale University Press, 1967), 209–10, 220–26, 229–32; Charles Buell Mitchell, "Martin Bucer and Sectarian Dissent: A Confrontation of the Magisterial Reformation with Anabaptists and Spiritualists" (Ph.D. dissertation, Yale University, 1961), 195–97.

Therefore, whatever influence Bucer may have had on Calvin, it had a distinctively Oecolampadian flavor to it. The elements that Calvin added in the Ecclesiastical Ordinances of 1541 had been part of Oecolampadius's plan for Basel in 1530. Calvin's elders and the Consistory were thus an echo from Oecolampadius, but it was Calvin who made the Oecolampadian approach a permanent part of the Reformed tradition and a powerful competitor to the earlier Zwinglian scheme. This happened, however, only after a long period of conflict with the magistrates of Geneva over the control of discipline and excommunication.

Calvin's conflict with the magistrates in Geneva was rooted in a deeply held view on the nature of the Christian community. His mature view is found in the 1543 edition of his *Institutes*. There he spoke of the jurisdiction of the church, "an order framed for the preservation of the spiritual polity," which was "quite distinct from the civil polity." Ecclesiastical courts had existed for discipline and excommunication since the beginning of the church. When Paul spoke of the ruling offices in the church (1 Cor. 12:28; Rom. 12:8), he did not refer to the magistrate, but to the pastors and elders. Christ himself had entrusted the discipline of excommunication to his church (Matt. 18:17-18).

Calvin then denied that Christ's granting of excommunication to the church had been valid only temporarily until magistrates became Christians. Here he undoubtedly had a distorted version of Bullinger's viewpoint in mind. Such people, he continued, "do not notice how great a difference and unlikeness there is between ecclesiastical and civil power. . . . The church does not assume what is proper to the magistrate; nor can the magistrate execute what is carried out by the church." With these words, Calvin echoed Oecolampadius.

Calvin was careful to distance himself from the papal use of excommunication. It was necessary to discriminate between the abuses of the papacy and the true use of the ecclesiastical jurisdiction in order "to overturn the kingdom of Antichrist and set up again the true Kingdom of Christ." In using this ecclesiastical jurisdiction, two matters had to be kept in mind: "that this spiritual power be completely separated from the right of the sword; secondly, that it be administered not by the decision of one man but by a lawful assembly. Both of these were observed when the church was purer." Then Calvin reiterated that in the ancient church this power was not in the hands of one man, "but in the hands of the assembly of the elders, which was to the church what the Senate is to the city."[12]

Calvin thus made a clear distinction between civil and ecclesiastical jurisdiction, and asserted that the ecclesiastical jurisdiction was to be exercised by a court made up of pastors and elders, like the Consistory, according to the

[12]*Institutes*, IV.11.1–6.

commandment of Christ and the example of Paul and the ancient church. In doing so, he explicitly rejected the point of view of Bullinger and Zwingli and the practice of all of the Reformed churches at the time that he wrote this in 1543. In the next chapter of the *Institutes*, he dealt more specifically with the mechanics of ecclesiastical discipline. The offender should first be admonished privately and then in the presence of witnesses. If necessary, he should then be called before the "assembly of the elders" for further admonition. If he still refused to submit and repent, he must be excommunicated. Then Calvin cautioned against too great a zeal: only open sins could be reproved, and only "crimes or shameful acts" merited the penalty of excommunication. At this point Calvin stated the three goals of church discipline: the purity of the church and the Eucharist; the protection of the good one from the bad example of the wicked; and the repentance of the sinner.[13]

The story of Calvin's struggles with the magistrates and his eventual victory in Geneva is fairly well known. The opposition to Calvin centered on the matter of ecclesiastical discipline. The conflict became intense during the late 1540s when Ami Perrin became the leader of the opposition. The Calvinists referred to the Perrinists as the "Libertines," although, except for a few individuals, they were not libertines in the sense of moral laxity. One might rather refer to them as "liberals,"[14] for, although the Perrinists were hostile to Calvin and his system of discipline, they were not hostile to the Reformation itself. During the early 1550s, the Council attempted to exercise a firmer control over the ministers and to weaken the effectiveness of the Consistory. There was also a growing tendency to criticize indeed to ridicule Calvin and the other ministers. Then, in 1553, the Perrinist faction won decisive control of the Council, with Perrin himself becoming First Syndic. From 1551 through 1553 Calvin was faced with a series of personal challenges—in each case, he sought Bullinger's support. At the height of controversy, when Calvin's prestige and authority were at their lowest point, Bullinger's influence was crucial.

The first crisis was a direct challenge to Calvin's doctrine of predestination. In October of 1551, Jerome Bolsec publicly denounced Calvin's teaching as unbiblical and heretical: it made God the author of sin. Bolsec was arrested and tried for heresy. He appealed to the judgment of the churches of Bern, Basel, and Zurich, and the Council agreed to request the advice of these churches. Their replies on the whole called for moderation and reconciliation. None of them totally supported Calvin's position, and generally they were more favorable to Bolsec than to Calvin.[15]

[13]*Institutes*, IV.12.1–5.

[14]As so convincingly argued by James MacKinnon, *Calvin and the Reformation* (New York: Russell & Russell, 1962), 103–4. For a succinct, engaging description of Calvin's travails and eventual victory in Geneva, see W. Fred Graham, *The Constructive Revolutionary: John Calvin and His Socio–Economic Impact* (Richmond, Va.: John Knox Press, 1971), 30–53.

[15]See MacKinnon, *Calvin and the Reformation*, 116–20 for a summary of the controversy. For the record of the controversy, including the correspondence, see Jean–François Bergier and

Calvin was bitterly disappointed when Bullinger refused to endorse Calvin's harsher doctrine of election and reprobation, instead reiterating his own characteristically mild doctrine of single predestination. He informed Calvin that many were offended by his doctrine and inferred from it that Calvin made God the author of sin.[16] Stung by this criticism, Calvin complained to Farel that the Zurichers had been rude in their official letters and that Bullinger himself "haughtily despises our necessities." He wrote to Bullinger that it was "extremely absurd" to defend Bolsec.[17] More than a year later, in April 1553, the two men repaired their friendship,[18] and none too soon, for Calvin was about to face the most severe test yet of his leadership and authority in Geneva.

The more spectacular, and by far the best known, incident during this period of crisis was the Servetus case, which must be seen within the larger framework of Calvin's continuing conflict with the Perrinist faction in Geneva. Some have argued that Servetus counted on the aid of Calvin's enemies, or conversely that the Perrinists meant to use the Servetus affair to discredit Calvin.[19] Calvin himself certainly saw a connection between the manner in which the Council handled the Servetus case and its enmity toward him. He wrote to Bullinger on September 7 that the Genevan magistrates would write to him for his judgment: "Even with our loud protests they give you this annoyance, but they have come to such madness and rage that everything we say to them is suspected."[20]

Others also presumed a connection between the Servetus case and Calvin's other problems in Geneva. Bullinger wrote to Johannes Haller at Bern: "I believe that he [Servetus] fled to Geneva by the providence of God so that she [Geneva] might cleanse herself from the charge of blasphemy and heresy among many people by giving him a deserving punishment. But I hear that they [the Perrinists] actually protect that most good-for-nothing fellow out of hatred for Calvin."[21] Wolfgang Musculus wrote to Bullinger from Bern that Servetus hoped "to make full use of the ill-will with which the magnates there attack Calvin."[22]

Robert M. Kingdon, eds., *Registres de la Compagnie des Pasteurs de Genéve au temps de Calvin. Tome 1: 1546–1553* (Genéve: Droz, 1962), 80–128; for an English translation, see Philip Edgcumbe Hughes, trans. and ed., *The Register of the Company of Pastors of Geneva in the Time of Calvin* (Grand Rapids: Eerdmans, 1966), 137–86 (hereinafter cited as Hughes, *Register*).

[16]*CO*, 14:col. 208, 210, 214–15. See Baker, *Heinrich Bullinger and the Covenant*, 34–36 for a fuller description of the correspondence on Bolsec, and 27–54 for Bullinger's doctrine of predestination.

[17]*CO*, 14:col. 218–19, 252; English translation in Jules Bonner, trans. and ed., *Letters of John Calvin* (New York: Burt Franklin, 1972), 2:328–29, 333.

[18]*CO*14: col. 510–11, 513–14; Bonner, *Letters* 2:402–404.

[19]For a treatment of these arguments, see Roland Bainton, *Hunted Heretic: The Life and Death of Michael Servetus, 1511–1553* (Boston: Beacon, 1960), 172–81.

[20]*CO*, 14: col. 611; Bonner, *Letters*, 2:427.   [21]*CO*, 14: col. 624.   [22]*CO*, 14: col. 628.

At about the same time, in mid-September, Haller wrote to Bullinger that dissension and bitterness was increasing at Geneva:

> The more powerful ones all but conspire against Calvin. He sets himself up against the most important men and is prepared to die to maintain the institutions of his church. And as I understand it, the primary cause of this entire controversy is the rigor of the ecclesiastical discipline that has been established there, whereby everyone is all but put under the feet of the ministers. It is oppressive and intolerable to the powerful, and hence they are not gracious enough to our Calvin because they feel that he claims too much for himself.[23]

Haller's sardonic words referred to the controversy over discipline that was reaching crisis proportions at this very time in Geneva.

The Perrinist faction had come to power in the February elections of 1553. Perrin and his associates felt that the time was ripe for a serious challenge to Calvin. Their attack was direct: they denied the Consistory the power to excommunicate. Philibert Berthelier, one of Calvin's most stubborn enemies, had been excommunicated by the Consistory in 1551. His excommunication had been repeatedly renewed because of his rebellious attitude and his refusal to accept the authority of the Consistory. In early September 1553 the Council annulled his excommunication and allowed him to communicate if he wished to do so, despite Calvin's vehement protests.[24]

At the height of the Servetus case, then, the long conflict at Geneva over discipline was entering its final and most crucial stage. The two issues, the Servetus trial and the crisis over discipline, were closely intertwined. The Perrinist faction maneuvered in the background to attempt to get an acquittal for Servetus. Perrin himself argued for a verdict of not guilty.[25] Calvin claimed that Perrin had even attempted to secure Servetus' release after he had been found guilty.[26] The majority of the Council knew, however, that Servetus had to be dealt with, and severely so, especially considering that the replies from the Swiss churches had been unanimously negative toward Servetus.[27] Nevertheless, at least in Calvin's mind, the hostility of the magistrates was clear in their insistence on consulting the Swiss churches rather than relying solely on him. Simultaneously they lifted Berthelier's excommunication, thus challenging both Calvin and the power of the Consistory.

---

[23]*CO*, 14: col. 625.

[24]Bergier and Kingdon, *Registres*, 1:147; Bergier and Kingdon, *Registres de la Compagnie des Pasteurs de Génève au temps de Calvin. Tome II: 1553-1564* (Génève: Droz, 1964), 48-49 (hereinafter cited as Bergier and Kingdon, *Registres*, 2); Hughes, *Register*, 205, 285-86.

[25]MacKinnon, *Calvin and the Reformation*, 148-50.

[26]*CO*, 14: col. 657.   [27]*CO*, 8: col. 808-23.

On September 7 the pastors appeared before the Council to protest the Council's annulment of Berthelier's excommunication, requesting that the magistrates follow the Ecclesiastical Ordinances. The councilmen answered that they did not intend to introduce any innovations, but rather "they wished what was contained in them to remain fixed and inviolable."[28] The Council's position, then, was that the Ordinances had never given the Consistory the power of excommunication, that this authority resided in the Council alone.

In response, the Company of Pastors sent a protest to the Council, declaring that the Ordinances gave the power of excommunication to the Consistory. On November 7 the Small Council announced that it would reserve to itself the right of "absolving those who had been banned from the supper," and two days later the Council of Two Hundred voted to take the right of excommunication away from the Consistory entirely. The Small Council then wrote to the councils of Bern, Basel, Zurich and Schaffhausen to ask their opinions about the matter.[29] The reply from Bern was short and to the point: in Bern there was no excommunication.[30] The response from Schaffhausen was apparently fairly positive, and that from Basel relatively negative toward the use of excommunication by a church court.[31]

The replies from Zurich though were decisive. The letter from the Genevan Council to the Zurich magistrates is dated November 30, a month after the execution of Servetus. Surely the Perrinists expected a reply from the Zurich magistrates favorable to their own point of view. Four days prior, however, on November 26, Calvin had written two letters to Zurich, one to all the pastors and a personal letter to Bullinger, in which he pleaded for their support. Both letters, sent secretly were delivered by a trusted confidant of Calvin.

In his letter to Bullinger, Calvin complained that his opponents had opposed ecclesiastical discipline for seven years and that things had come to such a state that the entire ecclesiastical order in Geneva would be destroyed unless the Zurichers came to his aid. The accompanying letter to all the pastors would apprise him of the details. What he needed from Bullinger was the assurance that the Zurich magistrates would make a reply favoring Calvin's position. He urged Bullinger to make certain that they would first agree that Calvin's form of discipline was "consonant with the word of God," and second that they would "disapprove of innovation." Calvin was certain that if Bullinger could obtain these two points from the Zurich Council, the victory

---

[28]Bergier and Kingdon, *Registres*, 2: 48–49; Hughes, *Register*, 285–86.

[29]Bergier and Kingdon, *Registres*, 2:49–54; Hughes, *Registers*, 286–89, 291–92. For the letter from the Gevevan Council to the Zürich Council, see *CO*, 14: col. 685–86.

[30]*CO*, 14: col. 691.

[31]The official responses have been lost. For information on the Schaffhausen position, see Rügerus to Bullinger, *CO*, 14: col. 710; on the Basel position, see Sulzer to the Genevan pastors, *CO*, 14: col. 711–13.

would be his. Calvin thanked Bullinger "for the faithful and pious response that you gave in the case of Servetus." Although that had not checked "the lawless and profligate ones," things would soon be better if Bullinger would once again give his assistance.[32]

Calvin's letter to the Zurich pastors was much longer. He apologized for again asking for their help so soon after the Servetus case, but certain "depraved men" made it necessary. The present problem with Berthelier was but one of many disputes stirred up by Satan in recent years at Geneva. But it was a particularly vexatious dispute. Berthelier had scorned the authority of the Consistory, and with the aid of that "godless faction" of men "who were not ashamed noisily to defend the cause of Servetus," Berthelier had been able to persuade the Council to annul his excommunication. This was, Calvin assured them, simply the culmination of a four-year attempt on the part of "evil men" to overthrow the Reformed church in Geneva. Now these same men hoped to use the Berthelier affair to conclude "a glorious victory over Christ and his doctrine and his ministers, in short over all his members."[33]

Only the Zurichers, Calvin continued, could save the Genevan church from Satan. The welfare of the Genevan church was entirely in their hands. Calvin felt that he, in order not to exacerbate the problems of the church, had been too flexible in the past. "But," he exclaimed,

> we cannot allow them this victory; we cannot knowingly and willingly hand over the entire jurisdiction of the church, not only because the authority of our ministry would be destroyed but also because the name of Christ would be subject to every foulest abuse. An unrestrained license for every evil would become more and more overbearing; the position of the pious would not only be exposed to every injustice, but absolutely shattered, it would be violently overthrown.[34]

Clearly Calvin felt extremely threatened by the situation.

Calvin made it clear to the Zurichers that he felt that all his problems in the past years were related: his opponents, the Perrinists, were, simply stated, attempting to overthrow true religion and godly discipline. The Zuricher's aid in the Servetus case had been crucial. Now Calvin took great pains to make sure that they understood that the battle was far from over. Godlessness and licentiousness would prevail in Geneva, the gospel itself might well be silenced, if the Zurichers did not once again come to his aid. So when the

---

[32]*CO*, 14: col. 674; Bonner, *Letters*, 2:441–42.

[33]*CO*, 14: col. 675–676; Bonner, *Letters*, 2:442–45.

[34]*CO*, 14: col. 677; Bonner, *Letters*, 2:445–46.

Genevan Council wrote for an opinion on excommunication, the Zurich pastors must persuade their magistrates to give the correct reply. In applying such pressure on Bullinger and the Zurich pastors, Calvin overstated the extent to which his discipline had already been established in Geneva (with his several references to the Council's fondness for "innovation" and "novelty")–but his plea for support was successful.

For, despite Bullinger's aversion to the idea of an ecclesiastical court with a jurisdiction independent from the magistrate, and despite the system of magisterial discipline in Zurich, both Bullinger and the Zurich magistrates did come to the aid of Calvin. In a letter of December 12, Bullinger revealed to Calvin that the Genevan Council had posed three questions to the Zurich Council: what was the correct scriptural practice of excommunication; could it be practiced without a consistory; and how did the Zurich church handle discipline?[35]

Bullinger explained that a committee of three magistrates and three pastors had been formed to formulate "an appropriate response." The committee had decided that the consistorial laws of Geneva were "pious and come near to the rule of the word of God," and therefore ought not to be altered. "It is sufficient that they preserve purity, especially in this day when men become increasingly worse." Even though the Genevan discipline did not correspond to that of Zurich, "nevertheless it is moderate considering the times, place and people." Bullinger made it clear to Calvin that he had gone to considerable trouble to prevent an unfavorable reply from the Zurich Council.[36]

As Bullinger predicted, the Zurich magistrates replied that the Genevans should retain their present system, for to change it would only bring more disorder rather than peace and unity. Although the Genevan system differed from that of Zurich, "each magistracy in such and other matters under its command must act according to the nature of its land and people." It was important, however, that the Genevan Council retain its leadership in order to do its duty to further the honor of God.[37] Therefore, while suggesting to the Genevan Council that no change be made, the Zurich magistrates still upheld magisterial control of the whole process.

Calvin was extremely grateful to Bullinger,[38] as he well should have been. Had Bullinger wished, he could have tipped the balance in Geneva toward Zurich's type of magisterial discipline. He did not do so because he accepted Calvin's description of his opponents as godless men who opposed all Christian discipline and wanted license and liberty to do what they wished. It was not then simply a choice between systems of discipline; rather it was a choice between supporting Calvin or supporting the Perrinists, who, Bullinger be-

---

[35]*CO*, 14: col. 697.   [36]*CO*, 14: col. 697–98.   [37]*CO*, 14: col. 699–700.

[38]*CO*, 14: col. 722; Bonner, *Letters*, 2:447. See also Beza's letter of thanks to Bullinger. *CO*, 14: col. 714.

lieved, had attempted to protect Servetus and who now wished to silence the gospel in Geneva.

The Genevan Council most surely counted on a reply from the Zurich Council negative to Calvin's ideas on discipline. Calvin wrote to Farel on December 30 that the Council would be disappointed in their reply.[39] In fact, the reply from Zurich must have been a total shock to the Genevan magistrates. In any case, this was the beginning of the end of Calvin's difficulties with the Genevan Council.

In January 1554 Calvin and the magistrates made peace.[40] Whether there was some informal understanding on the authority of the Consistory is unclear, but when the Consistory decided on March 22 that Berthelier's excommunication would remain in force, there was no opposition from the Council.[41] Then, in January 1555, all three councils agreed that the Consistory had the authority both to excommunicate and to admit a person to the celebration of the Eucharist as stated by the Ecclesiastical Ordinances of 1541.[42] The Perrinists lost their control of the Council in the elections of 1554, and their defeat was total in 1555.[43] Afterwards Calvin wrote to Bullinger, "Recently, after long struggles, the right of excommunication was at last confirmed to us. Then, in a quiet meeting, the syndics were elected in accordance with our wishes."[44]

The end to the struggle came in the spring of 1555, when in less than a month fifty-seven French refugees were admitted to the rights of citizenship. Calvin's opponents, fearful of such an increase in the number of citizens committed to Calvin, protested in vain. Then, in mid-May, a riot broke out, which the Council saw as the first step in an armed overthrow of the government. Some of the Perrinists were executed, and many fled from Geneva. Perrin and several others were sentenced to death *in absentia*. After nineteen years of struggle, Calvin had won a total victory.[45]

From 1555 to his death in 1564, Calvin wielded an enormous amount of influence in Geneva. During the decade of Calvin's dominance, the Consistory became more powerful and its efforts to direct the morals of the Genevans, more effective. A new edition of the Ecclesiastical Ordinances was

[39]*CO*, 14: col. 724; Bonner, *Letters*, 2:449.

[40]*CO*, 21: col. 567.

[41]Bergier and Kingdon, *Registres*, 2:54–55; Hughes, *Register*, 294.

[42]*CO*, 21: col. 593–94; Bergier and Kingdon, *Registres*, 2:59; Hughes, *Registers*, 305.

[43]MacKinnon, *Calvin and the Reformation*, 107.

[44]*CO*, 15: col. 449; Bonner, *Letters* 3:151.

[45]Bergier and Kingdon, *Registres*, 2:63; Hughes, *Register*, 309; Robert M. Kingdon, "Calvin and the Government of Geneva," *Calvinus Ecclesiae Genevensis Custos. Die Referate des International Kongresses für Calvinforschung vom 6. bis 9. September 1982 in Genf*, ed. Wilhelm H. Neuser (Frankfurt am Main: Peter Lang, 1984), 61–63; MacKinnon, *Calvin and the Reformation*, 107–9.

issued in 1561. It contained revisions that were based on several edicts issued by the Council in 1560. The first edict stipulated that a magistrate who was chosen as an elder would not act as a magistrate in the Consistory. The expressed purpose of the edict was to accentuate the distinction between civil power and the ecclesiastical jurisdiction. Then, the fourth edict put a fine point on the matter of excommunication: those who had been excommunicated by the Consistory would continue to be rejected until they repented and requested reconciliation with the church. In passing these edicts, the Council officially recognized the principles for which Calvin had fought for so long.[46]

Calvin's agenda, as expressed in the 1543 edition of the *Institutes*, had finally become official policy. The order of church discipline initially outlined by Oecolampadius in 1530 found its first practical application at Geneva in 1561. The ecclesiastical jurisdiction was now officially distinct from the civil polity. Christ's commandment in Matthew 18 had been obeyed with the creation of the order of elders and the Consistory, thus making it possible to preserve the purity of the Eucharist and the church by excluding any who were clearly unfit. Geneva was the only Reformed city where such a discipline existed in 1561. All the Swiss Reformed cities held to the Zurich approach to Christian discipline, with the magistracy in charge in varying degrees.

Although it would be too much to say that Bullinger assured Calvin of his victory, he did help Calvin avert defeat. The idea that Calvin may well have lost his battle in Geneva without the aid of Bullinger is full of irony. For after Calvin's death the Calvinist church polity became a powerful competitor to the Zurich point of view within the Reformed churches. The gesture on the part of Bullinger during the Berthelier affair had hardly signified consensus on discipline. On the contrary, the two traditions continued to oppose each other throughout the sixteenth and seventeenth centuries. The battlegrounds were France, Germany, the Netherlands, England, Scotland, and New England. In the end, Calvin's victory at Geneva assured not only the survival of the Oecolampadian-Calvinist system but also its eventual dominance among the Reformed churches.

[46]MacKinnon, *Calvin and the Reformation*, 169–70. For the edicts, see *CO*, 10: col. 120–23; for the 1561 *Ordinances*, see *CO*, 10: col. 91–105.

John Calvin, based upon a painting by Holbein.

Marriage in Calvin's Sermons

Claude-Marie Baldwin

This study deals with Calvin's French style as he speaks to the issue of marriage. It is in his sermons that his language is most vivid on the subject. Calvin's two fundamental principles appear clearly: the hierarchical order and the mutual accountability of husband and wife. His "sexist" views are tempered by his faithfulness to the scriptural texts.

WHEN SEEKING TO ADDRESS MARRIAGE in John Calvin's writings, we look in vain for treatises on this topic. In the *Institutes*, Calvin is mainly refuting the ordinance of the celibacy of priests as he briefly commends marriage: "They ... dare also call marriage 'pollution,' .... This, despite the fact that God deemed it not alien to his majesty to institute marriage [cf. Gen. 2:22]; that he declared it honorable among all men [Heb. 13:4]; and that Christ, our Lord, sanctified it by his presence, deigning to honor it with his first miracle [John 2:2, 6-11]!"[1]

In Calvin's commentaries, we find his doctrinal views expressed briefly when he deals with pertinent passages in both the Old and the New Testaments. But it is in his sermons that Calvin's fullest expression appears. As the preacher addresses his parishioners in Geneva, he fills out his views in order to reach the common man and woman.

This study deals with Calvin's French style as he speaks to the issue of marriage. I wish to illustrate Calvin's vivid language as he communicates his two fundamental principles about marriage: hierarchical order and mutual accountability.

For the purposes of this article, I have chosen portions from selected sermons in which Calvin exposits particular Bible verses dealing with marriage. In addition, I have selected the sermon on the Epistle to the Ephesians, chapter 5, verses 22–26 in its entirety because it is Calvin's richest stylistic elaboration on marriage.

---

[1]John Calvin, *Institutes of the Christian Religion* ed. John T. McNeill; tr. Ford Lewis Battles (Philadelphia: The Westminster Press, 1960) IV. 13.3.

In that sermon, Calvin clearly states the origin of marriage: "Now marriage was not instituted by men, we know that God is the author of it and that it is dedicated in His name: and Scripture says that it is a sacred covenant and calls it divine for that reason."[2] Upon that foundation, Calvin discusses the hierarchical order within marriage which has three bases: (1) nature itself, (2) punishment as a consequence of the rebelliousness of Adam and Eve, and (3) the present condition of mankind in a fallen universe.

The hierarchical order was God's ordained way before the Fall. "Before the sin and the fall of Eve and Adam, man was already head of woman."[3] For what reasons? First, Calvin sets Adam and Eve in the context of all creation: "But let us know that God put us into this world after having subjected to us the beasts and the birds of the sky, and the fish of the water, after having ordered all that for our usage, and constituted these two degrees between us, he wanted man to bear the mark of greater superiority and that woman should be next, but in a lower degree, be that as it may."[4] And Calvin, in his sermon on I Tim. 2:12–14, remarks that God wanted man to be preeminent and that the others (women) must acknowledge that God wanted to hold them in bridle. The following passage illustrates well Calvin's approach to his audience:

> Car quelle ingratitude sera-ce à la femme, si elle ne se contente pas d'estre en ce rang moyen où Dieu l'a mise? Les bestes brutes quand elles scauroyent parler, ne seroyent pas si ingrates: car elles pourroyent alleguer qu'elles sont creatures de Dieu comme nous. Et pourquoy est-ce que les chevaux sont assujettis à nostre service, les boeufs, les asnes, les moutons? que non seulement on en use pour les employer en un grand travail et penible tout le temps de leur vie, mais il faut que leur chair mesme nous serve de nourriture? Or nous cognoissons la grande liberalité et infinie de nostre Dieu en cela, qu'il nous a donné un tel usage sur ses creatures. Voilà la femme qui est en degré excellent, combien qu'elle soit sujette à l'homme, si est-ce neantmoins qu'elle porte encores l'image de Dieu en son endroit. Et ainsi, quelle ingratitude sera-ce, si elle ne se contente de ce qui luy est donné? quand nous alleguerons, tous ensemble, pourquoy c'est que Dieu nous a mis en ceste vie caduque, et que nous ne sommes point en tel degré que les anges de paradis, je vous prie, devons-nous estre receus à tels murmures?[5]

[2]Jean Calvin, "Sermons Ephesians 5, 22–26," *Calvini Opera*, 51, 736. This and all subsequent translations into English are mine.

[3]Calvin, Sermons Eph. 5:22–26, CO 51, 737.

[4]Calvin, Sermon Cor. 11:4–10, CO 49, 724–25.

[5]Calvin, Sermon Tim. 2:12–14, CO 53, 212: "What ingratitude there will be on the part of the woman if she is not content to be in this middle rank in which God has placed her? Brute

Calvin, in this short excerpt, asks five rhetorical questions. "What ingratitude on the part of the woman it will be if she is not content to be in this middle rank in which God has placed her?" and "Why are the horses subjected to our service, the oxen, the donkeys, the sheep?" and "That not only we use them to do great and arduous labor all during their lives, but even their flesh itself must supply us with food?" and "Therefore, what ingratitude will it be if she is not content with what is given to her?" and finally a sentence which ends with "I ask you, must we be listened to on such murmurings?" What is impressive here is how Calvin manipulates woman by seeking to shame her for not being grateful for her inferior station to man since she is superior to animals. In this way, he intends to convince her to accept her middle rank.

Several images illustrate just how Calvin views the relationship of woman to man. "Does a branch want to have a greater reputation than the root or the trunk of the tree? Here is a branch which has come out of a trunk, and contrary to what should be, she will seek glory. Where does that lead? Now, woman is like a branch who has come from man."[6] Likewise, woman is a part and an accessory to man. In another sermon, the preacher states that "man is like unto the head of mankind and women are like the body."[7]

Unfortunately we cannot examine Calvin's sermons on the verse in Genesis 2:21 in which God causes Adam to fall into a deep sleep while He removes one of his ribs, because these sermons were sold in the nineteenth century by the Librarian of the University of Geneva, one Senébier, to a bookseller for scrap paper. However, in his commentary on this passage, Calvin states: "'God created man . . . he made them male and female.' In this manner Adam was taught to recognize himself in his wife, as in a mirror; and Eve, in her turn, to submit herself willingly to her husband, as being taken out of him."[8]

---

beasts, were they to know how to speak, would not be so ungrateful: for they could plead that they are creatures of God like us. And why are the horses subjected to our service, the oxen, the donkey, the sheep? That not only do we use them to do great and arduous labor all during their lives, but even their flesh itself must supply us with food? Now, we know the great and infinite liberality of our God in that he has given us this kind of use of his creatures. Here is the wife who has an excellent standing even though she is subject to man, since nevertheless, she still bears God's image in her. And therefore, what ingratitude there will be if she is not content with what is given to her? When we will plead all together as to why God has put us in this decaying life and that we are not at the same level as the angels of paradise, I ask you, must we be listened to on such murmurings?"

[6]Jean Calvin, *Sermons sur l'épitre aux Corinthiens.* I Cor. 11:4–10, CO 49:728–729.

[7]Jean Calvin, *Sermons sur le livre de Deuteronome.* 23:24, 25–24: 1–4, CO 28:146.

[8]Jean Calvin, *Comm. in Genesin,* CO 23:48–49.

Throughout Calvin's sermons where marriage is mentioned, we find that one of his leitmotifs is that woman should be content with the station which God has assigned to her even though this subjection is hard to bear at times.

Calvin's second explanation of the present condition is that her lot has been made harder by sin. In fact, her present state is a punishment because of Eve's primary responsibility in the Fall. It comes from her side. In the following passage, Calvin's style reinforces this point most effectively:

> Mais puis qu'il n'y a autre remede sinon que les femmes s'humilient et qu'elles cognoissent que ça esté de leur costé qu'est venue la ruine et la confusion de tout le genre humain, que nous avons esté tous perdus et maudits et bannis du Royaume des cieux: quand (di-je) les femmes cognoistront que tout cela est venu d'Eve et du sexe feminin (comme sainct Paul le declare en l'autre passage), il ne reste plus sinon qu'elles s'humilient et qu'elles portent patiemment la subjetion que Dieu leur a mise sus, qui n'est sinon un advertissement d'humilité et de modestie. Or si elles s'eslevent contre leurs maris et qu'ils n'en puissent jouir en nulle facon, c'est comme si elles seelloyent le peché d'Adam et d'Eve et la rebellion qui a esté commise, et qu'elles declarassent qu'elles ne veulent point que Dieu guairisse ceste playe, voire qui est mortelle. Quand donc on fait ainsi la guerre contre la grace de Dieu, que peut-il advenir sinon une confusion extreme? Or les femmes qui ont mauvaise teste ne penseront point à cela: mais tant y a qu'il est enregistré devant Dieu, et faudra qu'elles en rendent conte à leur confusion extreme.[9]

Let us look more closely at this paragraph. We notice several pairs of words. In keeping with his legal training, Calvin habitually uses pairs of words for rhetorical balance. But I believe that, in this case, he is clearly using this device for emphasis. Notice the result of Eve's sin: "La ruine et la confusion," [ruin and confusion]; three adjectives "perdus et maudits et bannis," [lost, damned,

[9]Jean Calvin, Sermons Eph. 5:22–26, CO 51, 739. "Since there is no other remedy other than that women should humble themselves and know that it is from their side that the ruin and confusion of the whole of mankind came, that we have all been lost and damned and banished from the Kingdom of heaven: when (say I) women will recognize that all that came from Eve and from the female sex (as Saint Paul declares in the other passage), there is nothing left but for them to humble themselves and to patiently bear the subjection which God has put on them, which is nothing but a warning to be humble and modest. Now, if they rise up against their husbands who cannot enjoy them in any way, it is as if they were sealing Adam and Eve's sin and the rebellion which was committed, and that they were declaring that they do not want God to heal that wound which in truth is mortal. When one thus wages war against the grace of God, what can happen other than extreme confusion? Now women who are unruly will not think of that: but the fact remains that it is registered before God and they will have to give account of it to their extreme embarrassment."

and banished]; the source of perdition is "venu d'Eve et du sexe feminin" [from Eve and the female sex]: the remedy "qu'elles s'humilient et qu'elles portent patiemment la subjetion" [to humble themselves and patiently bear the subjection]; which is a warning of "humilité et de modestie" [humility and modesty]. esty]. Calvin shows the seriousness of Eve's sin in his use of terms such as "guairisse" [wound]; woman must be humbled so that God might *cure* this wound, which is indeed mortal. Woman would "fait ainsi la guerre", *be doing war* against God by not subjecting herself to her husband. Women who "ont mauvaise teste", *are unruly*, must realize that their attitude is "enrigistre", *registered* before God, and great will be their confusion when they must account for it before God.

Woman can live biblically by not repeating Eve's disobedience. Here, he is speaking for dramatic impact in the voice of a woman:

> Puis que Dieu m'a donné une telle condition, que je soye sujette à mon mari, il n'est point question que je hausse ici la teste comme une biche, et que je rejette le joug; car je ne desobeiray point à un homme mortel, je ne desobeiray point à un homme mortel, je no l'offenseray point seulement, entant que je luy ay promis la foy, de luy estre sujette et obeissante, et que je fay tout le contraire: mais j'offenseray celuy qui m'a assujettie à luy: c'est Dieu qui m'a donnee entre les mains de mon mari, et veut que je luy soye plus sujette qu'à pere et à mere.[10]

Notice the analogy to a deer in the imagery: "hausse ici la teste comme une biche" [raising my head like a deer]; and to a beast of burden "que je rejette le joug" [that I reject the yoke]. In vivid direct discourse, Calvin paints the portrait of the sensible wife. She thinks through what Scripture says and comes to the conclusion that if she disobeys her husband she will in fact be disobeying God. In depicting a model of the thought-process and the conclusion which the wife is to reach, Calvin is using a powerful didactic tool.

In addition to Eve's sin, there is the pervasiveness of sin in all human beings. This following quote illustrates how effectively Calvin describes the inner thought of his parishioners as they long to be rid of cumbersome spouses. Again he calls upon the vividness of direct discourse. This time the husband speaks: "J'ay une femme terrible et rebelle" [I have a terrible and rebellious wife]. Then he returns to the third person.

---

[10]Jean Calvin, Sermons Deut. 23:24–25, 24:1–4, 28, 149. "Since God has given me such a condition that I be subject to my husband, there is no question of my raising my head like a deer, and that I reject the yoke: for I shall not disobey a mortal man, I won't even offend him, in that I gave him my word, to be subject and obedient to him, and I am doing the very opposite; but I will offend the one who subjected me to him: it is God who gave me into the hands of my husband, and who wants me to be more subject to him than to father or mother."

Le mari pourra alleguer, J'ay une femme terrible et rebelle: ou bien elle est fiere, ou elle a mauvaise teste, ou elle est langarde. Apres, l'autre sera yvrongnesse, l'autre sera paresseuse, l'autre aura quelque complexion. Brief, il n'y a celuy qui ne puisse avoir quelque couleur, quand il ne gardera point la foy et l'honnesteté du mariage comme il appartient. La femme aussi de son costé ne sera point despourveue: car son mari souvent sera chagrin et rioteux: et bien peu regardent à quoi Dieu les a appelez. Les uns sont mauvais mesnagers, hantans les tavernes; ou bien ils se desbordent à jeux et autres dissolutions; Les autres sont paillars, les autres gourmans, les autres yvrognes. Or donc chacune femme pourra aussi bien pretendre quelque excuse pour s'exempter de son devoir. Mais quand nous venons à Dieu, il nous faut baisser la teste: car nous ne profiterons rien en nous rebequant à l'encontre de luy. Combien que les hommes se gouvernent mal d'un costé et les femmes de l'autre, si est-ce que Dieu ne veut point que le mariage soit rompu ni violé pour cela:. . . .[11]

This paragraph illustrates not only Calvin's vocabulary, but the balance in his thinking which it reflects. Notice the adjectives which describe an undesirable wife: "terrible et rebelle" [terrible and rebellious], "fiere" [haughty], "elle a mauvaise teste" [she is unruly], "langarde" [talkative], "yvrongnesse" [drunkard], "paresseuse" [lazy]. The pejorative adjectives descriptive of man include "chagrin et rioteux" [fretful and quarrelsome], "gourmans" [greedy], "yvrongnes" [drunk]. Despite this tableau of vices, the overriding principle remains that a wife must still be subject to and obey her husband.

Yet, these numerous troubles are mankind's doing. "That does not come from the nature of marriage; had Adam our father remained in his state of integrity, it is certain that marriage, since it is a help from God, would have led to a perfect and angelic life: but since we are corrupt, and that we have so many vices in us that it is pathetic, we convert good into evil: and what God had instituted for our glory, we often convert into ignominy."[12]

[11]Jean Calvin, Sermons Eph. 5:22–26, CO 51, 736. "The husband will be able to plead, I have a terrible and rebellious wife; either she is haughty, or she is unruly, or she is talkative. Then, the other will be drunkard; the other will be lazy, the other will have some temperament. In short, there will not be one who does not have a pretext, when he does not keep the faith and honesty of the marriage as is fitting. The woman also, on her side will not be wanting: because her husband will often be fretful and quarrelsome, and very few look to what God has called them. Some are bad providers, frequenting taverns: or they dissipate themselves in games and other dissolutions; others are ribald, others greedy, others drunk. Now therefore each wife will be able to claim some excuse to exempt herself from her duty. But when we come to God, we must lower our heads; for we will profit in no way by rebelling against him. Even though men, on the one hand, conduct themselves badly as do women on the other hand, nevertheless God does not want marriage to be severed or violated for that.

[12]Jean Calvin, Sermons Deut. 24:1–6, CO 28, 159.

In spite of the suffering of mankind in marriage as well as other estates, the hierarchical order created by God before the Fall was meant to be permanent and exceedingly good. In a fallen world where man is harsh and woman is rebellious, woman must bear the punishment of subjection, because of Adam and Eve's disobedience. "Il faut donc que je cognoisse ici la punition de mon peche."[13] In fact, in this twisted world, she is to be submissive even when her husband treats her poorly: "But the vices which are in the man must not prevent the woman from being subject to him and obeying him."[14]

We see in the texts above that Calvin reflected the predominant thinking of his time as he stated the biblical role of a woman and of a wife. His reasoning is offensive when he tells women to be content with their place since, after all, animals who are lower than women do not complain about theirs. His statement is distorted when he blames women wholly for the Fall. His thinking is harsh when he counsels women to submit to abusive treatment.

Yet, throughout the sermon portions in which Calvin deals with marriage, he is careful to state a second major principle of the husband-wife relationship, that of mutual obligation. Nowhere in Calvin's writings is the subject of mutual responsibility dealt with more clearly and vividly than in his sermon on Eph. 5:22–26. The biblical text itself rather obviously warrants this balance. But, I believe that Calvin also reveals his commitment to a middle way between strict hierarchy and unmitigated equality by so preaching. When we study Calvin's commentary on Eph. 5:22–26, we find succinct didactic exposition. Each verse is exposited in two paragraphs at the most in which Calvin's interpretation is stated as plainly and briefly as he can do so in clear French prose. On the other hand, his sermon on the same verses fills twelve pages of the small print of the *Opera Calvini*.

The careful structure of this sermon is striking. He introduces the topic by reminding his audience of mutual subjection of all men and of special subjection of wives, children, and servants. He then proceeds to speak to husbands and wives all through his homily. The balance is remarkable even as he addresses men and women. In dealing with the last verse, he points to Jesus Christ as the source of all grace and the one to whom all owe obedience in marriage.

In order to render his teaching effective, Calvin uses ten passages of direct discourse and twenty-two rhetorical questions in this text. These direct discourse monologues and rhetorical questions become more frequent as the sermon progresses, heightening the intensity of the message.

As the preacher deals with one verse after another, he repeatedly emphasizes the ultimate accountability of both spouses to God. He has the husband saying: "Why did God show himself so benign, so human, so pitying towards

[13]Jean Calvin, Sermons I Tim. 2:12–14, CO 53, 216.
[14]Jean Calvin, Sermons Eph. 5:22–26, CO 51, 736.

me? Now since he elevated me to such dignity, it is reason enough that I should conform to him. And now he expects me to relate to my wife in like manner as Jesus Christ treated me."[15]

On this basis, both spouses are to behave charitably towards one another while espousing the roles which have been assigned to them. In order to lead both man and wife to such an avowal, Calvin starts by depicting in very realistic words the husband and wife who scoff at God's commands. His language is delightfully colorful here. In this passage, the young bride decides that she is not about to obey her husband:

> Ho, voilà, je tiendray bon: et si mon mari veut faire du terrible, je luy monstreray que je ne m'en soucie pas: et puis quand j'auray continué quelques jours et qu'il verra qu'il perd son temps, il faudra qu'il quitte le jeu et qu'il me laisse faire.[16]

The wife calculates that she will outfox her husband and wear him down. Meanwhile, his monologue which follows hers reads; "Ho, qu'on m'en laisse faire; j'en viendrai bien à bout," reflecting a rather similar attitude to his wife's! Calvin explains that these attitudes in both man and woman despoil God of his due and that is why "Saint Paul applies the similarity of Jesus Christ, as much to one side as to the other."[17]

As the sermon unfolds, Calvin uses more monologues to indicate explicitly the progression which should take place in the spouses' behavior from rebellion and self-centeredness to submission and concern for each other.

The parallel is further evident in the duty of each spouse to serve God in being considerate of the other. And the sermon ends on a sublime note: "Now on the one hand, husbands must recognize here what they owe their wives, that is to say that they must be as precious to them at least as their own lives."[18] And the wives, "on the other hand must recognize, since God wanted marriage to be as a figure of the grace of our Lord Jesus Christ, that they not be too unappreciative, rather that they settle down where God calls them."[19]

Though adjectives such as "true" (10 times), "certain" (9 times) and "subject" (12 times) appear more frequently than "mutual" (3 times), the whole structure of the sermon emphasizes mutual responsibilities in marriage. In his commentary on this passage, Calvin sums up his carefully wrought views of

[15]Jean Calvin, Sermons Eph. 5:22–26, CO 51, 743.

[16]Jean Calvin, Sermons Eph. 5:22–26, CO 51, 741. "Oh, here, I will hold fast: and if my husband wants to be a terror, I will show him that I don't care: and then when I will have carried on for a few days and he will see that he is wasting his time, he will have to stop this game and will let me do as I wish."

[17]Jean Calvin, Sermons Eph. 5:22–26, CO 51, 741.

[18]Jean Calvin, Sermons Eph. 5:22–26, CO 51, 745.

[19]Jean Calvin, Sermons Eph. 5:22–26, CO 51, 746.

marriage; "And, to be sure, where charity reigns, there is mutual servitude."[20]

Because Calvin was a careful and balanced student of Scripture, he tempered his sexist views with a biblical view of reciprocity of commitment in marriage.

*   *   *

The main interest in studying these portions of selected sermons and the sermon on Eph. 5:22–26 lies in the fact that Calvin is eager to teach his parishioners a *modus vivendi*. In so doing he reveals more clearly his biases, his humanity, and his doctrinal views. It is through the rich texture of his French style that he invigorates and illustrates the exposition of the *Commentaries* on the same biblical passages. In this way, we can witness to Calvin's mastery of style to achieve the purpose of his preaching.

[20]Calvin, Epîtres aux Galates, Ephésiens Philippiens et Colossienes *Commentaires de Jean Calvin sur le Nouveau Testament 6* (Genève: Labor et Fides, 1965), pp. 222–23.

II

Influence

The Changing Face of French Protestantism: The Influence of Pierre Du Moulin*

Brian G. Armstrong

The earliest, shaping influences on French Protestantism came from its origin and reception in humanist circles, among the educated members of the bourgeois class, and by the hostile environment in which it developed. In this environment its adherents quickly sought the protection of the nobility, and so quite soon fell under the control of, and began to identify with, the privileged classes. By the early seventeenth century the upper class mentality had begun to dominate in French Protestantism, even among its pastors. In the first decade of the seventeenth century Pierre du Moulin (1568-1658) became its leading pastor and spokesman. A courtier as well as theologian/polemicist, Du Moulin's influence was decisive in solidifying the dominance of the privileged-class orientation of the movement, in establishing the scholastic theology which brought to it greater intellectual respectability, and even in pitching it toward Episcopacy which seemed more consonant with the absolutist mind-sent of the period. The result was a church which looked more and more like the Catholic Church against which it had originally formulated its teachings and structure.

FROM ITS ORIGINS UNTIL 1598 THE PROTESTANT CHURCH IN FRANCE was a "suffering" church. Persecutions and martyrdoms were the ordinary experience. Steps were taken to secure the safety of the congregations, especially by seeking the protection of the nobility which was estranged from the royal favor, but the fact remained that at any moment life, property, and privilege were in jeopardy. The nature and expression of the church was shaped by this hostile environment, whether considering its social alignment and expression, its political and theological positions, or the critical problem of division which plagued the church until its eventual expulsion from France.

I will not enter into the debate, renewed by Henry Heller's recent study,[1] over the alleged leading role of the artisan, and the estrangement of artisan and notable, in the early years of French Protestantism. What seems to be a consensus among scholars is that the hostile setting prevented any significant, long-term development of a populist-controlled Protestant church in France.[2]

---

[1] The *Conquest of Poverty: The Calvinist Revolt in Sixteenth Century France.* vol. 35 of *Studies in Medieval and Reformation Thought,* ed. Heiko A. Oberman, et al. (Leiden: Brill, 1986). Via a detailed analysis of the origins of the Protestant movement in seven key towns of France, Heller redocuments the thesis of H. Hauser that the origins and strength of the French reformation are to be found among the artisan class.

[2] Cf., for example, the thorough account by Robert M. Kingdon dealing with the quick demise of the "democratic" or "congregationalist" program of Jean Morely. Kingdon, *Geneva and the Consolidation of the French Protestant Movement, 1564-1572: A Contribution to the History of Congregationalism, Presbyterianism, and Calvinist Resistance Theory.* (Madison: University of Wisconsin Press; and Geneva: Droz, 1967).

As early as 1559, it has been estimated, 50 percent of the nobility had embraced Protestantism,[3] creating what H. Hauser has called "seigneurial, manorial" Protestantism.[4] But long before 1559, indeed from the very first, the leading figures of the movement sought identification with, and refuge at, the courts of the nobility (including that of the king's sister, Margaret of Angouleme), or in neighboring Protestant states. More importantly, almost without exception the leading ministers and publicists were from the privileged classes.[5] Additionally, the establishment of the synodal system assured the control of the notables. In the first place, the people naturally looked to the privileged classes for leadership; secondly, only the latter were able easily to find, and to afford, the means and the time required for travel to, and the lengthy meetings of, a national synod.

The role of the nobility of the sword increased during the Wars of Religion. In wartime the great nobles naturally assumed almost total control of the movement, for their traditional right to bear and wield the sword still held the day, in spite of the change in warfare.[6] The very conservative position taken by Calvin and his disciples prior to the Saint Bartholomew's Day massacre of 1572 regarding resistance also played its part, for if resistance were to be countenanced at all it must be under the aegis of the nobility, the so-called "lesser magistrates." As well, the powerful, nascent spirit of absolutism contributed its part to noble control, for the overweening, sometimes disgusting, deference paid to the nobles by the majority of the Protestants, as well as the Catholics, signalled an almost total obeisance to the nobility.[7] In this context, it is not surprising that the great noble, Philippe de Mornay, Sieur du Plessis-Marly, came to be known as the "pope of the Huguenots," assuming, along with the mantle of a major theological authority, even the religious sobriquet heretofore applied only to clerics.[8]

---

[3]Prestwich, *International Calvinism*, 73, citing Chaunu.

[4]H. Hauser, *La Prépondérance Espagnole (1559-1660)*, 2d ed., vol. 9 of *Peuples et Civilisations, Histoire Generale*, ed. L. Halphen & Ph. Sagnac, (Paris: Presses Universitaires de France, 1940), 46.

[5]See, inter alia, Michael Walzer. *The Revolution of the Saints: A Study in the Origins of Radical Politics*. (New York: Atheneum, 1968), 68 ff., and M. Prestwich, "Calvinism in France," 78 ff.

[6]See, inter alia, F. J. Baumgartner, "The Final Demise of the Medieval Knight in France," *Regnum, Religio et Ratio: Essays presented to Robert M. Kingdon*, vol. 8 of *Sixteenth Century Essays and Studies* (Kirksville, Mo.: Sixteenth Century Journal Publishers, 1987) 9–17.

[7]For an excellent presentation of the general situation including even the Protestant nobililty's part in the seige of La Rochelle in 1572-73, see Mack P. Holt, *The Duke of Anjou and the Politique Struggle during the Wars of Religion*. (Cambridge: Cambridge University Press, 1986). Cf. also P. Benedict, *Rouen during the Wars of Religion*. (Cambridge: Cambridge University Press, 1981), and J. H. M. Salmon, *Society in Crisis: France in the Sixteenth Century*. (New York: St. Martins Press, 1975).

[8]On de Mornay, see esp. Raoul Patry. *Philippe du Plessis-Mornay, un huguenot homme d'Etat*. (Paris: 1933).

In the political realm, the resistance literature which followed the massacres of 1572, although virulent, did not usually call for popular uprisings. Indeed, it served primarily to provide support for the campaign of Henry of Navarre to take his place as the heir-presumptive to the throne, and with the deaths of Alençon in 1584, and of Henry III in 1589, to take the throne itself. With Navarre's eventual assumption of the throne (1594), the Protestant resistance literature abruptly ceased, and after the promulgation of the Edict of Nantes in 1598 the main Huguenot publicists became firmly and consistently royalist. The result was a strengthening of the traditional order, including the powers and privileges of the notables.[9]

On the theological front, prior to 1598 the doctrinal position of the Huguenot church of France underwent no significant change from the so-called confession of La Rochelle. (Most likely authored in the main by Calvin, the confession was adopted in all its essentials at the first national synod, held in Paris in 1559.) The purpose and method of Huguenot theological treatises undergo some change as the slow evolution into scholasticism occurs, but the essentials of the faith remain the same, even with regard to the idea of resistance.

John Calvin and Theodore de Bèze are the best known, and often most influential, of the Huguenot theological publicists, writing from their port of refuge in Geneva. Their contributions have been thoroughly studied.[10] However, a closer look at the situation in France would, I believe, show the pervasive influence of Antoine de la Roche Chandieu, probably the premier French Huguenot minister during the latter half of the sixteenth century, but Chandieu's contribution has yet to be investigated thoroughly.[11] Accepting that Calvin, de Bèze, and Chandieu are the principal theological spokesmen of the Huguenots, what is common to these men is their aversion to any leading role by the lower classes, or even the artisans, and their nearly complete

[9]Cf. Myriam Yardeni, "French Calvinist Political Thought, 1534-1715," in M. Prestwich, ed., *International Calvinism*, 313–37, a convenient, informed overview, and E. Labrousse's fascinating "La doctrine politique des Huguenots: 1630-1685," *Etudes théologiques et religieuses*, 47 (1972): 421–29.

[10]Calvin's relation to the French church is dealt with in many works, but probably most thoroughly in two books by Robert Kingdon, *Geneva and the Coming of the Wars of Religion in France, 1533-1563*, (Geneva: Droz, 1956); and, *Geneva and the Consolidation*, cited above in n 2. Paul F. Geisendorf's biography, *Theodore de Bèze* (Geneva & Paris: 1949) is still the best overall on de Beze's relations with France. A major study on Beza on this topic is needed, especially in the light of the publication of the *Correspondance de Theodore de Bèze*. Aubert, Dufour, Meylan, et al., eds., (Geneva: Droz, 1960 ff).

[11]On Chandieu, see the biographical note in the *Bulletin de la Société de l'Histoire du Protestantisme Franßais* 2 (1853):385–86 (hereafter cited *BSHPF*); and Chandieu's autobiographical journal published by A. Bernus in *BSHPF* 37 (1888): 2–13, 57–69, 124–36, 169–91, 393–15, 449–62, 561–77, 617–35. (This document was also published separately at Paris, 1889.) Chandieu used many pseudonyms, the most common of which were Gamaliel and Sadeel (or Zadeel).

identification with the established order.[12] It is true, of course, that their emphasis on education does elevate the role of the schoolmaster, but the larger share of the schoolmasters was also from the privileged classes.

In short, the French Huguenot church, though having a strong appeal to the dispossessed and to the middle classes, was firmly in control of the nobility when Henry IV issued the Edict of Nantes in 1598. The Edict made of the French Huguenot church an official "established church," with all the attendant privileges. The extent of the changes the edict brought to the thinking and practice of the French Huguenots has yet, I believe, to be appreciated fully. Most of the anti-establishment program of the Huguenots, whether in the social, political, or theological realm, underwent a complete metamorphosis. And, the radical change in the nature of the movement signalled by the elevation to the status of "established church" created major problems for the Huguenot nobility, the one group least able to accommodate the metamorphosis.

The nobles were characterized by a fierce independence which had originally estranged them from the crown and led most of them to ally with the Huguenot cause. They now lost some of the authority and control which their privileged status had secured for them during the years of crisis. The clergy became a privileged class in its own right and was not dependent on the nobility for its "liberties." The very absolutism which had driven the nobility to ally with the estranged Huguenot movement was now strongly adopted by the ministers. Hence the strong "republicanism," if you will, of the nobility became an unacceptable element to the religious leaders. Furthermore, serious division would surface within the ranks of the nobility, for the only strong thread which had held them together was their common military cause against the crown—and against the leaders and proponents of the Roman Catholic church, the chief support of the crown in France.

II

Coterminus with the promulgation of the Edict of Nantes in 1598 was the acceptance by Pierre du Moulin of the call to become pastor of the Huguenot church of Paris.[13] Du Moulin was to dominate French Protestantism for the

---

[12]Both de Bèze and Chandieu were from noble families, while Calvin evidently inclined toward the aristocracy. For Calvin's reliance on royal and noble courts, see Prestwich, "Calvinism in France," 78 ff.

[13]When du Moulin arrived the Paris Huguenot church was meeting at Ablon, about ten miles outside the city walls. Through du Moulin's intercession the place of meeting was changed to ever-closer proximity to the city, finally being established at Charenton-St. Maurice, about one mile from the city. A great temple was constructed ar Charenton. It was burned by a Catholic mob in 1621, was rebuilt, and remained until it was razed in 1685 after the Revocation of the Edict of Nantes.

next sixty years like no individual before or since. Nearly all of the characteristic features of the Huguenot movement in the first half of the seventeenth century bear the impress of du Moulin's influence, whether social, political, or theological. We turn to a brief consideration of this remarkable man and some aspects of his pervasive and decisive influence on French Calvinism.

"As for our Monsieur du Moulin," the firmly Protestant son of the famed Francis Hotman wrote, "he is imprudent, impudent, and an ingrate, all in one."[14] Du Moulin's Catholic opponents styled him the "Reformed Rabelais," a sobriquet designed to categorize him as impious, while at the same time begrudgingly recognizing his great literary skill.[15] On the other hand, the modern biographer of du Moulin, Lucien Rimbault, styles him as "a classical pastor in a classical age."[16] What these testimonies all indicate is that no one, whether his contemporary or a modern scholar, finds it easy to be neutral when it comes to the bombastic du Moulin. But whatever the reaction to him, for the seventeenth-century French Huguenot he was a larger-than-life hero, the David who slew the Catholic Goliath.

Du Moulin was born in a chateau in Normandy in 1568. He was proud to record that it was in the same room in which Philippe du Plessis-Marly de Mornay had been born some twenty years before. Like de Mornay, du Moulin came from an old family of the nobility of the sword, related to the royal families of both France and England. Much of his character can be understood only in the light of his noble heritage. His father, Joachim, had forfeited much of his patrimony by adopting the Huguenot faith, and served as an ordained minister of the Huguenot church for some fifty difficult years. Hence young Pierre was brought up in the Calvinist tradition. He was educated in the Protestant state of Sedan and at the University of Cambridge in England. Arriving in the Low Countries in 1592, he taught philosophy and Greek in Leiden until he resigned his post in 1598 to take up the post as Pastor of the Paris Church. He served the Church at Paris until he was expelled from France in 1621 by King Louis XIII, on the pretense that he had involved himself in international politics. From 1621 until his death in 1658, du Moulin served as Pastor at Sedan, and Professor of Theology in the Protestant Academy in that place.

---

[14]Letter of 8 September 1612 from Hotman in Dusseldorf to Casaubon in London. Burney Ms. 367, fol. 23r., in the British Library, London. The original reads: "Quand a nost(re) M(onsieu)r du M(oulin) Il est Imprudent, Impudent, et Ingrat tout ensemble." Hotman was one of James I of England's ambassadors to the German states, and was clearly aligned with the humanist learning represented by Joseph Scaliger and Casaubon. Like Casaubon and Scaliger, he detested du Moulin's parade of learning solely for polemical, theological purposes.

[15]See, inter alia, F. Garasse, *Le Rabelais Reformée* (Bruxelles, 1618).

[16]L. Rimbault, *Pierre du Moulin, 1568-1658: Un Pasteur Classique à l'age Classique. Etude de théologie pastorale sur des documents inédits.* (Paris: Librairie Philosophique J. Vrin, 1966.) This is the only major study on du Moulin. In my judgment, Rimbault has failed to capture the essential du Moulin; whatever else he may have been, du Moulin was certainly not the "classical pastor."

It was during the twenty-two plus years at Paris that du Moulin gained his great reputation—as the greatest of the Huguenot polemicists and as the premier spokesman for French Protestantism. His greatest forté was as a champion of debate, both oral and written. The oral debates were held before large audiences in the public forum. He took on the best polemicists the Catholic Church could provide, and it is said that he was never bested. He loved the limelight, and never more than when engaged in the theological dueling which was so much a part of the *mentalité* of the nobility.[17] He possessed an unusually quick and facile mind, a prodigious memory, logical skills which were finely honed from his years of teaching logic, and a marvelous facility for quick repartee, sometimes scatalogical, when his opponent seemed to be winning the support of the audience. His great charisma and wit never failed him in these conferences.

His success in oral debate was equalled or exceeded by his literary skill and pungent polemical style.[18] His style is direct, terse, and unencumbered. One never encounters long, complicated sentences or phrases. And above all, it is witty and entertaining, drawn in the language of the common man. He delights to parody his opponents' arguments, revealing and playing upon logical absurdities and nonsequiturs.[19] He was not only a clever, witty and savage polemicist, but an incredibly prolific one as well. He produced nearly one hundred polemic treatises, (plus about 150 theses of polemical nature sustained under his direction). Their popularity is evidenced by more than 350 editions during his lifetime, with translations into English, Dutch, Italian, Romansch, German, and into Latin and French when written in another language. He was not a great scholar, but he was learned enough to hold his own in scholarly debate, and especially to use the façade of scholarship in the service of his "popularizing," at which he was a master.

[17]It is important to keep in mind that oral debate and the polemical treatise of the seventeenth century are the learned equivalent of the medieval duel, partaking of the same chivalric code according to which honor requires that any challenge be answered.

[18]In a letter to du Moulin dated 19 December 1611, speaking of du Moulin's *Defense de la Foy Catholique*, James I of England makes the following observation: "La verité seullement nous contraindra d'advouer ce seul point, que selon le peu de capacité que Dieu nous a donne, nous trouvons v(ost)re stile sy a propos, nerveux, & aigu, qu'a n(ost)re advis il est en cela Inimitable." Original in the Bibliotheque Nationale, Paris, Collection Dupuy 571, fols. 60r-63v; copy in the British Library, London. Additional Ms 24195, fols. 71r-76r. The quotation is taken from the original, fol. 60r.

In my judgment, du Moulin's literary skill is his greatest strength.

[19]For example, when dealing with the Roman church's doctrine of transubstantiation in his *Anatomy of the Mass*, chapter 19, one finds the following: "Accidents without a subject, said to be in the consecrated host, is another heap of absurdities, and ridiculous contradictions. For what greater incongruity is there than this, namely, that Accidentia non accidunt; as if one should say Albentia non albent,—that persons speaking are not speaking; . . . that there is color and nothing colored; that there is length and nothing long; that there is roundness and nothing round; which is as if one should pretend a sight without an eye; a sickness when there is no one sick; lameness but no leg; an eclipse of the moon when there is no moon."

Before turning to a consideration of his legacy to the Huguenot cause, it is only fair to remind the reader that the portrait drawn in the following pages is only a very small part of the story of Pierre du Moulin and his influence. He was a deeply spiritual man, producing many popular devotional treatises. There are more than eighty editions, for example, of a treatise dealing with one's preparation for the sacrament of the Lord's Supper, He was also an accomplished linguist in the Humanist mold, publishing treatises in Greek. He was addicted to the Humanist pastime of writing poetry, leaving among his papers many poems in Greek and Latin. He was interested in church union and was the principal figure in an attempt to unite all Protestant churches under the leadership of King James of England. He authored, and sent to James, the document on which the "Protestant union," which had been formed on the political level for defensive purposes, could be effectuated on the ecclesiastical level. He even sent this document to the Synod of Dordrecht requesting that it be given serious consideration—at the same time that he sent them his book designed to assist in the condemnation of the Arminians! In short, du Moulin was a very talented and complex man. His impact on French Protestantism goes far beyond that discussed below.

III

Du Moulin's particular legacy to French Protestantism owes in large part to his upper-class *mentalité* and lifestyle. Wherever he went, he gravitated toward those who held the high positions of state. At Leiden he ingratiated himself to the Dousa family[20] and, as his son tells us, became an intimate friend of de Buzanval, the French ambassador to the Low Countries.[21] At Paris du Moulin served as personal pastor of the sister of the king, and further positioned himself close to King Henry IV by securing the titles of "Conseiller du Roy" and "Maistre des Requestes de son hostel, maison et Couronne de Navarre."[22] He also positioned himself close to the English, Dutch, and German ambassadors to the court at Paris, becoming especially close friends with

[20]Some of his correspondence with the Dousas is preserved in the British Library, Burney Ms. 371, fols. 14 ff. Du Moulin owed his appointment as Professor of Philosophy at Leiden to the support of the a Dousa family.

[21]See the biography of his son, Pierre, which forms the preface of *The Novelty of Popery, Opposed to the Antiquity of True Christianity*. . . . (London, 1662). The son records: "That Ambassador was ever since his most real and intimate friend." sig. [** 4v].

[22]This information is taken from an unpublished letter of Pierre Bayle to his brother Jacob, dated 26 November 1678. I am grateful to Mme. Elisabeth Labrousse for supplying me with a copy of this letter.

Thomas Edmondes from England and Francis Aerssens from the Low Countries.[23]

After the assassination of Henry IV in 1610, du Moulin found himself isolated from the King's council in France and so turned to ingratiate himself to James I of England. He requested and received permission from James to write a defense of the confession, related to the oath James required of Catholics in England, against the attacks of Bellarmine and F. Coeffeteau. His response was issued in three parts.[24] Not only did he secure thereby James's close, lifelong friendship, but also gained for himself handsome payment.[25] During his years at Sedan du Moulin was intimate with the Duke of Bouillon who administered the principality. Though he failed in his attempts to win the favor of Charles I of England, he did maintain close ties with the Princes of Orange in the Low Countries, the latter partly through the offices of his brother-in-law, Andrew Rivet, who was preceptor and chaplain to the Prince.

It was from the advantage of high position, therefore, that du Moulin was able to exert his decisive influence on French Protestantism. And, it is important to note, the position of authority which he held was, at least in part, secured by deliberate intention. For example, although they were more honorary than real, his offices of "Conseiller du Roy" and of "Maistre des requestes de l'hostel du Roy" had to have been purchased. His role as an unofficial advisor to James I of England was secured through his constant requests to be of service in some cause.[26] He also, as we shall see, invested his ministerial office with as much authority as possible, even to the point that parlementary action was taken against him for the use of the title "Pastor of Paris," since such use greatly infuriated the Bishop of Paris and the Roman Catholic clergy in general.

[23]His extensive correspondence with Edmondes can be found in the Edmondes papers in the British Library, and in the State Papers, Foreign (France) in the Public Record Office, London, (PRO), plus a few letters in the National Library of Scotland in Edinburgh. Some of his correspondence with Aerssens is included in the State Papers, Foreign (Dutch), PRO, London, and a few letters to Aerssens have been published.

It is perhaps worth noting that du Moulin did not establish a close relationship with lord Herbert of Cherbury, who succeeded Edmondes as the English ambassador to Paris. The so-called "founder" of the Deist movement was not enamored of du Moulin, and it is probably not accidental that du Moulin's exposure as involved in international politics (via a letter to James I), and subsequent expulsion from France, came during Herbert's embassage.

[24]*Defense de la Foy Catholique Contenue au Livre de trespusissant & Serenissime Iaques I. Roy de la gra(n)d Bretagne & d'Irland, Defenseur de la Foy. . . .* (n.p., 1610, and Geneva, 1610), in 2 parts; and *Accomplissement des Propheties. Livre auquel sont exposees les Propheties de l'Escriture Saincte, concernantes le Pontife Romain & son seige* (La Rochelle, 1612, and Geneva, 1612.)

[25]See du Moulin's letter to the grand treasurer Salisbury of 10 October 1610 in which he expresses his thanks for the "deux cents livres qu'il a pleu au Roy me donner par les mains de Monsieur Edmond son Ambassadeur ordinaire. . . ." PRO, SP 78/56/303. The payment was for the first volume. Other payment was forthcoming, as will be described later.

[26]See, for example, the letter of William Becher, a member of James's ambassadorial staff in Paris, of 12 December 1609 (o.s.) to the count of Salisbury: "I sent your L(ordshi)p . . . one of Coeffeteau's bookes in answere to his M(ajes)ties, since when, one Mons(ieu)r du Moulin, a minister of this Chruch, did tell me that he had a great desire to reply vnto it, wherein I did encourage him, . . . " PRO, SP 78/55/13v.

Du Moulin was, then, authoritarian through and through, by nature, by birth, and by the positions he held. He was always dogmatic and bold, never doubting but that he possessed the very truth of God. His participation in the *mentalité* of the nobility, in which one's honor demanded a response to every challenge, coupled with his identification with the truth and cause of God, meant that he was constantly embroiled in some dispute, whether with a colleague or with a Roman Catholic.[27] He was duty-bound to defend both his own honor and the honor of God–and one doubts that he really separated the two! Any deviation from his understanding of God's truth, in any area, would precipitate a fiery response from du Moulin. He was clever in using any means, including threats to leave France if he did not get his way, in his frenzy to vindicate "the Truth."[28] Much of his surviving correspondence testifies to the constant counsel of his friends to moderate his methods and language.

It was through this authoritarianism that du Moulin impacted French Protestantism so strongly. The following material will document his impact in only two areas, the French Protestant view of the ministry, and the development of scholasticism in French Protestant theology.

IV

At the heart of the teaching on the ministry formulated by Calvin, following Luther, was the idea of the universal priesthood of all believers. While a theological idea, based on the idea that all are "ministers" (servants) of the Word, its great distinctive was its social dimension. Every believer is part of, and responsible to function in, a new social order, the community of

[27]He held public disputes, e.g., with the Roman Catholics Cayer, Bouju, du Perron, Coeffeteau, Cotton, Arnoux, Veron, and de Raconis, during his Paris days. He entered into nasty polemic with the Protestants Piscator, Tilenus, Arminius and followers, Cameron, Amyraut, and followers, and the Independents of England. An example of his precipitous actions relates to the Arminian affair. In 1617-18 he wrote his *Anatome Arminianismi* (Leyden, 1619; many editions thereafter) for the deliberations which were to take place at the Synod of Dordrecht. He dedicated it to the Estates of Holland, congratulating them on their condemnation of the Arminians as subversive heretics–even before the convocation of the Synod! (The Estates rewarded du Moulin with a gift of 200 gulden, plus the golden pfennig of the Synod.)

[28]See, for example, his letter to the national synod of Tonneins in 1614. The synod was to consider the bitter contention over the doctrine of justification between du Moulin and Daniel Tilenus, Pastor and Professor of Theology at Sedan. Du Moulin wrote to the synod demanding a judgment in his favor and the suppression of the writings of Tilenus. He concludes the letter by maintaining that Tilenus' behavior "est un acte si pernicieux que ie me promets q(ue) vous userez la dessus de l'authorité q(ue) Dieu vous a donnée, & donnerez un Jugement remarquable à la posterité, & ferez qu'un livre si injurieux ne soit plus veu. Que si d'autres considera(ti)ons plus importantes vous empeschent d'y pouvoir remedier, & q(ue) le livre ne soit point supprimé, vous ne trouverez pas mauvais, M(essieu)rs, si je me retire en lieu ou i'aye La Liberte de me defendre, et si i'accepte l'honneur et le repose qui m'est offert ailleurs plustost q(ue) vivre in lieu ou estant consumé de trauvail, cependant mon Ministere est deshonoré. . . ." Copy of letter from du Moulin, Paris, to the national synod of Tonneins, undated, (but certainly from the month of April, 1614). National Library of Scotland, Edinburgh, Ms. Wodrow XXII, fols 144r-148r.

the saints. The community, that good order may be observed, was responsible to select one to fill the office of minister (pastor)[29] whose primary function was the proclamation of the Word of God and the proper administration of the sacraments. The minister was thus, indeed, separated out for a special function, but only for an orderly functioning of the body of believers in worship. The minister had to show evidence of both an inner call and aptitude for the ministry, and was, further, always subject to dismissal by the community should he fail to adhere faithfully to the dictates of the Word of God. The hierarchical view of the priesthood found in the Roman Church was thereby denied, and along with it the formalized distinction between clergy and laity.[30]

The Confession of the French Reformed Church reflected these principles, emphasizing, in Article 30, that "all true pastors, wherever they may be, have the same authority and equal power under one head, one only sovereign and universal bishop, Jesus Christ; . . . " On the other hand, in Article 31, the Confession went on, following Calvin,[31] to specify the possibility of an "extraordinary call," which did not require the election process of the community, nor perhaps any special ordination ceremony, thus opening the possibility of a usurpation of the office. And, indeed, the category of the "extraordinary call" became the focus of heavy attack by the Roman Catholic polemicists in the latter sixteenth century. Using to excellent advantage both the horror of the sectarian Protestant excesses in the ministerial arena, and the search for order which characterized the age, the Romanists accused the Huguenots of harboring in their bosom a monster which would permit any wild-eyed soul entrance into the ministry.

In the face of the seeming advantage delivered to the Romanists by the "extraordinary clause," du Moulin's uneasiness with the system of presbyterial church government came to the fore. His predilection for a more authoritarian system is seen in several events:

a) In the first place, he felt the need for a change in the wording of the Confession on the point of church government. In 1603 he recommended to the national synod of Gap some modification of the language of the Confession. His suggestion was not followed however;

b) More specifically, there is evidence showing that du Moulin actually preferred the Episcopal system to the Reformed. In the letter quoted above from Hotman to Casaubon, Hotman indicates that he had heard du Moulin express his preference for the episcopal system, as well as his belief that the

---

[29]The term "pastor" is preferred by the French Protestant church, emphasizing the shepherding function, but for the sake of convenience I will use the term "Minister."

[30]It is debatable whether the radical, social dimension of the ministry implied here was, in fact, really practiced in any of the Protestant churches, but the principle was consistently affirmed.

[31]*Institutes*, IV.iii.4.

Church of England best preserved the teaching and ceremonies of the ancient church.[32]

c)Du Moulin's comportment on several occasions suggests that he thought of himself more as a bishop than as a Reformed minister of equal standing and authority. This is borne out by the way in which be behaved when elected as moderator of the national synod of Alais in 1620. The longest national synod held in France, its length was occasioned at least in part by resistance to du Moulin's attempts to impose his will on his fellow pastors and the elders meeting there. Even the vice moderator of the synod, Brunier, accused him of usurping over the synod a "papal authority."[33]

d) And, finally, there is the firm evidence that, incredible as it may seem, du Moulin actually requested, during his stay in England in 1624-25, that he be named the bishop of Gloucester.[34]

Beyond his audacious request to be elevated to an English bishopric, perhaps the most surprising aspect of du Moulin's career was his reversal of the general Protestant tradition against pluralism. His writings in defense of King James of England had ingratiated him to that monarch. In February of 1615 James invited him to England, where du Moulin spent three months. He was created Doctor of Divinity at Cambridge, and also made a prebend of Canterbury, which paid him one thousand francs per annum. He was quickly criti-

---

[32]" . . . luy ay ouy dire autre fois qu'il eust souhaitte' en france la mesme forme de gouvernment ecclesiastique qui est en Ang(leter)re, et lors, s'est passay plus outre, Que soit en la doctrine ou en Ceremonies nulle eglise aujourdhuy, telle qu'elle soit, approche d'auantage de celle des quatre premieres siecles." Hotman, Dusseldorf, to Casaubon, London, 9 August 1612: British Library, London (BL), Burney Ms. 367, fol 23r.

[33]O. Douen, *La Révocation de l'édit de Nantes à Paris*, (Paris, 1894), I. 175.

[34]See the two letters of du Moulin to this effect, one to King James I, the other to James's first secretary, Conway, dated 23 October 1624. PRO, the former SP 78/62/129r, the latter SP 78/73/254r. The letter to James I reads:

> Sire
> Mon devoir estoit de me transporter moy mesme vers V(ostre) M(ajeste) plustost que de luy escrire si mon indisposition n'eust permis de me mettre aux champs. Vostre Royale grandeur aura agreable que ces lettres suppleent a ce defaut desquelles seruiront a supplier V(ostre) M(ajeste) que puis qu'il a pleu a Dieu appeller de ce monde Monsieur l'Evesque de Gloster, & que par !a, commodité se presente de pourvoir a mon establissem(ent) il luy plaise commander a Monseigneur le garde des Seaux de me pourvoir suivant l'ordre qu'il a pleu a V(ostre) M(ajeste) luy prescrire Par ce moyen elle sera delivree de mon importunité & ie seray de plus en plus obligé a prier Dieu pour la prosperité & conserua(ti)on de V(ostre) M(ajeste) de laquelle ie suis
> Sire
>> Treshumble & tresobeissant serviteur
>> Du Moulin

142   *Calviniana*

cized by his Roman Catholic opponents for allying with a foreign nation, and for practicing what the Protestants had so severely censured in Roman Catholicism. In a letter to King James after his return to France, du Moulin reports the criticism, and glibly remarks: "But I shut them up, saying that I would surrender this prebend when the Italians would surrender the benefices which they have in France."[35]

When he fled from Paris to Sedan in 1621 du Moulin demanded and received a double salary—500 livres per annum for his work as pastor, 1,000 livres per annum for his position as Professor of Theology in the Academy.[36] For three years, at least—perhaps throughout his life—he continued to receive his salary as pastor of the church at Charenton/Paris. In addition to the salary from the prebend at Canterbury. By August of 1624, he was also receiving a living from Llan Rayader in Wales.[37] By November of 1624, he had been awarded an additional living of 200 livres per annum, although he didn't even know the source of the income![38] Three weeks later he was nominated for the deanery of Rippon, but it is not clear whether he ever received any stipend therefrom.[39]

Thus, du Moulin was receiving at least five different livings in 1624 and perhaps as many as seven. This is probably the most remarkable example of pluralism among the French Protestant clergy. It amply testifies to the need to

[35]Letter, from Paris, to King James, dated 17 August 1615. PRO. SP 78/63/268r-269r. Passage quoted from fol. 269r. Du Moulin went on to say in the letter "Dieu veille continuer la paix a nos pouvres Eglises, mais s'il advenoit autrement, je me suis destine ce lieu la pour retraitte, afin d'y estudier sans trouble, & y achever mes jours. . . ."

[36]Throughout his life du Moulin would continue to receive the double salary, making his salary at least one-third more than his colleagues with similar appointments. See the account records for Sedan in *BSHPF* 54, (Year?): 108–17, showing du Moulin received 1500 livres per annum, Rambours (holding similar positions) 500.

[37]Letter of du Moulin to King James, undated, (but obviously from July or August since it was answered by Secretary Conway on 2 September: see PRO SP 14/214/77r) in the British Library, Additional Ms. 19402, fol. 150r. In the letter du Moulin, thinking he was ill unto death, asked that his livings in England would devolve unto his children: "J'ay donc a vous supplier, SIRE, treshumblement que deux de mes fils dont l'vn est pres d'estre receu au sainct Ministere & l'autre estudie en Theologie, ayent la survivance des deux beanefices que V. M. de sa grace m'a fait auoir, dont l'un est une prebende a Cantorberie, l'autre est le Donatif de Llan Rayader au pays de Galles, que i'ay par la cession de Monseigneur le Garde des Seaux."

[38]In a somewhat brusque letter to Secretary Conway, dated 8 November 1624 (two weeks after he had requested the Bishopric of Gloucester), du Moulin writes: "I'eusse bien desiré qu'en vos lettres eust esté exprimé le nom du Donatif & l'Evesché ou il est situé. Item le nom de la personne a laquelle je me doibs addresser pour auoir les deux cens livres." PRO, SP 14/174/37r.

[39]Letter of John Packer, Westminster, to secretary Conway, dated 27 November 1624. PRO, SP 14/175/86r. On 20 November du Moulin had signed the following receipt: " . . . I Peter Moulin doctor of Divinity Receaved from Richard Oliver, servant to my Lord Duke of Buckingham by appoyntment from his grace, the some of two hundreth pounds of currant & lawful English money given unto me of free guift by his Ma(jes)tye of w(hi)ch some I hold my selfe well and fully satisfied. Witness this my hand and seal." PRO SP 14/175/21r. The reason for this enormous gift is not given. It would surpass the amount of both his salaries at Sedan, being equivalent to at least 2,000 livres, probably considerably more.

recognize that the "benefits of clergy" and other clerical excesses against which the early Reformers had inveighed were, in the early 1600s, practiced by French Protestants. Many examples in France and elsewhere can be added to underline the fact that the Protestant clergy of the seventeenth century behaved the part, and took advantage of the prerogatives, of a privileged class. The mythology about the abolition of the distinction between clergy and laity in Protestantism, which permeates much of the literature, needs, at least as a general interpretation, to be abandoned.[40]

It is clear, then, that du Moulin was not in accord—in theory or in practice—with the French Reformed doctrine on the matter of the ministry, and it is to be wondered why he would undertake to defend it, as he did in 1618 when he published his *De la Vocation des Pasteurs*.[41] However, our query is answered in the preface, where he tells us why he took up his pen on this issue. First, he had been asked by many of the pastors of France to "defend the honor of the sacred ministry." Never one to back away from his chivalric duty to fight when his honor was in question, and never one to pass up an opportunity to propel himself into the limelight of a celebrated polemical confrontation, he responded by launching an attack on the Catholic position and a defense of the Huguenots "to repair the breaches in the church." So he will "defend the honor of the ministry . . . show the validity of our calling, and the nullity and corruption of theirs."

Never content nor comfortable with the defensive position, du Moulin developed his argument in such a way that he first attacks the validity of the Roman Catholic ministerial office. In five pages he completely dismisses the Catholic ministerial office as an invalid, manmade invention which overturns the Christian faith. There are, he says, three matters at issue: 1) Is the office of the pastors of the church divinely ordained and therefore valid? 2) Is the process of ordination valid? 3) Is the commission and succession from the Apostles?

Only the first of these, he argues, is of crucial importance, for the aspects of that question are established by the Word of God. That is, these are matters of doctrine, matters which will affect everyone's salvation. If the ministry in its nature and purpose is not instituted by God, then it is of human origin and therefore of no value whatsoever in the matter of salvation. Now it is the matter of the sacerdotal work of the priest in Roman Catholicism which has no support in scripture, indeed it runs counter to scripture; it follows, then, that the Roman Catholic ministry is corrupt and invalid. On the other hand, since the central aspect of the Reformed ministry, the proclamation of the Word of God, is enjoined by scripture, it follows that the Reformed ministry is good, holy, instituted by God, and therefore valid.

[40]As Professor James McGoldrick has pointed out to me in private correspondence, the Protestants did, however, maintain their strict anti-sacerdotal position.

[41]Published at Sedan in 1618.

Du Moulin turns to the matters of ordination and Apostolic succession. They are not essential matters, he argues, having to do only with form and practice, of "histoire" as he calls it. His position on ordination is that the Reformed practice is reasonable, therefore acceptable. He is careful not to present anything which would deny the Anglican position, arguing against the Roman Catholic position on the basis of the "superstition" which attends it.

On the matter of Apostolic succession, he departs significantly from the ordinary Reformed position. Most Reformed overtly denied the propriety of the idea of a "succession." Du Moulin, on the other hand, while arguing that a succession of chairs is finally impossible to prove due to the unreliability of the evidence, does not deny the idea. Indeed, he labors mightily to prove that the Reformed have a true succession, a doctrinal succession rather than a succession of chairs, to be sure, but surely what the early fathers of the church meant when they discussed the succession. Hence he accommodates to the general idea of a succession. At this point he surely knew he was at variance with the mainstream of his tradition.

The manner in which he "repaired the breaches" is therefore quite surprising for a Huguenot minister of the seventeenth century. It is surely evidence of the extent to which the Huguenot church in France had moved toward episcopacy that it occasioned no hue and cry within their ranks; indeed, on the contrary, it became one of du Moulin's most popular books.[42] Because he was in a very delicate position as an unofficial advisor to James I, as a holder of livings in England, and as a proponent of the union of Protestantism, one can appreciate that he was in a ticklish spot when writing the book. He tried to satisfy both the Anglican and the presbyterial (firmly so, at least as far as their discipline was concerned) Huguenots. In the end he satisfied neither,[43] but the slant toward episcopacy—or at the very least, the accommodation of episcopacy—was strong in the treatise. Robert M. Kingdon and others have questioned in print why the Huguenot refugees generally became Episcopalians. The answer to the question may, in large part, be attributed to the pro-Anglican, as he believed, interpretation of the ministerial call provided by du Moulin.

---

[42]It was extremely popular, even for one of du Moulin's books. I have been able to identify a dozen printings in 1618 alone, and there were probably more. Du Moulin indicates that it was printed twenty times in the first year.

[43]Witness his correspondence with Lancelot Andrewes, Bishop of Winchester, regarding the issues (published in Latin in Andrewes' Works). These letters were translated into English and published under the title : *Of Episcopacy. Three Epistles of Peter Moulin, Doctor and Professor of Divinity. Answered by the Right Reverend Father in God Lancelot Andrews*, (n.p., 1647).

On the Huguenot side, few dared to take issue with du Moulin, but it is almost certain that Moses Amyraut's *Six Livres de la Vocation des Pasteurs* (Saumur, 1649) was an attempt to re-state, and hopefully to restore, the presbyterial/syodal authority. (Du Moulin had argued that the system had disgraced itself, and so lost its viability, by failing to condemn the Amyraut "heresy.")

V

In the theological realm there is a parallel metamorphosis to that detailed in the position taken regarding the ministry and the privileged station of the pastor. The theology of a persecuted minority religion is a very different type from that of an official church, sanctioned by the state. The content of theological expression may remain essentially the same, but the manner of expression changes dramatically. For the members of an established church the interests shift to concerns having to do with respectability, with equal standing, and with the defense of the position already won. In so doing, it was necessary to enter into intellectual debate on the grounds, and using the methods, of the opponent, especially since the opponent had the weight and authority of tradition on his side. Ostensibly, the allegedly Biblical truths for which the Huguenots had fought were now recognized. The primary function then became that of showing that the doctrines, even the rationale, of the faith were reasonable and intellectually respectable.

In the move from affirmation to validation, from the proclamation of a message to its defense, methodology became equally as important as, if not more important than, the message itself. In that process both the nature and the content of the religious teaching gradually underwent change. This, plus other factors, precipitated the full-fledged development of the phenomenon known as scholasticism in French Protestantism.[44] Reason became at least an equal partner with revelation; mystery became more an embarrassment than a profound aspect of one's relationship with an infinite deity; careful, precise

---

[44]The problem of defining Protestant scholasticism remains a major bug bear of late sixteenth and seventeenth century research. We have in recent years made major advances because of the renewed interest in the "epigones" who followed Luther and Calvin. Works by J. Bray on Beza, J. P. Donnely on Vermigli, Olivier Fatio on Danaeus, O. Gruendler on Zancheus, I. McPhee on Beza, J. Platt on the phenomenon in general, J. Raitt on Beza, D. Sinnema on the synod of Dordrecht, and perhaps especially the extensive work of Richard Muller, have all contributed to a better understanding of the problem with respect to Calvinism. Yet, I feel we continue to bring to the problem many erroneous presuppositions. In particular, there is the suspicion that by indicating change from the primary reformers one is making a negative value judgment. This suspicion should be obliterated from our thinking. The historian never has the luxury of such value judgments, but does have the responsibility to show the change. Whether the original was better or worse than the later developments is not our task to determine. Additionally, we seem to assume a monolothic Calvinist theological position when there was none, and we often fail to integrate into our thinking and work the presence of many influences in any one individual. We dare not, it seems to me, argue that because there are humanist elements present in someone like du Moulin therefore he cannot be a scholastic. All kinds of combinations of influences are not only possible, but common. Du Moulin, for instance, surely reveals the strong influence of mysticism, of apocalypticism, of hermeticism, of humanism, of rationalism, and even some influence of the skeptical tradition.

So when it comes to the issue of Protestant scholasticism the question must be, first, Is scholasticism present in a theologian's program? And second, does scholasticism seem to dominate that program? This still leaves the question, of course, of how to define Protestant scholasticism. There seems to be no consensus at this point. I remain generally committed to the "definition" I attempted in *Calvinism and the Amyraut Heresy* (Madison: University of Wisconsin, 1969), 31 ff.

definition and distinction replace an emphasis on only the central teaching in as simple and uncomplicated a manner as possible; and a logical system became an essential, indispensable part of theology.

In France, in the work of men such as Antoine de la Roche Chandieu and Daniel Chamier—to name but two—one or all of these trends can be found now and again prior to the promulgation of the Edict of Nantes, but it was only during the time and career of Pierre du Moulin that they became the normal program, almost the exclusive program, of the theological enterprise.[45]

Du Moulin was admirably suited to the demands of the situation, by training, experience and temperament. We have indicated above that he began his public career as a lecturer in philosophy at Leiden. His first major publication sprang from his lessons at Leiden and was entitled *Elementa logica*.[46] It was nothing but a simplified and popularized Aristotelian logic. The commitment to Aristotelianism which it indicates was commonly an aspect of Protestant scholasticism, (though one could be a scholastic and not be an Aristotelian).

His experience, once he reached Paris in early 1599, was dominated by constant polemic with the Roman Catholic theologians of France. In the pursual of that polemic, indeed in the great glee he took in this polemical activity, he necessarily had to enter into the fray on the grounds already established by the Catholic foe. Most of his opponents were Jesuits, and they were commonly trained, above all, in the scholastic teaching of Suarez. Consequently du Moulin adopted the scholastic type of argumentation—the scholastic method, if you will.

His temperament has to be classified as "type A" in current psychological terms. Something of a manic-depressive,[47] when in the prevalent manic state

[45]It is important, however, to recognize that, even compared with earlier theologians such as Zanchi or Vermigli, du Moulin's scholasticism is quite mitigated. If he is compared with his contemporaries such as Sibrandus Lubbertus, Johannes Maccovius, or Franciscus Gomarus of the Low Countries, his scholasticism is very mild. Nevertheless, there is a very perceptible change in the theological enterprise in France under his influence, a change that can only be described as a scholasticizing one. Perhaps of special significance is the change that can be seen in the positions of du Moulin himself with regard to both content and method. He early declared that the questions which were being posed to Arminius, for example, were inappropriate and foolish. Within ten years he was making these very questions the basis of his own attack on Arminianism. Or, in the bitter struggle with his colleague Amyraut, one can easily show that he condemned in Amyraut theological positions which he had himself espoused only a few short years before. Finally, it should also be recognized that the change which occurred was a natural and inevitable one. We should not naively think that one can continue simply to repeat, in the same terms and according to the same methodology, the program promulgated nearly one hundred years before. It is surely no criticism that du Moulin and colleagues were anxious not to become obscurantists!

[46](Lugduni Batavorum, 1598). This handbook on logic was immensely popular. I have identified at least eighteen editions in Latin, twenty editions in French (it was even published at Paris with the "Privilege du Roy"), and two editions in English.

[47]He suffered long bouts with "melancholia," as he called it. For nearly six months, on one occasion, he refused to come out of his room. His family and friends were accustomed to "cover"

he had to dominate, to be in control. He cleverly used various means to accomplish this control, but normally it was accomplished through his superior logical skills. He had complete trust in his ability to discover truth via logic and reason. Consequently, he was always sure of his position, and equally as sure that anyone who differed from his position was being irrational. There was no gray area for du Moulin; all was clear-cut, either right or wrong, and he was right because he could show the logic of his position.

The logic that he used was based on syllogistic reasoning. This was the one and only true method of determining truth, including theological truth. It was, further, he argued, a natural endowment of all men. " . . . there is a Natural Logic which man naturally uses without working at it. Even the peasants frame syllogisms without thinking about it."[48] He therefore employed the syllogism as the principal weapon in his polemics, and he was aghast that he had to defend the validity of the syllogism when his opponents eventually took refuge in a skeptical/fideist position.[49] He complains that "these new disputants are intolerable in that they reject all syllogisms and all arguments."[50] In a passage revelatory of what I consider a definitive mark of his scholasticism, he ruefully complains: "If we form a demonstrative argument, they mock it, saying that syllogisms are a human discourse, and an invention of Aristotle which ought not to rule our faith."[51] The passage makes it clear that for du Moulin syllogisms did rule the faith, and that he was convinced they should. It is certainly ironic that the Catholics use against du Moulin the very complaint that Luther had used against the medieval scholastics—reliance on that "damned rascal Aristotle" and his syllogisms.

A final example of du Moulin's scholastic orientation is his increasing interest in speculative, metaphysical theology. In his treatise on logic in 1598 he characterized metaphysical questions as those "which resemble crayfish where one may pick a lot but eat very little, and which do not serve any civil or religious function."[52] In a letter of 1619 to Secretary Calvert in England he castigated the speculative interest of some of the reformed theologians, stating that the supralapsarian teachings of de Bèze, Piscator, Gomarus, and Tronchin were the cause of the Arminian problems of the Dutch churches.[53] But after

for him, indicating to the outside world that he was in his study writing, but on this occasion it was hard to sustain that "cover" and there is a letter in the Leiden archives from his nephew, de l'Angle, to his brother-in-law, Andrew Rivet, describing his "catatonic state."

[48]*Elements de la logique* (Geneva, 1625). Preface, signature a ii, recto-verso.

[49]See R. Popkin, "Skepticism and the Counter Reformation in France," *Archiv für Reformationsgeschichte* 51 (1960), 58–86.

[50]*Des Traditions et de la perfection et suffisance de l'Escriture Saincte* (Sedan, 1631), 284.

[51]Ibid., 270.

[52]*Elements de la logique* (Geneva, 1625), Preface, signature a ii, verso.

[53]Du Moulin, Paris, to Calvert, London, dated 23 December 1619. London, PRO, SP 78/68/264r-v. (In the letter du Moulin went on to say that the Synod of Dordrecht and Calvin were more moderate on the question of the decrees.)

the death of King James in 1625, whose influence may have been a strong moderating force in du Moulin's theology, du Moulin reversed his position and aligned himself so strongly with the speculative approach that by the end of his life he was basing almost the whole structure of his theology on it. I will provide two examples of this.

On 8 December 1628, on the occasion of the inauguration of Abraham Colvinus as Doctor of Theology, du Moulin addressed the faculty and guests of the Academy of Sedan on the topic "De Sacra Theologia," or, as the title of the published address reads, "Oratio de laudibus theologiae."[54] The main thrust of the address was to show the primacy of scripture for all human knowledge, arguing that all pagan traditions have their origins in the scripture. One sees clearly in this the old assumption that theology is the "Queen of the Sciences," the source of all other knowledge, and du Moulin's debt to Thomas Aquinas seems to be evident. But whether or not one agrees that he is drawing on Aquinas for his argumentation, one sees here the unmistakable sign of one of the main characteristics of scholastic theology—the attempt to incorporate all knowledge within the parameters of Christian theology.

Beyond laying the basis for theology as the universal science, one of the questions with which du Moulin deals in this address, a question common in medieval scholasticism, is, "Whether theology is speculative or practical?" One would expect that he would opt for the latter position. Calvin clearly had stressed the useful, the practical, in his theology, and I know of no Protestant theologian prior to du Moulin who had departed from that fundamental position. But the unpredictable du Moulin unabashedly concludes, "I will boldly state that theology is more contemplative than practical, inasmuch as contemplation is the reason for action, for by good works we aspire to the vision of God."[55] The scholastic orientation of that statement is clear, right down to the idea behind the phrase "the vision of God."

In late 1635 or early 1636 he penned his *Examen de la doctrine de MM. Amyrault & Testard*,[56] a treatise circulated throughout France to show the heresies of those two colleagues. The treatise is a broad attack on Amyraut, principally charging that he had corrupted Reformed theology on many points.[57] Reversing his earlier sentiments upon the foolhardiness of dealing with the decrees of God, du Moulin's entire approach in this work is calibrated upon the order of the decrees. His opening section deals with the order of the decrees. His fundamental criticism of the position of Amyraut (which he identifies with Arminianism) is based on the argument that a faulty "order of decrees is

---

[54](Sedan, 1629). It is also to be found as the first entry in Volume 1 of *Thesaurus desputationum theologicarum in alma Sedanensi academia variis temporibus habitarum* (Genevae, 1661).

[55]*Thesaurus disputationum* vol. 1, page 5.

[56](Amsterdam, 1638), published without his knowledge or consent.

[57]For a fuller discussion see my *Calvinism and the Amyraut heresy*, 84 ff.

the base of everything in Arminianism, and from that all their errors emanate."[58] Rather than placing the blame on the supralapsarians as he had done in his letter to Calvert in 1619, he now places the blame on the Arminians for their faulty order of the decrees! The question, "Who can know the mind of God?" which he had earlier answered in the negative he has now answered positively, at least as far as the order of the decrees is concerned. The assurance that the mind of God can be known in such matters is another strong indication of du Moulin's espousal of Protestant scholasticism.

We have looked at two areas in which du Moulin pitched French Protestantism toward a full scholastic program. These are only a small part of the story of du Moulin's influence in that direction. I hope to show in a forthcoming volume on his life and work a fuller, perhaps more balanced, picture.

[58]Page 5 of the revised edition published under the title *Esclaircissement des controverses Salmuriennes* (Leiden, 1648).

*For an excellent, informed overview of French Protestantism from 1555 to 1685, see the two articles "Calvinism in France, 1555-1629" and "Calvinism in France, 1598-1685," the latter by the remarkable Elisabeth Labrousse, the former by Menna Prestwich in *International Calvinism, 1541-1715*, ed. M. Prestwich, (Oxford: Clarendon 1985). I am endebted to both of these articles; beyond that, to Elisabeth Labrousse, whose knowledge of seventeenth and eighteenth century French Protestantism is probably unsurpassed; my debt extends over many years, both on the personal and professional levels. The preceding essay is dedicated to her.

Calvin appears before the Genevan city council upon his return in 1541.

Calvin and Puritanism: The Career of William Whittingham

Dan G. Danner

During the critical years of 1554 to 1558 English Protestants settled in Geneva during the Marian exile. There are few scholars who would not recognize that the roots of the radical form of English Protestantism designated "puritan" were either planted in Calvin's Geneva, or at least nurtured and cured there during Mary Tudor's reign. Some have concluded that these English Exiles became Calvinists and brought a form of Calvinism back to England. The life of William Whittingham presents a case study against this historical matrix.

One result of Whittingham's work was the 1560 English edition of the Geneva Bible. When Whittingham finally returned to England in the mid-1560s, there is no doubt that he was very much in the puritan camp. Subsequent activities of his life will demonstrate that he was influenced by Calvinist views, but there are enough points of departure from Calvin's teachings to show that what Calvin and Geneva were able to contribute to English Protestantism was a fertile and welcome atmosphere where English refugees could nurture and foster their own brand of Protestantism which was evident in later English puritanism.

STUDENTS OF THE REFORMATION HAVE long been interested in the Marian exile and in particular the English Protestants who settled in Geneva during the critical years, 1554 to 1558. In fact, Geneva has become synonymous in English Reformation studies with a radical form of English Protestantism which has become designated "puritan." There are few scholars who would not recognize that the roots of this tradition were either planted while the English refugees were in Calvin's Geneva, or unquestionably nurtured and cured there during Mary Tudor's reign. As a result, some interpreters have concluded that these English exiles indeed became Calvinists and brought back to England an incipient, or even developed, form of Calvinism.

The life of William Whittingham presents an intriguing case study against this historical matrix. Whittingham was probably the most important and productive of the English exiles at Geneva. He was well educated, especially in languages, and demonstrated some excellent literary skills and talents both during his exile on the Continent and during much of his life as a leader of the Protestant cause in England. At the age of sixteen he entered Brasenose College, Oxford, graduated with his B.A., and was elected Fellow of All Soul's in 1545. In 1547 he became senior student of Christ's Church, receiving his M.A. in February of 1548. It was likely at Oxford that he befriended Christopher Goodman and the two became life-long friends and theological comrades. That he was preferred at Oxford substantiates Wood's claim that

Henry VIII wanted to replenish Oxford with some of the "choicest scholars in the University." He was granted leave to travel in 1550, and was in France at the University of Orleans for a short time before visiting Geneva and Germany. He returned to England in May of 1553.[1]

Whittingham seems to have been an acquaintance of Peter Martyr. He had been instrumental in getting Martyr to London where the latter supported Cranmer's reforms of the mass; when Mary ascended to the throne, Whittingham used his influence and past French diplomatic experience to appeal in behalf of Martyr, asking for a honorable passport from England to the Continent with "permission to remove all his goods."[2] Whittingham himself left for Germany, arriving in Frankfurt on 27 June 1554. Christina Garrett is convinced that a personal vendetta between Whittingham and John Ponet, exiled at Strasburg, was part of the troubles at Frankfurt. Ponet, former Bishop of Winchester, was desirous of maintaining a type of episcopal control of the English churches in exile. She further postulated that the "Cecil aristocratic circle" at Strasburg was very different from the more democratic ethos that prevailed at Frankfurt and which later became the ordinate fixture of the Geneva exiles' church.[3]

Whittingham met John Knox at Frankfurt and the two began a revision of the Second Edwardian Prayerbook, attempting to bring it closer in line with Reformed practice. During this time, Whittingham was corresponding with Calvin and drawing up the prospectus for a new church order to be used by the English church at Frankfurt. Calvin's letter of 18 January 1555 shows his favoritism to Knox's and Whittingham's efforts, and this surely helped to win over to the cause other reformers such as Goodman. When Richard Cox, John Jewell, and others arrived in Frankfurt on 3 March 1555, things became very unruly. Eventually, Whittingham, who had kept Calvin fully informed of the troubles, followed Knox to Geneva. He arrived with the first group on 13 October 1555.

[1]Anthony Wood, *Athenae Oxonienses*, ed. P. Bliss (London: F. C. & J. Rivergton, 1813), 1:446–50; A. F. Pollard, *Dictionary of National Biography*, [hereafter *DNB*] ed. Leslie Stephen (New York: Macmillan, 1908), *s.v.* Whittingham, William.

[2]Christina Garrett, *The Marian Exile: A Study in the Origins of Elizabethan Puritanism* (Cambridge: Cambridge University Press, 1938), 327–30; see also Mary Anne Everett Green, ed., *Life and Death of Mr. William Whittingham*, from a ms. in Anthony Wood's Collection, Bodlian Library, Oxford (printed for the Camden Society, 1870), p. 3, and J. Hay Colligan, *The Honourable William Whittingham of Chester* (London: Simpkin Marshall, 1934), *passim*.

[3]Ibid. For an opposing view, see Ronald J. Vander Molen, "Anglican Against Puritan: Ideological Origins During the Marian Exile," *Church History* 42 (March 1973): 45–57. Vander Molen believes that Garrett is wrong in saying that the Puritans were more democratic or represented a lower social status. He affirms that the main distinction between the Anglicans and Puritans was intellectual, i.e. that the lay-oriented Knox party was a "death knell for humanistic scholarship." After all, the Cox party was still willing to use Calvin's ideas and church polity, and they certainly were more Calvinistic than were the Knox company on matters of political obedience.

It is conjectured that Whittingham married Calvin's sister in 1550, but this is surely inaccurate because he married Katherine Jaquemayne of Orleans while he was in Geneva. Two children were baptized during Whittingham's stay in Geneva as recorded in the *Livre des Anglois*. He was elected an elder of the church on several occasions, a deacon once, but never a minister. Pollard acknowledges that Whittingham became a minister with the encouragement of Calvin in 1559, a matter of much consternation in his later experiences in England.[4]

Whittingham was a prolific writer and translator during his exile. In 1557 John Bodley published from Geneva a translation of the New Testament with annotations; it was Whittingham's. It was doubtless he who was the main force behind the issuance of a complete Bible edition, with fuller annotations and other literary paraphernalia. The 1560 edition of the Bible was the result, and Whittingham with a few others remained in Geneva until it was published in May of 1560, even though other English had left for home as the news of Elizabeth's accession reached the Continent. Whittingham also published many psalms turned into meter. Seven of these are included among the fifty-one psalms in 1556 as part of the service book which Whittingham had already drawn up at Frankfurt; the others were revisions of Sternhold's Psalter. A metrical version of the Ten Commandments by Whittingham was appended to the service book as well. His knowledge of Hebrew in these efforts is quite apparent. His other literary activities were consigned to prefacing important tracts by Nicholas Ridley on the Lord's Supper and by Goodman on the right of resistance, and translating Beza's treatise on predestination in 1556.

Whittingham's return from Geneva was initially characterized by travel. He accompanied the Earl of Bedford on his mission to the court of France. Later, he went with the Earl of Warwick in the latter's defense of Newhaven against the French, where be became preacher to the military forces. He gained a high opinion from the Earl and it was probably due to Warwick's influence and similar plaudits from Cecil that Whittingham became Dean of Durham. He preached before the Queen on 2 September 1563, and wrote to the Earl of Leicester in 1564 concerning his opposition to vestments. Two years later he addressed the same letter, minus the personal references to the Earl of Warwick, to "my faythful Brethren now afflycted. . . ." The letters were characteristically puritan in ethos and form and show in no uncertain way that Whittingham was very much in the puritan camp in the mid-1560s.[5] However, it would appear that Whittingham softened his tone in the next several years. Wood thinks that when Cecil became treasurer, Whittingham changed his stance on the wearing of vestments by agreeing with one of

[4]Pollard, *DNB*.

[5]See John Strype, *The Life and Acts of Matthew Parker* (Oxford: Clarendon, 1821), 3:76–84.

Calvin's comments that the ministry of the church should not go unheeded or be prohibited by external adiaphora. It was probably this that got him the chiding letters from some of his former exiled compatriots.[6]

John Strype reports that on 24 March 1564, the use of the scholar's gown and cap were enjoined and the surplice required at all divine administrations, as well as the observance of the prayerbook, and that Whittingham was one of the one hundred and ten who signed *volo* to the requirements. In 1563 Cecil had persuaded the Queen to send letters to the Archbishop of York to make sure the "office of prayer and fasting" was being implemented in that province. This would have affected Durham, and Whittingham addressed a letter on 19 December to Cecil explaining what was happening with religious activities under his direction. This was still during Whittingham's more radical puritan phase.[7]

Perhaps it was in 1569 that Whittingham began to make a change. The question of how much he was following the enforcements of Elizabeth's *via media*, heretofore clear, came to a head over his ordination. It began when Thomas Lever, erstwhile Genevan exile and Master of Sherburn House, a hospital near Durham, complained to the Bishop of Durham, James Pilkington, and also fellow exile in Geneva, about some of the "works of impiety" in Durham. Rumor had it that several stone coffins, belonging to the priors, had been taken up and used as troughs for horses and swine, and that the covers were then being used to cover the dean's own house! Furthermore, Whittingham was accused of defacing various icons of the monastery, even using some of the stones to build a washing-house. The two holy water stones, made of fine marble and artificially engraven, were taken away and used to steep beef and saltfish in, so intense was the anti-monastic fervor.[8] The matter was attended by Pilkington who favored Whittingham and who knew also that Lever, even though he had spent some time in Geneva, was not liked by Knox and his sympathizers. It is difficult, of course, to ascertain exactly what had happened and why Whittingham became the brunt of Lever's accusations. In 1576 Whittingham was the target of a hearing, requested by the Queen, which included Pilkington and the Dean of York, both Whittingham supporters, and the Archbishop of York, Edwin Sandys. Strype reports that the archbishop was refused a visitation by the Deanery of Durham in the following year, 1577, and that the matter seemed to have ended in confusion because of the fiery nature of the commission. Sandys concluded that things were a

[6]Wood, *Athenae Oxonienses.*

[7]John Strype, *The Life and Acts of Edmund Grindal* (Oxford: Clarendon, 1821), 145; cf. Strype, *Parker*, 1:267–68.

[8]Benjamin Brook, *The Lives of the Puritans* (London: James Black, 1813), 1:229–36.

mess in Durham, that the appointed orders were not being implemented, and that there was little else to do short of excommunication.[9]

In 1578, however, another commission was sent by Elizabeth to look into the unresolved Whittingham case. The commission was to visit the cathedral church in Durham and to investigate Whittingham's papers of ordination. The commission subsequently became divided on their findings, for one member reported that Whittingham was not suitably ordained while the president of the commission was more sympathetic to the more informal kind of ordination which Whittingham received in 1559 at Calvin's insistence while in Geneva. What this entailed is not known; no mention of it appears in the *Livre des Anglois* and most of the English had by then returned to England.[10]

Whittingham brought forward two certificates of ordination, signed by eight persons, dated 8 July 1578, which proved his ordination "by lot and election." Archbishop Sandys remonstrated that this was to no effect, but Whittingham countered with citations from Calvin "who affirmeth, that the election was not, nor is to be drawn into example." A month later Whittingham presented a notary-sworn certificate, signed by eight persons, with some changes in wording to which objection had been made, and the addition of wording suggested by the commission. The report of the chancellor concerning the affair invalidated Whittingham's ordination—something the Queen wanted all along—owing to there being no "*externae solemnitates, authontatem ordinantis*" as signatories of the certificate. John Bodley was the only name approved by the commission.[11]

The matter was further complicated, moreover, by the sympathy of the president of the commission who filed his minority report. He was willing to accept the Genevan ordination if only for the pragmatic reason that all ordinations in Continental Reformed churches would thereby not be called into scrutiny by the English! Furthermore, he argued, the commission was not unanimous in its rendering, especially because of the violent disagreements between Archbishop Sandys and Whittingham. Such should not be sufficient to deprive Whittingham. How far the matter was belabored Strype is uncertain. Whittingham was to die six months later.[12]

The question remains as to what Whittingham was doing or allowing to be done in Durham which caused the furor. Was it simply a matter of nonconformity regarding the vestments and the prayerbook, or the insensitive and iconoclastic practice of some form of sacrilege? Both Wood and Brook are

---

[9]John Strype, *Annals of the Reformation* (Oxford: Clarendon, 1824), 2:ii, 107–09. Cf. Mervyn James, *Family, Lineage and Civil Society: A Study of Society, Politics and Mentality in the Durham Region, 1500-1640* (Oxford: Clarendon, 1974), 58–59.

[10]Ibid., 167–74; cf. Green, *Life and Death of Whittingham*, 47–48, and A. F. Mitchell, ed., *Livre des Anglois* (no colophon or date), 3.

[11]Ibid.   [12]Ibid.

convinced that Whittingham was involved, at least to some extent, in the bizarre happenings in Durham of the kind charged by Lever.[13] It is indeed difficult to imagine that for one whose love for music brought him to such heights of "allowing singing in the church" and being careful to provide the best songs and anthems "that could be got out of the queen's chapel to furnish his choir with" would have stooped to such degrees of iconoclasm by deprecating other forms of artistic expression. But such was often the nature of puritanism, at least of the kind that was represented by Genevans such as Whittingham. Perhaps the chiding of fellow exile, Thomas Wood, had had its effect, for Whittingham remained faithful to his puritan position until his death on 10 June 1579. He may have wavered at some point on the practicality of remaining obstinate to vestments, but the account above would seem to undergird what was most important in his mind: following the apostolic pattern as overlaid in the Bible, and giving one's life to the proclamation of the gospel for the edification of the godly. He was buried in the cathedral church in Durham, where ironically, in 1640, the Scots defaced the tombstone which covered his grave.[14]

Whittingham's literary contribution to English Protestantism prior to his leading role in the translation of the Geneva Bible had consisted mainly of turning various Psalms into meter for liturgical use and certain prefaces which were appended to works by Nicholas Ridley, Beza, Goodman, and Knox. In 1556 he published at Geneva fifty-one Psalms turned into meter as part of the service book which Whittingham and his colleagues had been appointed to draw up at Frankfurt. His other liturgical contributions were the revision of Sternhold's Psalms and a metrical rendering of the Ten Commandments which were appended to the Psalter of Sternhold and Hopkins. His eminence as a Hebraist allowed him to contribute more than any of the other exiles to the formation of the liturgy of the English church at Geneva.[15]

In 1556 Whittingham wrote a brief preface to Ridley's treatise on the Lord's Supper, giving his approval of Ridley's arguments and conclusions. One would therefore expect an examination of this work to divulge some reflection of Whittingham's own eucharistic ideas as well as the kind of eucharist theology prevalent with the English church at Geneva. Particular attention should be given Ridley's treatment of the doctrine of transubstantiation.

[13]Wood, *Athenae Oxonienses*; Brook, *Lives of Puritans*.

[14]Wood, *Athenae Oxonienses*.

[15]Pollard, *DNB*. The authorship of *A Brieff Discours off the Troubles Begonne at Franckford, 1554-1558 A.D.* has been ascribed to Whittingham (e.g. A. W. Pollard and G. R. Redgrave, *A Short Title Catalogue of Books Printed in England, Scotland, and Ireland . . . 1475-1640* [London: Bernard Quaritch Ltd., 1926]), but Patrick Collinson has made a good case for Thomas Wood as the author. See his "The Authorship of *A Brieff Discours off the Troubles Begonne at Franckford*," *Journal of Ecclesiastical History* 9 (October 1958): 188–209, and his *Elizabethan Puritan Movement* (Berkeley: University of California Press, 1967), 153.

Ridley's comprehensive examination of this doctrine began by asserting that if it be Christ's own natural body which is present in the substance of bread, then it must be granted that transubstantiation has indeed taken place and that the substance of the bread has become the natural body of Christ. It would follow that the carnal and corporeal presence of Christ's body is present in the eucharist and that the sacrament should be adored with the honor due to Christ himself. Therefore, whoever partakes of the sacrament—be he murderer, adulterer, or faithful servant—receives also the natural substance of Christ's own blessed body, both flesh and blood.[16] But if it can be shown from scripture that after the bread and wine had been blessed, the substances which remained were still bread and wine, then the argument for transubstantiation falls to the ground, the sophistry of such theologians as Scotus notwithstanding.

At this point Ridley followed Paul's rehearsal of the Lord's Supper in 1 Corinthians. The apostle's statement, "The bread which we break, is it not the partaking or fellowship of the Lord's body?" clearly showed that after the thanksgiving it was bread which the apostle broke. The substance was still bread, therefore, and did not change into the body of Christ. The same argument follows from what Christ said to his disciples concerning the cup: "I say unto you, I will not drink henceforth of this fruit of the vine until I shall drink that new in my Father's Kingdom." Christ called the cup the fruit of the vine, and the substance had not changed but remained "very natural wine." Ridley affirmed that it should be clear from the words of scripture that the substances had not changed but remained the same.[17]

Ridley believed that his case was strengthened by the words of Paul when he recorded these words of Christ: "This cup is the new testament in my blood; this do as often as ye shall drink it in the remembrance of me." Does this not require the same magnitude of miracle as what the Romanists have done with the statement of Christ regarding the bread? Would they not be more consistent to affirm that the cup is transubstantiated into the New Testament rather than the blood of Christ? Ridley thought so, and bore no mercy in showing the inconsistency of the papists whom he believed to be deceived by arguments from sophistry rather than depending upon the sure and simple word of God. Ridley then retreated to the interpretation of Augustine, which he took to be figurative, and insisted that the body and blood of Christ are obtainable to the Christian only figuratively and only by faith.[18]

[16]*Certen godly, learned and/Comfortable conferences, between the/two Reuerende Fathers, and holve martyrs of/Christ, D. Nicolas Rydley late Bysshoppe of Wor-/cester, during the time of theyr empryson-/mentes. Whereunto is added./A Treatise agaynst the error of Transubstan-/tiation, made by the sayd Reuerende Father D./Nicolas Rydley./M.D.LVI* (no colophon); cf. the text in T. H. L. Parker, *English Reformers* (Philadelphia: Westminster, 1965), 298–99.

[17]Ibid., 302.

[18]Ibid., 306.

Since Christ's body is "really" in heaven, it cannot be said to be on earth. To affirm that his body is "really" present in the bread "maketh precious things common to profane and ungodly persons, and constraineth men to confess many absurdities." If transubstantiation were true, many whoremongers, murderers, even dogs and rats, eat the corporeal body of Christ! But the sixth chapter of John, where Jesus gave his sermon on the "bread of life," should adequately refute such a ludicrous doctrine if only the Romanists were true to scripture.[19]

Ridley wanted to leave the distinct impression, however, that he was not a thoroughgoing Zwinglian.

> I say and confess . . . that the bread on the which thanks are given is the body of Christ in the remembrance of him and his death. . . .
> I say and confess the bread which we break to be the communion and partaking of Christ's body. . . .
> I say and believe that there is not only a signification of Christ's body set forth by the sacrament, but also that therewith is given to the godly and faithful the grace of Christ's body, that is, the food of life and immortality.[20]

It was the blood of Christ in the chalice, but the point at issue was "how" it was, for it was the blood of Christ indeed, but not in the same form as that which sprang from the side of the Lord at Calvary. This blood which we drink is by sacrament; likewise the bread, for it is indeed the body of Christ which we break, but only by sacrament. They nourish and sustain our spiritual bodies, just as baptism, ordained in water, regenerates our spiritual bodies.[21]

It was also in 1556 that Whittingham translated Theodore Beza's *Summa totius Christianismi, sive descriptio et distributio causarum salutis electorum et exitii reprobatorum ex sacris literis collecta*, written by the Genevan in 1555. The English title was *A Brief declaration of the chiefe poyntes of Christian Religion, set forth in a Table*, and Whittingham's preface was appended to the work. The hallmark of Beza's treatise on election, the only part of the work translated by Whittingham, was the power and purpose of God. From everlasting "God hath purposed and decreed . . . to create all things at their seasons to his glory." Thus God had elected from the foundation of the world, and by his steadfast mercy, those whom he would choose to be saved and those whom he would

---

[19]Ibid., 313.

[20]Ibid., 313–14.

[21]Ibid., 320. Cf. Gordon E. Pruett, "A Protestant Doctrine of the Eucharistic Presence," *Calvin Theological Journal* 10 (1975): 142–74.

leave in their sins. Reprobation lay hidden in God, albeit the "whole fault remain within themselves." The purpose of election in the will of God preceded the election of the saved in Christ and is the primary cause of salvation. Consequently, God has shown his mercy in the salvation of the elect and manifested his just judgment in the condemning of the reprobate, "that he might find matter of just damnation in those, unto whom it is given neither to believe, neither yet to know the mysteries or secrets of God."[22]

God did not create humankind in sin because he created them after his own image, "that is, in cleanness and holiness." Beza's sublapsarianism kept God from being the author of evil. It was man's will which caused him to sin, thereby showing that the reprobate receive what they justly deserve. God's laws bring about a remembrance of sin in the hearts of humankind thus producing fear. The law and its consequences, however, shows us that we "should flee unto that only mediator Jesus Christ." The severe and sharp preaching of the law is followed by the "grace and gentleness of the Gospel," yet with the condition that they believe in Christ who alone can deliver them from condemnation and give them the power and right to obtain the heavenly inheritance. The outward preaching of the word of God is accompanied by the inward power of the Holy Spirit, which does not renew the remnants of free will "as Sophisters do suppose," but rather "turneth their hearts" and opens "their sense, heart, ears, and understanding." The Spirit of God creates faith in the elect and brings them to a knowledge of their election in Christ, "so that they begin to will and do the things which are of God."[23]

Christians are initiated into this faith by the sacrament of baptism, and faith is sealed by the sacrament of the Lord's Supper. Thus Christians may not lose faith, for "they still have the seeds of the love of God and neighbor within them." On the other hand, the reprobate are not allowed to be saved. God justifiably hates them, for they are corrupt, "showing forth his just anger upon some of them, as soon as they are born." They suffer in ignorance, therefore, and although they might strive to improve themselves, they know no sense of salvation, which is known only by God as he has revealed himself as father in Christ. There is no natural revelation of God. The reprobate simply cannot understand or believe the gospel; it is foolishness or a stumbling block to them. There may be some, like the demons, who believe in their trembling, but they cannot be saved. Moreover, among the reprobate there are those who lapse from what might appear to have been faith; they were not among the elect, for they voluntarily and willingly returned to their old ungodly ways, so that, as

---

[22]*A Briefe declaration of the chiefe poyntes of Christian Religion, set forth in a Table* (Geneva: Printed by Jo. Rivery, 1556), found also in *The Treasure of Truth, touching the grounde work of man his salvation, and chiefest pointes of Christian Religion* . . . , and newly turned into English, by Iohn Stockwood (London, 1581), fo. D1, v.

[23]Ibid., fols. F4v–F6r.

a matter of speech, it is said that God hardens their hearts, blinds their eyes, and stops their ears.[24]

Beza was convinced that it was not within human power to identify the elect or the reprobate, but in visiting the sick it might be of some comfort to assure them of their election, or by pointing out the evils of the reprobate, they may be struck by the judgment of God! No person can pluck away our treasure in Christ.

> . . . And when thou hearest the voice of God sounding in thine ears and mind, which calleth thee unto Christ the only mediator, consider by little and little, and search diligently . . . whether thou be justified and sanctified, that is, made righteous and holy, by faith in Christ, for these are the effects by the which, faith, the very cause of them indeed is known. And this thou shalt know . . . partly by the spirit of adoption crying within . . . : partly also by the power and working of the same spirit in thyself: namely if thou feel, and also indeed shew, that although sin do swell in thee, it doth not reign in thee.[25]

John Stockwood put together this tract of Beza, with an enlargement of Whittingham's preface by his own hand, together with the 1556 treatise on election by Anthony Gilby and John Foxe's tract on the same subject. It was published in 1581 and entitled *The Treasure of Truth*. Although Whittingham wrote nothing about predestination himself, his translation of Beza's treatise and sponsorship of Knox's work on predestination in Geneva in 1559 clearly indicate the keen interest that he had in the subject. It thus would be no accident that under his direction the doctrine of predestination permeated the annotations and prefaces of the Geneva Bible.[26]

In 1558, Whittingham wrote a preface to the controversial book of Christopher Goodman, *How Svperior Powers Oght to be Obeyd*. There is little doubt that Whittingham concurred with Goodman's position in 1556, even though a somewhat different stance was taken in the notes on the New Testament in the 1560 edition of the Geneva Bible.[27] Whittingham urged his brethren in England to "be persuaded in the truth of that doctrine concerning

---

[24]Ibid., fol. H4v.

[25]Ibid., fols. K6 v–K9, r. Cf. John S. Bray, *Theodore Beza's Doctrine of Predestination* (Nieuwkoop: DeGraaf, 1975), and R. T. Kendall, *Calvin and English Calvinism to 1649* (New York: Oxford University Press, 1979), 210.

[26]See Dan G. Danner, "The Contribution of the Geneva Bible of 1560 to the English Protestant Tradition," *Sixteenth Century Journal* 12 (Fall 1981): 5–18; Dewey Wallace, "The Doctrine of Predestination in the Early English Reformation," *Church History* 43 (June 1974): 201–15.

[27]Danner, "Geneva Bible." See also my "Christopher Goodman and the English Protestant Tradition of Civil Disobedience," *Sixteenth Century Journal* 8 (October 1977): 61–73.

obedience to the magistrates, and so glorify God with us." If England wanted to know her true duty to the monarch, she was advised to "read this book and thou shalt well understand it," and if she wished for Christian liberty, "come and see how it may easily be had."[28]

The *Régistres de Conseil* of Geneva recorded that on 13 November 1559, William Whittingham, John Baron, and John Knox were involved in a literary effort relative to a certain treatise on predestination. These men asked for permission to have it printed in Geneva, in English, because certain Englishmen elsewhere had written against it. Permission was granted, provided that the treatise would not bear a subscription that it had been "imprinted at Geneva." Whittingham and Baron promised to be responsible for the piece, assuring the council that there would be nothing contrary "to the catholic and orthodox doctrine" in it.[29]

The author of the treatise was John Knox, and Whittingham revised it for printing at Geneva in 1560. Although he did not attach any literary effort of his own to the document, an examination of the arguments and conclusions of Knox would certainly show some of the translator's thinking, and since this motif is one of the salient emphases in the Geneva Bible, it would be valuable to notice how much Knox's doctrine of predestination influenced the compilers. The title of Knox's treatise was *An Answer to a Great Nomber of blasphemous cauillations written by an Anabaptist, and aduersarie to Gods eternal Predestination.*

Whittingham's career upon Elizabeth's succession to the throne has already been highlighted. His letter, "To my faythfull Brethren now afflycted, and to all those that unfaynedly loue the Lorde Jesus," written probably sometime in 1566, showed that he was then the radical puritan many believed him to be. In the letter, for example, his opposition to the vestments was very much in line with the polemic of other puritans such as Anthony Gilby and Thomas Sampson.[30] "The thing which otherwise by nature is indifferent," he wrote, "doth degenerate and become hurtful" if certain conditions and circumstances were prevalent. How could God's glory be advanced by vestments when superstition was still attached to the "popish garments"? They did not edify but rather brought "doubt of religion" for common Christians. Surely something so controversial and closely aligned with Romish policies could not be deemed indifferent.[31] Leaning heavily on passages from Augustine, Tertullian, and Jerome, Whittingham advised that Christians should not practice anything not clearly commanded in scripture; the argument that since vestments were

---

[28]*How Svperior Powers Oght to be Obeyd,* fo. Aii, v, from the preface.

[29]*Régistres de Conseil,* Archives, Hôtel de Ville, Geneva, fo. 144, 13 November 1559, quoted in David Laing, *The Works of John Knox* (Edinburgh: James Thin, 1895), v, 16.

[30]Cf. Dan G. Danner, "Anthony Gilby: Puritan in Exile—A Biographical Approach," *Church History* 40 (December 1971): 412–22.

[31]Fol. Aiir–Aiiv.

not forbidden in scripture they were expedient was inane to him. Things indifferent should induce a better life for those involved and should not cause offense.

> Now if any man would say, that we do this rather of singularity than of conscience, and that we are so addicted to our own manners, that we will not change for better, he may understand that if our apparel seem not modest and grave as our vocation requireth, neither sufficient to discern us from men of other callings, we refuse not to wear such as shall be thought to the Godly and prudent Magistrates for these uses most decent, so that we may ever keep ourselves pure from the defiled robes of Antichrist, would to God that this sentence of St. Ambrose were well weighed whereas he saith, as the robe setteth forth the Senator, as husbandry, the husbandman so nothing setteth forth a Bishop, but the works of a Bishop. . . .[32]

Whittingham had written the same letter, with the addition of a few personal remarks, to the Earl of Leicester, "to use his interest that conformity to the habits might not be imposed." It had been written from Durham in 1564.[33] That he would later be chided for acquiescing to the indifference of wearing the vestments, especially in light of the strange and bizarre events in Durham, is one of the enigmas of the English Reformation. It probably indicates the lack of adequate sources of information as much as the ambivalence of one of the most effective and influential English exiles who had fled abroad during Mary Tudor's reign. It may, indeed, represent also the kind of influence that John Calvin had on many of the Marian exiles; Calvin's influence was more political, therefore, as a figurehead within the reform movements on the Continent. His influence as a theologian was not so great.

The life of William Whittingham would clearly suggest that English Protestantism, of the radical variety we have dubbed "puritan" herein, had a character and ethos of its own, and that it had indigenous roots not directly removed from the Continent. It would be unfair and inaccurate, therefore, to attribute the contributions Whittingham made to English Protestantism to Calvin or Geneva. There is no question of Calvin's influence, but it should be clear that Whittingham did not get his ideas of reform from the Genevan. Whittingham's interest in the doctrine of the Lord's Supper, evident within the Geneva Bible marginalia and indirectly reflected in Ridley's treatise, is unique to the English Protestant theological tradition and shows no direct

---

[32]Fols. Av,v–Avi,r.
[33]See Strype, *Parker*, 3:76–84.

linkage to Calvin's eucharistic thought. The doctrine of predestination like-wise was already deeply implanted within the English Protestant tradition, due to the work of Whittingham's fellow exile, Anthony Gilby, and bears comparison with only Calvin's later thought in the 1559 edition of the *Institutes*. That Whittingham translated Beza's tract on predestination merely indicates corroboration of a biblical notion the exiles believed important to stress anew. The exiles' view resembles more the thought of Beza than Calvin, but they did not borrow their predestinarian ideas from Geneva. It is true that Knox's treatise on the subject, sponsored by Whittingham, was more in line with Calvin's earlier treatments. Moreover, it is well known that Geneva was embarrassed by the tracts of Goodman and Knox on civil disobedience; the exiles did not get their vision of the state and resistance to the ungodly magistrate from Calvin.

What Calvin and Geneva were able to contribute was the provision of a fertile and welcome atmosphere where English refugees could nurture and foster their own brand of Protestantism. That Whittingham seemed to waver somewhat late in his life on the vestiarian question, perhaps agreeing with Calvin's less radical position, is not really surprising. After all, it was exceedingly important to do things in Bible ways and to believe and practice only what the scripture explicitly warranted. What was of greater importance to many puritans, among them Whittingham, was the edification of the godly.

Calvin and the syndics visit the newly founded Genevan Academy.

Some Aspects of Death and Dying in Puritanism

Donald K. McKim

Historians have only recently examined the attitude of Puritanism towards death, viewing not only funeral customs and burial practices, but how the larger society was perceived, what its belief systems were, and how the ordinary person died, as well as seeing how theologians and preachers taught Christians to prepare for death. This essay explores, in a preliminary manner, one line of some of the aspects of death and dying in Puritanism, and may thereby direct our thinking toward a culture and an ethos which still has a powerful influence on our own.

THE TOPIC OF PURITANISM'S ATTITUDES TOWARD DEATH has only recently been taken up by historians.[1] Emergence of works from the social sciences on the culture, sociology, and economics of Puritan England and New England will prove increasingly valuable for exploring different facets of this subject. It is important to know what funeral customs and burial practices were like, how the larger society was perceived, what its belief systems were, and how the ordinary person died as well as to understand the pronouncements from pulpits and the teachings of theologians on how to face death and prepare for it as a Christian.

In the case of Puritanism, the theological beliefs of the Reformed tradition stemming from John Calvin (1509-64) have been formative. One of the mediators and architects of this tradition in sixteenth-century England was William Perkins (1558-1602). As a leading theologian at Cambridge University during the reign of Elizabeth I, Perkins was especially concerned with the application of Biblical and theological teachings to the lives of those who read his books and heard him preach. His works display the interaction between his theological perspectives, which are indebted much to Calvin, and his ethical concerns for the renewal and reformation of the English church. In giving attention to death and dying, Perkins attuned his Calvinism to a specific personal issue that was significant and immediately relevant to his readers.[2]

The present essay will explore some aspects of death and dying in Puritanism and focus particularly on the prescriptions by Perkins of how one should face death and "die well." The theological foundations of his views as well as the tensions, preparations, and questions they entailed are set in the wider context of some aspects of death and dying in the early modern period.

[1]See David E. Stannard, *The Puritan Way of Death: A Study in Religion, Culture, and Social Change* (New York: Oxford University Press, 1977).

[2]On Perkins's life and work as well as his Calvinism, see Donald K. McKim, *Ramism in William Perkins' Theology* (Bern: Peter Lang, 1987), ch. 1.

165

Mortality Rates

As the cemetery stood at the center of the village, so death stood at the center of life for families of early modern times. In France, the death rate was four or five times higher than it is today. In a village of one thousand people, at least fifty would die each year. These would be mainly infants, children, and young adults.[3] In the 1640s, the life expectancy of English babies was thirty-two years. While the highest mortality rates were among newborn infants, in London by 1764, 49 percent of all recorded chidren were dead by age two and 60 percent by age five. Rural England seems to have had a better situation than France. But still, between one-quarter and one-third of all the children born to English peers and peasants died before age fifteen throughout the sixteenth and seventeenth centuries.[4]

Such figures brought with them their own peculiar psychological and attitudinal effects. In a time when relatively few died at "a ripe old age," the association of death with the aged alone was not so strong. Young adults between twenty and fifty died very frequently. This led to a strong sense of the precariousness of life. Affective relationships were at the mercy of sudden and unexpected death. The family life of Sir John Gibson was summed up in 1655 when he wrote:

> Twelve sons my wife Penelope
> And three fair daughters had,
> Which then a comfort was to me
> And made my heart full glad.
> Death took away my children dear
> And at the last my joy,
> And left me full of care and fear,
> My only hopes a boy.[5]

While members of the rural elite (squires of wealth and those higher on the social scale) who reached age twenty-one could hope to live into their sixties, even they were not immune to any one of a multitude of fatal disasters. They could live in the country away from cities and epidemics and thus have a better chance for longer life. Compared to their social inferiors, they were well off indeed. Yet their hold on life was still a constant gamble. Those

[3]See Lawrence Stone, *The Family, Sex and Marriage in England 1500-1800* (New York: Harper & Row, 1977), 66-73.

[4]Ibid., 68. The rates should probably be even higher since ecclesiastical lawyers and theologians said that "a child before he is baptized is not a child of God but a child of the Devil." Yet a number of newborn babies who died within several days of birth were almost certainly not yet baptized. See W. H. Hale, *A Series of Precedents and Proceedings from the Act Books of Ecclesiastical Courts in the Diocese of London* (London, 1847), 162.

[5]*North Country Diaries*, 2, Surtees Society 124 (1914): 52.

who did survive till later years were venerated since they were so few in number compared with all the thousands who died before attaining old age.

Causes of Death

The intensely insecure environment of the early modern period and the high mortality rates were caused by a number of factors. The supply of food was always unreliable. About one of every six harvests proved to be a total failure.[6] Death by starvation in the streets was not uncommon. A 1674 parish register in Staffordshire recorded: "John Russel being famished through want of food (Josiah Freemen being overseer), was buried with the solemnity of many tears."[7] In 1631 it was pointed out that "the poore of parishes are faine to bee relieved by the Farmer, the Husbandman, and the middle rank, or else they must starve, as many upon my own knowledge did this last Snowie-winter."[8] While alternatives were available, even those were not possible for everyone. A 1623 report from Lincolnshire stated that "dog's flesh is a dainty dish, and found . . . in many houses."[9]

Even in times of plenty, many people complained of "sore eyes" and incidences of rickets caused by deficiencies of vitamins A (butter and green vegetables) and D (milk and eggs).[10] Inadequate diets in infancy led to the deformation of many children due to rickets. Unbalanced diets among the rich caused more than one in twelve of late sixteenth and early seventeenth century peers to suffer through agonizing years of "stones" in the kidneys or bladder. The most common causes of infant deaths were intestinal worms and fever brought on at teething time. Inadequate milk supplies from the mother or wet-nurse, poisoning from pewter dishes, lack of fresh air, and excessive swaddling were other major causes of death as well.[11]

Widespread ignorance about personal and public hygiene among both rich and poor meant contaminated food and water were constant threats to life in early modern times. The stagnant waters of city ditches were frequently used as latrines. Butchers threw the entrails of their slaughtered animals into the streets. In London by the early eighteenth century, a special problem was caused by the "poor's holes." These were large, deep, open pits where

---

[6]See the data in W. G. Hoskins, "Harvest Fluctuations and English Economic History, 1480-1619," *Agricultural Historical Review* 12 (1964) and "Harvest Fluctuations and English Economic History, 1620-1759," *Agricultrual Historical Review* 16 (1968).

[7]Peter Laslett, *The World We Have Lost: England Before the Industrial Age* (New York: Scribner's, 1965), 117.

[8]Carl Bridenbaugh, *Vexed and Troubled Englishmen, 1590-1642* (New York: Oxford University Press, 1968), 377.

[9]P. Bowden, "Agricultural Prices, Farm Profits, and Rents," *The Agrarian History of England and Wales 1500-1640*, ed. Joan Thirsk (Cambridge: Cambridge University Press, 1967), 4:632.

[10]Keith V. Thomas, *Religion and the Decline of Magic* (New York: Scribner, 1971), 6.

[11]Stone, *Family, Sex and Marriage*, 77.

the corpses of the poor were laid side by side, row upon row. Only after the pit was completely filled with bodies was it covered over.[12]

These conditions fostered the periodic outbreak of the most dreaded of all scourges, the Bubonic plague. The plague spread throughout the English towns. In the one hundred fifty years before 1665, there were only about a dozen years in which London was free from the deadly killer. In the sixteenth and seventeenth centuries, death from the plague is thought to have produced these casualty figures in London:

1563   20,000 deaths

1593   15,000 deaths

1603   36,000 deaths (over one-sixth of the population)

1625   41,000 deaths (another one-sixth)

1636   10,000 deaths

1665   68,000 deaths (at least)[13]

The terrifying suddenness of the plague and its virulence produced devastating social effects. The upper classes fled the city and the poor were left there to die. Unemployment, food shortages, violence, and looting usually resulted. The practice of quarantining infected families in their houses frequently produced further violence. As a preacher commented, the plague was   .

> the most dreadful and terrible; . . . then all friends leave us, then a man or woman sit[s] and lie[s] alone and is a stranger to the breath of his own relations. If a man be sick of a fever it is some comfort that he can take a bed-staff and knock, and his servant comes up

[12] A contemporary exclaimed, "How noisome the stench is that arises from these holes so stowed with dead bodies, especially in sultry seasons and after rain." See M. D. George, *London Life in the Eighteenth Century* (London: Kegan Paul, Trench & Trubner, 1925), 97; 340 n66; 342 n90; 344 nn114, n 117; 345 n 124. Cf. Stone, *Family, Sex and Marriage*, 77-78.

[13] See J.F.D. Shrewsbury, *A History of Bubonic Plague in the British Isles* (Cambridge: Cambridge University Press, 1970) *passim*. Cf. Thomas, *Religion and Decline of Magic*, 7-8; Bridenbaugh, *Vexed and Troubled Englishmen*, 104ff., 187; and Laslett, *World We Have Lost*, 117ff. In one small hamlet "a parish register informs us, more or less incidentally, everyone died, and the last full-grown man to get the disease actually dug his own grave in the yard and buried himself in it. He seems to have taken this strange action because he was certain he must die and because he knew that the servant-girl and the boy who were alone would be left alive, would never be able to get his body out of the house. This was at Malpas in Cheshire in September, 1625," J. C. Cox, *The Parish Registers of England* (London: Methuen, 1910), 175.

and helps him with a cordial. But if a man be sick of the plague then he sits and lies all alone.[14]

The psychologically shattering fear of contagion shattered the bonds of family solidarity all the more.

In addition to the plague, there were periodic outbreaks of influenza, typhus, dysentery, and in the seventeenth century, smallpox. This last, newer disease did not kill so frequently (the mortality rate was about 16 percent in the early eighteenth century), but it left its victims either completely blinded or pockmarked and disfigured for life. Between 1670 and 1689, approximately thirty thousand people died of smallpox in London. Thirty percent of the reported deaths in London in the seventeenth century were due to epidemics.[15] The poet Oliver Goldsmith (1730-74) wrote in 1760:

> Lo, the smallpox with horrid glare
> Levelled its terrors at the fair;
> And, rifling every youthful grace,
> Left but the remnant of a face.[16]

Medical practitioners did little to aid and much to harm those afflicted by most contemporary illnesses. The theories on which many of their treatments were based were usually wrong. Normally a physician devised "blood-letting" to evacuate evil "humours." The doctor tried to induce vomiting and prescribed frequent applications of purges and enemas to rid the stomach and bowels of their contents. The prescriptions of reputable physicians often differed little from those of that "great multitude of ignorant persons"–the herbalists, wise women, or empirics whom Parliament had denounced in 1512.[17]

For apoplexy, a "cure" was to swallow a glass of the urine of a healthy person mixed with salt in order to induce vomiting. For gout, one was to apply live earthworms to the affected areas until they began to swell. Robert Boyle, the "Father of Chemistry," advised blowing dried and powdered

---

[14]*The Works of the Rev. William Bridge* (London, 1845) 1: 468-69. Cf. Thomas, *Religion and Decline of Magic*, 8.

[15]C. Creighton, *A History of Epidemics in Britain*, 2d ed. (London: Cass, 1965), 2, 454-55.

[16]Oliver Goldsmith, "The Double Transformation," *Poems of Thomas Gray, William Collins and Oliver Goldsmith*, ed. R. Lonsdale (London: Harlow, Longmans, 1969), 586.

[17]See Thomas, *Religion and Decline of Magic*, 12. The Royal College of Physicians established in 1518 to supervise and license physicians who practiced in London and within a seven mile radius exercised its monopoly in a jealous and restrictive way. The ratio of population to physicians in London was never better than 5,000:1 and usually much greater. But on the whole, even these physicians were too expensive for the bottom half of the population to afford. See Sir G. Clark, *A History of the Royal College of Physicians of London* (Oxford: Clarendon, 1964-66), 1:70, 71, 132, 188, 190, 304, 315, 356; 2:736-39.

human excrement into the eyes to remedy cataracts. Robert Hooke took medicines composed of a powdered human skull among other ingredients.[18]

All this gives some indication of the environment of sixteenth-century England. Poverty, sickness, and sudden disaster were familiar features. The process of death and dying was so common and so open that everyone was exposed to it from the very earliest ages. As a result, family life in the early modern period was marked by impermanence. Whether from the point of view of husbands and wives or parents and children, none had much reason to expect to remain together for too long a time. The stark reality was that death was a part of life and had to be treated as such.

Attitudes Toward Death

It has been argued by Philippe Ariès that Western attitudes toward death can be traced through four stages. The first attitude, labeled "Tame Death," is the oldest and longest tradition. It is summarized by the phrase *et moriemur* ("and we shall all die"). Dying is "the familiar resignation to the collective destiny of the species." In the twelfth century a second tradition arose which focused more attention on the individual self. "One's own death" (*la mort de soi*) was the stress and the expression. Third, death took on a new meaning with the eighteenth century. "Thy death" (*la mort de toi*) captures this attitude which shifted the emphasis away from the self and toward the "death of the other." Finally, in the nineteenth and twentieth centuries, "forbidden death" became the theme. Death has become shameful and forbidden. The accent has now fallen on an "acceptable death," that is, "'an acceptable style of living while dying' . . . an acceptable death is a death which can be accepted or tolerated by the survivors."[19] The initiative in death has passed (since the eighteenth century) from the dying person to the family and now to the doctor and hospital team. The stress is on the avoidance of any public display of emotion.

Ariès traced the twelfth century new concern for the individual as a displacement of the older idea of the collective destiny of the species through four phenomena. These are: (1) the portrayal of the Last Judgment at the end of the world; (2) the displacing of this judgment through the end of each life, to the precise moment of death; (3) macabre themes and the interest shown in portrayals of physical decomposition; and (4) the return to funeral inscriptions and to a certain personalization of tombs.[20]

---

[18]Stone, *Family, Sex and Marriage*, 80.

[19]Philippe Ariès, *Western Attitudes Toward Death: From the Middle Ages to the Present*, trans. Patricia M. Ranum (Baltimore: The Johns Hopkins University Press, 1974), 89. Each of the four chapters of this book is devoted to one of these topics. Attitudes toward life, death, and immortality in the early church theologians are surveyed in Jaroslav Pelikan, *The Shape of Death* (Nashville: Abingdon, 1961).

[20]Ariès, *Western Attitudes Toward Death*, 28ff.

To judge from the art and literature of the Middle Ages, the physical horrors of deterioration and death were prominent concerns. The "cadaver" (*transi*: "the perished one") or *charogne* made its appearance at this time. Pierre de Nesson (1383-1442) wrote:

> O carrion, who art no longer man,
> Who will hence keep thee company?
> Whatever issues from thy liquors,
> Worms engendered by the stench
> Of thy vile carrion flesh.[21]

Yet the horrors of decomposition were not limited to *post mortem*. In the illness of old age (*intra vitem*), the poet proclaimed:

> I am nothing but bones, I seem a skeleton,
> Fleshless, muscleless, pulpless. . .
> My body is diminishing to the point where
> everything becomes disjointed.[22]

This was far more than merely the language of the "preacher." The poets were aware of the presence of corruption universally. The worms which devour the cadavers at death sprang from within:

> Each conduit [of the body]
> Constantly produces putric matter
> Out of the body.[23]

Even in altarpieces and murals, the physical horrors of death and deterioriation were protrayed. In the predella below the Madonna by Giovanni del Biondo in the Vatican, an unprecedented representation (for Tuscan art) showed a corpse decayed and consumed by snakes and toads. A

---

[21]Pierre de Nesson, "Vigiles des morts: Paraphrase sur Job," quoted in *Anthologie poétique française, Moyen Âge*, ed. Garnier (Paris, 1967), 2:184 cited by Ariès, *Western Attitudes Toward Death*, 41.

[22]P. de Ronsard, "Derniers vers," Sonnet 1, *Oeuvres complètes*, rev. ed., ed. P. Laumonier (Paris: Silver and Le Beque, 1967), 18, pt. 1, 176-77. Cf. Ariès, *Western Attitudes Toward Death*, 42.

[23]Pierre de Nesson quoted by A. Tenenti, *Il senso della morte el l'amore della vita nel Rinascimento* (Turin, 1957), 147. Cf. Ariès, *Western Attitudes Toward Death*, 42.

bearded old hermit points to it with an admonishing gesture while a man and his dog recoil from it in terror.[24] Other examples could also be cited.[25]

Coexistent in the Middle Ages with this strong horror of the physicalness of death and decay of the body was the Christian optimism of the resurrection of the body. The hope of heaven was always real. Death in the late Middle Ages was "a ghastly visitation upon the *body* of man, but fear of the soul's fate . . . remained blunted by the Christian tradition."[26] The poet François Villon combined the physical and spiritual aspects when he wrote:

> Death trembles him and bleeds him pale.
> The nostrils pinch, the veins distend,
> The neck is gorged, skin limp and frail.
> Joints knot and sinews draw and rend.
> O Woman's body, so suave and tender,
> So trim and dear, must you arrive
> at such an agony in the end?
> Oh yes, or rise to Heaven live.[27]

In literature and art, this was also the age of graphic descriptions of the Last Judgment—that day of whose coming no one knew when the blessed would be received into Paradise and the wicked pass to everlasting damnation.[28] But even the *Ars Moriendi* (Art of Dying) woodcuts (ca. 1450) was not "a doleful book—no clarion call to repentance. There is little stress upon hell, only hope of heaven. Always is Moriens encouraged and consoled."[29] In the closing scene, the dying man has resisted the temptations

[24]Millard Meiss, *Painting in Florence & Siena After the Black Death* (New York: Harper & Row, 1951; rpt. 1964), 74, and the photograph, Fig. 52.

[25]See the pictures in Stannard, *Puritan Way of Death*, 16 (Fig. 2) of the tomb of François de Sarra (ca. 1400), and 18 (Fig 3) of Mathias Grunewald's "The Damnation of Lovers" (fifteenth century). Stannard notes that even when the subject of resurrection was discussed, there was "an intense emphasis placed on the problems thus posed for the disintegrated corpse." He cites sections in Aquinas's *Summa Theologica* and the popular "myth of Lazarus" which claimed that following Lazarus's resurrection by Jesus, he lived in constant torment knowing he would have to endure the physical act of dying once again, 17, 19.

[26]Stannard, *Puritan Way of Death*, 19.

[27]François Villon, *The Legacy, The Testament, and Other Poems*, trans. Peter Dale (London: Macmillan, 1973), 51. Cf. Stannard, *Puritan Way of Death*, 17.

[28]See the accounts and pictures in T.S.R. Boase, *Death in the Middle Ages*. Library of Medieval Civilization, ed. Joan Evans and Christopher Brooke (New York: McGraw-Hill, 1972), *passim*, especially ch. 2.

[29]Mary C. O'Connor, *The Art of Dying Well: The Development of the Ars Moriendi* (New York: Columbia University Press, 1942), 5. Johan Huizinga wrote: "The dominant thought, as expressed in the literature, both ecclesiastical and lay, of that period, hardly knew anything with regard to death but those two extremes: lamentation about the briefness of all earthly glory, and jubilation over the salvation of the soul," *The Waning of the Middle Ages* (London: E. Arnold & Co., 1924), 135. See his whole chapter 11, "The Vision of Death."

of the demons who lie in disarray at his feet, and he has died peacefully. His soul (shown issuing from his mouth) is received by a company of angels.

Thus the medieval fear of death as displayed in the grotesque physical depictions of cadavers and corpses was met by the equally potent optimism of Christianity. One strand of the Christian tradition which had a counter-balancing effect to the medieval fascination with the physical textures of death was the *contemptus mundi*. This reached its fullest expression near the middle of the medieval period. Illustrative of this ascetic stream was the influential work of Pope Innocent III, *De Contemptu Mundi: Liber de Miseria Humanae Conditionis*. This work was a type of "ascetical *summa*."[30] Its message simply was that depravity, vileness, and corruption was the lot of humankind. Only by pursuing an ascetic and celibate ideal that renounced mortal passions and concentrated on the spiritual glories of God and heaven could true humility and salvation be found. With this attitude, the inner tensions wrought by the dramatic confrontations with horrible death in art and literature could be resolved.

With the waning of the Middle Ages, intense preoccupation with death began to fade. The growth and acceptance of the idea of Purgatory helped to lessen concern with the dreaded awe of judgment and damnation.[31] Renaissance poetry has been described as laying stress on

> immortality and afterlife. The word 'death' was often avoided and replaced by euphemisms . . . [and] depiction of the realistic aspects of death was carefully suppressed. . . . In the early sixteenth century, poets dwelt upon fame and immortality rather than death. . . .[32]

The *contemptus mundi* was still powerful. A certain "yearning for death" became "the center of belief, for it [meant] the rejection of the world–sin–and the affirmation of God."[33] In 1554, Sir John Harington wrote:

> Death is a porte whereby we pass to joye;
> Lyfe is a lake that drowneth all in payne;

[30]This characterization is from Donald R. Howard, "The Contempt of the World: A Study in the Ideology of Latin Christendom with Emphasis on Fourteenth-Century English Literature," (Ph.D. dissertation, University of Florida, 1954), 144. Cf. Stannard, *Puritan Way of Death*, 21.

[31]See Gaby and Michel Vovelle, *Vision de la mort et de l'audelà en Provençe* (Cahiers des Annales 29, 1970) and Stannard, *Puritan Way of Death*, 22.

[32]Edelgard Dubruck, *The Theme of Death in French Poetry of the Middle Ages and the Renaissance* (The Hague: Mouton, 1964), 152, 154. Cf. Stannard, *Puritan Way of Death*, 22.

[33]Luis Klein, "Die Bereitung zum Sterben: Studien zu den frühen Reformatorischen Sterbebüchern," (Ph.D. dissertation, Georg-August-Univesität, Göttingen, 1958), 121. Cf. Stannard, *Puritan Way of Death*, 22.

Death is so dear, it killeth all annoye;
Lyfe is so lewd, that all it yields is veyne.
For, as by lyfe to bondage man was brought,
Even so by deathe all freedom too was wrought.[34]

Even by the seventeenth century Jeremy Taylor (1613-67), the Anglican Bishop, wrote of death that "it is so harmless a thing, that no good man was ever thought the more miserable for dying, but much the happier."[35]

Yet this tradition did not go unchallenged. Erasmus, for example, when he was a young monk had written a tract in 1488 or 1489 on contempt for the world; but thirty years later, after finding that copies of the document were still being circulated, he added a preface and a new final chapter in which he referred to the tract as a "trifling piece with which I amused myself while a mere boy in practicing the art of composition." Significantly, Erasmus's last chapter attacked the monasteries. He reversed his earlier position of praise for the celibate, silent, monastic life. He now argued that life in the world could be as pure as life in a monk's cell.[36]

A further powerful effect in relaxing the *contemptus mundi* tradition was the work of Calvin. Instead of withdrawing from the world, Calvin urged full participation in it. This included far-reaching concerns in areas of politics, economics, and the common life.[37] When Calvin wrote of the "contempt for the world," it was in terms of his larger vision for eternal life in the world to come: "Whatever kind of tribulation presses upon us, we must ever look to this end: to accustom ourselves to contempt for the present life and to be aroused thereby to meditate upon the future life."[38] While the present life is full of allurements and the human heart is "occupied with avarice, ambition, and lust" so it is "so weighed down that it cannot rise up higher" (III.9.1). Calvin said God calls us "not to be captivated by such panderings"

[34]*Nugae Antiquae: A Miscellaneous Collection of Original Papers . . . by Sir John Harington*, ed. Henry Harington and Thomas Park (London, 1804), 2:332-33. Cf. Stannard, *Puritan Way of Death*, 23.

[35]Jeremy Taylor, *The Rule and Exercise of Holy Dying* (1651; London, 1869), 95.

[36]See Albert Nyma, *The Youth of Erasmus* (Ann Arbor: University of Michigan Press, 1931), 167-81; Howard, "Contempt of the World," 213-18, and Stannard, *Puritan Way of Death*, 23, 25.

[37]There is much literature on this. See for example W. Fred Graham, *The Constructive Revolutionary: John Calvin and His Socio-Economic Impact* (Richmond: John Knox Press, 1971); Andre Biéler, *La pensée economique et sociale de Calvin* (Geneva: Librairie de l'université, 1959); and studies of the Calvinist tradition such as Max Weber, *The Protestant Ethic and the Spirit of Capitalism*, trans. Talcott Parsons (New York: Scribner, 1930), and Michael Walzer, *The Revolution of the Saints: A Study in the Origins of Radical Politics* (Cambridge: Harvard University Press, 1965).

[38]*Calvin: Institutes of the Christian Religion*, ed. John T. McNeill, trans. Ford Lewis Battles, Library of Christian Classics (Philadelphia: Westminster, 1960), III.9.1. Further citations from the *Institutes* are in the text.

(III.9.2) but to come away from a "perverse love of this life" to a "desire for a better one" (III.9.4). This is "that blessed inheritance of his life and glory" (III.9.5).

Yet this "meditation on the future life" (*meditatio futurae vitae*) does not mean withdrawal from participation in the present life. It points instead toward not loving the things of this world inordinately. For Calvin, the earthly life "is never to be hated except insofar as it holds us subject to sin; although not even hatred of that condition may ever properly be turned against life itself" (III.9.4). For "this life, however crammed with infinite miseries it may be, is still rightly to be counted among those blessings of God which are not to be spurned" (III.9.3).

Calvin advocated here a full Christian involvement in the present world, accepting God's good gifts with thankfulness, and being vigorously active in all arenas of life–while at the same time looking toward the blessedness of eternal life after death. As he commented on 1 Tim. 4:8:

> We must remember to distinguish between the blessings of the present and those of the future. For in this world God blesses us in such a way as to give us a mere foretaste of His kindness, and by that taste to entice us to desire heavenly blessings with which we may be satisfied.[39]

In the meantime God has called Christians to work in this world. In commenting on the denunciations by Saint Paul of those who are "idle" and "disorderly" (2 Thess. 3:6-7), Calvin claimed Paul used the term "disorderly to apply not to those who lead a dissolute life or whose reputation is stained by flagrant misdeeds, but to idlers and nonentities [*ignavos, et nihili homines*] who do not have any honourable or useful occupation."[40] To his followers, these words of Calvin seemed a perfect description of those who lived the monastic life.

Death and Dying in Puritanism

THEOLOGICAL FOUNDATIONS. Along with other aspects of Calvin's theology, English (and later American) Puritanism inherited Calvin's contempt for the *contemptus mundi* as it had come to be expressed in medieval

---

[39]Comm. I Tim. 4:8 *Calvin's New Testament Commentaries*, ed. David W. and Thomas F. Torrance (Grand Rapids: Eerdmans, 1959-72), 10:244; hereafter cited as *CNTC*. These views of Calvin's constitute a kind of *via media* between the "brutish love of this world" (3.9.1) characteristic of the sinful self and the final perfection and blessedness the saints will experience in the Kingdom of God (III.9.6). This stance is characteristic of Calvin's theological method itself. See Donald K. McKim, "John Calvin: A Theologian for an Age of Limits," *Readings in Calvin's Theology*, ed. Donald K. McKim (Grand Rapids: Baker, 1984), 291-310.

[40]*CNTC* 8:416.

Catholicism.[41] For William Perkins, a "vocation" or "calling" was "a certaine kinde of life, ordained and imposed on many by God, for the common good."[42] A person lived out a "calling" in the midst of the church and commonwealth. Those who have renounced the world, such as "Monkes and Friars," Perkins said:

> challenge to themselves that they live in a state of perfection, because they live apart from the societies of man in fasting and prayer: but contrariwise, this Monkish kind of living is damnable; for besides the generall duties of fasting and praier, which appertaine to all Christians, every man must have a particular & personal calling, that he may be a good and profitable member of some society and body. And the auncient Church condemned all Monkes for theaves and robbers, that besides the generall duties of praier and fasting, did not withal imploy themselves in some other calling for their better maintenance.[43]

To Perkins and the Puritans, God had created the world and God's people must work within it. Perkins wrote of "the maine end of our lives": "That is, to serve God in the serving of men in the workes of our callings."[44]

Intertwined with this view of vocation in Puritan theology were highly developed doctrines of election, providence, and predestination.[45] Salvation was not based on good works or ritualistic expressions of penance. Salvation

---

[41]The term "Puritanism" is used in a general sense here in line with the definition by Basil Hall: "Puritan is the regular word for those [clergy and laity] of the established Chuch of England whose attitudes ranged from the tolerably conformable to the downright obstreperous, and to those who sought to presbyterianise that Church from within." From 1640 to 1662, the more precise terms "Presbyterian," "Independent," and "Anabaptist" are better used. See Basil Hall, "Puritanism: The Problem of Definition," *Studies in Church History* 2, ed. G. J. Cuming (London: Thomas Nelson & Sons, 1965), 294. Robert S. Paul notes that "undoubtedly the Puritans were (on the whole) Calvinists . . . [but] many regarded as Puritans questioned particular parts of Calvinism." See his "The Accidence and the Essence of Puritan Piety," *Austin Seminary Bulletin* 93 (May 1978): 8, 37 n6.

[42]*The Works of William Perkins*, 3 vols. (Cambridge: John Legatt, 1616-18), 1:750. Further references in the text are to this edition. The archaic spellings have been preserved. On vocation see also Robert S. Paul, "Weber and Calvinism: The Effects of a 'Calling,'" *Canadian Journal of Theology* 11 (January 1965): 25-41.

[43]*Works of Perkins*, 1:755-56; cf. 1:586; 3:237, 375. Richard Sibbes later picked up on Calvin's view that the world requires active maintenance and that "worldly things are good in themselves, and given to sweeten our passage to Heaven . . . [since] this world and the things thereof are all good, and were all made of God, for the benefit of this creature," *The Saints Cordials* (London, 1637), 188.

[44]*Works of Perkins*, 1:757. See Paul, "Accidence and Essence of Puritan Piety," 26ff. on "The Call to Public Service."

[45]See for example William Perkins, *A Golden Chaine* (1:11-116) and his *A Christian and Plaine Treatise of the Manner and Order of Predestination* (2:603-41).

was a free gift of God, mysteriously given to some (the Elect) through God's eternal decree. One could not choose one's election; the choice was God's. In the same way, God's decree from all eternity has "determined all things (Eph. 1:11; Matt. 10:29; Rom. 9:21)," wrote Perkins (1:15). The will of God was "the cause of causes" (2:610). Ultimately, behind every event and circumstance of the universe stood the will of God. With this as a theological foundation, far-reaching effects ensued for every area of life. Especially strong was the Puritan notion of God's will and providence directing the course of history–both corporate and individual.[46] This, coupled with an expectancy of Christ's imminent second coming (intensified at different periods in the seventeenth century), produced the Puritan "saint" who saw the hand of God at work in everything–including death.[47]

THEOLOGICAL TENSIONS. These strong theological presuppositions created a certain tension or paradox in Puritanism's attitudes toward death and dying. On one hand, life was a "pilgrimage," directed by God (e.g. Bunyan's *Pilgrim's Progress*). It was "even a vapour that appeareth for a little time, and afterwarde vanisheth away."[48] Death was thus a blessing, a merciful deliverance by God from all the sorrows and trials of this vale of tears with all the ravages of disease, suffering, and the uncertainties of the precarious life of early modern times. Puritans did not hold this world strictly in contempt–as their views of vocation show–but they believed the truest and highest happiness that creatures could attain is found in the eternal glories of heaven. William Perkins described death as a blessing since it "gives an entrance to the soul, that it may come into the presence of the everlasting God, of Christ, and of all the Angels and Saints in heaven." In that sense, death was desirable.[49]

On the other hand, Puritans were also aware of a different side of the biblical description of death. Perkins took the Pauline text, "by one man sinne entred into the world, and death by sinne" (Rom. 5:12) with stark seriousness. He saw death as "a punishment ordained of God and imposed on man for his sinne. . . . ordained as a meanes of execution of God's justice

[46]Donald K. McKim, "The Puritan Veiw of History or 'Providence Without and Within,'" *The Evangelical Quarterly* 52 (October-December 1980): 215-37.

[47]On eschatological aspects see Christopher Hill, *Anti-Christ in the Seventeenth Century* (London: Oxford University Press, 1971); *Puritans, the Millennium, and the Future of Israel*, ed. Peter Toon (Cambridge: James Clarke, 1970). Cf. Thomas, *Religion and Decline of Magic*, Chap. 4 on "Providence."

[48]James 4:4 from the Geneva Bible (1560).

[49]*Works of Perkins*, 1:494. None of the religious doubted the reality of heaven. John Preston said in a sermon to the lawyers of Lincoln's Inn and the Parliament as they met at Oxford in 1625, "There is a certain Heaven which all Saints goe to," *The Golden Sceptre*, 268. Cf. Irvonwy Morgan, *Puritan Spirituality* (London: Epworth, 1973), 117.

and judgment."[50] No one was immune from the dreadful punishment for the sin of Adam. As a tombstone said simply:

> Death which came on man by the fall,
> cuts down father, child and all.[51]

THEOLOGICAL PREPARATIONS. With the prevalence of death in the culture and the theological underpinnings of a strong sense of predestination and providence, the Puritan faced the ambiguities of death. According to the prevailing theology, death was at once a wonderful blessing and also "a most terrible calamity." As a phenomenon in itself (as in the Middle Ages), death took on a prominence among other Puritan preoccupations. In the writings of Puritanism there is a whole genre of works devoted to the preparations one should make for death.[52]

One work illustrating Puritan thinking on death with its ambivalence and tensions is William Perkins's *A Salve for a Sicke Man or, A Treatise Containing the Nature, Differences, and Kindes of Death; as also the right manner of dying well* ([1595] *Works of Perkins* 1:487-514). It was particularly designed for "Marriners when they goe to sea; Souldiers when they goe to battell; and Women when they trauell with childe." The text for Perkins's treatise was Ecc. 7:3, "The day of death is better than the day that one is borne."

After Perkins distinguished the nature, differences, and kinds of death as well as some objections to the biblical text, he divided his work into three parts. The meaning of the text was that "the time of bodily death in which the bodie and soule of man are severed asunder, it is better then the time in which one is brought into the world" (*Works of Perkins* 2:490).

The first major part was devoted to the "uses" of this text; namely, how a person may "die well." How should one prepare to die? Perkins found two requirements for this in God's Word: "A preparation before death, and a right behaviour and disposition of death" (2:495). In the former, there were general and particular preparations. Generally "a man prepares himselfe to die through the whole course of his life" (2:495). This was done through five duties: meditation on death during one's lifetime (2:496); the endeavor to take away from one's own death the power and sting thereof (2:497); the duty in this life to enter into the first degree of life eternal (2:498); learning to die little by little through this life (2:499); and the doing of good while there is still time (2:499, citing Gal. 6:10).

[50]*Works of Perkins*, 1:489. Leonard Hoar later spoke of death as "the greatest evil in the world," *The Sting of Death* (Boston, 1680), 3. See Stannard, *Puritan Way of Death*, 77.

[51]Allan I Ludwig, *Graven Images* (Middletown, Conn.: Wesleyan University Press, 1966), 88, from the gravestone of John Hull, Cheshire, Connecticut.

[52]See Gordon S. Wakefield, *Puritan Devotion* (London: Epworth, 1957), chap. 9, "Holy Dying". Cf. chaps. 10-11.

Particular preparations for death came at times of sickness. Then, Perkins urged his readers, one should practice the duties of being reconciled to God and to one's neighbors (2:501). Dying persons were reconciled to God through a renewal of their former faith and repentance (2:501). Perkins's strong sense of predestination came through at this point. He wrote:

> So soone as a man shall feele any manner of sicknes to seize upon his body, he must consider with himselfe whence it ariseth: and after serious consideration, he shall find that it comes not by chaunce or fortune, but by the speciall providence of God. This done, he must goe yet further, and consider for what cause the Lord should afflict his body with any sicknes or disease. And hee shall finde by God's Word, that sicknes comes ordinarily and usually of sin. *Wherefore is the living man sorrowfeull? Man suffereth for his sinnes*, Lam. 3:39.[53]

In the Puritan ethos, some people spared no effort in probing for the cause or sin that resulted in sickness or calamity. Often the victim or a member of the immediate family was blamed. When Adam Martindale's sister went up to London in the early seventeenth century and caught smallpox and died, Adam took it as her punishment for disobeying her father who had forbidden her to go.[54] Sometimes people put blame on themselves for an illness in the family. When Ralph Josselin's daughter had an ague, he regarded it as a punishment for his own sins.[55] When the infant son of the fourth countess of Warwick fell ill, the countess wrote:

> My conscience told me it was for my backsliding. Upon which conviction I presently retired to God; and by earnest prayer begged of him to restore my child, and did then solemnly promise to God, if he would hear my prayer, I would become a new creature.[56]

The doctor was astonished, but the child promptly recovered.

Perkins urged the sick person to take concern for both soul and body. One help for the soul was to focus the mind on the blessed estate to be enjoyed after death. A second help was to "looke upon death in the glasse

---

[53] *Works of Perkins* 2:501. The methodological movement from "general" to "particular" is characteristic of the Ramist method that Perkins employed in this and his other works. See McKim, *Ramism in Perkins' Theology*, 111.

[54] *Life of Adam Martindale*, Chetham Society, 1st ser., 4 (1845): 6. Cf. Stone, *Family, Sex and Marriage*, 210.

[55] Alan Macfarlane, *The Family Life of Ralph Josselin: A Seventeenth Century Clergyman* (Cambridge: Cambridge University Press, 1970), 175-76.

[56] *Autobiography of Mary Rich, Countess of Warwick*, ed. T. C. Croker, Percy Society 22 (1848): 17-18. Cf. Stone, *Family, Sex and Marriage*, 210.

of the Gospel, and not in the glasse of the law" (2:503). Those who are sick should also take concern for their souls by meditation: on the special providence of God; on the promise of God for the righteous (Rev. 14:13); on the estate of all them that are in Christ whether alive or dead; and on God's promises to the sick–the lessening of their pains, the comforting of their spirits, and the ministry of good angels (2:504).

A sick person took concern for the body by the right use of the available means. Here Perkins took a positive view of doctors and medicine. He wrote: "The meanes is good and wholesome physicke, which though it be despised of many as a thing unprofitable and needless, yet must be esteemed as an ordinance & blessing of God" (2:505). He cited biblical examples from the use of a lump of dry figs by the prophet to restore King Hezekiah to health (2 Kings 20:7) through the commendation of the Samaritan for binding up and pouring wine and oil on the wounds of the man who fell among robbers (Luke 10:34). Physicians chosen should be those who were "knowne to bee well learned, and men of experience, as also of good conscience and good religion" (2:505). Perkins warned vehemently against "meanes as have no warrant. Of this kinds are all charmes or spels, or what wordes so ever they consist: characters and figures either in paper, wood, or waxe: all amulets, and ligatures. . . ." (2:506). But readers were to keep in mind too that they should humble themselves before God before they took any medicines. They should accompany the use of "physicke" with prayer. And they should remember the proper "end" of physicke: it does not serve to prevent old age or death itself; it merely prolonged natural life in order that we might have more time to prepare ourselves for God's kingdom (2:506). Perkins also saw it as the physician's duty to admonish dying patients to repent of their sins. When the doctor saw "manifest signes of death in his patient," he was "not to depart concealing them, but first of all to certifie the patient thereof" (2:507).

The sick person had a duty to be reconciled to neighbors–to forgive them and desire their forgiveness. Those who were rulers or governors were to see they left their charges in good estate whether they were magistrates, ministers, or householders. This was how one was to prepare for death.

Perkins then went on to explain how one was to behave at death. The first duty here was to die in or by faith. This may be expressed through praises and thanksgivings to God and through one's last words. Perkins then listed famous last words uttered by great saints of the church (2:509-10). The second duty was to die in obedience, that is, "ready and desirous to goe out of this world, whensoever God shal cal him, and that without murmuring or repining, at what time, where and when it shall please God." The third duty was to "render up our soules into the hands of God" (2:511).

Perkins concluded his treatise by dealing briefly with the other two major questions: In what sense should death be feared, in what sense should it not be feared? He claimed that the children of God "are not to feare death overmuch" (2:512). Their fear of death has two causes: "Death is the destruction of humane nature in a mans own selfe and others" and second, it is "the losse of the Church or Commonwealth, when we or others are deprived of them which were indeede or might have bin an helpe, stay and comfort to either of them, and whose death hath procured some publike or private losse" (2:513).

Yet the other side of the theological tension was there as well. In another sense, Perkins claimed, we are to be glad of death for a number of reasons: it shows our subjection and obedience to God; it abolishes sin; brings the dead body into a better condition; gives the soul passage to eternal life; and gives opportunity for God to judge the wicked (2:513).

Perkins's final comments were in the form of a question: whether it be lawful to desire death since the day of one's death is better than the day of one's birth? His answer was that "this desire must not be simple, but restrained with certain respects" (2:513). These were: death may be desired as a means to free us from the corruption of our natures; to bring us into immediate fellowship with Christ and God in heaven; and it may be desired in respect to the troubles and miseries of this life, provided this desire was not immoderate and was joined with submission and subjection to the good pleasure of God. Yet while death for the Christian was "blessed," for the unbelieving and unrepentant, it was in every way "cursed and most horrible."

THEOLOGICAL QUESTIONS. From this consideration of Perkins's work and the streams traced above, two final questions arise. One is to what extent did the triumphant note or the fearless attitude toward death actually prevail in the lives or deathbed scenes of those influenced by Puritan theological writings? There are indications that despite the fundamental Christian doctrinal belief in the "triumph over death," the theological tensions still remained very strong till the end.[57]

Perkins himself was not unaware of the possibilities that at the time of death even true saints could experience pangs of anxiety. He observed that

---

[57]See Stannard, *Puritan Way of Death*, 79ff. for a discussion. He challenges Perry Miller's view of the Puritans' "cosmic optimism" in the face of death. Stannard's view is that "the Puritans were gripped individually and collectively by an intense and unremitting fear of death, while *simultaneously* clinging to the traditional Christian rhetoric of viewing death as a release and relief for the earthbound soul," 79. See Perry Miller, *The New England Mind: The Seventeenth Century* (Boston: Beacon, 1939; rpt. 1961), 37-38. The example of Increase Mather is a case in point. In 1715 he said: ". . . how glad should I be, if I might dye before I stir out of this pulpit." When he was dying eight years later, however, his son Cotton Mather reported his father's "expressions of some Fear lest he might after all be Deceived in his *Hope* of the *Future Blessedness*." See Increase Mather, *Several Sermons* (Boston, 1715), 59-60, and Cotton Mather, *Parentator* (Boston, 1724), 207.

not only wicked and loose persons despaire in death, but also repentant sinners, who oftentimes in their sickness, testifie of themselves, that being alive, and lying in their beds, they feel themselves as it were to be in hell, and to apprehend the very pangs and torments thereof.[58]

But how widespread was deathbed anxiety? Did the "King of Terrors" terrify till the end? Could all people resolve their lives into Perkins's neat dichotomies and "prepare to die well" while not fearing death "overmuch"?[59]

The second question raised by these aspects of death and dying in Puritanism has to do with the reason why this tension in the Puritan view of death took on such tremendous importance. The ultimate question, which overshadows all lesser questions about *how* to die is the theological question: "How do I know that I am among the Elect?" Perkins's "preparations for dying well" were sharply divided into different "steps" and "duties." Underlying his discussion and the basic tensions, he exhibits in his view of election, predestination, and his doctrine of the assurance of salvation. Humankind is in utter and total sinful depravity. Salvation rests solely on the electing work of God. There is the threatening reality of divine judgment on one hand; the glorious eternal bliss of heaven on the other. How could one be *sure* of one's election? Despite all strivings and preparations for death, could one be positive on the deathbed that, in the ultimate sense, death need not be feared "overmuch"? Could one have absolute certainty that the day of one's death would be better than the day of birth? These questions made Puritan discussions of death and dying take on most crucial dimensions.

Tracing Puritan views on the assurance of salvation is complicated, for this issue is also linked with developed doctrines of "preparation for salvation."[60] There was variety and development in the Puritan tradition on these points. While assurance of salvation was a desirable goal and there was much to say in describing the "signs" or "marks" of election, there was also difficulty and confusion. This was because of the constant danger of deception. For many Puritans, there was always a lingering doubt whether

[58]*Works of Perkins*, 2:492. Three accounts of Perkins's own death have survived. By one, he died crying, "Mercy, mercy!" By another he cried, "Hold, hold. Do not pray so; but pray the Lord to give him faith and patience, and then let him lay on me just what he please" after hearing someone pray for the mitigation of his pains. The third account says simply that when he was asked what he wanted, he answered, "Nothing but mercy." See Ian Breward, "The Life and Theology of William Perkins 1558-1602," (Ph.D. dissertation, University of Manchester, England, 1963), 33-34.

[59]The "King of Terrors" is a description by Samuel Willard, *A Compleat Body of Divinity* (Boston,1726), 234, from a sermon on October 31, 1693 (Sermon 66).

[60]See Norman Petit, *The Heart Prepared: Grace and Conversion in Puritan Spiritual Life* (New Haven: Yale University Press, 1966). Cf. Patricia Caldwell, *The Puritan Conversion Narrative: The Beginnings of American Expression* (Cambridge: Cambridge University Press, 1983).

the "signs" of salvation were being properly read and interpreted. This tension was tightened because it was precisely this doubt that was essential to the whole enterprise, for the danger of *false* assurance was always real. The surest way to be falsely assured of salvation was to be complacent–to have no doubts. Put succinctly, "The best sign of assurance was to be unsure."[61]

Later in New England the Antinomian Controversy, the Halfway Covenant, and other theological disputes were the upshot of questions about preparation, conversion, and assurance. At the risk of oversimplifying the whole development, the line seems to have moved from a position taken by Perkins that assurance is "when the elect are perswaded in their hearts by the Holy Ghost, of the forgiveness of their owne sinnes, and of God's infinite mercie toward them in Jesus Christ" (1:363) to the view of Jonathan Edwards (1703-58) that "assurance is not to be obtained so much by self-examination as by active piety."[62] The dynamics of the introspection gave way to a heightened concern for outward signs or "good works" to display one's "active piety." Eventually even Edwards's view was removed from its rigidly predestinarian framework. The doctrine of assurance then was developed by "perfectionism" and revivalism–movements which William Perkins and other Puritans would have attacked as Pelagian or semi-Pelagian.

As this theology changed, so did cultures and churches. In America, new attitudes and responses to death and dying arose. An age of romantic sentimentality followed.[63] Some aspects of the Puritan way of death are still forcefully present today. But there is also present an "American way of death"–a way far removed from the cemetery at the center of the early modern village.

[61]Stannard, *Puritan Way of Death*, 75. Perkins was aware of this problem. One of his answers, however, was that all who received the gift of true faith "have also another gift of discerning whereby they see and know their owne faith" (1:547).

[62]See Jonathan Edwards, *An Humble Inquiry* (Boston, 1749), 36. In other words, "Experience shows, says Edwards . . . that Christians who have passed from doubt into assurance exercise most grace. Life is most evident, in the summer when the trees are bearing fruit, not in the winter when the leaves are dead. In other words, the more grace a [person] practices, the more assurance [one] feels; the more assurance [one] feels, the more grace [one] practices," John H. Gerstner, *Steps to Salvation: The Evangelistic Message of Jonathan Edwards* (Philadelphia: Westminster, 1960), 172.

Perkins was also concerned with the need for good works as a sign of the regenerated life. See *Works of Perkins*, 1:292. To Perkins, "unfallible certainty" of one's salvation came "first of all & principally by faith; & then secondly, by such workes as are unseparable companions of faith" (1:540, 541). On this problem see also Gordon J. Keddie, "'Unfallible Certenty of the Pardon of Sinne and Life Everlasting,' The Doctrine of Assurance in the Theology of William Perkins (1558-1602)," *The Evangelical Quarterly* 48 (October-December 1976): 230-44, and R. T. Kendall, *Calvin and English Calvinism to 1649* (Oxford: Oxford University Press, 1979), Part II.

[63]See Ariès, *Attitudes Toward Death*, 56, who speaks of the nineteenth and twentieth centuries as being marked by "the new cult of tombs and cemeteries and the romantic, rhetorical treatment of death."

A group of students listening to one of Calvin's lectures.

A Working Bibliography of Writings by John Knox

Ian Hazlett

Even though David Laing's *The Works of John Knox* contains almost all of Knox's writings, it does not provide a list as such of Knox's published works, and it is inconvenient for students and researchers to search Laing's introductions to each piece to find out whether it was published or not. Further, the nature of Knox's writings make them, bibliographically speaking, relatively complex. Most were occasional in character, containing two or more separate pieces of different dates or subjects under one title in some places, or as unspecified separate pieces in others, making it difficult to rely simply on "titles". The principle in this bibliography has been to itemize each of Knox's published compositions separately, but with reference to its host volume, to present a clearer conspectus of his editions and their sequence. Until a more comprehensive and analytical bibliography is undertaken, it is hoped that this bibliography, used in conjunction with Laing's standard edition, will aid Knox scholars and researchers.

THE PRIME REASON FOR COMPOSING THIS Knox bibliography is that, somewhat surprisingly, none already exists. In the absence then of such a catalogue, the aim of this bibliography is simply to provide a reasonably reliable quick reference list of Knox's published writings, and of others in which he was involved. Almost all of Knox's writings are contained in David Laing's *The Works of John Knox*. But Laing does not actually provide a list as such of Knox's published works. The tables of contents in each of the six volumes juxtapose published and unpublished writings without further indications, so that one has to search the introductions to each piece to find out whether it was published or not. This is clearly a matter of great inconvenience for students and researchers.

A further ground for devising a guide to Knox's works is that while he was not a prolific writer, the nature of his publications is, bibliographically speaking, relatively complex. Most of his writings were markedly occasional in character. Further, they were often composite editions, in which more than one tract was included. Also, in several instances one of the included pieces was something he had actually written several years before; and in these composite editions, sometimes the title page indicates everything in the book, sometimes not. In some cases, in fact, a Knox publication consists of two or three tracts with separate title pages just bound into one volume at the time. The result of this situation is that relying on the "titles" of some of Knox's publications—and above all on convenient short titles—can be very hazardous indeed. Short titles can be all the more confusing because several of Knox's tracts have similar sounding titles. Moreover, a few tracts were republished, but with different or new titles.

185

In view of these considerations, a principle in this bibliography has been to itemize each of Knox's published compositions separately, but with reference to the host volume. It is hoped that thereby a clearer conspectus of Knox's editions and their sequence will be established until such time when someone will undertake a comprehensive and analytical bibliography of Knox's works in conformity to modern standards. In this bibliography, I have restricted myself to providing the titles in the original, the publisher, the place, and date of publication. Additional if minimal bibliographical information can be found by consulting Laing, as well as (1) *A Short-Title Catalogue of Books Printed in England, Scotland and Ireland and of English books published abroad,* 2d ed. and H. G. Aldis, *List of Books printed in Scotland before 1700.*

As a rule, I have not cited subsequent re-editions of Knox's works except when it appears under a different title, when it is revised or enlarged, or when published by different publishers resulting in variant texts, as in the case of the *Scots Confession.* I have confined myself to the *editio princeps* of the *Book of Common Order* along with its predecessors. And while the bibliography is meant to be restricted to the sixteenth century, I have in fact included the Genevan Latin translation in 1612 of the *Scots Confession.* This is because that was the sole version of the Confession which was to be known on the Continent of Europe for nearly three centuries.

All items found in Laing have been indicated. Some of Knox's writings have of course been edited in modern times, such as *The History* by W. C. Dickinson, *The First Blast of the Trumpet* and others by M. A. Breslow, *The Scots Confession* by Theodor Hesse, the *Genevan English Service Book* by W. D. Maxwell, and the *First Book of Discipline* by James K. Cameron; but for the practical purposes of immediate orientation, this bibliography is used in conjunction with Laing's standard edition.

In the early stages of this exercise I was assisted by Mr. Andrew Woolsey B.A. B.D. and Rev. Valerie Watson M.A. B.D. Th.M. whose efforts brought home to me the labyrinthine nature of Knox's publications. Their work of reconnaissance helped to generate what is here below.

A WORKING BIBLIOGRAPHY OF WRITINGS OF JOHN KNOX PUBLISHED IN THE 16TH CENTURY

1552

1. **Declaration on kneeling** (= 'The Black Rubric', in the Second
    Prayer Book of Edward VI.)
    [London] 1552.   (Parker Society ed. p. 285)

1554

2. **A Percel of the .vi. psalm expounded.**
    [London?, J. Day?, 1554].

2a. Another: entitled ... **Exposition upon the syxt Psalme of David
    wherin is declared hys crosse: complayntes and prayers ...**
    [Wesel?, H. Singleton?, 1556?].   (Laing 3: 119-56)

2b. Another, (revised by Abraham Fleming), entitled ... **A Fort for the
    afflicted.**
    London, T. Dawson, 1580.

3. **An Admonition or warning that the faithful Christians in Lon-
    don, Newcastel, Barwycke and others may avoide Gods
    vengeaunce, both in thys life and in the life to come.**
    Wittonburge, N. Dorcastor [= London? J. Day?], 1554.   (Laing 3:
    165-216)

3a. Another entitled ... **A godly letter sent too the fayethfull in Lon-
    don, Newcastell, Barwyke, and to all other within the realm off
    Englande that love the comminge of oure Lord Jesus.**
    Rome [= Wesel? J. Lambrecht? for H. Singleton], 1554.

4. **A confession and declaration of praiers added thereunto ...
    upon the death of ... king Edward VI ...**
    Annexed to Nr. 3a.   (Laing 3: 89-156)

5. **A Faythfull admonition made by Johnn Knox unto the
    professours of Gods truthe in England, wherby thou mayest
    learne howe God wyll have his Church exercised with troubles,
    and how he defendeth it in the same.**
    Kalykow [= Emden, E. van der Erve], 1554.   (Laing 3: 257-330)

1556

6. A comfortable Epistell sente to the afflicted church of Chryst, exhorting them to beare hys crosse wyth pacience ... with a prophecy of the destruction of the wycked.

    Annexed to Nrs. 2a & 2b.   (Laing 3: 237-49)

7. A most wholsome counsell, how to behave oureselves in the myddes of thys wycked generation touching the daily exercise of Gods most holy and sacred worde.

    Annexed to Nrs. 2a & 2b.   (Laing 4: 133-40)

8. The copie of a letter sent to the ladye Mary dowagire, Regent of Scotland.

    [Wesel? H. Singleton? 1556.]   (Laing 4: 73-84)

8a. Another ... nowe augmented and explaned by the Author.

    Geneva, J. Poullain and A. Rebul, 1558.   (Laing 4: 429-60)

9. A Notable sermon, made by the sayde John Knox, wherin is evydentlye prouved that the masse is and alwayes hath ben abhominable before God and Idolyatrye. (1550)

    Annexed to Nr. 8 only.   (Laing 3: 33-70)

10. A summe, according to the Holie Scriptures, what opinioun we Christians haif of the Lordis Supper, callit The Sacrament of the Bodie and Blude of our Saviour Jesus Christ.

    Annexed to Nr. 8 only.   (Laing 3: 73-75)

11. (Co-editor): The form of prayers and ministration of the Sacraments, etc., used in the Englishe Congregation at Geneva: and approved, by the famous and godly learned man, John Calvyn.

    Geneva, J. Crespin, 1556.   (Laing 4: 141-214)

11a. Ratio et forma publice orandi Deum, atque administrandi Sacramenta, et caet[era] in anglorum ecclesiam, quae Genevae colligitur recepta: cum iudicio and comprobatione D. Iohannis Calvini.

    Geneva, J. Crespin, 1556.

11b. (enlarged ed.): The Forme of prayers and ministration of the Sacraments, etc ... whereunto are also added the praiers which thei use there in the Frenche Church. With the confession of faith whiche all they make that are received into the universitie of Geneva.

Edinburgh, R. Lekpreuik, 1562.

11c. (Book of Common Order): **The Forme of prayers and ministration of the Sacraments used in the English Church at Geneva,
approved and received by the Churche of Scotland, whereunto
besydes that was in former bokes, are also added sondrie other
prayers, with the whole Psalmes of David in English meter.**
Edinburgh, R. Lekpreuik, 1564. (Laing 6: 293-340)

1558

12. **The first blast of the trumpet against the monstrous regiment of
women.**
[Geneva, J. Poullain & A. Rebul], 1558. (Laing 4: 363-420)

13. **The appellation of John Knoxe from the cruell and most unjust
sentence pronounced against him by the false bishoppes and
clergie of Scotland.**
Geneva, [J. Poullain & A. Rebul?], 1558. (Laing 4: 465-520)

13a. **Supplication and exhortation to the nobilitie, estates, and
communaltie of [Scotland].**
Annexed to Nr. 13. (Laing 4: 523-38)

14. (Summary of the proposed **Second Blast of the Trumpet.**)
Annexed to Nr. 13. (Laing 4: 539-40)

1559

15. **The copie of an epistle sent by John Knox one of the Ministers
of the Englishe Church at Geneva unto the inhabitants of
Newcastle and Barwike.**
Geneva, 1559. (Laing 5: 473-94)

16. **A brief exhortation to England for the spedie imbrasing of
Christs Gospel heretofore by the tyrannie of Marie suppressed
and banished.**
Annexed to Nr. 15. (Laing 5: 501-22)

17.   The Names of some part of those most faithful Servants and
       deare Children of God, which lately in thee, and by thee, O En-
       gland! have bene most cruelly murthered by fyer and imprison-
       ment, for the testimonie of Christ Jesus and his eternal
       veritie. . . .
       Annexed to Nr. 15.   (Laing 5: 523-26)

1560

18.   An answer to a great nomber of blasphemous cavillations writ-
       ten by an Anabaptist, and adversarie to Gods eternal
       predestination.
       Geneva, [J. Crespin], 1560.   (Laing 5: 19-468)

18a.   Another . . . London, [R. Field] for T. Charde, 1591.

1561

19.   (Co-author): The confessioun of faith professit and belevit be the
       Protestantes within the Realme of Scotland.
       [Edinburgh], J. Scotte, 1561.   (Cf. Laing 1: 94-120)

19a.   Another . . . The Confessione of the faythe and doctrine . . .
       [London], R. Hall, 1561.

19b.   Another . . . The Confessione of the fayht and doctrine . . .
       Edinburgh, R. Lekpreuik, 1561.

19c.   Another . . . in: Acts of Parliament of James VI.
       Edinburgh, R. Lekpreuik, 1568.

19c.   (Translation by Patrick Adamson): Confessio fidei et doctrinae per
       Ecclesiam Reformatam Regni Scotiae receptae . . .
       Andreapolis [= St. Andrews], [Lekpreuik?], 1572.

19d.   (Translation by Gaspard Laurent): Scoticana confessio fidei. In:
       'Corpus et syntagma confessionum fidei . . . '
       Geneva, 1612.

1563

20.   **Heir followeth the coppie of the ressoning which was betuix the Abbote of Crosraguell and John Knox, in Mayboill concerning the masse ...**
Edinburgh, R. Lekpreuik, 1563.   (Laing 6: 169-220)

1564

21.   **Prayers, etc. subjoyned to Calvin's Catechism** – 'The catechisme or Maner to teache Children the Christian Religion.'
Edinburgh, R. Lekpreuik, 1564.   (Laing 6: 341-60)

1566

22.   **A sermon preached by John Knox Minister of Christ Jesus in the Publique audience of the Church of Edenbrough, within the Realme of Scotland, upon Sunday, the 19th of August, 1565.**
[London? H. Denham?] 1566.   (Laing 6: 227-73)

23.   **The Ordour and doctrine of the generall faste, appointed be the Generall Assemblie of the Kirkes of Scotland.**
Edinburgh, R. Lekpreuik, 1566.   (Laing 6: 391-428)

1569

24.   **The Ordoure of excommunicatioun and of publict repentance, used in the Church of Scotland ...**
Edinburgh, R. Lekpreuik, 1569.   (Laing 6: 447-70)

1571

25.   **To his loving brethren whome God ones gathered in the church of Edinburgh.**
Striuling [= Stirling], R. Lekpreuik, 1571.

1572

26. An Answer to a letter of a Jesuit named Tyrie, be Johne Knox.
St. Andrews, R. Lekpreuik, 1572   (Laing 6: 479-514)

27. To his loving Mother, Maistress Elizabeth Bowes ...
Annexed to Nr. 26.   (Laing 6: 515-20)

1575

28. A Brieff discours off the troubles begonne at Franckford in
Germany Anno Domini 1554. Abowte the Booke off common
prayer and Ceremonies ...
[Geneva, for Cartwright?], 1575.   (Laing 4: 7-68)

1583

29. A notable and Comfortable exposition of M. John Knoxes, upon
the fourth of Mathew, concerning the tentations of Christ ...
(Edited by John Field)
London, R. Walde-grave for T. Man, [1583].   (Laing 4: 89-114)

1584

30. John Knox, the bound servant of Jesus Christ, unto his best
beloved brethren of the Congregation of the Castle of St.
Andrewes, and to all Professours of Christs true Evangell ...
(1548)
Prefixed to Henry Balnaves' 'Confession of Faith'.
Edinburgh, T. Vautrollier, 1584.   (Laing 3: 5-11)

31. A briefe sommarie of the work by Balnaves on justification.
Annexed to Nr. 30   (Laing 3: 13-28)

1587

32.   [The first (second-thirde) book of the history of the reformation of religion within the realm of Scotland.]
(Pp. 17-560 only. Includes text of the Scots Confession and the first
four heads of the First Book of Discipline [1560])
[London? T. Vautrollier, 1587.]   (Laing 1 & 2)

Calvin makes his farewell journey to the Genevan city council.

John Calvin and Menno Simons: Reformation Perspectives on the Kingdom of God

Timothy George

Despite obvious differences between the reformers John Calvin and Menno Simons, a study of their earliest writings reveals parallel concerns and distinct approaches to the motif of the Kingdom of God. An examination of each reformer's trajectories at the beginnings of their own renewal movements and a comparison of their respective construals of the Kingdom of God during their fluid period from about 1535 to 1539, before their definitive theologies were fully hammered out, provide a sense of the deep visceral concerns which led both reformers to break with their religious past. Even though Calvin and Menno were each preoccupied with the Kingdom of God, and expounded their ideas in strikingly similar ways, there were significant contrasts in their foci: Calvin asserted the supremacy of the Kingdom of God over and within the church political and local civic institutions; Menno espoused suffering and martyrdom, and was committed to a profoundly other-worldly spirituality.

IN 1536 JOHN CALVIN PUBLISHED THE first edition of his *Institutes of the Christian Religion* and shortly thereafter was called as a minister of the recently reformed church of Geneva. In the same year, Menno Simons resigned his parish church in Friesland, openly espousing the Anabaptist cause. Both of these events, Calvin's call to Geneva and Menno's espousal of Anabaptism, have been celebrated recently in festivities, commemoration services, and learned symposia.[1] The celebrations in Geneva were marred only by the vandalism of certain unknown perpetrators—could they have been liberal Protestants?—who mischievously splattered paint on the freshly cleaned statue of John Calvin at the famous "Mur de la Réformation."

Already in the sixteenth century both Calvin and Menno were recognized, from the perspective of the Catholic Reformation, as heresiarchs of the first order. Explaining how all of the heretics had arisen from the bosom of Mother Church, one apologist wrote: "They have all gone out from here, from us, that is, from our monks, such as Luther, Bucer, Oecolampadius; from

---

[1]The papers presented at the Amsterdam Colloquium on Anabaptism, May 20-24, 1986, will be published in a special issue of the *Mennonite Quarterly Review* (Spring 1988). The proceedings of the International Calvin Symposium, Montreal, Canada, Sept. 29-Oct. 3, 1986, was published as a separate volume by the Faculty of Religious Studies, McGill University, under the editorship of E. J. Furcha (Sept. 1987): *John Calvin, 1509-64: In Honour of John Calvin.*

195

our priests, such as Karlstadt, Zwingli, Brenz, Menno Simons; from our laity in the congregations, such as Calvin, Philip Melanchthon."[2] While Calvin and Menno never met each other personally, both were acquainted with the other's writings. They did not hesitate to characterize each other in pejorative terms. Menno referred to Calvin as a man of blood because of his role in the execution of Servetus.[3] Calvin, grouped with Menno by one of their common opponents, retorted with an air of *hauteur*: "He put me in the company of that unspeakably fantastic Menno, with whom I have no more in common than water has with fire."[4] Again, there is this insulting lambast from Calvin against Menno: "One cannot imagine anything to be prouder than an ass, more impudent than this dog."[5] Two of Calvin's ablest disciples, Jan Laski and Martin Micron, held extensive discussions with Menno and wrote refutations of his teaching that Christ became incarnate without taking his flesh and blood from Mary's body. As Menno put it, Christ became a man *in* Mary but not *of* Mary. Calvin was well aware of this debate and, indeed, used Menno's heavenly flesh Christology as a major foil in his own delineation of the Incarnation in the definitive edition of the *Institutes* in 1559.[6]

Despite obvious differences between the two reformers, a study of their earliest writings reveals parallel concerns and distinct approaches to the motif of the Kingdom of God. Both Calvin and Menno emerged into the limelight as advocates of a persecuted minority; both appealed directly to the *Obrigkeit* for toleration and leniency; each sought to distinguish his own religious community from more radical, revolutionary dissenters. In this paper we shall first examine briefly the trajectories of the two reformers which by the mid-1530s had placed them at the center of fledgling renewal movements; then, we shall compare their respective construals of the Kingdom of God as set forth in their

[2]"Sij (sc. de ketters) zijn seijt hij, van ons, dat is, van onse monnicken, als Lutherus, Bucerus, Oecolampadius; Wt onse priesters, als Carolstadius, Zwinglius, Brentius, Mine Simens; wt onse Leecken ende gemiente, als Calvinus, Philippus Melanchton, Ottomanus." Quoted in Wiebe Bergsma, *Aggaeus van Alabada (c. 1525-1581), schwenckfeldiaan, staatsman en strijder voor verdraagzaamheid* (Meppel: Krips, 1982), 68.

[3]*The Complete Writings of Menno Simons*, ed. John C. Wenger (Scottdale, Pa.: Herald Press, 1956), 939 [hereafter *CWMS*].

[4]*Ioannis calvini Opera quae supersunt omnia*, eds. G. Baum, E. Cunitz, and E. Reuse (Brunswick/Berlin, 1863-1900), 9:593 (hereafter *CO*]. Apparently Calvin first learned of Menno in a letter from Hardenberg in 1545. Cf. Willem Balke, *Calvin and the Anabaptist Radicals* (Grand Rapids: Eerdmans, 1981), 202–08.

[5]*CO*, Xa, 176.

[6]At the request of Martin Micron, Calvin wrote a specific refutation of Menno's doctrine, the *Contra Mennonem*: *CO*, Xa, 167f. Most comparative studies of Calvin and Menno have focused on their contrasting interpretations of the Incarnation. Cf. William Keeney, *Dutch Anabaptist Thought and Practice, 1539-1564* (Nieuwkoop: 1968), 90–100, 207–25. More recently J. R. Loeschen has compared Calvin and Menno's respective treatment of the doctrine of the Trinity: *The Divine Community: Trinity, Church, and Ethics in Reformation Theologies* (Kirksville, Mo.: Sixteenth Century Publishers, 1981). Cf. also Timothy George, *Theology of the Reformers* (Nashville: Broadman, 1988).

early writings, that is, from about 1535 to 1539. By focusing on this early, fluid period before their definitive theologies were fully hammered out, we can perhaps get a better sense of the deep visceral concerns which led both reformers to break with their religious past in quest for that city which hath foundations, that Kingdom which, in the words of Menno, "shall never be overthrown, perverted, nor weakened by angel or devil."[7]

Trajectories of Two Reformers

It is often pointed out that Calvin was a reformer of the second generation. When he was born at Noyon in 1509, Luther was already giving lectures as *Sententiarius* at the University of Erfurt and Zwingli hurried about his pastoral duties in Glarus. By the time Calvin became associated with the tenuous Protestant movement in France in the early 1530s, Zwingli was dead, Erasmus was dying, and Luther was besieged by *Schwärmer* on the right and papists on the left, as he put it reversing the modern positioning.[8] The first Protestant martyr in France was the Augustinian monk Jean Vallière who was burned alive at Paris in August, 1523, the same month in which Calvin arrived to begin his formal training at Europe's most famous university. During the next ten years Calvin advanced from his scholastic training at Paris through a thorough legal education at Orléans and Bourges to an embrace of the *bonae litterae* proper, marked by the publication of his first book in 1532, an edition of Seneca's treatise *On Clemency*, complete with a textual apparatus and lengthy commentary.[9]

Calvin's transition from humanist to reformer was marked by what he once described as a "sudden conversion" (*subito conversio*).

> My mind which, despite my youth
> Had been too hardened in such matters,
> Now was readied for serious attention.
> By a sudden conversion
> God turned and brought it
> To docility.[10]

---

[7]*CWMS*, 225.

[8]*Luther's Works*, ed. Helmut T. Lehmann (Philadelphia: Fortress, 1958), 40:129.

[9]*Calvin's Commentary on Seneca's De Clementia*, eds. Ford L. Battles and André M. Hugo (Leiden: Brill, 1969).

[10]This, Calvin's most revealing autobiographical confession, was written in the preface to his *Commentary on the Psalms* in 1555. I have followed the strophic translation of Ford L. Battles, *The Piety of John Calvin* (Grand Rapids: Baker, 1978), 31. The first English translation was made by Arthur Golding and published at London in 1571. Cf. *CO* XXXI, 22.

This famous conversion has proved notoriously difficult to date; the guesses range from 1527 to 1536.[11] However sudden the final turning point may have been, we can be sure that Calvin did not embrace the new gospel in a quick or facile manner. He later wrote: "Offended by the novelty, I lent an unwilling ear, and at first, I confess, strenuously and passionately resisted . . . for it was with the greatest difficulty I was induced to confess that I had all my life long been in ignorance and error."[12]

Calvin's conversion propelled him into the center of the French evangelical movement which was increasingly coming under fire from the king Francis I. On All Saints' Day, 1533, exactly sixteen years to the day after Luther had posted the famous theses on indulgences on the church door in Wittenberg, Nicholas Cop, a friend of Calvin and rector of the University of Paris, delivered a convocation address which shocked his hearers. Not a hot-gospel sermon really, it had enough evangelical content to upset the defenders of Catholic orthodoxy. Cop was forced to flee for his life. Calvin too was implicated in the event. According to an old legend, he escaped Paris in the nick of time, his friends hoisting him down out of a window on bed sheets while the police were knocking at the door—shades of Saint Paul's hurried flight from Damascus in a basket! About a year after Cop's address, some of the more advanced Protestants in Paris decided to make a startling, radical display of their faith. A fiery attack on the mass and its accoutrements—"bell-ringing, anointings, chantings, ceremonies, candlelightings, censings, disguises, and such sorts of buffooneries"—was printed on a single sheet, called a placard, and posted all over the city.[13] One even appeared, mysteriously, on the door of the king's bedchamber. Now the forces of persecution were unleashed against the French evangelicals. Calvin left the country in haste, finding refuge in the Reformed city of Basel.

Calvin did not make a big splash in Basel: "I dwelt there hidden, as it were, and known only to a few people."[14] But he was not idle. His first three writings as a Protestant come from this period. They will form the basis of our analysis of his understanding of the Kingdom of God. First, there is his preface to Pierre Robert Olivétan's French translation of the New Testament. This brief but eloquent statement contains *in nuce* much that will be more fully developed in the *Institutes* of 1536. Here he speaks already of the knowledge of God in creation—"the little birds that sing, sing of God; the beasts clamor for

[11]The best case for a later dating has been made by Alexandre Ganoczy, *Le Jeune Calvin* (Wiesbaden: Franz Steiner Verlag, 1966). T. H. L. Parker, *John Calvin: A Biography* (Philadelphia: Westminster, 1975) argues for an earlier conversion, as did Emile Doumergue, *Jean Calvin: Les hommes et les choses de son temps* (Lausanne: George Bridel, 1899), 1:467.

[12]*Calvin's Tracts and Treatises*, tr. Henry Beveridge (Grand Rapids: Eerdmans, 1958), 1:62.

[13]"The Placards of 1534" is translated as Appendix I in Ford L. Battles, *The Institution of The Christian Religion, 1536* (Atlanta: John Knox Press, 1975), 437–40

[14]Battles, tr. *Piety of Calvin*, 31.

him; the elements dread him; the mountains echo him, the fountains and flowing waters cast their glances at him, and the grass and flowers laugh before him."[15] Yet human beings, "despoiled . . . deprived . . . defaced . . . divested of all their glory" because of sin required the special revelation of God unfolded in the history of salvation.

> And it was our Lord and Savior Jesus Christ, the true and only eternal Son of God, who had to be sent and given to mankind by the Father, to restore a world otherwise wasted, destroyed, and desolate.[16]

The nature of Christ's Kingdom was foretold by the Old Testament prophets, its foundation secured by Christ's life, death, resurrection, and ascension. Believers in Jesus Christ are "heirs of the Kingdom," "citizens of the Kingdom." In the gospel they have the key to knowledge of God "which opens the door of the Kingdom." Still, Calvin warns, we should not look for a life without conflict and suffering, since the Kingdom is present in this life only in hope. Its final fulfillment awaits the *parousia* when "Jesus Christ shall appear in majesty with his angels."[17]

Calvin's first theological treatise proper, the *Psychopannychia*, was originally written in 1534 to refute the doctrine of soul sleep, which Calvin attributed to the "nefarious herd of Anabaptists."[18] Some of Calvin's interpreters have wondered why Calvin would expend so much energy combatting such a relatively obscure heresy. For Calvin, however, the way one viewed life after death had important implications for the way one lived life before death. The doctrine of soul sleep not only misconstrued the proper nature of soul and body; it also obscured the inviolate nexus between Christ and the believer:

> If, therefore, the life of Christ is ours, let him who insists that our life is ended by death, pull Christ down from the right hand of the Father, and consign him to the second death. If he can die, our death is certain; if he has no end of life, neither can our souls ingrafted in him be ended by any death.[19]

---

[15]*Calvin's Commentaries*, ed. Joseph Haroutunian (Philadelphia: Westminster, 1958), 60.
[16]Ibid., 61.   [17]Ibid., 68.

[18]The first printed edition of *Psychopannychia* of which we have an extant copy appeared in Strasbourg in 1542 published by Wendelin Rihel. This edition carried the title: *Vivere apud Christum non dormire animis sanctos, qui in fide Christi decedunt*. The same printer brought out a second edition three years later in March, 1545, but with a revised title: *Psychopannychia, qua refellitur quorundam imperitorum error, qui animas post mortem usque ad ultimum iudicium dormire putant*. A modern critical edition appeared as *Joh. Calvin, Psychopannychia*, ed. Walther Zimmerli (Leipzig; A. Deichertsche Verlagsbuchhandlung, 1932). An English translation is found in Beveridge, tr. *Tracts and Treatises*, 3:414–90. Cf. Timothy George, "Calvin's *Psychopannychia*: Another Look," Furcha, ed., *John Calvin, 1509-64*, 297–329.

[19]Beveridge, *Tracts and Treatises*, 3:439.

Throughout this treatise Calvin points out several times that the church is "still a pilgrim on the earth." The *regnum Christi* consists both in the progress of believers (*profectus fidelium*) and the building up of the church (*aedificatio ecclesiae*).[20] The church as a pilgrim community is often enough the church "under the cross," *ecclesia militans*, the church at war with the principalities and powers of this present age. This is the church which is sustained amidst all its struggles by the assurance of its union with Christ, which not even death can sever, and by its expectation of the ultimate victory of that Kingdom not made with hands.

The themes touched upon in the *Psychopannychia* and the preface to Olivétan's French New Testament were developed with remarkable clarity in Calvin's first real masterpiece, *Christianae Religionis Institutio*, published at Basel in March, 1536.[21] Scholars have been primarily concerned to compare this volume with later editions of the *Institutes*. It is better understood, however, in the context of the two works we have just reviewed. Ostensibly modeled on Luther's *Small Catechism*, the first five chapters deal with the law, faith, prayer, and sacraments true and false. This material is bracketed, however, by the famous dedicatory epistle to Francis I on the one side, and by chapter six which deals with Christian freedom, ecclesiastical power, and political administration on the other. Both of these units of material are essentially apologetic in character. They offer an eloquent plea for the toleration of the persecuted evangelicals in France and also a nuanced statement of Calvin's political theology. We shall return to these more fully, but at this point it is well to note that in his exposition of "Thy Kingdom come," in the Lord's Prayer, Calvin stresses the same eschatological tension we have observed in the *Psychopannychia*. The Kingdom of God is present here and now; it may "in some measure be beheld." And yet we continue to pray "Thy Kingdom come," because it will only properly come when it is completed.

> While we pray in this way that 'God's Kingdom come,' at the same time we desire that it may be at last perfected and fulfilled, that is, in the revelation of his judgment. On that day he alone will be exalted, and will be all in all, when his own folk are gathered

[20]Cf. T. F. Torrance, *Kingdom and Church* (Edinburgh: Oliver and Boyd, 1956), 90–139. Also helpful are the earlier studies by Heinrich Quistorp, *Calvin's Doctrine of Last Things*, tr. Harold Knight (London: Lutterworth, 1955), and Karlfried Frölich, *Die Reichgottesidee Calvins* (Münich: Chr. Kaiser Verlag, 1922). Heinrich Berger has set Calvin's ecclesiology in the context of his understanding of salvation history: *Calvins Geschichtsauffassung* (Zürich: Zwingli-Verlag, 1955).

[21]The Latin text of the 1536 *Institutes* is given in *Ioannis Calvini Opera Selecta*, ed. Peter Barth (Münich: Chr. Kaiser Verlag, 1926), 1:21–280.

and received into glory, but Satan's kingdom is utterly disrupted and laid low.[22]

We have noted that 1536 was a pivotal year in the reforming careers of both Calvin and Menno. Some five months after the *Institutes* rolled off the presses of Thomas Platter in Basel, Calvin had his famous encounter with Guillaume Farel in Geneva. When Farel sought to enlist the young theologian in the work of reform, Calvin demurred, preferring as he later wrote to Cardinal Sadolet, "the enjoyment of literary ease, with something of a free and honorable station."[23] Farel, twenty years Calvin's senior, was undaunted by the younger man's meager excuse and declared that God would curse him and his studies if he refused to give himself to the work. Confronted with such an adjuration Calvin conceded, and thus was drawn, kicking and screaming as it were, into the ranks of the reformers.

Menno's decision to embrace the Anabaptist cause in January, 1536, was not less difficult, although his personal trajectory had prepared him for it in a quite different way. Menno was born in 1496, precisely thirteen years after Luther and thirteen before Calvin. The son of a dairy farmer in the village of Witmarsum, he was ordained a priest in his twenty-eighth year at Utrecht.[24] First at Pingjum, then in his home village of Witmarsum, Menno performed the perfunctory duties of a country priest, though not without inward doubts and struggles. The dogma of transubstantiation troubled him. He later expressed his feelings thus:

> Yes, I have said to a weak, perishing creature that came forth from the earth, that was broken in a mill, that was baked by the fire, that was chewed by my teeth and digested by my stomach, namely, to a mouthful of bread, Thou hast saved me. Thus did I, a miserable sinner, toy with the harlot of Babylon for many years.[25]

In time Menno also came to question another pillar of the established tradition, infant baptism. The execution in 1531 of an itinerant tailor in the nearby

[22]Ibid., 1:109. Cf. Battles, *Institution*, 107–8. Elsie McKee makes the following comparison between the 1536 *Institutes* and later recensions: "In 1536 Calvin was not asking to organize the church but to purify and reform it. He was not concerned so much with polity as with doctrine and correcting abuses." "Calvin's 1536 Institutes: The Church's Book," in *Calvin Studies* 3, ed. John H. Leith (1986), 36.

[23]"Id unum dicere contentus ero, quod in summus votis fuisset, mihi non fuisse difficile illic adipisci: nempe ut otio literario cum honesta aliqua, ingenuaque conditione fruerer." *Opera Selecta*, 1:460.

[24]On Menno's life and career see the article by Cornelius Krahn in *Mennonite Encyclopedia*, 3:577–84; Christoph Bornhaus, *Leben und Lehre Menno Simons'* (Neukirchen: Neukirchener Verlag, 1973); Jan A. Brandsma, "The Transition of Menno Simons from Roman Catholicism to Anabaptism as Reflected in his Writings" (unpublished B. D. treatise, Baptist Theological Seminary, Rüschlikon-Zürich, 1955).   [25]*CWMS*, 76.

city of Leeuwarden because he had been baptized a second time made a lasting impression on Menno. On the basis of his own study of the Bible he came to the radical conclusion that "all were deceived about infant baptism."[26]

The early 1530s was a time of great social unrest which witnessed the rise of apocalyptic Anabaptism in the Low Countries. The earlier predictions of Thomas Müntzer and Hans Hut had given way to those of the furrier, Melchior Hoffman who declared that Christ would return to Strasbourg in the year 1534. Although Hoffman counseled his followers to wield only the "sheathed sword," that is to absorb violence but not to inflict it, his drastic predictions and scathing invective against emperor, pope, and "bloodsucking anti-Christian Lutheran and Zwinglian preachers" created an atmosphere in which the overtly revolutionary kingdom of Münster could flourish.[27] Possessed of Hoffman's eschatological urgency, Jan Matthijs and Jan of Leyden moved the site of New Jerusalem from Strasbourg to Münster which they took over in a storm of violence. When Jan of Leyden assumed the leadership after Matthijs's death, he had himself crowned "king of righteousness over all." This experiment in theocracy ended in a bloody holocaust when the city of Münster was besieged by Protestant and Catholic troops fighting side by side against the violent Anabaptists within.

Menno did not break with the Roman Church until he was deeply stirred by events surrounding the tragedy of Münster. As early as 1532 some people in the area of Witmarsum had been rebaptized. Some of these were also drawn into the vortex of the revolutionary kingdom of the two Jans at Münster, including even Menno's own brother, Peter Simons. In an abortive attack on an old cloister at Bolsward, Peter and several hundred Anabaptists were savagely slain. This event precipitated a crisis in Menno's life.

> After this had transpired the blood of these people, although misled, fell so hot on my heart that I could not stand it, nor find rest in my soul.

Menno realized that he had not lived up to the light which he had received. He now implored God for forgiveness and a new life in Christ. "My heart trembled within me. I prayed to God with signs and tears that he would give me, a sorrowing sinner, the gift of his grace."

From April, 1535 until January, 1536, Menno tried to use his position as the priest of Witmarsum to carry out an evangelical reform. Whereas before

---

[26]Ibid., 8.

[27]Hans-Jürgen Goertz, ed., *Radikale Reformatoren* (Münich: Beck, 1978), 163. Hoffman referred to the emperor, pope, and false teachers as the "hollische Dreieinigkeit." On Hoffman's influence on the revolutionary Anabaptists, see Klaus Deppermann, *Melchior Hoffman: Soziale Unruhen und apokalyptische Visionen im Zeitalter der Reformation* (Göttingen: Vandenhoeck und Ruprecht, 1979).

he had dissimulated and compromised, he now spoke out clearly and without hesitation. His first writing, *The Blasphemy of Jan of Leyden*, comes from this period. This is a stirring tract in which Menno opposes the kingship of Christ to the false pretensions of "King John." He shows the un-Christlike character of the "proponents of the sword philosophy" and calls for a life of nonresistance: "It is forbidden to us to fight with physical weapons. . . . This only would I learn of you whether you are baptized on the sword or on the cross?"[28]

In the same month that Jan of Leyden was tortured to death, Menno made his decisive break with the Church of Rome. Feeling a special compassion for the "poor misguided sheep" who wandered about without a shepherd, Menno began "to teach and to baptize, to labor with my limited talents in the harvest field of the Lord, to assist in building up his holy city and temple and to repair the dilapidated walls." Sometime in 1537 he accepted a new ordination at the hands of Obbe Phillips, thus becoming not only an *ana*baptist but also a *re*ordinationist. During the next years he lived the life of a hunted heretic, preaching by night to secret conventicles of brothers and sisters, baptizing new believers in country streams and out of the way lakes, establishing churches and ordaining pastors from Amsterdam to Cologne to Danzig. In 1544 he lamented that he was a "homeless man" who could not find a cabin or hut in which to hide his wife Gertrude and their three children.[29]

In the aftermath of Münster, Menno's writings appealed to many disillusioned Anabaptists who were prepared to follow neither David Joris in his radical spiritualizing of the Melchiorite message, nor the Batenburgers and others who still sought to evoke the Kingdom of God by fits of terrorist violence.[30] A series of pamphlets from Menno on "The Spiritual Resurrection," "The New Birth," and a "Meditation on the Twenty-Fifth Psalm," stressed the themes of repentance, regeneration, and rigorous discipleship. These themes were expanded and placed in the context of a comprehensive apologetic in the *Foundation of Christian Doctrine*, Menno's *Fundamentboek* of 1539. This work is comparable to Calvin's *Institutes* of 1536. Like the latter it also underwent several revisions and new editions. For example, in 1539 Menno could still refer

---

[28]*CWMS*, 45, 49. The authenticity of *The Blasphemy of Jan of Leyden* has been questioned by Calvin Pater who refers to it as "a pious seventeenth-century forgery" on the grounds that the first known imprint is from 1627. *Vide* his *Karlstadt as the Father of the Baptist Movements* (Toronto: University of Toronto Press, 1984), 250 n 67. However, *The Blasphemy* could well have circulated in manuscript form. The stylistic discrepancies alleged by Pater are not substantial enough to call into question its authenticity. Cf. James Stayer who refers to *The Blasphemy* as a "proto-Melchiorite essay" of Menno in *Anabaptists and the Sword* (Lawrence, Ks.: Coronado Press, 1973), 310.

[29]*CWMS*, 424.

[30]On the relation between Menno and David Joris see James M. Stayer, "Davidite vs. Mennonite," in *The Dutch Dissenters*, ed. Irvin B. Horst (Leiden: Brill, 1986), 143-59.

to the Münsterites as "our dear brethren" who had "erred slightly" in trying to protect their faith through resistance. This passage was excised in later editions perhaps to more clearly distance Menno and his followers from the bloody events in Westphalia.[31] Having surveyed the reforming careers of Calvin and Menno through their first major writings, we turn now to a comparison of their respective approaches to the Kingdom of God.

Construals of the Kingdom
 1. *The Kingdom and the Covenant.* Both Calvin and Menno interpret the Kingdom of God in terms of a thoroughgoing Christocentrism. The Kingdom of God *is* the *regnum Christi*. We have noted how Calvin in his preface to Olivétan's New Testament relates the Kingdom to the Old Testament prophecies. The whole sum of Scripture is to know Jesus Christ; he is "the beginning, the middle, and the end" of our salvation.[32] All of the Old Testament worthies are really types of Christ. He is Isaac, the willingly sacrificed son. He is Jacob, the watchful shepherd; Joseph, the compassionate brother; Moses, the sovereign lawgiver; David, the victorious king. "He is the magnificent and triumphant king Solomon, governing his kingdom in peace and prosperity."[33] Of all the events in the *ordo salutis*, Calvin places special emphasis on the ascension of Christ. By ascending into heaven, Christ "took possession of it for us." He sits at the Father's right hand a King, made Lord and Master over all, so that he may restore all that is in heaven and on earth."[34] The reign of Christ on earth is linked directly to his session in heaven. In his dedicatory epistle to Francis, Calvin asserts: "And we must not doubt that Christ has reigned on earth ever since he ascended into heaven."[35] From heaven the ascended Christ, in the company of the vigilant, wakeful souls of the departed faithful, sustains and protects the *ecclesia militans* on earth. "Surely the church of Christ has lived and will live so long as Christ reigns at the right hand of the Father."[36]
 Menno, no less than Calvin, stresses the crucial role of Christ as the "Lord King both of the earth and of his faithful church."[37] The title of Menno's magnum opus, *The Foundation of Christian Doctrine*, echoes I Cor. 3:11, "For other foundation can no man lay than that is laid, which is Jesus Christ." This verse

[31]The translation of the *Foundation* in *CWMS* follows the 1558 Dutch edition. A critical edition of the 1539 *editio princeps* was brought out by H. W. Meihuizen, ed., *Dat Fundament des Christelycken Leers* (The Hague: Nijhoff, 1967), Cf. Meihuizen's comments on the "dear brothers" passage: ibid., xvii-xxii.
[32]Haroutunian, ed., Commentaries, 69.
[33]Ibid.
[34]Ibid., 64.
[35]Battles, *Institution*, 15. "Nec dubium nobis esse debet, quin semper in terris regnaverit Christus, ex quo coelum ascendit." *Opera Selecta*, 31.
[36]Battles, *Institution*, 12.
[37]*CWMS*, 35.

appeared on the frontispiece of every published writing of Menno. Against the pretensions of Jan of Leyden, Menno devises his own catena of Old Testament allusions, almost identical to Calvin's: Christ is the true Melchisedec, the strong Samson, the pious David, the wise Solomon, etc. Yet Menno's appeal to the Old Testament is much more qualified than that of Calvin. Calvin stresses the continuity of the two testaments; for him there is really only *one covenant in two dispensations*. This principle enabled him, along with Zwingli and Bullinger before him, to justify infant baptism by analogy to its Old Testament counterpart, circumcision, and also to find in the Old Testament a pattern for church-state relationships. Menno denied the legitimacy of this appeal to the Old Testament by pointing to the *normative* status of the New Covenant. The radical newness of Christ's Kingdom has displaced the mandate of the Old Covenant.

For Menno it is not the ascension so much as the Incarnation which inaugurates the *regnum Christi*. The emphasis he places on the celestial flesh of Christ underscores the uniqueness and discontinuous character of the Incarnation. This principle enabled him to oppose not only pedobaptism as a ceremony of human invention, "a horrid stench and abomination before God," but also the Münsterite appropriation of "the external kingdom of David."[38] Perhaps nowhere in the entire Reformation was religious experience and biblical prototype more closely joined than in the tragi-comic exploits of the Münster heroes, Jan Matthijs and Hille Feickes. Jan, like Gideon *redivivus*, tried to disperse the besieging army with only a handful of warriors, while Hille, playing Judith to the bishop's Holofernes, attempted to enter the camp of Franz von Waldeck in order to behead him.[39] Against this bold reenactment of the Old Testament precedents, Menno admonishes his followers to "leave the armor of David to the physical Israelites and the sword of Zerubbabel to those who built the temple of Zerubbabel in Jerusalem." The only arms with which a Christian may fight is the Word of God. The motive for this injunction is not only a strict appeal to the New Testament over the Old, but also a desire to follow in literal imitation the example of Jesus.

> Christ did not want to be defended with Peter's sword. How can a Christian then defend himself with it? . . . Christ has not taken his Kingdom with a sword, but he entered it through much suffering.[40]

[38]Ibid., 272, 41.

[39]Cornelius Krahn, *Dutch Anabaptism: Origin, Spread, Life and Thought* (The Hague: Nijhoff, 1968), 140.

[40]*CWMS*, 45, 49. Cf. Calvin's interpretation of Peter's attempted defense of Christ with the sword in his Commentary on John 18:11. *Calvin's Commentaries*, eds. D. W. Torrance and T. F. Torrance (Grand Rapids; Eerdmans, 1961), 5:157.

For Menno, then, the blueprint of Christ's Kingdom is the New Testament Scriptures, on the basis of which he positions himself against his Catholic and Protestant opponents on the one side and his misguided "dear brethren," the revolutionary radicals on the other. Calvin, while acknowledging a qualitative difference between the two dispensations, sees more continuity between the Kingdom in this present age and what he often calls "l'ancien église." For Calvin the incarnate Christ is not so much a model for the Kingdom as he is the bringer of it through his death, resurrection, and especially ascension.

2. *The Kingdom and the Cross.* In the writings we are surveying both Calvin and Menno developed their views of the Kingdom of God as theologians of suffering communities of faith. Both went to great pains to emphasize the eschatological tension between the partial realization of the Kingdom in this present age and its final consummation in the age to come.

"So long as the church is a sojourner in the world," writes Calvin, "it is to wage war under the perpetual cross."[41] On the eve of being expelled from his native country, he wrote:

> Will there be banishments, proscriptions, privation from goods and riches? But we know that if we shall be banished from one country, the whole earth is the Lord's, and if we be thrown out of the earth itself, nonetheless we shall not be outside of his Kingdom.[42]

He speaks of the shattering effects of persecution on the French evangelicals: "Some of us are shackled with irons, some beaten with rods, some led about as laughingstocks, some proscribed, some most savagely tortured, some forced to flee. All of us are oppressed by poverty, cursed with dire execrations, wounded by slanders, and treated in most shameful ways."[43] It is possible that Calvin himself had witnessed the execution of Etienne de la Forge in 1528. This may even have been a factor in his subsequent conversion. He quotes with approval the statement of Tertullian that the blood of the martyrs is the seed of the church. In the face of oppression and violent opposition again and again Calvin counsels perseverance and patience—not patience in the modern attenuated sense of passive forbearance, as when we wait in line at the post office or grocery store, but patience in the New Testament sense of *hypomoné*, "let us run with *hypomoné*, with courage and steadfast endurance, with revolutionary patience, the race that is set before us" (Heb. 12:1–2). So he can write to the beleagured Protestants in France: "Let us not lose our comfort when we see all earthly powers and forces against us; . . . let us not be desolate, as though

[41]John Calvin, *Concerning Scandals*, tr. John W. Fraser (Grand Rapids: Eerdmans, 1978), 30.

[42]Haroutunian, ed., *Commentaries*, 67.

[43]Battles, *Institution*, 5.

all hope were lost, when we see true servants of God die and perish before our eyes."[44] The true condition of Christ's Kingdom cannot be determined by its outward circumstances. Out of this perspective will be born that tradition of Protestant hagiography and martyrology so ably developed by John Foxe in England and by Jean Crespin in France.

When we turn to Menno we are struck by his remarkably parallel emphasis in the inescapability of the cross. It is well to recall that just as Calvin was deeply moved by the martyrdom of Etienne de la Forge, so Menno's confidence in his priestly vocation was shaken by the execution of the Anabaptist tailor at Leeuwarden in 1531. Martyrdom is an ever present possibility. If Socrates died for the teachings of his religion, if Marcus Curtius died for the city of Rome, if the Jews and Turks did not fear fire and death for their fatherlands, why should I not the rather offer my soul for the brethren and for the institutions of Jesus Christ?[45] The cross of Christ may in no wise be avoided, for the lamb will never be at peace with the wolf, the dove with the eagle, Christ with Belial. Menno encourages his followers that, despite their present sufferings, the true kingdom awaits those who are faithful.

> Although you must now for a short time bear the heat of the sun, yet you know right well that the kingdom of honor in eternal joy is promised and prepared. . . . Fear not, little flock, for it is the Father's good pleasure to give you the kingdom. Not the perishing kingdom of Assyria, of the Medes, of Macedonia, nor of Rome, but the kingdom of the saints, the kingdom of the great King, of David, the kingdom of peace, of grace, and eternal peace, that shall never pass away but abide and stand forever.[46]

Menno's word, "*lydsaemkeit*," which might be better rendered by the German *Gelassenheit* rather than the English "suffering," referred to the complete sacrificial surrender exemplified by Christ himself.[47] "If the Head had to suffer such torture, anguish, misery, and pain, how shall his servants, children, and members expect peace and freedom as to their flesh?" It was necessary, then, not only to suffer the cross, as Christ had done, but also to suffer the cross *in the same way* as Christ had done. For the most part the Anabaptist martyrs followed the teaching of Menno and prayed for their persecutors even in their own moments of distress. A famous example of this is the story of Dirk Willems who, when he saw that his pursuer had fallen through the ice and

---

[44]Haroutunian, ed., *Commentaries*, 68.

[45]*CWMS*, 86.

[46]Ibid., 223.

[47]This is a recurrent theme in the *Fundamentboek*: "Gods volck sal triumpheren, niet mot geweer unde wapen, dan allene doer lydsaemkeit met hoers Heren woort." Meihuizen, ed., *Dat Fundament*, 137. Cf. ibid., 192.

was about to drown, rather than taking advantage of this situation to make sure his escape, returned to save his pursuer whereupon Willems was at once arrested by the man and delivered over to his death. Not all Mennonite martyrs were so altruistic however. Maria van Beckum, for example, although she prayed that God would forgive her captors, was nonetheless emboldened to remind one of them, "Friend, consider what you are doing . . . repent, lest you burn for it in hell."[48]

Both Calvin and Menno, then, understood the church as caught in the vortex of a great cosmic-historical conflict between the forces of light and those of darkness. Upon learning of the death of his fellow minister Antoine Courault, Calvin wrote to Farel in 1538: "Let us stand resolutely upon the watch-tower even to the end, until the kingdom of Christ, which is now hidden and obscured, may shine forth."[49] There is remarkable consonance between Menno's advice to the persecuted Anabaptists and Calvin's exhortation to the oppressed French Protestants. We must now examine the various ways they expected the civil authorities to assist or make allowance for the shining forth of the Kingdom.

3. *The Kingdom and the Obrigkeit.* Both the *Institutes* of 1536 and the *Fundamentboek* of 1539 were addressed to civil authorities; both contained impassioned pleas for the toleration of persecuted religious minorities. Calvin laments the condition of the "poor little church" (*paupercula ecclesia*) which has been wasted and overwhelmed by the sheer unprovoked violence of the king. Calvin at no point disputes the authority of the king to suppress genuine threats to the order of his realm. If the accusations hurled against the French evangelicals were true, then no one would doubt that its authors would be "worthy of a thousand fires and crosses."[50] But it is through ignorance and malice that the true Christians are confused with "the Catabaptists and other monstrous rascals."[51] While Calvin exculpates the Protestants from any rebellious intention, he nonetheless holds the king responsible for his cruel oppression. The question which ought to concern the ruler is "how God's glory may be kept safe on earth, how God's truth may retain its place of honor, how Christ's Kingdom may be kept in good repair among us." Any earthly sovereign whose reign does not serve God's glory, Calvin avers, "exercises not kingly rule but brigandage."[52] This is an echo of Saint Augustine's dictum, "Remove justice, and what are kingdoms but gangs of criminals on a large

---

[48]Thieleman J. van Braght, *The Bloody Theater or Martyrs' Mirror* (Scottdale, Pa.: Mennonite Publishing House, 1951; originally published in Dutch in 1660), 468.

[49]*The Letters of John Calvin*, ed. Jules Bonnet (Philadelphia; Presbyterian Board of Publication, 1858), 1:100.

[50]Battles, *Institution*, 2.

[51]Ibid., 16.

[52]Ibid., 3.

scale?"[53] Calvin pleads for a fair hearing against his false calumniators; he swears dutiful allegiance and loyalty—we pray for the prosperity of your kingdom even in our exile from it. Still, he closes the dedicatory epistle to Francis I with an appeal to divine retribution which contained more than a single charge of political dynamite. If the King will not relent from his persecution, then we must await the "strong hand of the Lord, which will surely appear in due season, coming forth armed to deliver the poor from their affliction and also to punish their despisers. May the Lord, the King of Kings, establish your throne in righteousness, most Mighty and most Illustrious King."[54] Calvin's insistence that the Lord is the King of Kings who must be obeyed before and above all human authorities is given a particular twist by his doctrine of the resistance of the lesser magistrates. While no private individual may avenge the despotism of earthly rulers, God has established lesser magistrates, such as the ephors of ancient Sparta or the three estates in sixteenth-century France, to serve as a check against the fierce licentiousness of kings. The way in which this concept was developed by Theodore Beza, François Hotman, and others to justify the Huguenot struggle in France, and the way in which by analogy the same argument was applied by revolutionary Calvinists from Poland to Scotland is a part of the history of what Robert Kingdon has called "militant forms of Christian witness." Our purpose here is to note that at least the seeds of this development are found already in Calvin's first theological manifesto.[55]

When we turn to Menno's plea for toleration, we remember that he, like Calvin, was a fugitive from his native land of Friesland. In 1542 the Emperor Charles V published an edict against the Anabaptist leader and offered 100 gold guilders for his arrest. Menno addresses his appeal to "all our dear and gracious rulers" from the emperor to the lowest civil magistrate, "everyone in his calling, dignity, and rank." He, like Calvin, distinguishes his group from the "harmful sects" (i.e. the Münsterites and Batenbergers). In reality, however, it is the persecuting authorities and the seditious sects who have much in common: both have bloodied their hands with the sword which Menno and his followers have renounced:

[53]"Remota itaque iustitia quid sunt regna nisi magna latrocinia?" *St. Augustine: The City of God* (Cambridge: Harvard University Press, 1963), 2:16: Bk. 4, ch. 4.

[54]Battles, *Institution,* 19. " . . . et manum Domini fortem expectemus, quae indubie tempore aderit, et sese armata exeret, tum ad pauperes ex afflictione eruendos, tum ad vindicandos contemptores. Dominus, Rex Regum, thronum tuum iustitia stabiliat, et solum tuum aequitate, Fortissime ac illustrissime Rex." *Opera Selecta,* 1:36.

[55]Ibid., 279. Cf. Robert M. Kingdon, *Church and Society in Reformation Europe* (London: Variorum Reprints, 1985). Cf. Frölich's comment in Frölich, *Reichgottesidee,* 23: "Und zwar ist Calvins Geschichtsauffassung eine durchaus dynamische. Das gesamte, im Strome der Zeit dahinflutende Weltgeschehen steht *sub specie aeternitatis.* Blitzartig vermag dieses geschichtliche Empfinden das ganze Sein dieses Mannes zu charakterisiern. In allem, was er ist, in allem, was er tut, in allem, was er denkt, bricht der Sinn für das Dynamische durch. . . . Das Verhältnis des Reiches Gottes zur Geschichte gilt er daher zunächst zu betrachten, um der Sache selbst näher zu Kommen."

> Our wagon fortress is Christ, our weapon of defense is patience,
> our sword is the Word of God. . . . Iron, metal, spears and swords
> we leave to those who (alas) consider human and pig's blood of
> about the same worth.[56]

Menno appeals to the common humanity of the rulers and their victims in urging them to clemency. "Show some natural reasonableness and human charity toward your poor subjects," he pleads. "Together with you we are descended from the same father, Adam, and from one mother, Eve, created by the same God. . . . We are clothed with the same nature, yearning for rest and peace, for wives and children, as well as you, and by nature fearful of death as are all creatures." "Oh dear sirs, sheathe your sword!" he exclaims.[57]

However, sensing perhaps that such an argument may not be persuasive, Menno, like Calvin, reminds the rulers of the consequences of their harsh deeds. "Acknowledge your superior, Christ Jesus, who is made to you a Prince and a Judge," he says. He warns that their abuse of the crown rights of Christ the King will issue in dire judgment:

> [All of you, be he emperor or king] came into this sorrowful world
> as we did, and you are but vapor, frail flesh, a withering flower,
> dust and ashes, as are we all. Today you are kings and exult in great
> and high honor; tomorrow you are laid low, and must be food for
> snails and worms.[58]

While earthly rulers are to be obeyed in all temporal affairs which are not contrary to God's Word, they are not to usurp "the judgment and kingdom of Christ, for he alone is the ruler of the conscience." Menno, however, never goes so far as to counsel the lower magistrates to resist with force the evil actions of their superiors. He does hold them accountable for their execution of the bloody mandates. "It did not help Pilate," he reminds them, "that he crucified Christ in the name of the emperor."[59] To refuse compliance with such evil laws would require, in effect, a conversion to the gospel of nonresistance. This leads us to a final point of comparison between Calvin and Menno: their respective views on the Christian character of civil authority.

4. *A Christian Magistracy?* Calvin's letter to Francis I was more than an *ad hoc* plea on behalf of the persecuted Protestants. It belongs to the genre of "mirrors for magistrates." Seneca had written *De Clementia* for the young Nero, and it is not perhaps fortuitous that Calvin chose this particular treatise

[56]*CWMS*, 198.
[57]Ibid., 117.
[58]Ibid., 119, 194.
[59]Ibid.

to edit and comment upon when he was still an aspiring humanist. Already in his preface to Olivétan's New Testament, Calvin designated the magistrates as "the officials and lieutenants of God," "the guardians of the church." This theme is more fully developed in the final chapter of the 1536 *Institutes* which is entitled, significantly, *"Politica ordinatio ecclesiae necessaria,"* that civil order is necessary for the well-being of the church.[60]

It is important to note that Calvin, who so often has been interpreted as the architect of theocracy, drew a definite distinction between civil and ecclesiastical governance. In language strongly reminiscent of Luther, Calvin can speak of two kingdoms, the spiritual and the political. The former has to do with the life of the soul; it resides in the mind within; the latter has to do with the concerns of the present life and regulates outward behavior. There are within the human, so to speak, "two worlds, over which different kings and different laws have authority."[61] At the beginning of his treatment of civil government in the *Institutes*, Calvin avers that the outward kingdom "pertains *only* to the establishment of civil justice and external morality" (*ad instituendam civilem duntaxat externamque morum iustitiam pertinet*). As Calvin develops his argument, however, it becomes clear that he does not mean this "only" to be taken literally. Indeed, the civil authority exists not merely for the sake of civil justice and outward morality, but also to provide certain "helps" to the spiritual government, i.e. the church. "Let no one be disturbed," Calvin says, "that I now commit to civil government the duty of rightly establishing religion, which I seem above to have put outside of human decision." What are the "helps" Calvin envisaged the Christian magistrate providing to the church? They include the suppression of idolatry, the prevention of blasphemy and public offenses against religion, the public institution of pure worship and right teaching, and the enforcement, by threat of capital punishment if necessary, of both tables of the Ten Commandments. Calvin goes to great lengths to show how godly magistrates can both love and kill their enemies at the same time. Indeed, by executing the vengeance ordained by God they hallow "by cruelty their hands, which by sparing they would have defiled."[62] It is not surprising, then, when Calvin refers to civil authority as a "most holy office," it is in fact "by far the most honorable of all callings in the whole life of mortal men."[63]

[60]*Opera Selecta*, 1:283.

[61]Battles, *Institution*, 252. Among the many studies of Calvin's views on church and state, the following are particularly helpful: Edouard Chenevière, *La penseé politique de Calvin* (Geneva: Labor, 1936); Josef Bohatec, *Calvins Lehre von Staat und Kirche* (Aalen: Scientia, 1961; originally published in 1937); John T. McNeill, "John Calvin on Civil Government," *Journal of Presbyterian History* 42 (1964), 71–91. Harro Höpfl's recent controversial study is also worthy of note: *John Calvin's Christian Polity* (Cambridge: Cambridge University Press, 1983).

[62]Battles, *Institution*, 293.

[63]Ibid., 288.

Menno's view of the magistrate falls somewhere between Calvin's high estimation and the radical apoliticism of the Swiss Anabaptist tradition embodied in the Schleitheim Confession. All agree that the civil authority is ordained by God; but, according to Schleitheim, it is to be exercised only "outside of the perfection of Christ," that is, outside of the church.[64] Menno holds a more mediating view. The duty of the magistrate, he holds, is to chastise and punish manifest criminals, to do justice between citizens, to deliver the oppressed out of the hand of the oppressor. There is the further task however of restraining the deceivers who mislead the poor helpless souls into destruction. It is the duty of magistrates to restrain such deceivers whether they be priests, monks, or preachers, baptized or unbaptized. Moreover, the magistrate is to refrain from introducing "ridiculous abuses and idolatry." All of this is to be done, Menno insists, "without force, violence, and blood." Even the restraint of the deceivers must be accomplished "by reasonable means, that is, without tyranny and bloodshed." In this way, Menno says to the magistrates, "you may enlarge, help, and protect the kingdom of God with gracious consent and permission, with wise counsel and a pious, unblamable life."[64]

Such a program implies that the magistrate may indeed be a Christian. Menno in fact assumes that this may be the case although he is not optimistic about the number of rulers who will fulfill their vocation in a Christian manner. He admonishes,

> Dear sirs, wake up, it is yet today. Do not boast that you are of royal blood and are called gracious lords, for it is but smoke, dust, and pride. . . . Do not boast that you are mighty ones upon the earth, and have great power, but boast in this rather if so be you rule your land in the true fear of God with virtuous wisdom and Christian righteousness to the praise of the Lord. . . . Seek the kingdom and country that will endure forever, and remember that here on earth you are but pilgrims and sojourners in a strange land, no matter how much held in honor.[65]

Menno assumes that a magistrate can also be a Christian; he does not, with Calvin, set forth a doctrine of Christian *magistracy*. In Menno's view, magisterial initiative in religious matters should be essentially passive: restraint, consent, permission, toleration. All of this must be done without coercion, without resort to violence. "Punish the evil in a Christian manner," Menno advises.[66] Even capital punishment is contrary to the Christian law of love and must be shunned. For Calvin the supportive ministry of the godly magistrate

[64]*CWMS*, 193.
[65]Ibid., 206.
[66]Ibid.

extended far beyond such concessive matters. "It is not enough merely to confess Jesus Christ and to profess to be his own . . . to you it belongs especially
to see to it that the gospel is heard, to have it published in your lands, in order
that it may be known by the people who have been committed to your charge;
in order that they may know you as servants and ministers of this great King,
and may serve and honor him, by obeying you under his hand and under his
guidance."[67] In line with this perspective the Council of Two Hundred, the
ruling magistracy of Geneva, pledged on February 2, 1554 "to live according
to the Reformation, forget all hatreds and cultivate concord."[68] To live according to the Reformation implied that they would seek to bring the laws of
Geneva into harmony with the Word and will of God thus fulfilling the vocation of a Christian magistracy.

Conclusion

Calvin and Menno died within three years of each other; Menno at
Wüstenfeld in Holstein in 1561, Calvin at Geneva in 1564. Ironically both reformers, who had spent so much time counselling candidates for martyrdom
and whose own lives were in jeopardy on numerous occasions, died natural
deaths comforted to the end by their close friends. From the beginning of their
ministry, both reformers were preoccupied with the theme of the Kingdom of
God. We have observed how, from very different contexts and sometimes
with quite different connotations, Calvin and Menno expounded on this
theme in strikingly similar ways. If we were to trace this theme through the
rest of their writings, no doubt the contrasts would become more pronounced.
At Geneva, Calvin struggled to assert the supremacy of the Kingdom of God
over and within both church political and local civic institutions. A recent interpreter of Calvin's social and political ethos has written, "His ability to distinguish the spiritual and the temporal was uncommon for his day; his refusal
to allow the spiritual to be subject to the temporal was uncommon for Protestantism in his day; his ability to suffuse the temporal with the values of the
spiritual without robbing the former of its identity is instructive for our day."[69]
As a minister of the Word, Calvin was, of course, primarily concerned with
the integrity of the church; but as one who refused to draw a precise correlation between the Kingdom of God and its institutional embodiment, he was
also able to assert the rule of God *etiam extra ecclesiam*.[70]

[67]Haroutunian, *Commentaries*, 72.

[68]John T. McNeill, *The History and Character of Calvinism* (New York: Oxford University
Press, 1954), 187.

[69]W. Fred Graham, *The Constructive Revolutionary* (Richmond: John Knox Press, 1971), 158.

[70]Cf. Heiko A. Oberman, "Die 'Extra'-Dimension in der Theologie Calvins," in *Geist und
Geschichte der Reformation*, ed. H. Liebing (Berlin: K. Scholder, 1966), 323-56.

Roland Bainton once remarked that when Christianity takes itself seriously, it must either forsake or master the world and at different points it may try to do both at once. The legacy of Menno Simons illustrates the tension inherent in this dual process. In their espousal of suffering and martyrdom, the Anapabtists forged a spirituality which was at once profoundly other-worldly and yet unswervingly committed to the purposes of God within history. If their ideals of religious toleration, the noncoercive character of faith, and the inviolability of the individual before God were with few exceptions unacceptable to, and unaccepted by, the religious and civil authorities of their time, this in no way detracts from their genuinely revolutionary character, in the original Copernican sense of revolution as a return to point of origin. However, far from embracing Calvin's notion of a Christian magistracy, later Mennonites abandoned even Menno's allowance of a Christian magistrate. If the blood of the martyrs was the seed of the church, increased toleration, ironically, spawned laxity and spiritual malaise. Menno's generation had been hardier. In his *Fundamentboek*, Menno had written: "This is my only joy and heart's desire: to extend the kingdom of God; [for this] I have renounced name and fame, honor and ease, and all, and have willingly assumed the heavy cross of my Lord Jesus Christ."[71] For Menno and his followers the gospel of nonresistance did not imply the path of least resistance. Their vision has been ably described by the philosopher Ernst Bloch:

> Despite their suffering,
> their fear and trembling,
> in all these souls
> there glows the spark from beyond,
> and it ignites the tarrying kingdom.[72]

---

[71]*CWMS*, 189.

[72]"Soviel Leid, soviel Furcht und Zittern auch gesetzt sein mag, so gluht in allen Seelen doch neu der Funke von druben, und er entzundet adas zogernde Reich." I follow the translation in Hans Jürgen Goertz, ed., *Profiles of Radical Reformers*, tr. Walter Klaassen (Kitchener, Ontario: Herald Press, 1982), 9.

The Schools of Brandenburg and the "Second Reformation": Centers of Calvinist Learning and Propaganda

Bodo Nischan*

This article shows how Elector John Sigismund of Brandenburg (1608-19) and his Calvinist advisors tried to use the Mark's leading institutions of learning to transform the country's Lutheran into a Reformed church. Their effort failed, largely because this "Second Reformation" was an elitist movement which lacked popular support. Instead, Brandenburg's rulers, with the encouragement of Reformed irenic professors from Frankfurt University, had to settle for a confessional compromise that ultimately led to the devlopment of religious toleration in early modern Brandenburg-Prussia.

THE PURPOSE OF THIS CHAPTER IS FIRST to show how Calvinists in early seventeenth century Brandenburg tried to use the country's leading schools to transform its Lutheran church into a Reformed church, and second to assess the degree to which they succeeded. The Second Reformation, which continued and completed the earlier ("first") Lutheran reformation,[1] began in

*Dedicated to the memory of Wilkins B. Winn, friend and colleague at East Carolina University. An abbreviated version of this essay was presented at a meeting of the Southern Historical Association in New Orleans on 12 November 1987. The research for this article was funded in part by grants from the American Philosophical Society and the Southern Regional Education Board.

[1]On the concept of the "Second Reformation," see Jürgen Moltmann, *Christoph Pezel (1539-1604) und der Calvinismus in Bremen* (Bremen: Einkehr, 1958); Thomas Klein, *Der Kampf um die Zweite Reformation in Kursachsen 1586-91* (Cologne and Graz; Böhlau, 1962); Franz Lau, "Die zweite Reformation in Kursachsen. Neue Forschungen zum sogenannten sächsischen Kryptocalvinismus," in *Verantwortung, Untersuchungen über Fragen aus Theologie und Geschichte. Zum 60. Geburstag D. Gottfried Noth*, ed. Ev. Luth. Landeskirchenamt Sachsen (Berlin: EVA, 1964), 137–64; Gerhard Zschäbitz, "Zur Problematik der sogenannten 'Zweiten Reformation,'" *Wissenschaftliche Zeitschrift der Karl-Marx-Universität Leipzig, Gesellschafts- und Sprachwissenschaftliche Reihe* 14/3 (1965): 505–9; Heinz Schilling, *Konfessionskonflikt und Staatsbildung: Eine Fallstudie über das Verhältnis von religiösem und sozialem Wandel in der Frühneuzeit am Beispiel der Grafschaft Lippe* (Gütersloh: Mohn, 1981); idem, *Die reformierte Konfessionalisierung in Deutschland: Das Problem der 'Zweiten Reformation'* (Gütersloh: Mohn, 1986), especially the essay by Rudolf von Thadden, "Die Fortsetzung des »Reformationswerks« in Brandenburg-Preußen," 233–50; and Henry J. Cohn, "The Territorial Princes in Germany's Second Reformation, 1559-1622," in Menna Prestwich, ed., *International Calvinism 1541-1715* (Oxford: Clarendon, 1985), 135–65.

Brandenburg on Christmas Day, 1613, when Elector John Sigismund together "with about fifty people," mostly members of his court and government, took communion in the Reformed manner in Berlin's Holy Trinity Cathedral.[2]

Early in his life John Sigismund had developed a profound dislike for the traditional Catholic pomp and ceremony, which had been retained in Brandenburg's Protestant church, and for the rigidity of the Lutheran Formula of Concord (1577). These sentiments grew even stronger when he and his younger brother John George visited the court of the Palatine Elector Frederick IV in 1607. At Heidelberg, the center of German Reformed learning, the two young princes became convinced that the Lutheran understanding of the Lord's Supper, contemptuously referred to by Calvinists as the dogma of "ubiquity," was wrong. Luther, John Sigismund observed later, had done much to set the gospel free, but "still had remained deeply stuck in the darkness of the papacy . . . and therefore had not been able to extricate himself completely from all human teachings." His view of the real presence was too "papal" and certainly was "false, devisive, and highly controversial."[3] "All of which proved," the elector's supporters explained, "that the Lutheran church and religion needed another reformation" in which "the leftover papal dung is to be swept completely out of Christ's stable."[4] The result, the Reformed claimed, would be a "fully reformed Evangelical" or a "reformed Lutheran church."[5]

Elsewhere in Germany, where the Second Reformation had succeeded—in the Palatinate, Nassau, Bremen, Lippe, Hesse, and Anhalt—Reformed or Calvinist churches had been established. John Sigismund and his advisors likewise aimed at transforming the Mark's Lutheran into a Reformed church.[6] A detailed blueprint, developed early in 1614 by the privy council under the presidency of Margrave John George, the elector's brother, made it clear that the country's schools, especially the Joachimsthal Gymnasium in the

[2]See "Calvinische Abendmahl gehalten zu Cöln an der Spree in der Domkirche, genannt zue Heiligen Dreyfaltigkeit, Anno Chri. 1613 am Heiligen Christtage," Niedersächsische Staats- und Universitätsbibliothek, Göttingen (hereafter cited as UB Göttingen), Cod. MS. hist. 189.I: ff.10f.

[3]"John Sigismund to Estates, 28 March 1614," UB Göttingen, Cod. MS. hist. 189.I: f.47; another copy of this letter at Geheimes Staatsarchiv Preussischer Kulturbesitz, Berlin (West). X. HA Rep.8 (Prenzlau), Nr.414, ff.14–24, (hereafter cited as GStAPK).

[4]Adam Agricola, *Widerlegung der Schlussreden D. Lucae Backmeisters, Superint. zu Güstrow* (n.p., n.d.), 166; Abraham Scultetus's Introduction to the "Confession of Germany's Reformed Churches," reprinted in Brandenburg under the title *Auff sonderbahren Befehl und Anordnung Des Durchlauchtigsten Hochgebornen Fürsten und Herrn/ Herrn Johannis Sigismunds/ Marggraffens zu Brandenburg/ . . . Glaubensbekenntnus der reformirten Evangelischen Kirchen in Deutschland* (Frankfurt a.d.O, 1614).

[5]UB Göttingen, Cod. MS. hist. 189.I: ff.86, 108.

[6]For details, see Bodo Nischan, "The Second Reformation in Brandenburg: Aims and Goals," *Sixteenth Century Journal* 14/2 (1983): 173–87.

Uckermark and the University of Frankfurt on the Oder River, were expected to play a leading role in this process.[7] The privy councillors emphasized the urgent need for Reformed pastors and teachers "to educate the young in the proper and pure evangelical religion free of all human trash." Teachers already openly sympathetic to the Reformed faith–the Räte mentioned Schäller in Stendal and Pelargus in Frankfurt as examples–should be encouraged. If not enough Brandenburgers could be found, Calvinist pastors and teachers should be recruited abroad. Stipends should be set aside for advanced study at Heidelberg. Above all, special attention should be paid to the country's leading institutions of learning: the prince's school at Joachimsthal had to become a Reformed academy; and only "people of our religion are to be appointed to the theological faculty of the University of Frankfurt."[8] A new Reformed Kirchenrat, modelled after the Palatinate church council, was to function as a supervisory agency and see to it that this "Reformationswerk" was carried out properly.

These recommendations were endorsed and reiterated in separate memoranda by Frederick Pruckmann, the Mark's vice-chancellor, and Abraham Scultetus, the well-known Heidelberg theologian, who arrived in Berlin in April 1614 to help John Sigismund with his reformation. Scultetus especially stressed the dire need for more native teachers and pastors, noting that "there is already talk among the citizens that the elector has only borrowed preachers and that the thing will not last."[9] Neither he nor any of the elector's other advisors, though, recommended any systematic indoctrination of the young, nor did they propose any sweeping elementary school reforms through general visitations.[10] Instead they focused on the country's two elite institutions to

---

[7]Similarly in other German principalities schools had played a key role in promoting the Second Reformation. See Gerhard Menk. *Die Hohe Schule Herborn in ihrer Frühzeit, 1584-1660* (Wiesbaden: Historische Kommission für Nassau, 1981); idem, "Territorialstaat und Schulwesen in der frühen Neuzeit. Eine Untersuchung zur religiösen Dynamik an den Grafschaften Nassau und Sayn," *Jahrbuch für westdeutsche Landesgeschichte* 9 (1983): 177–220; Gerhard Schormann, "Das Lemgoer Gymnasium zwischen Luthertum und Zweiter Reformation," *Lippische Mitteilungen aus Geschichte und Landeskunde* 49 (1980): 7–32; and idem, "Zweite Reformation und Bildungswesen am Beispiel der Elementarschulen," in Schilling, *Konfessionalisierung*, 308–16.

[8]This blueprint was contained in a memorandum sent to the elector on 21 February 1614: "Der Churfl. Brandenb. Stadthalter u. Räte Bedenken wie die Reformation Fortzuführen," Zentrales Staatsarchiv, Dienststelle Merseburg, German Democratic Republic. Rep.47.16, ff.66–77, (hereafter cited as *ZStA*). In addition the Räte recommended the formation of a Reformed Kirchenrat, a Reformed confessional statement for the Mark, colloquies with the principality's Lutheran pastors, an anti-polemics edict, stricter censorship laws, and specific liturgical reforms to eliminate all remaining "relics of popery." Surprisingly, they did not suggest a general visitation, nor was such a visitation ever carried out in the seventeenth century.

[9]See "Vizekanzler Pruckmanns Gedanken wie die Reformation sei anzustellen (1614)," *ZStA*, Rep.47.16, f.32. Scultetus's memorandum is found in Karl Pahncke, "Abraham Scultetus in Berlin," *Forschungen zur Brandenburgischen und Preussischen Geschichte* 23 (1910): 43–47.

[10]This procedure had been used in Brandenburg and other German principalities to introduce and consolidate the Lutheran reformation in the sixteenth century; decisive for Brandenburg were the church ordinances of 1540 and 1573, and the general visitation in 1600. For additional

do most of the educating and propagandizing. As late as December 1615 Margrave John George, one of the most ardent supporters of this Calvinist reformation, still was telling the elector:

> It is very important that well-known and highly educated professors and preceptors be appointed at the prince's school and at the university. Special care must be taken that only people who confess the true Reformed faith are chosen as teachers.[11]

As the "proper seminaries for church and state" these two institutions, then were to promote the Second Reformation and produce the much-needed ecclesiastical and secular bureaucrats for the new Calvinist state.[12]

Implementation

In announcing his conversion to Calvinism, John Sigismund evidently hoped that most of his subjects, convinced as he was of the need for further reformation, would readily follow suit and convert as well. But such a popular groundswell never materialized. Instead most Brandenburgers reacted to John Sigismund's efforts with either apathy or outright hostility. Whenever a Reformed preacher entered the pulpit of the Berlin Dom, where the elector worshipped, "the common mob behaved very disorderly . . . and, shouting curses and blasphemies, ran out" of the cathedral.[13] In several cities–at Berlin, Brandenburg, Lindau, and Stendal–riots erupted in 1614/15 when attempts were made to introduce Calvinist teachers or pastors.[14] The country's Lutheran clergy and estates condemned the new reformation as a "dangerous deformation," and made it quite clear that they would not tolerate any infringement of their political rights and religious privileges.[15]

---

information, see Friedrich Wienecke, "Die Begründung der evangelischen Volksschule in der Kurmark und ihre Entwicklung bis zum Tode König Friedrichs I., 1540-1713," *Zeitschrift für Geschichte der Erziehung und des Unterrichts* 3 (1913): 16–36; and Wolfgang Neugebauer, *Absolutischer Staat und Schulwirklichkeit in Brandenburg-Preußen* (Berlin and New York: Walter de Gruyter, 1985), 66–78 and 211–28. Note also the recent debate over the impact of public education and indoctrination during the Reformation: Gerald Strauss, *Luther's House of Learning: Indoctrination of the Young in the German Reformation* (Baltimore: Johns Hopkins University Press, 1978); and James Kittelson, "Successes and Failures in the German Reformation: The Report from Strasbourg," *Archive for Reformation History* 73 (1982): 153–75.

[11]John George's "Memorial," 12 December 1615, *ZStA*, Rep.47.16, f.197.

[12]"Die rechten seminaria . . . ecclesiae et politicae," *ZStA*, Rep.2.10.

[13]UB Göttingen, Cod. MS. hist. 189.I: f.147.

[14]For details, see Daniel H. Hering, *Historische Nachricht von dem ersten Anfang der Evangelisch-Reformirten Kirche in Brandenburg und Preussen* (Halle, 1778), 279–301, 313–22; and Eberhard Faden, "Der Berliner Tumult von 1615," *Jahrbuch für brandenburgische Landesgeschichte* 5 (1954): 27–45.

[15]For a sampling of the Lutheran reaction, see Simon Gedicke, *Pelargus Apostata* (Leipzig, [1617]); [Matthias] Hoe [von Hoenegg], *Wolgegründete/ und zufördert denen Evangelischen Christen*

Much of the opposition originated at the University of Königsberg in neighboring Prussia where John Behm, a professor of theology, was the leader of a vociferous anti-Calvinist campaign.[16] Behm urged the estates to use their influence and stop the elector.[17] The Junkers needed little encouragement. Aware of the importance of the schools in this confessional struggle, they already were demanding that John Sigismund permit "our glorious university in Frankfurt a.d.O. and the Fürstenschule in Joachimsthal . . . to abide by our true religion."[18] When exhortations did not work, they tried economic pressure by withholding funds and donations which they had pledged earlier.[19] Such opposition slowed the reformers' efforts, but could not stop them from turning these schools into Calvinist institutions. Partly this was due to the fact that both had strong Philippist traditions which made their faculties more susceptible to Calvinism. Mostly, though, it was because the elector, rather than the country's estates or clergy, controlled faculty appointments at these institutions.

The grammar school at Joachimsthal in the Uckermark had been founded by Elector Joachim Frederick, John Sigismund's father, in 1607 to educate at public expense talented young Brandenburgers for state and church service.[20]

---

in der Chur und Mark Brandenburg/ zu nothwendiger nachrichtung/ verfertigte Verantwortung/ Wider das zu Berlin newlich ausgeflogene Calvinische Lästergespräch (Leipzig, 1614); and Leonard Hutter, *Calvinista Aulico-Politicus Alter. Das ist: Christlicher unnd Nothwendiger Bericht/ von den fürnembsten Politischen Haupt Gründen/ durch welche man/ die verdampte Calvinisterey/ in die Hochlöbl. Chur und Mark Brandenburg einzuführen/ sich eben starck bemühet* (Wittenberg, 1614). For additional information, see Bodo Nischan, "Reformation or Deformation? Lutheran and Reformed Views of Martin Luther in Brandenburg's 'Second Reformation,'" in *Pietas et Societas: Recent Trends in the Social History of Reformation and Society*, eds. Kyle C. Sessions and Phillip N. Bebb (Kirksville, Mo: Sixteenth Century Journal Publ., 1985), 202–15.

[16]On the University of Königsberg as a center of opposition, see August Tholuck, *Das akademische Leben des siebzehnten Jahrhunderts*, 2 vols. (Halle, 1853-54), 2: 73–81; Daniel H. Arnoldt, *Ausführliche und mit Urkunden versehene Historie der Königsbergischen Universität*, 3 vols. (Königsberg, 1746-56), 2: 119–229; and Götz von Selle, *Geschichte der Albertus-Universität zu Königsberg in Preußen* (Würzburg: Holzner, 1956), 76–78; and Fritz Gause, *Die Geschichte der Stadt Königsberg in Preussen* (Cologne and Graz: Böhlau, 1965), 382. On John Behm (1578-1648), see Arnoldt, 2: 162–4; Christian G. Jöcher, *Allgemeines Gelehrten-Lexikon*, 11 vols. (Leipzig, 1750-1897), 1: 913 f; and *Allgemeine Deutsche Biographie*, 56 vols. (Leipzig: Duncker & Humblot, 1875-1912), 2: 283 f. (hereafter cited as *ADB*).

[17]Johannes Behm, *Gantz Trewhertzige Warnung/ An alle und jede des Herzogthumbs Preussen Untersassen/ Sich für der verdämlichen Zwinglianischen oder Calvinischen Sect zu hütten* (Königsberg, 1614); and idem, *Christliche Landtags Predigt/ Bey Zusammenkunfft der sämbtlichen Stände des löblichen Herzogthumbs Preussen den 21. Novemb. Anno 1616 zu Königsberg . . . gehalten* (Königsberg, n.d.).

[18]"Estates to John Sigismund, 2 October 1614," *ZStA*, Rep.47, 17–18; another copy of this letter at UB Göttingen, Cod. MS. hist. 189.I: ff.59 f

[19]See John George's "Memorial," 12 December 1615, *ZStA*, Rep.47.16, f.197.

[20]See "Fundation des Joachimsthalschen Gymnasiums, Grimnitz, 24 August 1607," in Melle Klinkenborg, ed., *Acta Brandenburgica. Brandenburgische Regierungsakten seit der Gründung des Geheimen Rates*, 3 vols. (Berlin: Gsellius, 1927-30), 3: 172–80. A copy of the original charter is also found at *ZStA*, Rep.60.1.

Joachim Frederick viewed the school as a Protestant bulwark against the many Jesuit schools that had sprung up all over Germany in the late sixteenth century. The school was well-endowed with a capital of 40,000 thalers and a fine library. In addition, it received annual donations of grains, meats, wine, cloth, and paper.

Although founded as a Lutheran school "for the preservation and promotion of pure doctrine," Joachimsthal, very much like its founder, was never fanatically orthodox or anti-Calvinist.[21] With the exception of its first rector, the quarrelsome and abrasive Charles Bumann, who led the school from 1607 to 1610, its faculty was generally Philippist.[22] Many expressed serious reservations about the Formula of Concord and the Lutheran view of the Lord's Supper. Bumann's successor, the Heidelberg-educated Samuel Dresemius, who headed the school until it was destroyed and temporarily disbanded during the Thirty Years' War, was more sympathetic to Calvinism.[23] Christoph Pelargus, the Mark's Philippist-turned-Calvinist general superintendent, also played an important role.[24] At the gymnasium's opening ceremonies, on Bartholomew's Day 1607, he had delivered a festival oration "On the Dignity, Necessity, and Usefulness of Schools." He continued to visit Joachimsthal regularly, and after 1614 saw to it that only Calvinist teachers were appointed. Abraham von Dohna and Frederick Pruckmann on the privy council likewise promoted the school's calvinization. When the elector—stunned by the unexpected Lutheran criticism that his conversion precipitated—appeared to hesitate, they reminded him very pointedly that the gymnasium had to be reformed immediately if their enterprise was to succeed. They urged John Sigismund either to send instructions on how to proceed, or else to authorize them to take appropriate action. Since Scultetus, the Heidelberg court chaplain, was in Berlin, they suggested that he be dispatched to visit the school. Dohna and Pruckmann also sought to counter fears that

---

[21]Klinkenborg, 3: 172. On the history of the school, see F. L. Brunn, *Einige nähere Nachrichten von der Gründung, frühern Einrichtung und den Schicksalen des jetzigen könig. joachimsthalschen Gymnasiums bis zu seiner Vernichtung und Wiederherstellung* (Berlin, 1825); Carl Euler, "Das königl Joachimsthalsche Gymnasium," *Brandenburgia*, 7 (1898/99): 294–307; Erich Wetzel, *Die Geschichte des königl. Joachimsthalischen Gymnasiums 1607-1907* (Halle, 1907), 1–21; and Siegfried Joost, *Das Joachimsthalsche Gymnasium* (Wittich: Knopp, 1982), 2–16.

[22]See "Biographisch-bibliographisches Verzeichnis der Lehrer des Joachimsthalschen Gymnasiums von der Gründung der Anstalt bis 1826," *Kgl. Joachimsthalsche Gymnasium Berlin, Programm* nr.57 (1899/1900): 1–17; and Wetzel, 8 f. Bumann's administration is discussed in Brunn, 24–38.

[23]On Samuel Dresemius (1578-1638), see Martin Seidel, *Bilder-Sammlung* (Berlin, 1751); 173 f; and Brunn, 39 f.

[24]On Christoph Pelargus (1565-1633), see Johann C. Beckmann, *Notitia Universitatis Francofurtanae* (Frankfurt a.d.O., 1706), 122–33; Christian W. Spieker, *Beschreibung und Geschichte der Marien- oder Oberkirche zu Frankfurt an der Oder* (Frankfurt a.d.O., 1835), 251–71; and *ADB*, 25: 328–30.

Joachimsthal's calvinization might lead many Lutherans to boycott the school, noting that "there are enough foreigners . . . who would gladly take advantage of this electoral benefice if our native sons refuse to attend."[25]

John Sigismund responded quickly : on 21 September 1614 he visited the school together with Abraham Scultetus.[26] Since Dresemius, the rector, and the faculty supported the Second Reformation, Joachimsthal was quickly and smoothly converted. An ordinance, issued shortly afterwards, confirmed its new status as a Calvinist academy.[27] Worship services at the school chapel were reformed through the deletion of all so-called "papal ceremonial practices." German replaced Latin where it had still been used during the service—for instance, in the singing of hymns, the litany, kyrie, epistle, and gospel. Henceforth the sacraments were to be celebrated in the Reformed manner; anything alluding to the hated Lutheran doctrine of "ubiquity" was deleted. The elector's ordinance specifically noted that "in the Lord's supper the *fractio panis* rite, used in the primitive and all orthodox churches, is to be used. Holy Baptism is to be administered . . . without exorcism."[28] The Heidelberg Catechism was declared normative for all religious instruction. "The rector, pastor, deacon, and all teachers at the school were to confirm the *Confessio Sigismundi* by signing a revers."[29] They were instructed to watch carefully "that false Ubiquistic, Flacian, Schwenkfeldian, or similar abominable teachings do not find their way in the Fürstenschule." Without much delay or difficulty the Second Reformation thus had been introduced at the principality's leading secondary school.[30]

---

[25]"Privy Councillors to John Sigismund, 4 September 1614," *ZStA*, Rep.47.17–18.

[26]Gustrav A. Benrath, ed., *Die Selbstbiographie des Heidelberger Theolgen und Hofpredigers Abraham Scultetus (1566-1624)* (Karlsruhe: Evang. Presseverlag, 1966), 69.

[27]For the following, see "Newe Kirchen Ordnung Uberantwortet von den Herren Visitatoribus . . . in Valle Joachimica A⁰ 1616," *ZStA*, Rep.60.24.

[28]Both the fraction in the Lord's Supper and exorcism in Baptism became important "ceremonial tests" of one's confessional allegiance in the late Reformation: Lutherans opposed the fraction but generally retained exorcism, while Calvinists favored the fraction and opposed exorcism. For additional information, see Bodo Nischan, "The 'Fractio Panis': A Reformed Communion Practice in Late Reformation Germany," *Church History* 53 (1984): 17–29; and idem, "The Exorcism Controversy and Baptism in the Late Reformation," *Sixteenth Century Journal* 18 (1987): 31–51.

[29]John Sigismund's Reformed confession, also known as the *Marchica*, published in the summer of 1614, is found in Heinrich Heppe, ed., *Die Bekenntnisschriften der reformierten Kirchen Deutschlands* (Eberfeld, 1860), 284–94; and Wolfgang Gericke, *Glaubenszeugnisse und Kirchenpolitik der Brandenburgischen Herrscher bis zur Preussischen Union, 1540 bis 1815* (Bielefeld: Luther-Verlag, 1977), 122–31. See also Philip Schaff, ed., *The Creeds of Christendom, with a History and Critical Notes*, 3 vols. (New York and London: Harper, 1919), 1: 554–58.

[30]Christian T. Schosser, *Kurtze jedoch Gründliche Beschreibung der gantzen Churfürstlichen Marck zu Brandenburgk* (Magdeburg, 1617) matter-of-factly describes Joachimsthal as "eine newe Stat mit einer Churfürstlichen reformirten Schulen".

Even more important for the propagation of the new faith was the University of Frankfurt an der Oder, the Viadrina.[31] The school, founded in 1506 by Elector Joachim I, had been lutheranized in 1539. Andrew Musculus and Cristoph Corner, who helped write the Formula of Concord, had taught there and in the late sixteenth century had established the university's reputation as a citadel of Lutheran orthodoxy. Significantly, though, few professors at Frankfurt shared their religious zeal. The faculties of law, medicine, and philosophy never subscribed to the Formula, even though they were urged repeatedly to do so. There was dissent even among the theologians. Urban Pierius, a Musculus student, and somewhat later, Christoph Pelargus and John Heidenreich signed the Formula, but only reluctantly while voicing their objections to the doctrine of ubiquity.[32]

Their reservations undoubtedly were related to the university's strong humanistic tradition.[33] Early in the Reformation and again towards the end of the century Melanchthon's disciples had set the tone at the Viadrina. George Sabinus, Melanchthon's son-in-law, was named professor of rhetoric at the university in 1538 and became the leader of a group of early Philippists which included Alexander Alesius, one of the first well-known Scottish Lutherans, and Christoph Preuss, a philosopher and physician from Slovakia, who also served as the elector's private secretary. These Philippist tendencies, which suffered a temporary setback while John Agricola (d. 1566) was general superintendent and Musculus taught at Frankfurt, re-emerged late in the century under Pierius, Pelargus, and others. The suppression of Philippism in neigh-

[31]On the University of Frankfurt an der Oder, see Carl R. Hausen, *Geschichte der Universität und Stadt Frankfurt an der Oder*, 2d ed. (Frankfurt a.d.O., 1806); Tholuck, 2: 251-65; Hermann Fricke, *Gesicht und Maske der Viadrina* (Berlin: n.p., 1957); Günter Mühlpfordt, *Die Oderuniversität Frankfurt (1506-1811)* (Frankfurt a.d.O: Frankfurt-Information, 1981); Günther Haase and Joachim Winkler, eds., *Die Oder-Universität Frankfurt. Beiträge zu ihrer Geschichte* (Weimar: Böhlaus, 1983); and Gerd Heinrich, "Frankfurt an der Oder, Universität," *Theologische Realenzyklopädie*, vol. 1- (Berlin & New York: Walter de Gruyter, 1977-). 11: 335–42, (hereafter cited as *TRE*).

[32]Tholuck, 2: 252. On John Heidenreich (1542-1617), see *ADB* s.v. "Heidenreich, Johannes H." On Urbanus Pierius (1546-1616), see Seidel, 151–53; and Thomas Klein, "Zur Biographie des Urban Pierius," 14–54 in Urban Pierius, *Geschichte der kursächsischen Kirchen- und Schulreformation*, ed. T. Klein (Marburg: Elwert, 1970). Pierius later claimed "er hette beyde, Musculum und Cornerum, gebetten, sie wolten ihm dess zeugen sein, dass er nicht simpliciter subscribiret, und hetten sie ihm solchess zu thun zugesagt, so offt es die notturfft erförderen würde," 619.

[33]For the following, see Heinrich Grimm, *Meister der Renaissancemusik an der Viadrina. Quellenbeiträge zur Geisteskultur des Nordostens Deutschlands vor dem Dreißigjährigen Kriege* (Frankfurt a.d.O. & Berlin: Trowitzsch, 1942), 13–50; Hermann Fricke, "Ars Poetica an der Viadrina, *Forschungen zur Brandenburgischen und Preussischen Geschichte* 54 (1943): 115–29; Friedrich Weichert, "Die Oder-Universität Frankfurt und ihre Reformbestimmungen aus dem 16. Jahrhundert unter besonderer Berücksichtigung der theologischen Aspekte," *Jahrbuch für Berlin-Brandenburgische Kirchengeschichte* 55 (1985): 113–56; and Mühlpfordt, *Die Oderuniversität Frankfurt*, 23–27. For a more general assessment of the influence of humanistic ideas at German universities during the age of confessionalism, see Lewis W. Spitz, "The Importance of the Reformation for the Universities: Culture and Confession in the Critical Years," in James M. Kittelson and Pamela J. Transue, eds., *Rebirth, Reform, and Resilience: Universities in Transition 1300-1700* (Columbus, Ohio; Ohio State University Press, 1984), 42–67.

boring Saxony brought many Melanchthon students to Frankfurt making it a sort of "Ersatz-Wittenberg."[34] Close ties between Frankfurt and Leiden University, then the center of northern humanist and Calvinist learning, further encouraged these developments.[35] Francis Hildesheim on the Frankfurt medical faculty, later the personal physician of Electors Joachim Frederick and John Sigismund, corresponded with Justus Lipsius, the Neo-Stoic from Leiden and foremost northern humanist in the late sixteenth century.[36] Lipsius' political ideas were taught at Frankfurt; an edition of the *Politicorum Libri VI*, his major work on political Stoicism, was published there in 1612.[37] In such an intellectual environment the Formula of Concord never gained much of a following. Not surprisingly, the revised university statutes of 1610 no longer made it obligatory for the school's faculty.[38]

Since the Hohenzollerns, like other sixteenth-century rulers, had come to view the university as an agency of the state rather than the church, they sought to increase their involvement in the school's administration. As the university's chancellor, a post his father had acquired in 1598, John Sigismund had the right to appoint and promote faculty members.[39] He used these constitutional privileges to turn the institution into a full-fledged Calvinist school. By decree he also changed its theological statutes on 17 August 1616, ordering "that henceforth the doctrine of ubiquity . . . and the manducation of Christ's body in the Lord's Supper no longer are to be taught at this university."[40]

[34]Mühlpfordt, *Die Oderuniversität Frankfurt*, 27.

[35]For details, see Heinz Schneppen, *Niederländische Universitäten und Deutsches Geistesleben* (Münster/W.: Aschendorf, 1960), 9–31 and 80–85; and Gerhard Oestreich, "Politischer Neustoizismus und Niederländische Bewegung in Europa und besonders in Brandenburg-Preussen," in idem, *Geist und Gestalt des frühmodernen Staates* (Berlin: Duncker & Humblot, 1969), 101–56.

[36]Oestreich, "Politischer Neustoizismus und Niederländische Bewegung," 141. On Francis Hildesheim (1551-1614), see Seidel, 149 f; and *ADB* s.v. "Hildesheim, Franz."

[37]Oestreich, "Politischer Neustoizismus und Niederländische Bewegung," 141; Mühlpfordt, *Die Oderuniversität Frankfurt*, 27. On the appeal of Lipsius's neo-stoicism at the turn of the century, see Schneppen, 117–22; Jason L. Saunders, *Justus Lipsius: The Philosophy of Renaissance Stoicism* (New York: Liberal Arts Press, 1955); Gerhard Oestreich, "Justus Lipsius als Universalgelehrter zwischen Renaissance und Barock," in Theodoor H. Lunsingh Scheurleer, ed., *Leiden University in the Seventeenth Century* (Leiden: Brill, 1975), 176–201.

[38]See "Leges et statuta Academiae Viadrinae cum confirmatione Electoris Joh. Sigismundi, xiii. die Aprilis Anno MDCX," in Christian Mylius, *Corpus Constitutionum Marchicarum* 11 vols. (Berlin and Halle, 1737) I/2, no. 8, cols. 31-34; and Paul Reh, ed., *Die allgemeinen Statuten der Universität Frankfurt a.O. 1510-1610* (Breslau, 1898), 47 f.

[39]Conrad Bornhak, *Geschichte der preussischen Universitätsverwaltung bis 1810* (Berlin: Reimer, 1900), 6–19; and Otfried Schwarzer, *Das Kanzleramt an der Universität Frankfurt a.O.* (Diss., Breslau, 1900) esp. pp. 11 and 70-76. On the "Verstaatlichung" of sixteenth-century German universities, see also Peter Baumgart, "Universitätsautonomie und Landesherrliche Gewalt im späten 16. Jahrhundert: das Beispiel Helmstedt," *Zeitschrift für historische Forschung* 1 (1974): 23–53; idem, "Die deutsche Universität des 16. Jahrhunderts: das Beispiel Marburg," *Hessisches Jahrbuch für Landesgeschichte* 28 (1978): 50–79; and Menk, *Herborn*, 97–115.

[40]The decree is found at *ZStA*, Rep.51.68, f.14, and reprinted in Ernst C. Cyprian, *Abgetrungener Unterricht von kirchlicher Vereinigung der Protestanten*, 2 vols. (Frankfurt and Leipzig, 1726) 2: 75–77; and Hering, *Historische Nachricht*, 325–27.

Vacancies on the theological faculty gave him the opportunity to appoint Reformed professors there. With the deaths of Andrew Wenzel (d. 1613) and James Ebert (d. 1614), the theological faculty had shrunk to half its normal size, consisting now only of Christoph Pelargus and John Heidenreich.[41] Both men were well disposed towards the elector's new religion, but unable to provide the leadership needed at Frankfurt. Heidenreich was old and weak; his death in 1617 would create yet a third vacancy. Pelargus was busy with administrative responsibilities and had his hands full defending himself against the vociferous attacks of the Lutherans. Additional appointments to the theological faculty therefore had to be made, if Frankfurt truly was to become the center of Calvinist learning and propaganda which the elector and his Reformed advisors envisioned.

The first Reformed teacher whom John Sigismund appointed was John Bergius, a young Pomeranian, who had graduated from the University of Heidelberg and also had studied at Saumur, Cambridge, and Leiden.[42] Named associate professor of theology in 1614, he was promoted to full professor in 1616. Bergius would serve the Hohenzollern rulers for nearly half a century and exert a decisive influence on the Mark's religious and political affairs. Another Reformed theologian to join the faculty was Wolfgang Crell.[43] Educated at Bremen and Marburg, he had briefly served the Calvinist Count Maurice of Hesse-Kassel before accepting a call to Frankfurt in 1616. A third newcomer was Gregory Franck who was selected in 1617 to fill the vacancy created by Heidenreich's death.[44] Franck, who previously taught Greek at the university, had spent several years in France; he too had visited the Reformed academy at Saumur and met Duplesis-Mornay and other Huguenot leaders.

With these three appointments the theological faculty again was fully staffed and, more importantly, clearly Reformed. "The Oder university thus became the easternmost bastion of Calvinism."[45] The new teachers had been educated at some of Europe's finest schools and, the privy councillors thought, "could well compete with the theological faculties of other academies."[46] None of the new appointees was a native son; all of them, though, settled per-

[41]Beckmann, *Notitia Universitatis Francofurtanae*, 57.

[42]On John P. Bergius (1587-1658), see Beckmann, *Notitia Universitatis Francofurtanae*, 133–56; Johann C. Müller and Georg G. Küster, *Altes und Neues Berlin* (Berlin, 1737), 149–58; *ADB*, s.v. "Bergius, Johannes;" and n. 76 below.

[43]On Wolfgang Crell (1593-1664), see Beckmann, *Notitia Universitatis Francofurtanae* 166 f; and Müller and Küster, *Altes und Neues Berlin*, 158 f.

[44]On Gregory Franck (1585-1651), see Tholuck, 2: 254.

[45]Mühlpfordt, *Die Oderuniversität Frankfurt*, 29. Note also L. Spitz's observation: "From the death of Melanchthon until the end of the Thirty Years' War, the universities became increasingly agents of confessionalism. . . . These changes in the confessional position of established universities were particularly significant since Calvinism was not to receive official recognition and tolerance in the Empire until the Peace of Westphalia and could not therefore receive imperial credentials for new universities," 56.

[46]"Privy Councillors to John Sigismund, 23 March 1618," *ZStA*, Rep.51.70.

manently in the Mark and became enthusiastic promoters of the Second Reformation. Frankfurt University not only was to educate new Reformed leaders but also help stem the tide of Lutheran criticism that John Sigismund's reformation had precipitated. To silence his critics at home John Sigismund issued an edict on 24 February 1614 ordering "all superintendents, inspectors, and ministers . . . in the Mark of Brandenburg . . . to cease, eschew, and avoid all berating and abuse of other churches, which are not in your charge."[47] As the principality's chief censor the university supervised all publications in the Mark and was expected to help enforce the decree. Especially publishers of religious works had to consult its theological faculty and would find themselves in serious trouble if they dared to produce anything that could be construed as anti-Reformed propaganda. Even Frederick Hartman, head of one of Frankfurt's leading publishing firms which had long enjoyed a close relationship with the university, was not immune to criticism.[48] In the spring of 1615 he was severely reprimanded for producing a new edition of "Heilbrun's and Westphal's writings against John Calvin."[49] Margrave John George charged that this violated the elector's anti-polemics edict and showed disrespect for the Reformed religion. Hartman protested that he had merely printed a new edition of a previously approved book.[50] He pointed to his past publication record, which clearly demonstrated that he was sympathetic to the new religion.[51] If a mistake had been made the fault was not his, but lay in the often confusing and contradictory instructions he had received from Frankfurt's theological faculty. To avoid similar problems in the future, he suggested that clearer and more specific guidelines be provided.[52]

[47]Copies of the decree are found at *GStAPK*, XX. HA StA Königsberg EM Abt.37a, Nr.33, f.9, and X. HA Rep.8 (Prenzlau) Nr.414, ff.25–27. The text is also found in Mylius, I/1, no. 12; Gericke, *glaubenszeugnisse und Kirchenpolitik*, 132–36; and, excerpts in English, in C. A. Macartney, ed., *The Habsburg and Hohenzollern Dynasties in the Seventeenth and Eighteenth Centuries* (New York: Harper, 1970), 223–27.

[48]On Friedrich Hartman (1565-1631), see Heinrich Grimm, "Der Verlag und die Druckoffizin der Buchdrucker 'Hansen Vnd Friderichen Hartman. Vater Vnd Sohn Buchhendler zu Franckfurt An der Oder' (1588-1631)," *Gutenberg Jahrbuch* 35 (1960): 237–54; and Josef Benzing, *Die Buchdrucker des 16. und 17. Jahrhunderts im deutschen Sprachgebiet* (Wiesbaden: Harrassowitz, 1963), 133 f.

[49]"John George to John Sigismund, 16 March 1615," *ZStA*, Rep.51.64.

[50]The "Verzeichnis der Bücher/ welche von Hansen und Friderichen Hartmann/ Vater und Sohn/ Buchhendlern zu Franckfurt an der Oder/ gedruckt/ verlegt/ und bey ihnen neben andern ein und Außlendischen Büchern zu bekommen. Anno 1606" lists *Synopsis doctrinae Calvinianae, Summarischer begriff und widerlegung der Calvinisten Lehr D. Jacobi Heilbrunneri*; for the list, see Ernst Consentius, "Von Druckkosten, Taxen und Privilegien im Kurstaat Brandenburg während des 16. und 17. Jahrhunderts," *Forschungen zur Brandenburgischen und Preussischen Geschichte* 34 (1922): 219.

[51]His publications, indeed, support this claim; see, for instance, *Glaubensbekenntnis der reformierten Kirche* (1614); Abraham Scultetus, *Berlinische Reformation* (1614); and Martin Füssel, *Confessio Oder Kurtz Glaubens-Bekentnuß* (1615). Grimm notes (p. 250) that Hartman was responsible for producing much of John Sigismund's "kirchliche Amtsliteratur."

[52]"Friedrich Hartman to John Sigismund, 20 March 1615," *ZStA*, Rep.51.64.

If the university was to function as an effective propaganda agency for the new faith, its own house had to be kept in order. To avoid any potential embarrassment, John Sigismund ordered that no professor was to publish anything without prior authorization except "programs, personal announcements, and wedding or funeral poems." Everything else "had to be censored first by the [author's] dean and faculty; copies of all publications were to be sent to court for an evaluation by the privy council and had to be approved by His Electoral Highness." John Sigismund only modified these stern provisions after each faculty agreed to take a solemn pledge not to print anything that "would belittle either the Reformed religion or its supporters."[53] Individuals who still dared to deride the elector's faith were threatened with dismissal. For instance, Samuel Scharlach, a somewhat outspoken Lutheran on the medical faculty, was bluntly reminded "that he had been hired as a professor of philosophy, not as an inspector of consciences" and that he could leave if he no longer liked his job.[54] John Heidenreich on the theological faculty did not specifically criticize Calvinism but managed to incur the elector's ire by publishing a book critical of the Consensus of Sendomir, an agreement drawn up in 1570 between the Lutherans, the Reformed, and the Bohemian Brethren in Poland. John Sigismund, who ruled Prussia as Polish fief, feared that Heidenreich's publication would further damage relations with the Lutherans and hurt him politically in Poland. He therefore ordered "that all copies of the book be bought and destroyed"; he also instructed his "theologians in Frankfurt to defend their doctrines in general, but not to get involved in any specific issues."[55]

Margrave John George even went so far as to charge the university's law faculty with anti-Reformed malice because it had ruled in favor of two journeymen who had been falsely accused of starting anti-Calvinist riots on Trinity Sunday in June 1615. The professors thought that the margrave's claims were preposterous and totally unjustified. They noted that all the professors on the law faculty "except one had been Reformed for some time;" the sole remaining Lutheran was hardly in a position to force an anti-Reformed majority decision. Even more important, they thought, was the fact that their decision in favor of the accused was based on legal, and not religious, principles. If religion had influenced their judgment, the professors observed, "we hardly would be worthy of the honorable office to which his Electoral Highness has appointed us at this university."[56] The incident is significant because it indicated just how far the elector's more ardent advisors were prepared to go to use the school on behalf of their cause. It also suggested, though, that there

[53]*ZStA* Merseburg, Rep.51.64.

[54]"John Sigismund to Samuel Scharlach, 14 June 1614," *ZStA*, Rep.47.19.

[55]"John Sigismund to Prussian Oberräte, 25 October 1614," *GStAPK*, Ostpr. Fol. 1225, ff.139 f.

[56]"Frankfurt law faculty to John George, (July 1615)," *ZStA*, Rep.47.19.

were definite limits to what Calvinists could accomplish in Brandenburg even under the most favorable of circumstances.

Results

A) FAILURE: How effective, then, were the Joachimsthal Fürstenschule and the University of Frankfurt in promoting the Second Reformation in Brandenburg? While both had been transformed quickly and smoothly into Calvinist schools, their long-term influence is debatable. Most Brandenburgers remained quite hostile to the changes that had taken place. Indeed, the opposition of the Markish population, its clergy, and especially the estates—specifically the Junkers—soon demonstrated that the country's Lutheran church would not be as easily transformed as the elector and his advisors initially had hoped.[57]

Since the impecunious elector was heavily dependent on the financial backing of the estates, they were able to exert considerable leverage and force him to accept a "Recess" (on 5 February 1615) declaring

> that whosoever in the land wishes it may remain attached to the doctrine of Luther and the unchanged Augsburg Confession . . . and also to the Book of Concord. Such person shall not be subjected to any pressure or compulsion to relinquish it.[58]

The Second Reformation thus would remain what it had been at its inception: a *Fürstenreformation*,[59] a prince's reformation that could be implemented successfully only in institutions, such as the two schools, that were directly under the elector's control. Yet even here, where the Reformed cause enjoyed strong support and such auspicious beginnings had been made, setbacks and failures were experienced.

In spite of its endowment the Joachimsthal Gymnasium soon ran into financial difficulties that seriously jeopardized its mission. As early as 1614 complaints were voiced about the irregular payment of teachers' salaries; also, opponents of the new religion withheld the wood, meat, and other donations

---

[57]The problems Calvinists encountered in Brandenburg are well documented in the correspondence between the elector at Königsberg and his privy councillors in Berlin; see especially "Privy councillors to John Sigismund, 23 March 1617," and the elector's reply of 3 May 1617, ZStA, Rep.47.17–18.

[58]"Revers des Churfürsten Johann Sigismunds, so bey der Versammlung derer Landstände disseits der Oder gegeben worden, Cölln an der Spree, den 5. Febr. 1615," Mylius, VI/1, no. 79; also cited in Hering, *Historische Nachricht*, 233–35; English translation from Macartney, *The Habsburg and Hohenzollern Dynasties*, 227.

[59]On the use of this term in Reformation historiography, see Zschäbitz, "Zur Problematik," 507; and Schilling, *Konfessionskonflikt*, 50. Note also Heiko Obermann, "Stadtreformation und Fürstenreformation," in Lewis Spitz, ed., *Humanismus und Reformation als kulturelle Kräfte in der deutschen Geschichte: Ein Tagungsbericht* (Berlin and New York: De Gruyter, 1981), 80–103.

they had pledged earlier.[60] As feared by some, the Mark's population boycotted the school causing a precipitous decline in its enrollment at the very time that John Sigismund was trying to turn it into a citadel of Calvinism. By 1620 the school's economic difficulties had reached such crisis proportions that the Berlin government decided to reorganize it by consolidating its economic resources and drastically reducing the maximum size of the student body from 170 to 74 boys.[61]

These reforms alleviated but did not end the school's financial woes. Teachers continued to complain about low and irregular salaries; because of rabid inflation they requested to be paid in "old coins" rather than in the less valuable newer currency.[62] School attendance also remained a problem; the new ceiling figure of 74 was barely, if ever, reached. In 1624 the visitors reported only "a small handful of hardly 36 boys" at the school; a year later they noted merely "a modest number of pupils", and by 1629 this number had gotten "so small that we can only weep and pray that God in his mercy will increase it again."[63]

The coming of the Thirty Years' War aggravated Joachimsthal's plight further. "The danger of war increases daily," noted Rector Dresemius in early May 1627; by October he was reporting "quite a bit damage which has been caused by marauding soldiers."[64] Gregory Franck, who visited the school in 1634, observed "disorder, fire damage, and devastation," but urged George William to do everything humanly possible "to save this gem of our principality."[65] Yet there was little that the elector could do: in the night of 5 January 1636 it was occupied and ransacked by Saxon troops.[66] The *Fürstenschule* did not resume operations until after the war when it was rebuilt by the Great Elector.[67]

Designed as an elite school to train future leaders of church and state, the Joachimsthal gymnasium never did have a large student body. It has been esti-

---

[60]Euler, "Das königl Joachimsthalsche Gymnasium," 301; and Wetzel, *Die Geschichte des königl.*, 11.

[61]The document, dated St. Michael's Day [29 September] 1620, provided; "Nachdem . . . sich daargewiesen, das die anzahl der 170 Knaben gaar nicht behalten werden konte, als ist solche anzahl bis uf sechstische, oder vier und siebenzig Knaben, eingezogen;" *ZStA*, Rep.60.1.

[62]"Visitation report by Pelargus and Omichius, 24 October 1622," *ZStA*, Rep.60.6.

[63]"Visitation reports of 1624, 1625, and 1629," *ZStA*, Rep.60.2. See also "Gesamtfrequenz, 1607-1907," in Ernst Bahn et al., *Zur Statistik des königl. Joachimsthalschen Gymnasiums*, Festschrift zum Dreihundertjährigen Jubiläum des Königl. Joachimsthalschen Gymnasiums am 24. August 1907, Part II (Halle: Buchhandlung d. Waisenhauses, 1907), Table I.

[64]"Dresemius to Pruckmann, 9 May and 9 October 1627," *ZStA*, Rep.60.22.

[65]*ZStA*, Rep.60.2.

[66]Brunn, *Einige nähere Nachrichten*, 44; and Wetzel, *Die Geschichte des königl.*, 14 f.

[67]Already in 1640, when Frederick William (the Great Elector) succeeded and while the war was still raging, the Räte requested that funds be made available to rebuild this "Edell Cleinoth;" see "Privy councillors to Schwarzenberg, 27 November 1640," *ZStA*, Rep.47.2.6.

mated that in the twenty-eight years of its existence some 788 pupils attended the school; of these only 56 eventually went on to the University of Frankfurt.[68] Many, if not most, attended before the school became a Reformed academy. Joachimsthal's impact as a Calvinist nursery thus was rather limited.

The University of Frankfurt soon experienced similar problems.[69] Matriculation figures, which by the turn of the century had reached nearly five hundred per year, making Frankfurt the fourth largest German university, remained fairly high until the mid-1620s. While many Lutherans now avoided the university, students from neighboring Lusatia and Silesia, where Philippism and Calvinism exerted a strong influence, continued to frequent it, particularly after the fall of Heidelberg in 1619 made Frankfurt the leading Calvinist school in Germany.[70] War and natural disaster, however, did take their toll. The plague, which visited the city in 1613, 1622, 1625, and 1631-32, repeatedly forced teachers and students to evacuate to nearby Fürstenwalde. Severe floods in 1622 and 1625, food shortages, and worst of all, the coming of the war—the city was stormed and sacked by Swedish troops on 3 April 1631—added to the university's woes and kept students away.[71] Like the Joachimsthal gymnasium, the university thus never did play the part John Sigismund and his advisors had assigned to it.

Results

COMPROMISE: Nevertheless, the Viadrina's role was not completely without significance. In spite of many problems, the university did play an important part in helping to modify and adjust the original goals of the Second Reformation to the given political and confessional realities in Brandenburg. Since Elector John Sigismund decided not to impose—indeed, because of the powerful opposition of his estates could not impose—his religion on his subjects, and most of them refused to convert, Brandenburg became the first principality in the Empire where a limited religious toleration not only was proclaimed but actually practiced. The early Reformation's *cuius regio eius religio* principle thus gave

[68]Euler, "Das königl Joachimsthalsche Gymnasium," 301.

[69]For the following, see Daniel H. Hering, *Beiträge zur Geschichte der Evangelisch-Reformirten Kirche in den Preussisch-Brandenburgischen Ländern*, 2 vols. (Breslau, 1784-85), 1: 38–51; Tholuck, *Das akademische Leben*, 2: 257 f; and Fricke, *Gesicht und Maske der Viadrina*, 17–19.

[70]Franz Eulenburg, *Die Frequenz der deutschen Universitäten von ihrer Gründung bis zur Gegenwart*, Abhandlungen der Philosophisch-Historischen Klasse der Königl. Sächsischen Gesellschaft der Wissenschaften, vol. 24 (Leipzig: Teubner, 1904), 110, 290 f; Tholuck, 2: 251–65; Grimm, *Viadrina*, 22–31; Gottfried Kliesch, *Der Einfluß der Universität Frankfurt (Oder) auf die schlesische Bildungsgeschichte, dargestellt an den Breslauer Immatrikulierten von 1506-1648*, Quellen und Darstellungen zur schlesischen Geschichte, v.5 (Würzburg: Holzner, 1961); and Othmar Feyl, "Die Viadrina und das östliche Europa," in Haase and Winkler, 105–39. Note also Alexander Persijn, *Pfälzische Studenten und ihre Ausweichuniversitäten während des Dreißigjährigen Krieges* (Ph.D, Diss., Universität Mainz, 1959), 36 f.

[71]Hausen, *Geschichte der Universität*, 15 f; and Spieker, *Beschreibung und Geschichte*, 265–69.

way to a "poly-confessionalism" that allowed the elector's court Calvinism to coexist with the country's popular Lutheranism.[72]

Ideologically this policy was buttressed by Reformed irenicism; politically it was encouraged by the Thirty Years' War. The Frankfurt theologians—Christoph Pelargus, Gregory Franck, and John Bergius—all were Reformed irenicists.[73] Attempts were also made to hire other well-known irenicists, such as George Calixt from Helmstedt University and John Allstedt from Herborn.[74] Pelargus's moderate theological tone and conciliatory attitude earned him the reputation as a "Markish Irenaeus."[75] Bergius, who served the Hohenzollern rulers for nearly half a century—from 1614 to 1658, first as a professor at the university and then as court chaplain in Berlin—especially deserves credit for translating the ideas of Reformed irenicism into religious toleration and for modifying the original goals of John Sigismund's reformation.[76] In 1619 he and Pelargus both refused to attend the Synod of Dort, largely because they feared that the condemnation of Arminianism by orthodox Calvinists there would hurt relations with Lutherans at home.[77] Bergius' encouragement of the electors to participate in the religious colloquies at Leipzig (1631) and Thorn (1645), and his own efforts on behalf of greater Protestant cooperation in the war show how he actively helped shape the policies of the house of Brandenburg. Significantly, the Leipzig Protocol of 1631 and the Thorn Declaration of 1645, which he helped formulate, came to constitute together with John Sigismund's *Marchica* the official confessional position of Brandenburg's Reformed church.[78] The Leipzig Protocol in partic-

[72]Gerd Heinrich, "Absolutismus, Konfessionalismus, und Territorialismus (1613-1740)," *TRE*, 7: 114. Hartmut Lehmann, *Das Zeitalter des Absolutismus: Gottesgnadentum und Kriegsnot* (Stuttgart: Kohlhammer, 1980) speaks of a "konfessionell paritätischen Staat," p. 84. H. J. Cohn notes (p. 163) "the compromise . . . in Brandenburg, where on the foothills of toleration, a Calvinist court was to rule over a Lutheran people." See also Hans R. Guggisberg, "The Defence of Religious Toleration and Religious Liberty in Early Modern Europe: Arguments, Pressures, and some Consequences," *History of European Ideas* 4 (1983): 35–50.

[73]On irenicism at the University of Frankfurt, see Mühlpfordt, *Die Oderuniversität Frankfurt*, 28–32; Feyl, "Die Viadrina," 116–120; and *TRE*, 11: 338–40.

[74]"Brandenburg Kirchenrat to Calixt, 1 January 1617," UB Göttingen, Cod. MS. phil. 110.I: ff.16 f; Menk, 65.

[75]Spieker, *Beschreibung und Geschichte*, 252.

[76]Elsewhere I have tried to show how Bergius's theological views directly affected the development of toleration in seventeenth-century Brandenburg; see "John Bergius: Irenicism and the Beginning of Official Religious Toleration in Brandenburg-Prussia," *Church History* 51 (1982): 389–404.

[77]See "Bergius to Martin Füssel, 23 February 1619," in Phillipp van Limborch, *Historia Vitae Simonis Episcopii* (Amsterdam, 1701), 210 f; see also Beckmann's account of the Synod of Dort in *ZStA*, Rep.92.III 2/2, chpt. 13, 1: ff.186–192.

[78]See *Die Drey Confessiones, oder Glaubens-Bekäntnüsse/ Welche in dem Chur-Fürstl. Brandenb. die Religion betreffenden Edictis zu beachten befohlen werden* (Cüstrin, 1695). The three confessional statements also are found in Gericke, *Glaubenszeugnisse und Kirchenpolitik*, 122–33.

ular is noteworthy for here the term "toleration" for the first time was used explicitly to describe Lutheran-Reformed relations.[79] The influence of the Frankfurt irenicists and the impact of the ravages of war encouraged Brandenburg's Calvinist leaders to modify their goals: since a full reformation of the country's church had proved impossible, they now were seeking greater harmony and parity with the Lutherans.

A memorandum by the university's theological faculty, from the early summer of 1633, when a general visitation was contemplated (it never was carried out), provides additional evidence. Franck and Pelargus, who drafted the document, thought that further reforms would only cause "many absurd, injurious things." They therefore advised that

> for the time being, doctrines and ceremonies be left intact and each person be allowed to practice his faith as heretofore. For in this manner much more will be accomplished . . . than by rushing and forcing the issue. Let us hope that eventually all quarrels will cease by themselves.[80]

The reorganization of the almost defunct Lutheran consistory in 1637 likewise shows how the original goals of the Second Reformation had been modified. When Brandenburg's general superintendent Christoph Pelargus died, Elector George William offered the post to Bergius, who declined the offer because he realized that his appointment would only cause new disputes with the Lutherans. Instead Bergius and Gregory Franck proposed that the general superintendency be abolished entirely and that two ecclesiastical councillors be named to the consistory to administer the Lutheran and Reformed churches on a separate but equal basis.[81] George William liked the suggestion and had it implemented shortly afterwards.[82] The net effect of this reorganization was that "the idea of parity and evangelical unity" of the two Protestant confessions now had become firmly embedded in Brandenburg's church constitution.[83]

By the 1630s the original plan to staff Frankfurt's theological faculty exclusively with Calvinists also had been abandoned. Bergius's and Crell's per-

---

[79]Gericke, *Glaubenszeugnisse und Kirchenpolitik*, 34 and 152. For additional information, see Bodo Nischan, "Reformed Irenicism and the Leipzig Colloquy of 1631," *Central European History* 9 (1976): 3–26; and idem, "Brandenburg's Reformed Räte and the Leipzig Manifesto of 1631," *Journal of Religious History* 10 (1979): 365–80.

[80]See "Consilium Theologicae Francofurtanae ad Oderam de Anno 1633 de Visitatione generali et Reformatione in Marchia instituenda," Niedersächsisches Staatsarchiv, Wolfenbüttel, 37.Alt. 287 Bd.1, f.79; also printed in *Fortgesetze Sammlung von Alten und Neuen Theologischen Sachen* (Leipzig, 1728), 27–40.

[81]The memorandum, dated 13 April 1637, is summarized in Hering, *Beiträge*, 18.

[82]"Rescript of 16 May 1637," in Mylius, I/1, no. 13.

[83]G. Heinrich in *TRE*, 7: 115; see also Heinrich von Mühler, *Geschichte der evangelischen Kirchenverfassung in der Mark Brandenburg* (Weimar, 1846), 148–9.

manent transfers to Berlin and Pelargus' death had created new vacancies that needed to be filled. Significantly, Simon Ursinus, a Lutheran, was chosen to fill one of these slots (in 1639).[84] He and Franck agreed privately in 1641 to follow a strict rule of parity in filling future vacancies, so that henceforth an equal number of Lutherans and Calvinists would serve on the theological faculty.[85] Elector Frederick William did have some reservations about this rule, but eventually confirmed it.[86] These developments helped establish Frankfurt's reputation as a "Toleranz-" or "Avantuniversität."[87] The arrival of large numbers of French Huguenot refugees after the revocation of the Edict of Nantes in 1685, together with the growing influence of pietistic and enlightenment ideas assured that this poly-confessionalism of the early seventeenth century eventually blossomed into full-fledged toleration.[88]

C) CONCLUSIONS: This essay allows us to draw several conclusions about the effects of Second Reformation in Brandenburg generally and the role of the country's schools more specifically:

(1) First, this reformation clearly was an elitist movement essentially limited to the elector's court and government. Not surprisingly, its supporters pursued educational goals that were equally elitist.[89] They were preoccupied almost exclusively with the Joachimsthal Gymnasium and the University of Frankfurt, the country's two foremost centers of learning, where the ecclesiastical and secular bureaucrats of the new Calvinist state were to be educated.[90]

---

[84]Beckmann, *Notitia Universitatis Francofurtanae*, 57 f. On Simon Ursinus (1599-1644), see Jöcher, *Allgemeines Gelehrten-Lexikon*, 4: 1740; and Spieker, *Beschreibung und Geschichte*, 271–81.

[85]See "Convention oder Vergleichung: Christliche und politische Tolerantz, collegialische Societät und Freundschafft zwischen Lutherischen und Reformirten Professoren in Facultate Theol. Francof. von D. Gregorio Franco und D. Simone Ursino beliebet," Feb. 1641, in Cyprian, *Abgetrungener Unterricht* , 2: 87–97.

[86]Frederick William's "Resolution" is found in Tholuck, *Das akademische Leben*, 2: 259 f.

[87]Heinrich in *TRE*, 11: 340; and Mühlpfordt, *Die Oderuniversität Frankfurt*, 31.

[88]See Rudolf v. Thadden, *Fragen an Preußen: Zur Geschichte eines aufgehobenen Staates* (Munich: Beck, 1981), 113–16; Thomas Klingebiel, "Deutschland als Aufnahmeland: Vom Glaubenskampf zur absolutischen Kirchenreform," in Rudolf v. Thadden and Michelle Magdelaine, eds., *Die Hugenotten 1685-1985* (Munich: Beck, 1985), 85–99; Klaus Deppermann, *Der hallesche Pietismus und der preußische Staat unter Friedrich III. (I)* (Göttingen: Vandenhoeck & Ruprecht, 1961), 21–33; 173; and Mary Fulbrook, *Piety and Politics: Religion and the Rise of Absolutism in England, Württemberg and Prussia* (New York: Cambridge University Press, 1983), 153–73.

[89]Significantly, the "late-humanism" that most German Calvinists embraced was equally elitist. See Schneppen, 116; and Erich Trunz, "Der deutsche Späthumanismus um 1600 als Standeskultur," *Zeitschrift für Geschichte der Erziehung und des Unterrichts* 21 (1931): 17–53.

[90]This clearly contradicts the more traditional view of Hermann Pixberg, *Der Deutsche Calvinismus und die Pädagogik* (Gladbeck: Heilmann, 1952), 90: "Die Schulen des Calvinismus unterscheiden sich wesentlich von denen des Luthertums. In den lutherischen Gebieten steht die Schule neben dem landesherrlichen Kirchenregiment, durch die Gemeinde von oben her ihre Weisung empfängt. Im Calvinismus ruht sie auf der breiten Grundlage des allgemeinen Interesses." In his study Pixberg completely ignored the University of Frankfurt and the Joachimsthal Gymnasium.

(2) By contrast the type of education that would have reached the population at large, catechetical and elementary school instruction, which had played such a prominent role in the early decades of the Reformation, was virtually ignored by them. Mostly this was due to the fact that widespread Lutheran opposition would have made such mass indoctrination difficult; partly and paradoxically, though, the cause also appears to have been the new reformers' conviction that most people would readily convert once their leaders had been persuaded to embrace Calvinism.

(3) Since this assumption was faulty, John Sigismund's objectives were only partially achieved. As planned, the prince's school and the university were quickly and easily transformed into Reformed institutions. Neither, though, was able to fulfill its mission as a Calvinist propaganda center because the people and most of the political and religious leaders outside the electoral governing circle in Berlin remained adamantly opposed to the new religion. After nearly a century of Lutheranism the process of confessionalization in Brandenburg had reached a point where even a determined ruler could not simply impose a new religion on his subjects without considerable force and sacrifice. The initial goals of the Second Reformation therefore had to be abandoned and adjusted to existing political and confessional conditions.

(4) The University of Frankfurt played a decisive role in smoothing this transition. The irenical thinking of its Calvinist professors rendered them particularly well equipped for this task. Thus while the Reformed failed to achieve their original objectives—Brandenburg's calvinization—their reformation was important because it contributed directly to the development of the early modern Hohenzollern state characterized by religious toleration.

(5) Finally, our essay illustrates once again how events in the confessional age were determined more by regional than supranational factors.[91] John Sigismund and his associates occasionally may have glanced to Heidelberg or Leiden (but rarely to Geneva) for inspiration and guidance; in the end, though, local rather than international conditions decided the outcome of the Second Reformation in Brandenburg.

[91]Cf. Menk, *Die Hohe Schule*, 1–12; and Prestwich, *International Calvinism 1541-1715*, 1–14.

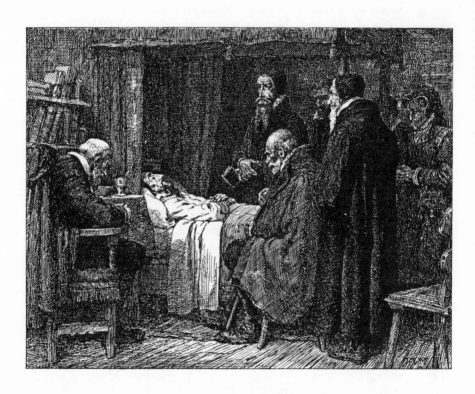

The death of Calvin, May 27, 1564.

Calvin's and Loyola's Letters to Women: Politics and Spiritual Counsel in the Sixteenth Century

*Charmarie J. Blaisdell**

An examination of the style and content of the letters of Calvin and Loyola to women finds them more focused on obtaining support and aid from these well-placed individuals than on offering spiritual support or comfort. Both movements appealed to women by offering unique opportunities to participate in spiritual life in the service of God. While there are certainly distinctive differences in the letters, there are striking similarities. Both Calvin and Loyola looked beyond the care of individuals' spiritual needs to the success of his movement.

THE LETTERS JOHN CALVIN AND IGNATIUS LOYOLA wrote to women are a small but significant part of their correspondence. There are over four thousand remaining letters of Calvin, directed to 307 persons and congregations; these extant letters probably represent only a portion of the letters that Calvin originally wrote and received.[1] During the last twenty years of his life, from 1544 until his death in 1564, Calvin corresponded with about eighteen women, mainly French noblewomen. Over sixty of these letters survive and there is evidence from the remaining letters that there were others which have disappeared.[2] We still have about seven thousand letters of Loyola to his followers of which over ninety are to women.[3] Again, as with Calvin, Loyola's

---

*An earlier version of this article was presented at the annual meeting of the American Historical Association, December 1985. I wish to thank Sherrin Marshall and Nancy Lyman Roelker for their criticism and suggestions.

[1]Calvin's letters are located in *Johannis Calvini Opera supersunt omnia*, ed. Johann Baum, et al. Brunswick, 1863-1900), 59 vols. Cited here as *CO*. A selection of Calvin's letters, including some to women, were translated by Jules Bonnet, *Lettres de Jean Calvin*, 2 vols., (Paris, 1854); some of the letters collected by Bonnet are also available in English translation, *Letters of John Calvin*, (Philadelphia: Presbyterian Board of Education, 1878). The variety and prestige of Calvin's correspondence and his letter-writing style have been the subject of several studies: Jean-Daniel Bénoit, "Calvin the Letter Writer," in William J. Courtenay, *Studies in Reformation Theology* (Grand Rapids: Eerdmans, 1966); Francis M. Higman, *The Style of John Calvin* (Oxford: Oxford University Press, 1967); Paul Marlin, *Un directeur spirituel au XVI siècle: Etude sur la correspondence de Calvin* (Montauban, 1886); Richard Stauffer, *L'Humanité de Calvin* (Neuchâtel: Delachaux et Niestle, 1964). As will become clear, I do not agree with these interpretations which see Calvin as a great spiritual counselor of women.

[2]Bénoit, "Calvin the Letter Writer," 67–70.

[3]*Monumenta Ignatiana: epistolae et Instructiones S. Ignatii*, 12 vols. (Madrid, 1903-1911) contain letters and instructions of Loyola, cited as *MI* I. Some letters have not been preserved in their entirety but are listed in the *Regesta, MI* I:2; R. Mendacha, *Epistolae Sancti Ignati Loyolae* (Bologna, 1837), 2d ed. contains some letters which Loyola received from women; Hugo Rahner, *Saint*

surviving letters show that others have been lost or destroyed. Women also wrote to both leaders but very few of these letters remain: nine to Calvin and fifty to Loyola. Probably, as one historian has suggested, these letters were more numerous than we might expect from the remainder but were kept for a short time and then destroyed as not important.[4] Certainly the correspondence of these two men with women is notably scanty when we compare it with the entire collection of their letters.

The contents of Calvin and Loyola's letters to women are important for a number of reasons. First they give us some access to understanding the role of women in the Reformation and Counter-Reformation. The popularity among women, especially royal or aristocratic women, of both these movements appears to have been related not only to the ideals of the movements but to the personalities of the leaders as well. Second, the letters give us some insight into the history of spiritual care for women in the sixteenth century. Third, they reveal some of the attitudes Calvin and Loyola had toward women. And, finally, the letters show the interest Calvin and Loyola had for their female correspondents for political reasons.

One of the most striking aspects in the letters of Calvin and Loyola is a difference in tone. Calvin's letters are businesslike even when he engages in angry scolding. He emerges more as the organizer of a movement than as a pastor to a newly formed flock. Loyola's letters, even when he is dealing with worldly issues such as donations and the foundation of new colleges, always contain a dimension of concern for the spiritual development of the recipient. Calvin seemed more concerned with the business of salvation, Loyola with the nurturing of souls. Yet both men, I would argue, were primarily motivated by a concern for the material growth of their respective movements.

From the time the Reformed regime was finally established in Geneva in 1555, France was the area that absorbed Calvin's interest. The problems of France stand out above all others in Calvin's letters as Calvin received and reported news of the political situation in his native country. Calvin knew very well that the hope for conversion of France lay with the powerful French nobility. For this reason, he initiated and maintained correspondence with members of aristocratic families, male and female.

Women were attracted to the Calvinist movement from the beginning and frequently took the lead in the "cause" in France, acting as intermediaries and negotiators between the rival Catholic and Protestant factions in the religious and political struggles following the sudden death of Henri II in 1559.

<hr />

Ignatius Loyola's Letters to Women, trans. Kathleen Pond and S. A. H. Weetman, (Herder, 1960) contains all of Loyola's letters to women in translation. I have depended on this collection heavily. For Loyola as a letter writer see V. Baesten, "St. Ignace d'apres sa correspondence," *Collection de précis historiques* 24 (1875): 410ff. Loyola's colleagues Polanco, Borgia and Lainez also wrote to women and some of the same ones.

[4]Rahner, *Loyola's Letters to Women,* 3.

Occasionally, they participated in subversive activities, supporting the Reform at great personal risk since they were either married to Catholic husbands or closely connected at Court. Many presided over families that had become Protestant largely due to their influence.[5] It is not surprising given their position at Court, their education, and their natural abilities that Calvin took a special and personal interest in both the political activities and the spiritual progress of many of these French noblewomen by writing to them to win their conversion, to exhort, to scold, or to offer service of some kind. I have argued elsewhere that this was primarily for political reasons.[6]

Calvin's female correspondents were primarily noblewomen. Even the letters to anonymous or unidentified female recipients appear to have been addressed to highly placed aristocratic women. In most cases it appears that Calvin initiated the correspondence. This was generally the case with women as well as with men, and fits with his policy to convert and keep the French nobility committed to the "cause." If the extant letters are a fair sample of Calvin's correspondence with women, his letters were generally politically motivated and he had more need of *them* than they had of *him*.

Seldom did he write with the sole purpose of offering spiritual direction or comfort. His letters were more often than not powerful monologues giving specific direction or advice. For Calvin the dignity and position of his female correspondents was all the more reason for them to understand and come to obedience to the message of the pure Gospel. For example in January 1563 Calvin wrote to Jeanne d'Albret on the death of her husband, Antoine. The letter began as a conventional letter of sympathy. But his real purpose was to urge Jeanne to carry through on her plan to establish the Reformed Church in Béarn.[7]

Like Calvin, Loyola attracted the attention and interest of women from the beginning. His earliest experiences giving pastoral care involved ministering to women.[8] Pious women of both aristocratic and middle classes were

[5]Nancy L. Roelker, "The Appeal of Calvinism to French Noblewomen in the Sixteenth Century," *Journal of Interdisciplinary History* 2 (Spring, 1972): 391–418; Roelker, "The Role of Noblewomen in the French Reformation," *Archive for Reformation History* 63 (1972): 168–95. The reader should also be aware of the literature, albeit limited, on the appeal of the Catholic Reform to women, especially recusant women. See for example, Sister Joseph Damien Hanlon, "These be but Women," *From the Renaissance to the Counter Reformation*, ed., Charles H. Carter (New York: Random House, 1965), 371-400; John Bossy, *The English Catholic Community, 1570-1850* (London: Darton, Longman and Todd, 1975), 152-78; Dom Hugh Aveling, "The Marriages of Catholic Recusants, 1559-1642," *Journal of Ecclesiastical History* 14 (1963); 68-83; W. J. Payley Wright, "Women and the Counter-Reformation in France," *Church Quarterly Review* 103-4 (1926-27): 115f.

[6]Charmarie J. Blaisdell, "Calvin's Letters to Women: The Courting of Ladies in High Places," *The Sixteenth Century Journal* 13 (no.3, 1982): 67-84.

[7]Nancy L. Roelker, *Queen of Navarre: Jeanne d'Albret* (Cambridge: Belknap Press, 1969), 208; CO, 19: (no. 3904) vols. 643–47.

[8]Rahner, *Loyola's Letters to Women*, 9-10; René Fulop-Muller, *The Jesuits: A History of the Society of Jesus* (New York: Capricorn, 1936), 49-51.

among his early circle of disciples, who promoted his ideas and pushed to become a part of the Jesuit Order and have Loyola himself as their spiritual director. Loyola was often under suspicion of the ecclesiastical authorities because
he attracted the interest and enthusiasm of so many women and his followers
were sometimes accused, like Calvin, of alienating wives from their
husbands.[9] Shortly before his death Loyola was still defending himself against
charges that the Society of Jesus owed its establishment to the patronage of
women.[10] Like Calvin, Loyola especially directed his attention toward aristocratic and politically influential women. And like Calvin, he consciously used
worldly patronage including political influence and monetary gifts from
women to further his Order. He once declared openly that "he who rejects the
opportunity of using worldly patronage for religious purposes has clearly not
learned to direct all things toward one goal."[11] For example, Loyola owed
much of his eventual acceptance by the House of Hapsburg to the friendly correspondence he carried on with the Hapsburg women, during the early days
of the Society.[12] In fact, the Infanta Juana, daughter of Charles V, was made
a member of the Society–the only female Jesuit in history–an event which
Loyola subsequently regretted and cancelled.[13] Juana remained active in the
world, never entered a convent, and lived a half-courtly, half-religious life
until her death. Indeed, much of the appeal of the Jesuits for women was the
opportunity to live a religious life in the world. One cannot help be reminded
of the work of Angela Merici and Mary Ward.[14] Loyola never hesitated to tap
the enthusiasm aristocratic women felt for his movement and generally was
able to channel their energies into charitable works for the Society.

Loyola took personal interest in both the worldly activities and spiritual
development of the women who were his correspondents and supporters. In
some cases he was the initiator of the correspondence, especially with royal
noblewomen.[15] In other cases women wrote him first as for example benefactresses and women who sought his spiritual counsel.[16] If the extant letters are

[9]*Monumenta Laini*, 8 vols. (Madrid, 1912-17), 1: 61 and especially 75.

[10]Rahner, *Loyola's Letters to Women*, 15.

[11]*MI* 2: 481. See also the Constitution of the Order where Loyola urged his followers to be
particularly solicitous to "persons of considerable importance," *Constitutiones Societatis Iesu*, 1540
(Rome: Typis Pontificare Universitatis Gregorianne, 1534-38), 3: 212.

[12]Rahner, *Loyola's Letters to Women*, 29–107 which contains the letters to the women of the
House of Hapsburg.

[13]Rahner, *Loyola's Letters to Women*, 52–67.

[14]For an interesting perspective on the Counter-Reformation movements and some attempts
by women to establish active female apostolates see Ruth Liebowitz, "Virgins n the Service of
Christ: The Dispute over the Active Apostolate for Women During the Counter-Reformation,"
in Rosemary Ruether and Eleanor McLaughlin, *Women of Spirit: Female Leadership in the Jewish and
Christian Traditions* (New York: Simon and Schuster, 1979), 132-71.

[15]See for example the letter to an unknown woman, "Dona Maria" in Paris, Rahner, *Loyola's
Letters to Women*, 186; to Senor Pascual, ibid., 177-78.

[16]See for example letter to Isabel Roser, ibid., 309-91.

any indication, the women who wrote to Loyola and who became ardent supporters had more need of *him* and his Society than he did of *them*, although he learned to accept their interest, enthusiasm, and offers of material help. The majority of Loyola's letters are either thanks for gifts or offers of spiritual advice or comfort. Unlike Calvin's letters, Loyola's have the quality of a dialogue with the recipient, offering continued interest and the concrete expectation of a reply.

There are similar and recurring themes in the letters to women of both Calvin and Loyola in spite of their difference in tone or style. In the first place both men entered into correspondence with politically influential women who were their social superiors. Second, the desire of women to participate actively as an integral part of these movements occupied the time and attention of both men. Third, both men were called upon to address the theme of separation and divorce among their female followers. Fourth, the need for ministers or confessors for the women was a theme frequently addressed in letters.

It is well known that Calvin's correspondence was almost entirely with French noblewomen such as Marguerite de Navarre, Jeanne d'Albret, Renée de France, Madame de Coligny, and less well-known women at the court of Catherine de Medicis, such as Perrone de Pesselieu (better known as Madame de Cany) and the Mesdames de Crussol, Grammont, Roye, and Lonjumeau. The dominant theme for these women was that they should remain firm in their newly acquired faith no matter what unpleasant circumstances they faced. The letters were more political advice than letters of spiritual counsel. Such letters were addressed to several women who were known to sympathize with the Huguenot cause, but who were understandably reluctant to make public profession of their faith.[17] The most renowned recipient of such letters was, of course, Renée de France, Duchess of Ferrara, with whom Calvin corresponded over a period of twenty years.[18] Calvin showed no mercy for Renée's reluctance to make a public profession of her faith in Ferrara where it was common knowledge that she worshipped secretly as a Protestant and gave refuge and material support to heretics. Renée had a more tolerant attitude in spiritual matters typical of the humanists and *évangéliques* than Calvin.[19] Her ambivalence once she had been instructed in the gospel infuriated Calvin on several occasions: in 1538 when she accepted the "Nicodemite" François Richardot into her entourage[20] and, again, in 1554 when her husband decided to bring

---

[17]Calvin à une Dame, n.d. *CO*, 20, col. 519–20, no. 4224; Calvin à une Dame, June, 1955, *CO* 15, col. 652–53, no. 2226; Calvin à Jeanne d'Albret, March 22, 1562, *CO*, 19, col. 347–49, no. 3748.

[18]Blaisdell, "Calvin's Letters to Women," 77–84. For a fuller discussion see Charmarie J. Webb (Blaisdell) "Royalty and Reform: The Predicament of Renée de France," (Unpublished Ph.D. dissertation, Tufts University, 1970).

[19]Blaisdell, "Royalty and Reform."

[20]Calvin à la Duchesse de Ferrare, n.d. (c. November, 1541) *CO*, 11, col. 325–26, no. 374.

her religious activities to a halt.[21] Thanks to the strategy and persistence of the Jesuit Father Pelletier she gave in and attended Mass openly and publicly. When Calvin heard of the Jesuit plan he sent a prominent French pastor François Morel to her court along with a letter of encouragement. The picture we have of these events is of a brief, stiff struggle between Jesuits and Calvinists for the Duchess's soul. For Calvin it was more important for Renée to convert openly than obey her husband. The dispatch of a pastor at a time when they were scarce indicates how important Calvin believed Renée's public conversion was for the success of his French policy. Calvin had no sympathy for Renée when she was forced to go to Mass, and, in a fury wrote, "the devil himself could celebrate this triumph."[22] Calvin never hesitated to use anger and sarcasm with women, to scold them for the evil people they associated with or listened to, or for their reluctance to publicly profess their faith. His advice was sometimes unsolicited, as in 1545 when he wrote Marguerite de Navarre regarding some unacceptable preachers she had at her court,[23] and in 1561 he wrote to Jeanne d'Albret prior to her conversion.[24] Instead of sympathy for the predicaments of undertaking Protestantism experienced by these women who were public figures and members of the French royal house, Calvin believed their position was reason enough for them to convert openly and lead others to do the same. Calvin was much less concerned with the personal dilemmas of these women than with winning their souls and support for the "cause."

Loyola's correspondence was primarily with women of the House of Hapsburg and with Italian and Spanish aristocrats, although there are some letters to middle class women, especially to mothers of Jesuits. Like Calvin, a significant part of Loyola's correspondence with women was politically motivated. Charles V's daughter Juana was an important figure in Loyola's correspondence and as we have seen, was the only woman who became a spiritual daughter and a permanent member of the Society. Loyola made use of Juana's devotion and offers of service although in her case he probably went further than he intended.

Loyola especially kept in touch with the benefactresses who helped him in his student days and in the establishment of the Order. He visited them and did special favors for them—sometimes against his better judgment. A case in point was Donna Maria Frassoni del Gesso, widow of the Estense Prime Min-

---

[21]Calvin à la Duchesse de Ferrare, August 6, 1554, CO col. 205-7, no. 194. For the Jesuit role in these events, especially that of Pelletier and Loyola's interest in the outcome see *Monumenta Historica Societatis Jesu: Chronicon Polanco* 4, annot 1554; *Monumenta Historica Societatis Jesu: Epistolae Mixtae* 5 vols. (Rome, 1898-1901) 4, 119-21 (letter of Pelletier to Loyola). Loyola himself never wrote to the Duchess as far as I know and she never wrote to him.

[22]Calvin à la Duchesse de Ferrare, February 2, 1555 CO 15, col. 418-19, no. 2105.

[23]Calvin à la Reine de Navarre, April 28, 1545, CO 12: col. 64-68, no. 634.

[24]Calvin à la Reine de Navarre, n.d. (c. January, 1561) CO 19: col. 313-14, no. 3622.

ister in Ferrara, who offered her services and became the foundress of the Jesuit College there. Out of gratitude, Loyola reluctantly made her a participant in all the spiritual merits of the Society. Like many of his female benefactresses, Donna Maria became a trial to Loyola's patience. It seems that her mothering of the Jesuits developed into ardor for individual Jesuits. He Jesuit spiritual advisor was limited to two visits a week at her house to avoid scandal. In 1554 she was given the title "Foundress by Merit" of the college. Loyola who cleverly turned her overweaning generosity and overbearing manner to the advantage of the Society, corresponded with her until his death.[25] Women supported the movement with time and material gifts demanded more and more opportunities to participate directly in the work of the Order and sometimes had to be told to suspend their activities with a Jesuit college or house because their presence called into question the morality of Loyola's sons.

Both the Calvinist and Jesuit movements seemed to appeal to women's need to be actively involved in the reform of the Church and society. The life of Donna Maria is but one example of the outlet for leadership that women—both Protestant and Catholic—found in religion in the sixteenth century. Calvin and Loyola seemed to encourage this by welcoming and accepting their political influence, physical energy, and material largesse. Yet neither man made a permanent place for women within the structure of his movement. Calvin sternly rebuked women such as Renée de France and Jeanne d'Albret when they attempted to play the traditional roles of princes by sponsoring and controlling Reformed congregations of their own lands. In reply to Renée's demand that she be allowed to play a more important role in the Church she founded at Montargis, Calvin wrote:

> Thus madam, to have a truly reformed church, it is more necessary to have men who have the supervision over the life of every individual.[26]

Before Calvin's arrival in Geneva women, such as Claudine Levet and Marie Dentière, were preaching to groups of men and women. Yet shortly after he settled in Geneva, women were even denied participation in the diaconate, further evidence that Calvin expected women to play traditional female roles in the organized Church.[27]

[25]For the correspondence relating to this episode of Loyola's overzealous admirer in Ferrara see Rahner, *Loyola's Letters to Women*, 188–202. For a fuller account see Pietro Tacchi-Venturi, *Storia della Compagnie di Gesu* 2 vols. in 3 parts (Rome; 1950) II/2; Ferruccio Pasini-Frassoni, "Donna Maria Frassoni e i Gesuiti in Ferrara," *Rivista del Collegio Araldico* (Rome, October, 1904), 505–94.

[26]Calvin a la Duchesse de Ferrara, January 8, 1564, CO 20: col. 230-33, no. 4067.

[27]For two discussions of women's roles in the Calvinist Church see: Willis P. De Boer, "Calvin on the Role of Women," in *Exploring the Heritage of John Calvin*, ed. David E. Holwerda (Grand Rapids, Eerdmans 1976), 236–72; Jane Dempsey Douglas, "Christian Freedom: What Calvin Learned at the School of Women," *Church History* 54, no. 2, (1984): 155-73.

Loyola initially welcomed women's enthusiastic support and even saw to the spiritual care of eager female followers during his early days in Manressa before the Order was organized. But he reversed his earlier position which permitted women to join the Order and struggled with the question of Jesuits sponsoring female convents. He eventually decided they should not. When one of Loyola's most enthusiastic and loyal benefactresses, Donna Isabel Roser of a noble Catalan family, formed a religious Order which she was determined to place under Loyola's spiritual care, he flatly refused to give his support. This act took courage because she had supported him financially as a poor student with money and books, had given a temporary home to his nephew, and offered to collaborate with Loyola in Rome using her own money and energy. Not accustomed to being rejected, she then applied to the Pope for permission to take vows along with two companions and for a papal command requiring Loyola to accept their vows. The Pope granted their request and on Christmas Day 1545, Donna Isabel and her companions made their vows and formed themselves into a female Order of Jesuits. Loyola tried to accept the *fait accompli* gracefully but from the beginning there was a struggle between himself and the headstrong Isabel. He finally had to renounce her and her Order.[28] In 1550, Loyola had to stop the project of Jeronimia Pezzani, a Modenese woman, who with seven others formed themselves into a female Jesuit Order.[29] In the very same year a similar project led by a persistent Jacoba Pallavicino and twelve followers resulted in a rapid-fire exchange of letters between Parma and Rome.[30] This enthusiasm of women drawn to active participation in the Calvinist and Jesuit movements, perhaps, indicates the extent to which women's spiritual needs had been unmet in the sixteenth century.[31]

As part of their pastoral work both Calvin and Loyola corresponded with women who were in marital crises. As we might expect, their attitudes toward marriage and divorce and the advice they gave were very traditional. Calvin, we recall, expected the Duchess of Ferrara to convert to Protestantism and remain with her husband in spite of his persecution of her which was well

---

[28]Rahner, *Loyola's Letters to Women*, 251–95 for the correspondence with Isabel.

[29]Ibid., 323–28 for the correspondence with Jeronimia.

[30]Ibid., 315–22 for the correspondence with Jacoba.

[31]Very little has been written about the spiritual care of women in the fifteenth and sixteenth centuries; the article by Liebowitz cited above is suggestive. See also brief mention of the subject in Steven Ozment, *the Reformation in the Cities* (New Haven: Yale University Press, 1975), 53-54. Francis Murray, "Feminine Spirituality in the More Household," *Moreana* (1970): 27-28, 92-102 is suggestive but does not go far enough; P. A. Becker "Marguerite Duchesse d'Alençon et Guillaume Briçonnet," *Bulletin de la société de l'histoire du protestantism français* 48 (1900: 393-477 and 661–67 is a thoroughgoing study of the relationship between one French noblewoman and her spiritual mentor. Studies of Italian women such as Isabella Bresegna and Vittoria Colonna suggest that the spiritual care of women in aristocratic circles in Italy was seriously lacking. It is interesting that Loyola became something of a folk hero among women in parts of Spain and Italy, including a popular patron saint of expectant mothers and women in childbirth.

known. In letters to several different female converts, Calvin offered specific advice on separation and divorce but typically showed little sympathy for the women's predicaments.[32] In each case the woman wished to be separated from her Catholic husband because she had experienced physical abuse since her conversion. Calvin was very reluctant to advise women to leave their husbands except in the extreme cases where their lives might actually be in danger. Instead he counseled patience, probably hoping for the eventual conversion of the husband and children. Calvin must have struggled with this particular issue since, following custom, he believed the husband was the head of the household and that the wife should be obedient to him. Yet Calvin was very clear that the husband's authority was "more that of a society than a kingdom" which is to say it was not license to oppress his wife.[33] In at least one case, Calvin's advice paid off. Perrone de Pesselieu, a woman who was often in public view as the sister of Madam d'Etampes, King François I's mistress, incurred the wrath of her husband when she converted. In 1553, she wrote Calvin asking if it were possible to leave her family and flee to Geneva. Calvin's advice (which she followed) was that she should remain with her husband. The following year, Calvin changed his view on the case and wrote advising her to come to Geneva. At just that moment, her husband converted. In 1561 their daughter married into a renowned family in a Protestant ceremony at Court. In this case, Calvin's initial advice paid off for the movement.[34] Obedience to one's husband was the theme of another exchange of letters, this time between the Company of Pastors and an unknown woman. Presumably Calvin was involved in the decision of the Company and the letter it inspired. Again this was the case of a noblewoman who was married to a militant Catholic who abused her, spied on her, confined her, and assaulted her "in body and spirit." She wanted to know if it was her Christian duty to remain with him or whether the Gospel would permit her to escape to a place where she could worship in liberty and peace. The reply (which was probably drafted by Calvin) was full of pity for her suffering. But the letter also made clear that according to Scripture, believers may not leave unbelieving partners. Christian wives should fulfill their duties to their husbands in such a way as they will eventually win them over to the faith. The woman should therefore pray for courage to resist demands her husband makes that might be a sin against God.[35] In a similar vein, Calvin wrote in 1559 to another woman "to bear with patience the cross

[32]Une dame aux ministres de Genève, June 24, 1552, *CO* 14, col. 337–40, no. 1634; Ministres de Genève à une dame, June–July, 1559, *CO*, 17: col. 519, no. 3064.

[33]*CO*, 51, col. 735–36, esp. 740. See also André Biéler, *L'Homme et la femme dans la morale Calviniste* (Geneva: Droz, 1963), 515 ff; Biéler, "Calvin on Marriage," in *John Calvin: A Collection of Essays* (Grand Rapids: Eerdmans, 1966).

[34]Calvin à Madame de Cany, June, 1553, *CO*, 14: Col. 536–38, no. 1751; *CO*, 16: col. 450–54, no. 1693.

[35]Calvin à une dame, June 4, 1559, *CO*, 17: col. 519, no. 3064.

which God has seen fit to place upon you; meanwhile not to deviate from the duty you have before God to please your husband. . . ."[36] In all of these letters there is an underlying theme: the husband's right to rule his wife even to the point of physical abuse. Calvin offered only two exceptions; if the wife was in life-threatening danger and if the husband's commands would cause her to sin against God. Calvin showed very little sympathy for the suffering a woman might have to endure with an abusive husband. Remaining in a marriage, even though life-threatening, was important because Scripture dictated it and because there were potential converts in husbands and children. His letters exhorted women to courage and reminded them that suffering strengthens one's receptivity to God's message. Calvin offered very little spiritual comfort to his suffering correspondents.

Loyola, too, was particularly concerned with the state of the marriage relationships of his female correspondents, benefactresses, and followers. Although he did not have to worry about religion splitting these marriages, the immorality of married couples and broken marriages were a prime focus of his spiritual care of women and a problem which he broached in his letters. "The whole foundation of Christian society rests upon the peaceful and honorable conduct of married people," he once stated. "But, in respect to matrimony, there reign disorders and bad example flourishes like a weed. Married women live without fear of God . . . they have separated from their husbands in open sin."[37]

To correct what he considered to be the abuses of the married state especially on the part of women, Loyola sponsored the foundation of a new religious house in Rome which he named for Saint Martha. Its purpose was to bring married women back to the discipline of married life and to prepare unmarried women for marriage. Women entered the house without taking final vows. Married women were free to leave and resume their marriages whenever they reconciled with their husbands. Unmarried women were permitted either to marry or to take the veil. The house was to be supported by the energy and generosity of noble and distinguished Roman women who were cleverly organized into a group of patrons called the *Compagnia della Grazia*. The house of Saint Martha in Rome became the model for similar houses in Florence, Bologna, Modena, Trapani, Messina, and Palermo. Eventually Loyola's pastoral work on behalf of primarily aristocratic women was extended to the foundation of a home, the *Compagnia della Vergeni Miserabili*, for young women "at risk" so they might be protected from the immoral life they seemed destined for and educated for a useful life in the world.[38]

---

[36]Calvin à Madame de Grammont, October 28, 1559, *CO* 17, col. 661, no. 3126.
[37]As quoted in Rahner, *Loyola's Letters to Women*, 17–18.
[38]Ibid., 17–20.

Like Calvin, Loyola intervened in the marital crises of his supporters, especially those politically prominent women who were in the public eye. Unlike Calvin, Loyola did not hesitate to intervene without invitation if he felt the situation warranted his counsel. He seems to have taken the initiative out of genuine concern for the maintenance of traditional Christian marriage. The most famous case was Loyola's temporary success in reconciling Joanna of Aragon and Ascancio Colonna who had lived separately for a number of years. Joanna's alienating their son from his father was a public scandal. Loyola's letter to Joanna touching on the matter followed his personal visit for the purpose of initiating the couple's reconciliation. What is most interesting and revealing about the letter which followed the visit are the insights that Loyola had into the feeling of the people involved and his ideas about how a reconciliation might be brought about. In his letter to Joanna he insisted that she should not set on Ascancio any conditions for reconciliation. He pointed out that one of the parties (probably Joanna) would have to bury pride and make the first move. Loyola appealed not only to the personal pride of Joanna and her political position and inner strength but also her loyalty to the Pope, the Emperor, and the Spanish nation—a surefire combination, we might suppose. While the reconciliation that took place didn't last long and fell apart for political reasons, Loyola's letter to Joanna reveals his gift for insight into human feelings and motivation.[39] Both Calvin and Loyola appear to have had quite traditional attitudes toward maintaining the married state at almost any cost; both seem to put the responsibility on the woman for holding the marriage intact or reconciling with the husband.

Responses to requests for ministers and confessors took up another significant portion of Calvin's and Loyola's correspondence. Indeed, perhaps one of the reasons we find very little spiritual counsel in Calvin's letters is that when he could, he sent ministers to the courts of his aristocratic female followers (as was the case with Jeane d'Albret and Renée de France) or assigned a minister to correspond with a particular woman, as for example Jacqueline de Rohan, the Marquise de Rothelin, who corresponded with Farel. As the Calvinist movement grew in the 1550s and 1560s, Geneva could not train and deploy ministers fast enough to meet demands for them. Calvin sometimes had to refuse the request from a noble ally for a pastor, as for example Madeleine Mailly the Comtesse de Roye, mother of the Princess de Condé and an extremely influential person at Catherine's court and one of the heroines of the movement. Calvin did take time in his September, 1561 letter to her to explain why he could not satisfy her request and to offer her both spiritual encouragement and congratulations for her accomplishments on behalf of the "cause." In the background of his words of spiritual encouragement to women, however, lay the obvious need to further the "cause." So important was this, it seems, that his

[39]Ibid., 134–45.

letters lack personal interest and empathy for the suffering of the individuals. For example, when writing to Madeleine de Mailly following her imprisonment for her activities, Calvin hardly mentions her recent incarceration. Instead he excuses himself for not sending her a pastor and counsels her to hold firm against the temptations and vanities of this world.[40]

In his letters to noblewomen as well as men, Calvin was respectful but never obsequious; he was forthright in his opinions and reprimands regarding weaknesses or errors no matter what the rank of his correspondents. But he remained a traditionalist in his attitudes towards women and openly expressed his opinion that they were the weaker sex. In a letter addressed to imprisoned Huguenot women, Calvin wrote,

> If men are fragile and esaily troubled, the weakness of your sex is even greater, according to the laws of nature.[41]

Yet Calvin also believed women were capable, with God's help, of overcoming their weaknesses and surpassing their male counterparts in faith. In the same letter he told them,

> Consider what has been the virtue and constancy of women at the death of our Lord Jesus Christ when the apostles seemed to forsake Him, they persisted in marvelous constancy and that a woman was a messenger to announce to the apostles the resurrection which they could not believe or comprehend.[42]

Perhaps in Calvin's favor it should be pointed out that in his letters to women he assumed they have a partnership with him in the work of spreading the Gospel. He included women in his invitation to individual activism in the work of reform, although, as we have already observed, his invitation did not extend as far as preaching, teaching, or participating in the diaconate.

Part of Loyola's work as a spiritual leader and reformer involved his responses to requests from both lay and religious women who were drawn to his Society for spiritual direction. So numerous were these requests from women that Loyola developed a very circumspect attitude toward the spiritual care of female souls which found concrete expression in the Constitutions of the Society.[43] As we have already seen, a part of his correspondence was devoted to the question of a female branch of the Society. After initially permitting it, Loyola thought better and forbade further development of a female Order in

---

[40]Calvin à Madame Roye, September 24, 1561, *CO*, 17: col. 736-37, no. 3532.
[41]Calvin aux prisonières de Paris, September 16, 1557, *CO* 16: col. 632–34, no. 2716.
[42]Ibid.
[43]*Constitutiones*, 3: 212.

spite of a continuous flow of requests.[44] A few of his noble female supporters had Jesuit confessors, but even this situation troubled Loyola and in some of his letters to the women of the House of Hapsburg he struggled diplomatically to recall their confessors to other duties—not always with success.[45] On that issue he had to tread very carefully, lest he upset the hard-won support of Charles V.

A second issue regarding spiritual care of women which troubled Loyola was the question of whether the Jesuits should undertake the spiritual care of those already in convents. Both in the *Constitutions* and in his letters Loyola strongly expressed the belief that spiritual care of women should not be the work of the society. This decision drew him into a lengthy correspondence with Sister Therese Radjilla, a nun of the Benedictine house of Santa Clara in Catalonia which was in serious need of reform.[46] Loyola made only one exception to his strict rule about giving spiritual direction to women. In 1547 he undertook the spiritual care of a group of *Murate* or cloistered nuns near Saint Peters who lived in enclosed cells and devoted themselves to prayer and giving spiritual counsel to visitors. Why he broke his self-imposed rule for these nuns is not clear.[47] Beyond this, his spiritual counsel to women was limited to letter writing. Letters written to royal and noblewomen for political reasons often also contained spiritual counsel; however, Loyola seldom wrote letters to women for the sole purpose of giving spiritual support. In this resptect Calvin and Loyola differed notably from Luther. For Loyola, the most obvious offers of spiritual support were sent in those letters intended to fend off a woman from overzealous involvement in the Order. It is striking too that while a significant number of Loyola's letters were occupied with discouraging women from participation in the Order, the majority of Calvin's letters contained exhortations to become more public and active followers.

[44]Letters requesting Loyola to found a female branch of the Order see letters of Juana Menses, Rahner, *Loyola's Letters to Women*, 307–8; Sebastina Exarch, ibid., 299–303; Juana de Cardona, ibid., 205–10; Guiomar Coutinho, ibid., 311–12; Leonor Mascarenhas, ibid., 417–18; Teresa Rejadella, ibid., 342–46.

[45]Loyola to Duchess Eleanor of Florence, February 2, 1555, Rahner, *Loyola's Letters to Women*, 100–1; October 13, 1555, 105–6; Princess Juana of Spain to Loyola, February 7, 1556, ibid., 62.

[46]Thérèse to Loyola, Rahner *Loyola's Letters to Women*, 348-49; 352; 360-61; 364-65; 366-67; Loyola to T herèse, ibid., 331-35; 336-37; 338-39; 341-46.

[47]Rahner, *Loyola's Letters to Women*, 369.

[48]Exceptions to this are found in letters from Loyola to Madonna Violante Gozzadini, December 22, 1554, Rahner, *Loyola's Letters to Women*, 220–21; to the Widow Boquet, August 16, 1554, ibid., 246–47; to Isabel de Vega, April 12, 1550, ibid., 454–55; ibid., November 1550, ibid., 458–60; to Isabel Vega, October, 1555, ibid., 476–77; to Isabel Roser, November 10, 1532, ibid., 264–67.

The movements of Calvin and Loyola had enormous appeal for women: both managed to harness women's enthusiasm and use it to their advantage. What was their appeal? Calvin and Loyola seemed to offer a means for expressing the ambitions of some powerful and enterprising women. Both elicited similar responses from these privileged and high-placed women who found in the reformers' ideologies opportunities to use their unique positions and capacities to be active in the world in a morally acceptable and constructive way. Calvinist emphasis on the Christian calling and Jesuit emphasis on education and an active life of Christian service appealed to these women. Neither movement offered women as much participation as the wanted, yet each did offer an escape from the idleness of their earlier lives as well as a partnership in a venture to reform religious life and society. Each offered women the opportunity to lead an active spiritual life.

The letters of Calvin and Loyola to women have some striking similarities. Both actively enlisted the help of women to intervene for them with higher authorities. Both held to the traditional point of view which prevented women from teaching and participating in church. Both had traditional views on marriage and divorce. Only in Calvin's permitting women to divorce their husbands for adultery and Loyola's defense of Elena Fantuzzi's right to remain single did they take exception to the marriage conventions of the time. Although they corresponded with some highly educated women, neither one engaged his correspondents in theological or doctrinal discussions; nor did women undertake to initiate such discussions. Each was blatantly political in enlisting female support and offering little in return but the satisfaction of serving God. While there are occasional offerings of spiritual comfort in their letters, neither Calvin nor Loyola was primarily concerned with spiritual care of women. Each looked beyond the care of individual female souls and put the success of his "cause" first.

Calvin's Letters to Women

Calvin to Marguerite de Navarre
    April, 1545
Calvin to Jeanne d'Albret
    January, 1561
    December, 1561
    March 22, 1562
    January 20, 1563
    June 1, 1563
    In addition, two letters from the Senate of Geneva: December, 1562 and January-February, 1564

Calvin to Renee de France, Duchesse de Ferrara
    November, 1536 (?) 1541 (?)
    August 6, 1554
    June 10, 1555 (probably to Renee although addressed simply "A Une
    Dame")
    July 20, 1558
    July, 1560
    January, 1561
    February 2, 1562
    May, 1563
    January 8, 1564
    January 29, 1564
    April 4, 1564
Calvin to Madame de Falais
    October 14, 1543 (?)
    June 24, 1544
    August 15, 1545
    September 18, 1545
    June 21, 1546
    October 19, 1546
    November 20, 1546
Calvin to Madame de Coligny
    September 4, 1558
    February 27, 1559
    September 24, 1561
    August 5, 1563
Calvin to Madame Cany
    January 8, 1549
    April 30, 1549
    s.d. (1552?)
    June 7, 1553
    July 24, 1554
Calvin to Madame de Roye
    September 24, 1561
    April, 1563
Calvin to Madame de Rothelin
    January 5, 1558
    May 26, 1559
    August,1559
    April, 1563
Calvin to miscellaneous women
    Madame de Crussol, May 8, 1563
    Madame de Grammont, October 28, 1559

Madame de Senighen, August 27, 1563
Madame de Pons, November 20, 1553
Madame de Longjemeau, December 14, 1557
Madame de Retigny, December, 1557
Madame de Retigny, April 10, 1558
Queen Elizabeth, January, 1559
Anne Seymour, June 17, 1549
Agnes Microw, December, 1555

There are 10 letters to "Unknown Women" who have never been identified. There is a letter dated June-July, 1552 from the Company of Pastors to an "Unknown Woman." Presumably Calvin had a part in writing it.

Loyola's Letters to Women

Queen Maria of Hungary
    Rome, March 26, 1552
Queen Catherine of Portugal
    Rome, March 12, 1552
Princess Juana of Spain
    Rome, January 3, 1555
Isabel of Portugal
    Rome, September 3, 1555
Margaret of Austria
    Rome, August 13, 1542
    Rome, August 16, 1550
    Rome, November 17, 1553
    Rome, December 17, 1553
    Rome, August 3, 1555
Duchess Eleanora of Florence
    Rome, September 23, 1553
    Rome, February 2, 1555
    Rome, October 13, 1555
Dona Magdalena, Lady of Loyola la Azpertia
    Rome, September 24, 1539
    Rome, May 24, 1545
Dona Isabel Borgia
    Rome, January 1, 1551
Dona Luisa Borgia
    Rome, August 20, 1553
Dona Juana de Menses
    Rome, June 1, 1551
Joanna Colonna

Rome, January 18, 1549
Rome, November, 1552
Dona Catalina de Zuniga, Marchioness of Dinia
Rome, September, 1552
Dona Catalina de Mendoza, Countess of Melito
Rome, June 1, 1552
Jacqueline de Croy
Rome, January 14, 1549
Rome, October 8, 1549
Rome, September 15, 1550
Ines Pascual (former landlady)
n.p. December 6, 1524/25
Paris, March 3, 1528
Paris, June 13, 1533
Dona Maria in Paris
n.p. November 1, 1536
Donna Maria Frassoni del Gesso
Rome, January 7, 1553
Rome, January 20, 1554
Rome, February 17, 1554
Rome, March 13, 1554
Rome, June 23, 1554
Donna Maria Margherita Gigli di Fantuzzi
Rome, May 30, 1551
Rome, December 24, 1552
Rome, July 28, 1554
Rome, April 6, 1555
Donna Constanza Pallavicini Cortesi
Rome, August 26, 1553
Rome, October 7, 1553
Rome, December 2, 1553
Rome, November 4, 1554
Madonna Violante Gozzadini
Rome, December 22, 1554
Rome, May 15, 1555
Donna Lucrezia di Storento
Rome, May 17, 1556
Dona Aldonza Gonzalex de Villasimplez
Rome, May 4, 1549
Rome, October 11, 1549
Rome, November 1, 1550
Dona Boquet, Widow of Don Juan Boquet
Rome, August 16, 1554

Dona Isabel Roser
    Paris, November 10, 1532
    Rome, December 19, 1538
    Rome, February 1, 1542
    Rome, October 1, 1546
    Rome, September 3, 1550
Dona Jacoba Pallavicino
    Rome, June 24, 1553
    Rome, February 17, 1554
Madonna Jeronima Pezzani
    Rome, December 2, 1553
Sister Teresa Rejadella
    Venice, June 18, 1536
    Venice, September 11, 1536
    Rome, November 15, 1543
    Rome, October 15, 1547
    Rome, April 5, 1549
An Anchoress of Salamanca
    Rome, July 24, 1541
Abbess Bartolomea Spadafora
    Rome, February 22, 1550
The Marchioness of Priego, Cordoba
    Rome, May 15, 1554
Juana de Valencia (mother of a Jesuit)
    Rome, September 5, 1555
    Rome, January 8, 1556
Madonna Cesare (mother of a Jesuit)
    Rome, January 28, 1554
The Widow Johanna Agnes Berze
    Rome, October 4, 1554
Magdalena Angelica Domenech
    Rome, January 27, 1553
    Rome, January 12, 1554
Dona Leonor Mascarehas
    Rome, June 28, 1545
    Rome, September 24, 1545
    Rome, January 19, 1546
    Rome, September 10, 1546
    Rome, June, 1552
    Rome, May 19, 1556
Dona Leonor Osorio
    Rome, July or August, 1547

Rome, August 11, 1548
Rome, October or November, 1548
Rome, December, 1548/49
Dona Isabel de Vega
    Rome, November, 1548
    Rome, April, 1550
    Rome, July 19, 1550
    Rome, November 1, 1550
    Rome, February 21, 1551
    Rome, March 7, 1551
    Rome, March 4, 1553
    Rome, November 5, 1553
    Rome, March 26, 1555
    Rome, April 25, 1555
    Rome, October 28, 1555
Indications of correspondence but no extant letters:
    Isabel de Josa
    Sebastiana Exarch
    Juana de Cardona
    Guiomar Coutinho

IOANNES CALVINVS, ÆTATIS SVÆ XLVIII.

Interpreting the Word by the Light of Christ or the Light of Nature? Calvin, Calvinism, and Barth

*James Torrance**

The question of which comes first, Law and then Gospel or Gospel and then Law is not only critical for interpreting the Scripture for Calvin and Calvinists of the early modern period as well as those of the nineteenth and twentieth centuries, but it is also critical for an understanding of the relevance of Calvin's ideas to contemporary struggles in South Africa and Northern Ireland. Whereas the Nature-Grace model of interpretation of Calvin has been influential in the rise of democracy and has been a source of social renewal, it no longer seems relevant in light of events in the world of the latter half of the twentieth century. A Barthian-Calvinist model that is biblical and christological is proposed as a new approach that would be true to the Word and to the reformers of the sixteenth century.

THE REFORMERS IN THEIR DEBATE WITH ROME took their stand upon the Bible as the sole Word of God. The reply of the Counter-Reformers was, "Yes, but how do you interpret it? Do you not require the teaching office of the Church to interpret it for you?"

Calvin was deeply sensitive to this issue, and wrote the *Institutes* in no small measure to answer this charge. So in his "Prefatory Address" to King Francis I of France he wrote, "Our adversaries cry out that we falsely make the Word of God our pretext and wickedly corrupt it."[1] He continued:

When Paul declared that all prophecy ought to be according to the analogy of faith (Rom. 12:6) he laid down a very clear rule for determining the meaning of Scripture. Let our doctrine be tested by this rule of faith and our victory is secure. For what accords better and more aptly with faith than to acknowledge ourselves divested of all virtue that we might be clothed by God, devoid of all goodness that we may be filled by Him, the slaves of sin that he may give us freedom, blind that he may enlighten . . . . to strip ourselves of all ground of glorying that he may alone shine forth glorious, and we be glorified in him? When we say these and like things, our adversaries interrupt and complain that in this way we shall subvert some *blind light of nature,* fancied preparatives, free will, and works that merit eternal salvation even with their supererogations. For they

---

*This article was read as a paper to an international centenary Barth Congress at the University of South Africa, Pretoria, on August 8, 1986.

[1]John Calvin, *Calvin: Institutes of the Christian Religion,* tr. John T. McNeill, ed. Ford Lewis Battles (Philadelphia: Westminster, 1960) 1.12-13.

cannot bear that the whole praise and glory of all goodness, virtue, and righteousness and wisdom should rest with God.[2]

The Word of God or the "Light of Nature"?

For Calvin, the formal principle of Reformed theology is Holy Scripture, interpreted in the light of revelation–that we interpret scripture out of scripture, and not by some prior "light of nature" or natural law. We interpret God out of God as he has revealed himself as our Father, and as he is only known in Christ the Son through the Holy Spirit–as this is set out in the Apostles' Creed, the *regula fidei* on which he structured the 1559 edition of the *Institutes*.[3] The material principle is *sola gratia*, that (as he so often puts it) "all parts of our salvation are complete in Christ our Head." Indeed, Calvin expounds *sola gratia* in terms of the twin principles: first, that God has done everything one hundred percent for us in Christ–the doctrine of the vicarious humanity and sole priesthood of Christ, expounded in Book II, and second, our participation in Christ through the Spirit, the doctrine of union with Christ, expounded in Book III. It is in terms of these twin doctrines (not one without the other) that Calvin examines each doctrine in turn and then, in Book IV, expounds the Church, the ministry, and the sacraments.

But, strangely, as Karl Barth has commented, he does not interpret Christologically his views on the State and civil government in chapter 20.[4] How does Calvin relate what he said in this chapter about the civil realm to all he has said so well in Books II and III about the Headship of Christ? This latter point Barth rightly believed to be a weaknesss in Calvin and the subsequent Calvinist tradition, a weakness Barth has sought to correct in his remarkable trilogy: *Gospel and Law,*[5] *Church and State*[6] and *The Christian Community and the Civil Community*[7] How far was Calvin at this point, in spite of the above Statement to the King of France, tacitly presupposing some concept of natural law discerned by the light of reason, some "light of nature," as the basis for civil order–the common inheritance of his day? If this is only implicit in Calvin's political views–for he never explicitly

[2]Ibid.

[3]Ibid., pp. xxix ff. For a discussion of the different editions of the *Institutio*, see F. Wendel, *Calvin, Sources et Evolution de sa Pensee Religieuse* (Paris: Presses Universitaires de France, 1950), 79; in English, *Calvin*, tr. Collins (Fontana Library), 1963.

[4]*Rechtfertigung und Recht*, No. 1 in the series Theologische Studien (Zollikon-Zurich: Evangelischer Verlag, 1938), [in English: *Church and State*, tr. G. Ronald Howe]. This was published with Karl Barth's *Gospel and Law*, 1935 and *The Christian Community and the Civil Community*, 1946 as a trilogy under the title *Community, State and Church* with an introduction by Will Herberg, (Gloucester, Mass., Peter Smith, 1968). See pp. 102 ff. for Barth's critical comments on Calvin, *Institutio* IV.20.

[5]Herberg, *Community, Church and State.*

[6]Ibid.

[7]Ibid.

employs the concept of natural law in his theology–it was certainly to become explicit in later scholastic Calvinism and be integrated into the whole structure of federal Calvinism in Puritan England, covenanting Scotland, and New England. Is there not here a failure to interpret the State, the civil realm, the social order, in the same Trinitarian, Christological way in which Calvin interpreted the Christian life of the individual, the Church, and her sacraments?

That Statement of method from Calvin's letter to the King of France in 1536 could also happily have been stated by Karl Barth in the Prolegomena of his *Church Dogmatics* when we think for example of his *Nein* to Emil Brunner's *Natur und Gnade*,[8] of his rejection of the concept of "orders of creation,"[9] or the words of the 1934 Barmen Confession, in Article one that "Jesus Christ, as he is attested to us in Holy Scripture, is the one Word of God which we have to hear, and which we have to obey in life and death. We regret the false doctrine that the Church could and should recognize as a source of its proclamation, beyond and besides this one Word of God, yet other events, powers, historic figures, and truths as God's revelation."[10]

Barth identified himself with Calvin's concern for a scientific theology, to interpret God out of God and not by some "light of nature." He sought on the basis of the confession that "Jesus is Lord" to build the doctrine of the Trinity, that we only know the Father through the Son and the Spirit–and know him not only as Redeemer, but also as Creator. In the manner of the theology of the Epistle to the Colossians, Christ is the One by whom and for whom all things were created; that God has reconciled all things to himself in Christ. To confess that Jesus is Lord is not only to confess his Headship over the Church, but over the State and over all nations.

Where there are differences between Barth and Calvin, and there are, they often arise because Barth has sought to carry through, more rigorously and consistently than even Calvin did, Calvin's own method of offering a Trinitarian Christological critique of every doctrine in turn. This more

[8]Both works were published in English as *Natural Theology*, Geoffrey Bles; (Centenary Press, 1946), tr. Peter Fraenkel, Introduction by John Baillie.

[9]The Lutheran concept of "orders of creation" was used by the German Christians to justify the distinction between Jews and Aryans in the Nazi era, and also by South African theologians to justify "separate development" on the basis of a God-created "ethnic diversity." This concept blended with Abraham Kuyper's idea of separate spheres of sovereignty in neo-Calvinism in South African social history in the theological support given to Nationalist policies by the Dutch Reformed Church. See John de Gruchy, *The Church Struggle in South Africa,* SPCK (London: Eerdmans, 1978), 10.

[10]Arthur C. Cochrane, *The Church's Confession Under Hitler* (Philadelphia: Westminster, 1962; reprinted Pittsburg: Pickwick Press, 1976). Also "The Barmen Declaration," a new English translation by Douglas S. Bax in *Journal of Theology for Southern Africa* 47 (June 1984): 78 ff. This latter is an excellent collection of essays on the Barmen Confession to mark the fiftieth anniversary of the Confession of 1934, interpreting its relevance in the South African scene.

rigorous approach we see in the handling of such subjects as election and the political social order. The fundamental question is: *is Christ as Mediator (the God-Man) the Head over all creation*, over Church, State, and human culture? *Or is he as Mediator only Head over the Church*, so that we interpret the State, politics, the nation, race relations, ethical issues in non-Christological terms, as in federal Calvinism? If at times Calvin might appear equivocal on this, Barth is unequivocally clear. Again, in the words of the Barmen Confession, "We reject the false doctrine that there could be areas of life in which we do not belong to Jesus Christ but to other lords, areas in which we would not need justification and sanctification through him."[11] Must not Romans 13 be interpreted in the light of the whole theology of the epistle? Is not the righteousness of which the State under God is the servant the same righteousness which for the Christian has been revealed in Jesus Christ and which is appropriated by faith alone? My concern in this article is to draw out the significance of these questions, which are of enormous importance for us today as we ask anew, as Barth did in his day, what is the relation between evangelization and humanization, the Gospel and the social order, the Church and politics, in the teeth of a deep all-pervading dualism in Western theology? Let us look at it in terms of the subject of Law and Gospel in the Calvinist tradition.

Law and Gospel in the Calvinist Tradition

When John Calvin wrote the first edition of the *Institutes* in 1536, he followed the order of Luther's *Short Chatechism*, expounding Law before Gospel, but after 1539 in subsequent editions he abandons this order, asserting the priority of grace over law. His understanding of the Old Testament as well as of Paul led him to see that the message of the Old Testament as well as of the New is fundamentally one of grace–of promise and fulfillment–and that law is given in the framework of grace, as the gift of grace, and designed to lead to grace. This is the same insight which Barth expounded in his short "Gospel and Law," and develops so fully in his *Church Dogmatics*"[12]

Western theology, both Catholic and Protestant, has too often inverted the order and misrepresented both Paul and Judaism. We see this not only in Lutheran thought but also in Puritanism and Calvinism, for in spite of Calvin's important insight, "federal Calvinism" (as enshrined for example in the Westminster Confession of Faith) was to be built on a dogmatic structure which asserted the priority of law over grace. If on the one hand this was

---

[11]Bax, "Barmen Declaration," 79.

[12]*Evangelium und Gesetz*, No. 32 of Theologische Existenz Heute series (Munich: Kaiser Verlag, 1935), translated into English by A. M. Hall in *Community, Church and State*, 71-100.

to be one of the sources of antisemitism in Christian history,[13] on the other hand here is one of the reasons why Calvinism has too often been associated with legalism and a rigid moralism, as in Scottish history. The development from Calvin to federal Calvinism is in no small way characterized by the inversion of the order of Gospel and Law.

This is of considerable importance politically, ethically, and socially, as well as theologically, and not least for our evaluation of Barth's understanding of Calvin.

The Covenant of Law and the Covenant of Grace
in Federal Calvinism (The Nature-Grace Model)

The central concern of the Reformation was the recovery of the meaning of *grace*–of justification by grace alone. One of the prime ways in which the Reformers contended for *sola gratia* was to say that that is the meaning of election. Our salvation is grounded in the free, unmerited grace of God without any prior consideration of worth or merit, not on any foreknowledge by God of our fulfilling prior conditions, as Calvin was to argue against Pighius. This line of argument was developed in the doctrine of "the double decree," especially in the hands of Calvin's successor Theodore Beza who proceeded to make the "double decree" (as Calvin had not done) the major premiss of his system of theology,[14] teaching the doctrine of a "limited atonement," that Christ is the mediator, not for all men, but only for the elect. God decrees all that happens, electing some, rejecting others, and then in grace sends Christ to execute the decree of salvation for the elect. If for Calvin (as later and more consistently for Barth) election is another way of saying *sola gratia*, for Beza and his successors, election is logically prior to grace.

The result was that in the period between 1550 and 1560 lively controversies[15] took place, raising such questions as: If God is sovereign over all men, and not just over the elect, how is he related to the whole human race–if Christ is only Head of the elect? If God decrees all for his own glory, is God responsible for sin and evil? What is the relation between the will of God and the will of man? Again, the elect, the saints who are justified by grace alone, must live responsibly in the world at large. How then do

[13]That is, the view that the Jews are "legalists," but we Gentile Christians believe in grace! So much recent scholarship has shown this view to be a travesty to authentic Judaism. See E. P. Sanders, *Paul and Palestinian Judaism* (London: S.C.M., 1977).

[14]Theodore Beza (1519-1605). The place given by Beza to the eternal decrees is seen clearly in his *Tabula praedestinationis* (or *Summa totius Christianismi*), 1555. This Table is reproduced in Heinrich Heppe, *Reformed Dogmatics*, tr. G. T. Thomson, foreword by Karl Barth (London: Allen & Unwin, 1950), 147-48. The table was adapted by William Perkins in his famous diagram and exposition, *The Golden Chaine* (Cambridge, 1596).

[15]See especially John T. McNeill, *The History and Character of Calvinism* (New York: Oxford University Press, 1954) for discussions of the controversies associated with Pighius, Bolsec, and Sebastian Castellio.

they interpret their existence in the realms of culture, public morality, and the State? There was a search for a basis for a social ethic.

With these questions doubtless very much in his mind, Zacharias Ursinus, the Heidelberg Lutheran who became a Calvinist, first put forward the concept of a *foedus naturale*[16] as a prelapsarian covenant, as a way of interpreting creation and the first three chapters of Genesis, something none of the magisterial reformers had done. When God created Adam, he created him the child of nature, to discern the laws of nature by the light of reason, and then on the basis of law (natural law and symbolic law) made a covenant or contract (*foedus*) with him, that if he obeyed and kept the covenant, God would be gracious to him and his posterity, but Adam transgressed, and brought down divine judgment on himself and all for whom he contracted. In this way, *man* was responsible for evil, not God. Adam had abused his God-given freedom. Here was a way of mitigating the harsher element of a high doctrine of the decrees and interpreting the relation between the sovereignty of God and human responsibility. On this approach, creation is being interpreted non-Christologically, but by the "light of nature."

For Ursinus, the concept of a *foedus naturale* was an answer to a genuine problem, but not a coordinating principle in his theology. But that is what it was to become before the end of the sixteenth century, in English Puritanism and Scottish Calvinism, and exercise such a powerful influence politically, in the rise of modern democracy. Among the many students who flocked to study in Heidelberg under Ursinus, Olevianus, and Zanchius, was an English Puritan, Thomas Cartwright, a friend of Beza and a Cambridge professor, who brought the concept back to England. In 1585 his friend Dudley Fenner wrote his *Theologia Sacra* (with an Introduction by Cartwright) where the concept of *foedus* was used as a basis for expounding Reformed theology, and where the phrase "covenant of works" (*foedus operum*) was first used. God has made two covenants, the covenant of works (the covenant of law or the covenant of nature) with all men, and the covenant of grace with the elect through Christ the Mediator. From this sprung the whole scheme of "federal theology," developed by William Perkins in England, and so to influence Puritanism in England, Scotland, and North America, and, through William Ames and Johannes Cocceius, Calvinism in Holland. The federal scheme became the absolute orthodoxy of the whole Puritan Calvinist world on both sides of the Atlantic, and found its first confessional status in the Westminster Confession of Faith. In these

---

[16]Zacharias Ursinus, *Major Catechism*, 1562, in Collegium Sapientiae, Heidelberg. See the important discussions of this in David A. Weir, "Foedus Naturale: The Origins of Federal Theology in Sixteenth-Century Reformation Thought," (unpublished Ph.D. thesis, St. Andrews, 1983, to be published by Oxford University Press). Also, J. B. Torrance "Calvin and Puritanism in England and Scotland: Some Basic Concepts in the Development of 'Federal Theology,'" in *Calvinus Reformator: His Contribution to Theology, Church and Society* (Potchefstrom, South Africa, 1982).

terms, theologians interpreted the relationship between creation and redemption, State and Church, the "civil" and "spiritual" realms. Reformed theology had been reformulated in terms of the Western nature-grace model, with its roots in medieval thought. The twin concepts were those of *natural law* and *foedus* (covenant or contract). The Mediatorial Headship of Christ, on this scheme, was restricted to the Church. Christ, as mediator of the covenant of grace, is known by the light of revelation. Natural law is discerned by the light of nature, by the kindly light of reason, as well as by scripture. Is this a legitimate way of interpreting Calvin's *duplex cognitio* of God as creator and redeemer? Or do we only know God as creator and redeemer in Christ by the light of revlation? Is Barth or is federal Calvinism the more faithful interpreter of Calvin?

The Political Significance of the Nature-Grace Model
    The political significance of the Nature-Grace model (apart from its theological implication) was enormous. Two events deeply disturbed Western Europe in the sixteenth century, after the Reformation. The first was the deposition of Mary Queen of Scots in 1567 (and her beheading in England in 1587), raising the question: What are the rights of a sovereign vis-á-vis his or her people? Have the people a right to depose their sovereign? The second event was the massacre of the Huguenots on the Eve of Saint Bartholomew in 1572, raising the complementary question: What are the rights of a people vis-á-vis the sovereign? Has the sovereign the right to massacre his people? How do you safeguard the rights of both king and people? The answer given was, "By covenant" *(foedus)*–by "contract of government." At the time of his coronation, a king makes a solemn covenant or contract with his people whereby they bind themselves together under law to guarantee each other's rights under specific conditions. This raised a very important set of questions. What is the nature and source of human rights? What constitutes lawful government? What is the seat of sovereignty in law? Is it in the monarchy, or in the people, or above both in God? Is the king above the law? Is violence ever justified in the defense of liberty? John Calvin argued that we must never resort to violence in the defence of religious liberty. But situations emerged in France, England, and Scotland where Reformed churchmen were prepared to use violence–but only lawfully, where a legal contract had been broken. Again the twin concepts of covenant and law, of *foedus* and natural law, were seen as foundations for civil law. *There was a passionate concern to maintain the universal reign of law.* Scholars searched the Bible, especially the Old Testament, and examined every conceivable passage where the word 'covenant' appears in order to find a basis for "lawful government," to defend their freedom against tyranny–using the Bible as a book of legal precedents. In the process they appealed to medieval notions of natural law and social contract (contract of society and contract of government). A wealth of literature appeared which was to be

enormously influential in the rise of modern democracy.[17] The common argument was that no one is above the law, neither king nor people. Civil law enshrines natural law (*foedus naturale*) discerned by Reason. Justification for these views was found in the Old Testament covenant passages, in medieval contractarian writers, and in historical precedents in European history.

Out of all this literature emerged two principles in the struggles against tyranny and the doctrine of "divine right of kings": (1) the passionate belief in *Justice*–the conviction that "right and not might" is the basis of all political society and of every system of political order in a true democracy; and (2) the passionate belief in *Liberty*–the conviction that will–human consent–and not force is the basis of true government.

It is important here to notice that in the Reformed world the Law-Grace model (the Nature-Grace model) was a powerful instrument for social renewal in the struggle for democracy. This can be seen in the American Declaration of Independence, in the conviction that God made all men equal, with inalienable rights to life, liberty, and the pursuit of happiness.

Paradoxically, in the American Civil War of 1859-61 Calvinists fought Calvinists, Presbyterians fought Presbyterians, on the question of slavery. What was the basis of their difference? Not the Nature-Grace model of federal Calvinism as such. That was the orthodoxy of the old Princeton school. There were no real differences on the subjects of grace, election, atonement, the need for personal salvation. The answer lies in two different views of natural law (and the orders of creation). Where the Northern theologians believed that all men are equal with equal rights, their Southern counterparts like Benjamin Morgan Palmer, Robert Lewis Dabney, James Henley Thornwell taught that God has created us with ethnic diversities– some black, some white, some masters, some slaves–and found biblical justification for their view of natural law. In terms of different concepts of natural law, each side exegeted the Old Testament differently, and found sanctions either for preserving the status quo (slavery) or for political renewal, for the emancipation of the slaves, with equal rights for all. The radical separation of Church and State, the Constitution of the United States, and the Bill of Rights all had their roots in the Nature-Grace model of Puritan Calvinism. But it is a dualistic model where the Mediatorial Headship of Christ is restricted to the Church. What controls political thinking is not the Gospel but an abstract notion of natural law and civil rights, with an appeal to the "light of nature" and the "kindly light of reason."

[17]For example, George Buchanan's *De Iure Regni Apud Scotos* of 1570; the *Vindiciae contra Tyrannos* by Junius Brutus (the French Huguenot Duplessis Mornay); and Samuel Rutherford's *Lex Rex* or *The Law and the Prince*, which was the political manifesto of the Scottish Covenanters. See James B. Torrance, "The Covenant Concept in Scottish Theology and Politics and its Legacy," *Scottish Journal of Theology* 34 (1981): 225-43, also in "Covenant or Contract? A Study of the Theological Background of Worship in Seventeenth-Century Scotland," *Scottish Journal of Theology* 23 (1970): 51-76.

The importance of this is seen today in the subject of apartheid in South Africa. Why is it that the same Puritanism worked itself out in one way in the development of democracy in North America and in another way in Afrikanerdom in South Africa?[18] The answer again lies in different views of natural law. While most Christians throughout the world feel that apartheid is a denial of human rights for the blacks, many in the Dutch Reformed churches in South Africa have found justification for separate development, both in Calvinist notions of natural law and in the concept of "orders of creation" of certain Lutheran missiologists who believe, like Gustav Warneck, that God, by nature, intends for there to be separate ethnic development.[19] If grace presupposes nature (natural diversity), does not destroy but perfects it, then divine sanction can be found for apartheid in civil law and in the church. In other words, the Nature-Grace, Law-Grace model of federal Calvinism has been used both as an instrument of renewal and of reaction. It is ambivalent. It gave rise to modern democracy and a concern for human rights, but it has also been used to justify slavery, apartheid, certain forms of rigid sabbatarianism, and other injustices.

In Ireland today we see behind the struggle between "nationalists" and "loyalists" different views of the Western Nature-Grace model. In Catholic Southern Ireland the State embodies in civil law the insights of natural law as interpreted by the ʻCatholic Church.[20] In Protestant Northern Ireland we can see the dualism of Westminster Calvinism in Presbyterians like Reverend Ian Paisley, who is on the one hand the ardent fundamentalist evangelist, preaching grace to the elect, the "born again," and at the same time he is the politician, the leader of the democratic unionists and an active member of Parliament. On both sides, what controls behavior in both "nationalism" and "loyalism" is not the Gospel but a fusion of the Law-Grace, Nature-Grace model with romantic loyalty to one's nation (*Volk*), be it pro-British or anti-British. As in the Germany of the 1930s, with the "German Christians" there was, as Barth and his colleagues saw, a *status confessionis* calling for the Barmen Declaration of 1934; so in Northen Ireland, two types of "Irish Christians" confront each other, each claiming divine–and historical–sanction for their politics. There is a *status confessionis* for the Church, with the need for a "Belfast Declaration" (!) to call all Christians to give their exclusive loyalty to Jesus Christ and to acknowledge that there is no area which does not belong to Christ.

Must we not ask ourselves, Why is it that in Lutheran Germany in the 1930s, in Calvinist South Africa and Puritan Northern Ireland, political

---

[18]William A. de Klerk, *The Puritans in Africa: A History of Afrikanerdom* (London: Pelican, 1976), 149 ff.

[19]De Gruchy, *The Church Struggle in South Africa*, 8 ff.

[20]For example, abortion and contraception.

situations have arisen where we see the weaknesses in the dualism of the Law-Grace, Nature-Grace model of very different forms of Western theology–Catholic, Lutheran, and Reformed? Do we not see a *status confessionis* in each situation, where, as Barth and Barmen have taught us, there is need to discover the Headship of Christ in every area of life, and unpack the anthropological, political, and social implications of the Incarnation? The question thus raised for us, as Barth raised it in his day, is this: Is our anthropology built merely on a concept of natural law (however we may interpret it), or is it based on our understanding of the Incarnation? Is it built on the "light of nature" or the "light of revelation," or a synthesis of the two?

Theological Comments on the Nature-Grace Model in Calvinism

For all that the Nature-Grace model was so influential in the rise of modern democracy and the concern for human rights, theologically it has great weaknesses, which highlight the importance of the question of the priority of grace over law and help us see how biblical and relevant for us today is Barth's critique of this model.

(1) It sees all as under the sovereignty of God, but not under the Mediatorial Headship of Christ as man. It does not do justice to the Pauline teaching of Ephesians and Colossians that God's concern is to reconcile and sum up all things in Christ. In its day it was an attempt to answer the question of how we relate justification and justice. Today there is a widespread debate over how to relate evangelism and social justice, evangelization and humanization. The Nature-Grace model leaves the two issues as parallel, but fails to see any organic Christological relation between them, based as I see it on inadequate understandings of the Incarnation, and the all-inclusive humanity of Christ. To hold out Christ to the world is not only to hold out personal salvation, but to give to all their humanity. All people, be they Jews or Gentiles, rich or poor, black or white, male or female, are meant to see in the Man Jesus their own humanity assumed, sanctified, and handed back to them. We do not have just an ethical mandate, but a Christological mandate for social action. In the name of the Gospel, and not just of natural law, we have a warrant to oppose all that dehumanizes–poverty, violence, unemployment, and other corruptions of justice. The Good News of the Gospel is that God has come to restore to all their lost humanity in Christ. What was lost in Adam is restored in Christ. This was the incarnational emphasis of Irenaeus and the Greek Fathers. In our Calvin studies, have we not read our Calvin too one-sidedly through Western Augustinian, Thomistic, Westminster eyes, and not enough in terms of Irenaeus, Athanasius, and the Cappadocian divines–as Barth would have had us do?

(2) In dualistic fashion, it separates creation and redemption. It fails to interpret creation Christologically. In the New Testament, Christ is presented as both Creator and Redeemer. By limiting grace and the

Mediatorial Headship of Christ to the "elect," Calvinism falls back on the concepts of "orders of creation" and "natural law" to interpret the State, race relations, social justice, ethnic diversity, anthropology. On this model there are two alternatives, either (a) to stress the radical separation of State and Church, as in pietism, or where politicians tell churchmen to keep out of politics, or (b) to effect false syntheses between Church and State, as in forms of Erastianism, or civil religion.[21] In the latter, divine sanction can be given to political ideologies or romantic concepts of the *Volk*. Then it is our concept of "nature" which controls our understanding of "grace," and not the Gospel.

(3) It builds theology on the view that Law is prior to Grace. This is clear in "federal theology" where the "covenant of works" (*foedus operum, foedus naturale*) is the major premiss of the whole system. Here the covenant of law is seen as the prime covenant, embodying God's primary intention for humanity in creation and the covenant of grace is seen as the God-given "means" whereby God secures the ends of the covenant of law for the elect. The older federalists said that God made the covenant of works twice–with Adam who broke it, and with Christ who kept it! But the danger is then that not only is the law prior to grace, but grace is subordinated to law, as the means of securing the ends of (natural) law. Is this the reason that in South Africa, in right-wing circles in the Verwoerd tradition, the State and the Church are seen to exist to secure the ends of nature, and divine sanction sought for apartheid in the State and in the Church?

(4) It has substituted a *legal* understanding of man for a *filial*. That is, God's prime purpose for man is legal, not filial. But this yields an impersonal view of man, as the object of justice, rather than the object of love. We can give a man his "legal rights" but not see him as our brother. In the New Testament, God's prime purpose in Creation, Incarnation, Atonement, and the gift of the Spirit at Pentecost is filial, not just legal–"to bring sons to glory."

(5) In the movement from Calvin to Calvinism, there was a basic shift in the doctrine of God, from a prime emphasis on God as Triune to a Stoic concept of God as the Lawgiver, and to an Aristotelian concept of God in whom there are no unrealized potentialities. The Triune God has his being-in-loving, and has created us for filial purposes that we might find our true being (humanity) in loving. The God of Stoicism is conceived of primarily in terms of legal justice, who has created man for legal obedience. The significance of this is seen in the writings of two outstanding Calvinists, John Owen in seventeenth-century England and Jonathan Edwards in

---

[21] Again, e.g., the "German Christians," "Irish Christians," or Afrikaner "Nationalists."

eighteenth-century New England,[22] who both taught that justice is the essential attribute of God, by which he is related to all men, but the love of God is artibrary, by which he is related (not by nature, but by will) to the elect. This may be the logic of the Law-Grace model of their high federal Calvinism, but it is not true to the New Testament. God is Love–he is Father, Son, and Holy Spirit in his innermost being–and what he is in his innermost being he is in all his works and ways. Classical high Calvinism has been dogged by a latent Sabellianism, that has created problems of assurance. God is loving towards the elect, but is he Love in his innermost nature? Does he love me? Or is there some hidden "horrible decree" that God might be other than what he reveals himself to be in Jesus Christ? Barth has even put this question to Calvin on the doctrine of election and so rightly has emphasized the ancient church's rejection of Sabellianism, asserting that what God is toward us in Christ, he is eternally and antecedently in himself–Father, Son, and Holy Spirit–holy Love. This is the ground of true joyful assurance.

(6) This shift in the doctrine of God and in anthropology is reflected in a shift in attitude to Holy Scripture–from scripture seen as the revelation of grace to scripture as a book telling us our duty. Where the first Helvetic Confession of 1536 interprets the *scopus scripturae* as to show forth the grace of God in Christ, the Westminster Confession and Catechisms of 1645 say that Scripture principally teaches "what man is to believe concerning God, and what duty God requires of man." The Bible is increasingly seen as a book of legal precedents and used at times to legitimate slavery, white supremacy, civil religion, and severe sabbatarianism. Such attitudes were too often justified in terms of a synthesis between the "self-evident light of nature" and the "evident light of revelation," as in the theology of Charles Hodge in the old Princeton school.

(7) Much modern evangelism has its roots in Puritan preaching which in turn adapted the Western *ordo salutis* from the medieval period; for example:

Man – Law – Sin – Repentance – Grace

The *order* lies behind federal Calvinism with its distinction between the covenant of law made with mankind in Adam, and the subsequent covenant of grace made for the elect in Christ. So the old preachers preached the law to give their hearers a sense of sin, in order to exhort them to repent and receive grace and forgiveness–what the Puritans called "law work." This order failed to distinguish the significance of Calvin's distinction between "legal repentance," where repentance is a condition of forgiveness, and

---

[22]John Owen, *The Death of Death in the Death of Christ* (London: Banner of Truth, 1956). See the discussion of Owen and Edwards in John McLeod Campbell, *The Nature of the Atonement*, 4th ed.,(London: James Clark, 1959), Ch. 3. Also, James B. Torrance, "The Incarnation and 'Limited Atonement'" in *Evangelical Quarterly* 55 (No. 2, April 1983): 83-94.

"evangelical repentance," where repentance is a response to grace and the Word of the Cross. In true "evangelical repentance," forgiveness (the Word of the Cross) is logically prior to repentance.[23]

* * *

The above considerations help us see the significance of Barth's concern, when following Calvin in the Reformed tradition, to work out a theology of the Word, where we seek to interpret the Bible by the light of revelation and not by an appeal to some "light of nature"–to interpret each doctrine by the "analogy of fatih," in terms of the Trinity, in terms of the person and work of Christ, in terms of *sola gratia*. The question we have posed is this: Is Barth or is federal Calvinism the more faithful interpreter of Calvin? Our concern is not to whitewash Calvin (or Barth!) nor to blacken federal Calvinism. The seeds of much of federal Calvinism are there in Calvin. But do we not see in Barth a concern to carry through Calvin's own program with a more radical, thorough consistency which is often truer to the biblical understanding of God than we have too often seen in Puritan Calvinism?

I have also suggested that what Barth and his colleagues at Barmen were doing in the context of the Nature-Grace, Law-Grace model of Lutheran Germany in the 1930s, we must do in analogous fashion in the context of the dualisms in our own Western Calvinist inheritance, be it in Northern Ireland, the United States, or South Africa.

For all that the Nature-Grace model has been so influential in the rise of democracy, as an instrument of social renewal, in the struggles for justice and liberty, today we must return to a more trinitarian, incarnational model, and rediscover the priority of grace over law and interpret law as within the Gospel. Some of the most burning issues of today are about humanity, the problems of poverty, war, nuclear armaments, race, tyranny, the women's movement. *For too long we have used simply the language of "rights"*–human rights, civil rights, women's rights–the language of natural law. *Is it not better to use the language of "humanity"*–the Irenaean model of the Greek fathers–*that what was lost in Adam is restored in Christ?* For this we need a more biblical, Christological model, if we would see the organic connection between justification and justice, evangelism and social concern, evangelism and humanization. *We need to recover the concept of the all-inclusive humanity of Christ, as Creator and Redeemer, to transcend the deep dualisms of our culture.* Have we not much to learn from Karl Barth if we would be true interpreters of the Word and heirs of the Reformation and, in the spirit of Barmen, *reject the false doctrine that there are areas of life in which we do not belong to Jesus Christ?* Jesus Christ is King of kings and Lord of lords.

[23]*Institutes*, 592 ff.

IOANNES CALVINVS.

Caluinum assidue comitata modestia ᵕuuum
Hoc vultu mambus tinxerat ipsa ius.
Ipsa àquo potuit virtutem discere ᵕvirtus.
Roma tuus terror maximus ille fuit.

Cum priuill.

Index

270 *Calviniana*

Gospel and Law, 256
impact of, on Lutheran theology, 14
influence of, on Wilhelm Niesel, 14

Basel, church and civil government in, 108-9, 108n1; heresy trial of Jerome Bolsec in, 112

Battles, Ford Lewis, 64, 65, 66

Bauke, H., *Die Probleme der theologie Calvins,* 64

Beckhum, Maria von, 208

Bede, Venerable, cosmology of, 79

Behm, John, , 219

Bergius, John, 224, 230, 231-32

Berkhof, Hendrikus, 14

Bern, church and civil government in, 108-9, 108n1; heresy trial of Jerome Bolsec in, 112

Berthelier, Philibert, Calvin's correspondence concerning, 115-16; excommunication of, 114-15

Beza, Theodore, 133, 159-60, 209; developer of "double decree," 259
tract of, on predestination, 163
treatise of, on election, 158-59

Bible
and civil government, 261
as word of God, 67, 72, 255
authoritative in Calvin's theology, 68, 75
distinct from Word of God, 66
interpretation of, 267
relationship of, with Spirit and Word of God, 69

Bill of Rights (American), roots of, in Nature-Grace Model, 262

Blaisdell, Charmarie J., "Calvin's and Loyola's Letters to Women: Politics and Spiritual Counsel in the Sixteenth Century," 235-53

Blarer, Ambrosius, 110

Blasphemy of Jan of Leyden, tract by Menno Simons, 203

Bloch, Ernst, 214

Bodley, John, 153, 155

Body, human, Calvin's negative attitude toward, 57

Bolsec, Jerome, heresy trial of, 112

Bonaventure, Saint, 82

Bouwsma, William, 9, 58, 63, 64;
John Calvin: A Sixteenth Century Portrait, 55
on anxiety of Calvin, 59
on social psychology, 60

Boyle, Robert, "Father of Chemistry," 169-70

Brandenburg, and toleration in, 229-30; Second Reformation in schools of, 215-33;

A Brief declaration of the chiefe poyntes of Christian religion, by William Whittingham, 158

Brunner, Emil, *Natur und Gnade,* 257

Bucer, Martin, 110; influence of, on Calvin, 111

Bullinger, Heinrich, 68
and Calvin's doctrine of election, 112-13
and Christian discipline, 109-10
and responsibility of magistrates, 109
and Servetus case, 113
correspondence of, with J. Haller, 114

Bumann, Charles, 220

Bunyan, John, *Pilgrim's Progress,* 177

Buridan, John, and natural science, 81

C

Call, inner, in French Protestantism, 140; in William Perkin's theology, 176

Calvin, Jean
advice of, to persecuted Christians, 53, 58-59, 206-7, 208
and Aristotelianism, 79, 86-87, 90-92
and astrological determinism, 84
and Bible, as word of God, 75
and civil and ecclesiastical authority, 211
and Christian discipline, 110-11
and Kingdom of God, 213
and Perrinists, 115
and political order, 58, 59-61
and predestination, 113
and Old Testament covenant, 18
and Servetus trial, 113
as spokesman for Huguenots, 133
attitudes of: toward natural philosophy, 80, 88-89; toward present life, 174-75; toward Menno Simons, 196; toward Spiritualists, 75
bibliography of letters to women, 248-50
Christology of: contrasted with Barth, 257-58; influenced by Chalcedonian Christology, 94
"Commentary on Seneca's *De clementia,*" 91, 96-97, 210-11
conflict of, with Genevan magistrates, 111
conversion of, 197-98
correspondence of, with Bullinger, 112-13, 115-16, 118; with Farel, 208; with William Whittingham, 152; with women, 235-53; with Zurich council, 115-16

Scripture References

The Authors

Brian G. Armstrong teaches in the History Department of Georgia State University, Atlanta, Georgia.

J. Wayne Baker teaches in the History Department of the University of Akron, Akron, Ohio.

Claude-Marie Baldwin is a member of the French Department of Calvin College, Grand Rapids, Michigan.

Charmarie Jenkins Blaisdell teaches in the History Department of Northeastern University, Boston, Massachusetts.

Dan G. Danner is a member of the Theology Department of Portland University, Portland, Oregon.

David Foxgrover teaches at Rockford College, Rockford, Illinois.

Richard C. Gamble is the Director of the H.H. Meeter Center for Calvin Studies, Grand Rapids, Michigan.

Timothy George is Dean at Samford Divinity School, Birmingham, Alabama.

W. Fred Graham teaches in the Religious Studies Program at Michigan State University, East Lansing, Michigan.

Ian Hazlett is a member of the Department of Theology and Church History of the University of Glasgow.

I. John Hesselink teaches Systematic Theology at Western Theological Seminary in Holland, Michigan.

Merwyn S. Johnson teaches in the Department of Historical and Systematic Theology of Erskine Theological Seminary in Due West, South Carolina.

Christopher B. Kaiser is a member of the Department of Historical and Systematic Theology of Western Theological Seminary, Holland, Michigan.

Donald K. McKim teaches Theology at the University of Dubuque Theological Seminary, Dubuque, Iowa.

Bodo Nischan teaches in the History Department of East Carolina University in Greenville, North Carolina.

James Torrance is a member of the Faculty of Divinity, King's College, University of Aberdeen

The Editor

Robert V. Schnucker teaches in the Philosophy and Religion Department and in the History Department, Northeast Missouri State University, Kirksville, Missouri.

Geneva as first seen by Calvin in 1536.

"Still more does this passage refute the madness of the fanatics who despise books and condemn all reading and boast only of the ἐνθυσιασμούς, their private inspirations by God. But we should note that this passage commends continual reading to all godly men as a thing from which they can profit."

Calvin's comments on 2 Tim. 4:13 as translated by T.A. Smail in *Calvin's Commentaries, The Second Epistle of Paul the Apostle to the Corinthians and the Epistles to Timothy, Titus, and Philemon,* ed. David W. Torrance and Thomas F. Torrance (Grand Rapids: Eerdmans, 1964), 341.